TERRIBLE FATE

TERRIBLE FATE

*Ethnic Cleansing in the
Making of Modern Europe*

BENJAMIN LIEBERMAN

Ivan R. Dee

CHICAGO 2006

www.ivanrdee.com

Library of Congress Cataloging-in-Publication Data:
Lieberman, Benjamin David, 1962–
   Terrible fate : ethnic cleansing in the making of modern Europe / Benjamin Lieberman.
     p. cm.
   Includes bibliographical references and index.
   ISBN 1-56663-646-9 (cloth : alk. paper)
   1. Genocide—Europe—History—19th century. 2. Genocide—Europe—History—20th century. I. Title.
D359.L676 2006
304.6'63'094—dc22

                                              2005023567

For Nancy

Contents

Preface

The towns and cities of Central and Eastern Europe, from Germany to Turkey, contain haunting traces of the vanished ethnic and religious communities that once called these places home. Germany today has restored synagogues and other reminders of the destruction of that country's Jews, but just to the east of Germany, in the Polish port city of Gdansk, one can find restored German buildings, though the Germans who built them are long gone. Still farther east, in the Ukrainian city of Lviv, stands a monument to Jews who died under Nazi occupation and another in honor of the Polish poet Adam Mickiewicz. But in Lviv today there are very few Jews or Poles.

In the Balkans, similar clues point to the ethnic and religious groups who have vanished from their former homes. The Greek city of Thessaloniki is the site of the former house of Mutafa Kemal Atatürk, the first president of Turkey, and the ruins of a vast Jewish cemetery lie buried under the city's university. But today nearly all of Thessaloniki's Jews and Turks are gone. Farther east, across the Aegean Sea in the Turkish port city of Izmir, one can find old buildings, remnants of the city's Greek past. And Armenian monuments and ruins are scattered across eastern Turkey where Armenians no longer live. Collectively, all these monuments, buildings, ruins, and cemeteries testify to the repeated removal—and sometimes the destruction—of ethnic and religious groups across a broad swath of land from Central Europe through Western Asia.

With few exceptions, this history of violence and expulsion is almost forgotten. The Holocaust, in which Nazis and their allies killed
half of Europe's Jews, is of course well known. There is also growing knowledge of the Armenian genocide, in which as many as 1.5
million people were killed; and the ethnic cleansing that ravaged the
former Yugoslavia during the 1990s attracted international attention. But the Holocaust, the Armenian genocide, and Yugoslavia are
more than a collection of atrocities from different times and places.
Each is also part of the much broader process of ethnic cleansing in
Europe and adjacent Asian lands.

In most cases the towns and cities that were swept clean of so
many of their former residents were once ruled by one of three large
empires: the Russian Empire, the Ottoman Empire, and the Hapsburg
Empire or, as it became known in its latter years, Austria-Hungary.
These empires were not nation-states. To use present-day terminology,
they were multinational, home to a multitude of ethnic groups. In
fact, few of the subjects of Europe's old empires possessed a strong
sense of national identity as we define it today. There was no Austro-
Hungarian "nation"; instead a diverse mixture of people—who spoke
German, Czech, Slovak, Polish, Italian, Slovenian, Romanian, and
Serbo-Croatian, among other languages—lived in Austria-Hungary.
These residents of the Hapsburg Empire were united not by any
shared national identity but because they were ruled by a common
sovereign. Similarly, there was no Ottoman nationality; the Ottoman
Empire was home to a mix of people who shared a common ruler, the
sultan, but who practiced many religions—including Islam, Judaism,
and numerous varieties of Christianity—and spoke many different
languages. In the Russian Empire, Russians made up a large part of
the empire's population, but the tsar's subjects lacked a common language, religion, or ethnic identity.

The rise of nationalism in the nineteenth century threatened
the survival of the old empires of Europe and Western Asia. Imperial subjects increasingly imagined themselves to be members of distinct nations.[1] Often these emerging nations were defined by language, like Czech, German, Polish, Bulgarian, or Greek. Sometimes

they were defined by religion, as in the case of the Zionists who sought to create a Jewish nation-state in Palestine or the "nations" within Yugoslavia: Serbs, Croats, and Bosnian Muslims are all Slavs who speak essentially the same language but are defined and divided by religion.[2] The Croats are Catholics, the Serbs Orthodox, and the Bosnian Muslims are Muslims. In some cases a group's religion and national identity became synonymous. Thus most Armenians worshipped in the Armenian church, and most Greek speakers worshipped in the Greek Orthodox church.

The rise of nation-states signalled the eventual deaths of the old empires. Carving homogenous nation-states out of empires meant moving borders or people, or both. As empires broke apart into nation-states, processes of ethnic cleansing and even genocide moved or eliminated many of the people who had once lived under imperial rule.

Europe's empires had their own traditions of inequality and discrimination, but nationalism nurtured intense new forms of hostility. Nineteenth-century nationalists initially praised fraternity among nations, but most soon took an aggressive tone toward other peoples. Neighboring nations, they argued, were competitors and even enemies. They crafted tales of national struggle with a basic common story line, in which their own nation, the hero or protagonist, was repeatedly victimized and betrayed by another nation. The villains of these stories often still lived alongside the victims, and one way to bring the story to a satisfactory resolution was to drive out or destroy the villains—even if they happened to be neighbors.

Once ethnic cleansing began, it occurred repeatedly. The ethnic cleansing of the region from Central Europe through Western Asia took place in three overlapping waves that corresponded to the expansion and fall of three different types of empire. The first wave began in the nineteenth century in the Russian and Ottoman empires and ended with the collapse of these empires during and immediately after World War I. At this time a second wave of ethnic cleansing was already under way and culminated with the rise and

fall of new nationalist and racist empire-building, most notably by
Nazi Germany during World War II. In the third and final major
wave, the collapse of Communist empires generated still more ethnic cleansing in the late twentieth century.

Misconceptions about the perpetrators of European ethnic
cleansing abound. In the examples of Nazi Germany and Stalin's Soviet Union, ethnic cleansing was engineered by powerful modern
states that controlled bureaucracies of terror and secret police: the
SS, the Gestapo, and Stalin's NKVD, predecessor of the KGB. But the
crimes of Hitler, Stalin, and their henchmen, while stunning in
their enormity, depart in many ways from more typical examples of
ethnic cleansing in Europe—they are not a template. While control
over a powerful government provides a means for ethnic cleansing,
it does not provide a motive. Leaders of strong states are not inherently predisposed to choose this process as a means to consolidate
their power. Ethnic cleansing in fact has frequently occurred under
struggling or even collapsing governments. It was often a crime of
dying states and of new and fragile governments—some such
regimes were barely recognizable as governments at all.[3]

The testimonies of victims provide additional clues to the causes
of ethnic cleansing. They have described crimes by secret police and
death squads, but many have also reported something even more disturbing: arson, assaults, and murders carried out by their own neighbors. While dictatorships such as Nazi Germany and the Soviet
Union enlisted ordinary people in terror campaigns, eyewitnesses
also depict genuine grassroots enthusiasm for ethnic cleansing.
Many Europeans decided that they truly wished to drive out their
neighbors. Because the Holocaust is the most widely known, most
chronicled mass murder in history, it is necessary to emphasize that
ethnic cleansing and genocide in Europe and Western Asia are not a
particularly German story. Many incidents of neighbors attacking
neighbors would have been seen as evidence of massive popular support for ethnic cleansing if the aggressors in such cases had been
Germans. But when other groups were involved a litany of excuses
has often followed: the killers and thieves were only a minority;

other members of their community displayed solidarity with victims; and the violence was spread by elites. Some of these claims may be true in some cases, but they do not explain how ordinary people could brutalize neighbors, acquaintances, colleagues, and classmates.

It is wise to avoid being too dogmatic in identifying the reasons why ordinary people have attacked their own neighbors. Even those who knew men who took part in ethnic cleansing have often lacked any explanation for their actions. Jasmina Dervisevic-Cesic, a Bosnian Muslim woman who was severely injured and lost her husband and two of her brothers in the war in Bosnia in the 1990s wrote: "I still find it hard to understand that one of the boys who played on my brothers' soccer team died with a gun in his hand, fighting . . . for a Greater Serbia that would mean the extermination of many of his old high school friends."[4] None of the obvious explanations, including orders from powerful leaders or personal greed, is adequate by itself. Dictators sometimes command deportations, but ethnic cleansing has often occurred under weak states. It is even more obvious that ethnic cleansing typically has included looting, but it is hard to imagine that the desire for wealth or property alone led ordinary people to break all accepted social norms and violently expel neighbors from their homes. Europeans did not simply drive out neighbors from different ethnic groups because they could: in many cases they saw ethnic cleansing as something good in itself. Crises and wars that appeared to confirm nationalist stories of victimization distorted ethnic relations. Individuals, accustomed to hearing stories of atrocities and historic betrayal, came to see neighbors from different ethnic and religious groups not as people with a shared past in work, school, and community life but as members of an inherently evil enemy nation who deserved punishment and removal.

Several related types of violence transformed the ethnic and religious map of the old imperial lands of Europe. The term "ethnic cleansing" refers to the removal, through violence and intimidation, of an ethnic group defined from a given territory. In 1993 a UN High Commission described the term in the context of Yugoslavia as

"rendering an area ethnically homogenous by using force or intimidation to remove persons of given groups from the area." This is a
useful definition, but there is no one single form of ethnic cleansing.[5] Both the degree of planning involved and the capacity to expel
an entire ethnic group may vary, and victims may be defined by ethnic identity, race, or religion, or by some combination of the three.

To understand the history of ethnic cleansing in modern Europe, it is helpful first to define several related terms, including
genocide. In cases of genocide, such as the Holocaust, the goal is not
simply removal but extermination of an ethnic, religious, or racial
group. Ethnic cleansing and genocide are not always distinct, however, because the violence employed in ethnic cleansing may escalate
to genocide.

On a spectrum of violence, pogroms, which are mob attacks
against a particular ethnic or religious group, fall short of both ethnic cleansing and genocide. Frequently pogroms have foreshadowed
later, more ambitious, and more violent cases of ethnic cleansing,
and pogroms have also taken place during ethnic cleansing campaigns.[6] When pogroms become increasingly widespread and frequent, they take on the character of ethnic war, especially when *both*
groups engage in the violence.

The process of ethnic cleansing may be achieved through several
mechanisms. Deportation most commonly refers to action by state
authorities to force an individual to leave a country, but deportation
may also describe the internal exile of an individual or a group. (Expulsion is a more general term.)[7] Population transfers refer to organized movement across state boundaries, typically under a diplomatic
agreement. Finally, forced migration is a much broader term that is
sometimes related to ethnic cleansing; it refers to the movement of
refugees displaced by natural or environmental disasters or public
works projects as well as by ethnic and political conflicts.

Uncovering and acknowledging the story of ethnic cleansing
and related violence in Europe transforms our understanding of European history. There has been little place for the ethnically cleansed
in standard histories of Europe because historians by custom tell the

stories of nations. A focus on ethnic cleansing shifts perspective. The story of the rise of the nation-state, a triumph of self-determination, becomes a story of tragedy for those who were driven out. Moments of liberation and victory become turning points in campaigns of terror and expulsion. National heroes become champions of bigotry, aggression, and exclusion. And in the case of ordinary people, the record of support for and participation in terror, violence, and theft adds a profoundly pessimistic note to the story of modern European progress.

The cleansing of the old imperial lands of Europe exemplifies the third major type of cleansing to occur since the end of the Middle Ages. The first began in Western Europe when rulers sought to create religious purity. Thus the monarchs who reconquered all of Spain in 1492 enforced religious conformity, driving away Jews or forcing many of them, and Muslims, underground. In France, when King Louis XIV ended toleration for Protestants in 1685, French Protestants or Huguenots scattered the globe despite a ban on emigration. In a second major type of cleansing, European settlers in the New World wiped out and displaced selected native non-Western populations. On occasion, Europeans even expelled other European settlers: in 1755 Britain drove the Acadians, French settlers, off their lands in Nova Scotia.[8]

But neither of these two earlier forms of cleansing extended to the multiethnic societies of Eastern and Central Europe and Western Asia. Both the tsar and sultan ruled over millions of subjects who did not share their respective faiths, and violence by European settlers overseas presented little threat to people who lived in Europe and Western Asia. The final phase of Western European colonial expansion in the late nineteenth and early twentieth centuries did encourage racist thinking, but except for Germany most of the European colonial powers (Britain, France, Belgium, Portugal, and the Netherlands) had no role in the ethnic cleansing that transformed much of Europe. The horrors of the Congo and other imperial ventures did not lead to mass killing in Europe. Ethnic cleansing in Europe and Western Asia was homegrown.[9]

TERRIBLE FATE

CHAPTER ONE

Bag and Baggage:
Ethnic Cleansing Begins

Today Sofia is the capital of Bulgaria. With a population of more than a million, it is Bulgaria's political, financial, and industrial center. But in the nineteenth century Sofia was a considerably different place. Not only was it much smaller, but as late as the 1870s it was a Turkish rather than a Bulgarian town. Approaching Sofia in 1850, the English traveler Edmund Spencer saw a town "rising up in the centre of a vast basin, with its domes and minarets." On closer inspection he found the town less than impressive. Amidst Greek and Roman ruins were mosques converted from former churches, but Sofia, with its "ill-paved narrow streets" and "badly-ventilated bazaars," was much like other towns of the region.[1]

The transformation of Sofia from a Turkish to a Bulgarian town was in part a by-product of the early forms of the ethnic cleansing that began to remake Europe's map in the nineteenth century. Although Sofia itself was not the site of the most violent attacks on Muslims, the shift in the town's makeup and identity was part of a broader violent redrawing of the ethnic and religious map of much of Bulgaria. A war that erupted in 1877–1878 between Russia and

Turkey marked the end of Sofia as a Turkish town and the beginning of its new identity as a Bulgarian city.

The term "ethnic cleansing" did not find common usage until
the wars for Yugoslavia in the 1990s, but the elements of ethnic
cleansing predated the term itself. Long before historians or legal
scholars had begun to use such terms as ethnic cleansing and
genocide, ordinary men and women suffered violent attack because of their ethnic identity. The first wave of modern European
ethnic cleansing emerged along the borders of two empires that
no longer exist: the Ottoman and Russian empires. Both empires
were frequently at war. Pressing to expand its power south into
the Caucasus and along the Black Sea, Russia fought against the
Ottoman Empire in 1801–1812, 1828–1829, 1853–1856, and
1877–1878. Over the same period, Ottoman forces confronted numerous rebellions and uprisings, including uprisings of Serbs in
1804 and 1815–1817, the Greek War of Independence from 1821
to 1830, rebellion in Bosnia and Herzegovina in 1875, rebellion in
Bulgaria in 1876, and rebellions on Crete in 1866–1868 and in
1896–1897.

"The Turk Shall Live No Longer . . ."

Early forms of ethnic cleansing developed on the southern border of
the Russian Empire and on the western borders of the Ottoman Empire. In the nineteenth century the European possessions of the Ottoman Empire were commonly known as "Turkey in Europe."
These were the regions in Europe conquered and still held by the
Turks. The Ottoman Turks first swept into the Balkans in the four-
teenth century; by the sixteenth century their empire in Europe
reached all the way to Hungary. Ottoman power declined in the
eighteenth century, but at the opening of the nineteenth century the
Ottoman rulers still held territory that today makes up Bulgaria,
Greece, Albania, Macedonia, Montenegro, Bosnia, Kosovo, and Serbia. The Ottoman sultan also appointed the rulers of principalities
on the Danube River that today make up much of Romania.

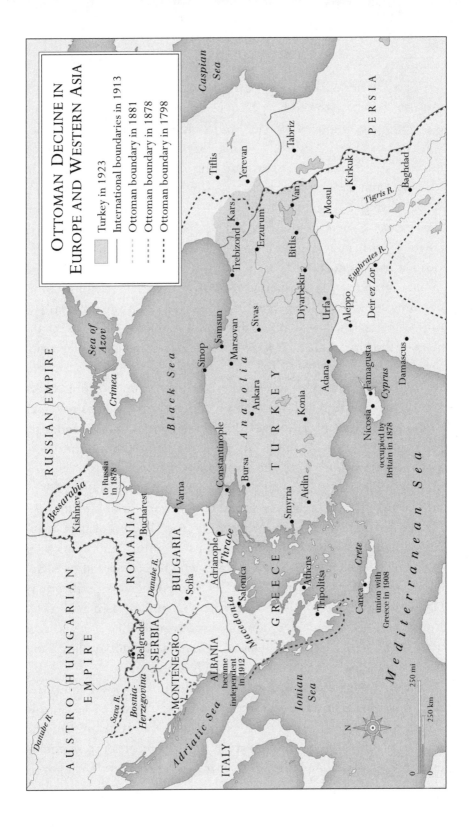

OTTOMAN DECLINE IN EUROPE AND WESTERN ASIA

Turkey in 1923
International boundaries in 1913
Ottoman boundary in 1881
Ottoman boundary in 1878
Ottoman boundary in 1798

RUSSIAN EMPIRE

Caspian Sea

PERSIA

Sea of Azov

Crimea

Tiflis

Yerevan

Tabriz

Van

Kars

Kirkuk

Mosul

Baghdad

Tigris R.

Erzurum

Trebizond

Bitlis

Diyarbekir

Urfa

Aleppo

Deir ez Zor

Euphrates R.

Black Sea

Sinop

Samsun

Marsovan

Sivas

Anatolia

Ankara

Konia

Adana

Damascus

Famagusta

Cyprus

Nicosia

occupied by
Britain in 1878

to Russia in 1878

Bessarabia

Kishinev

Varna

Bucharest

ROMANIA

Danube R.

BULGARIA

Sofia

Constantinople

Bursa

Smyrna

Aidin

TURKEY

AUSTRO-HUNGARIAN
EMPIRE

Sava R.

*Bosnia-
Herzegovina*

Belgrade

SERBIA

MONTENEGRO

Danube R.

Adrianople

Thrace

Salonica

Macedonia

ALBANIA
became
independent
in 1912

GREECE

Athens

Tripolitsa

Crete

Canea

union with
Greece in 1908

Mediterranean Sea

ITALY

Ionian Sea

Adriatic Sea

N

250 mi

250 km

0

0

The Ottoman Empire in Europe was extraordinarily diverse. Western travelers to the East frequently remarked on its bewildering religious, linguistic, and ethnic complexity. One such traveler was Austen Henry Layard, a young Englishman who later gained fame as an archaeologist excavating the ancient city of Nineveh in Mesopotamia. Layard traveled across the empire between 1839 and 1842, finding diverse populations almost everywhere he went. Soon after crossing the Ottoman border, he "passed through the bazaars crowded with men and women—Turks, Albanians, and Greeks of various tribes and races." At Salonica, today a Greek city, Layard found a growing port inhabited by Muslims and Greeks but dominated by Jews.[2] The language most often heard on the city's streets might be described as Spanish, the closest major language to the dialect of the city's Ladino Jews, whose ancestors had emigrated from Spain.

In Turkey in Europe as elsewhere in the Ottoman Empire, several of the groups that Layard observed were organized as religious communities known as millets.[3] Muslims enjoyed economic and legal privileges over non-Muslims, but other religious communities were also recognized, including the Orthodox Christian, Jewish, and Armenian millets. Muslims and the Orthodox millets accounted for by far the majority of people in Turkey in Europe. Many contemporaries referred to Muslims as "Turks," but the Muslims of Europe included both Turks who were descendants of immigrants from Anatolia, and descendants of Slavic peoples who had converted to Islam. Some Muslims spoke Turkish, others Slavic languages, still others Greek, but all were considered Muslims. In similar fashion, Greeks, Bulgarians, Serbs, and Macedonians, usually identified today as separate ethnic groups, were all part of a single Orthodox millet. Their millet's leader was the Greek patriarch in Constantinople.

In the nineteenth century a combination of external and internal pressures began to break Turkey in Europe apart. From outside the empire, foreign powers, most notably the Russian Empire, sought to diminish Ottoman power. From within the empire, inefficient tax collection and a lack of central authority over local governors and military leaders weakened the Ottoman hold on Europe. But the empire's troubles went far beyond finance and administration. Its very social structure was eroding as the rise of nationalism created new potential for conflict both between and within millets. In regions where members of different millets lived close to one another, nationalism gradually sharpened divisions between Orthodox and Muslim neighbors. In the case of the Orthodox millet, the idea of the nation also divided the religious community along linguistic and ethnic lines. Greeks and Bulgarians, once part of the same millet, gradually acquired separate national identities. The idea of a national identity gradually took root in Greek communities during the nineteenth century and emerged among other ethnic and religious communities, including Armenians, Bulgarians, Jews, and Turks.[4]

Turkey in Europe did not suddenly disappear—it contracted. By 1817 a Serbian principality, smaller than modern-day Serbia, gained considerable autonomy. In 1830 a Greek state, also much smaller than modern-day Greece, gained independence. In 1878 the Ottoman Empire lost Bosnia and Herzegovina and much of Bulgaria, and in 1881 it transferred Thessaly to Greece. With this disintegration of Ottoman power came major shifts in populations.[5] Many European Muslims left for regions still under Ottoman rule.

It was an era of violent attacks and the massacre of defenseless victims. Such massacres were a prominent feature of uprisings in Serbia at the start of the nineteenth century. A largely rural border province of the Ottoman Empire, beginning in 1804 Serbia was the site for a series of rebellions. Serbs killed Turks in Belgrade in 1806, and in 1813 Turks burned villages, killed men, and enslaved women and children.[6] But this rebellion was also different from more recent wars of ethnic cleansing in that it did not begin as a campaign to create ethnic purity. Serb rebels first fought against Janissaries, once-elite Ottoman soldiers who by the early nineteenth century had become little more than hired muscle for corrupt local warlords.

Soon after the uprisings in Serbia, Ottoman rulers faced new challenges from Greeks. Greek nationalist pioneers began to organize outside the empire; the leading Greek nationalist organization,

Filiki Eteria (Friendly Society), was founded in 1814 in the port city of Odessa on the Russian Black Sea coast. In March 1821 Alexander Ypsilanti of the Filiki Eteria led an invasion of the Danubian principalities in what is now Romania. A Turkish force defeated Ypsilanti in June, but a separate Greek rebellion led by Klephts (local leaders barely distinguishable from bandits) gained strength in the Morea (today known as the Peloponnesus), the large peninsula that juts out of southern Greece into the Aegean Sea.

In the early nineteenth century the Morea, the site of the Peloponnesian War between ancient Athens and Sparta, was inhabited by both Greeks and Turks. Some 400,000 Greeks and 40,000 Turks lived on the peninsula, with the Turkish minority concentrated in towns and fortresses. As in later cases of ethnic conflict, the Morea's Greeks and Turks shared common bonds. Like Bosnian Muslims, Croats, and Serbs in Bosnia in the 1990s, Greeks and Turks of the Morea shared a common language: both spoke Greek. But despite their similarities, the two groups displayed mutual hostility. Recalling a visit to the Morea before the Greek War of Independence, the English traveler Sir William Gell described two communities separated by a hill, "holding each other in universal abhorrence and sovereign contempt." Gell thought it odd that the religious doctrines that divided these communities were "preached to their followers in languages unknown to either, enjoining duties which neither followed nor knew."[7] In other words, he asserted that neither Orthodox Christian nor Muslims understood the language or followed the rules of their respective religions.

Nonetheless, war on the Morea was decidedly a war fought between Greeks and Turks. At least one Greek song suggested that the Greek rebels intended to drive out or even kill the Turks of the Morea: "The Turk shall live no longer, neither in the Morea, nor in the whole earth." This was not mere exaggeration: as in later cases of ethnic cleansing, this was war against entire civilian populations. Describing a war against all Turks, Kolokotrones, one of the leading Klephts and rebels sent instructions "to attack the Turkish inhabitants simultaneously, storming them in their different fortresses."[8]

Turks fled from the Morean countryside for towns with fortresses. But the fortresses soon became traps for Turkish forces, and Muslim and Jewish civilians there were besieged by Greek rebels. After taking the fortresses of Malvasia and Navarin, Greek forces massacred Turks. Reports of the killing at Navarin especially shocked British Vice Consul Green. When the massacre ended, Greeks left several hundred surviving Turks—"men, women, and children"—to die on a "small island in the middle of the harbour."[9]

The fall of the Turkish fortress of Tripolitsa in the central Morea on October 5, 1821, brought the single worst massacre of the war. Philhellenes, volunteers from Western Europe who had taken up the popular cause of Greek independence, witnessed the slaughter. A French volunteer described how the Greeks uttered a ululating cry, the "cry of the human tiger, of the man devouring man." Thomas Gordon, an English Philhellene, reported that the victors, "mad with vindictive rage, spared neither age nor sex—the streets and houses were inundated with blood, and obstructed with heaps of dead bodies." At least 8,000 Muslims and Jews died at Tripolitsa alone. Gordon was so horrified that he abandoned the Greek cause. Other slaughters of Turks gained less international attention, but massacres of Turks continued into 1822. Estimates of the total number of Muslims killed varied widely: the initial wave of massacres in April 1821 killed 15,000 of the Morea's Muslims, and the war's final death toll for Muslims may have exceeded 25,000.[10]

Christians also suffered violence, sometimes in reprisal for the massacre of Muslims. Soon after reports arrived of Ypsilanti's uprising on the Danube, the Orthodox patriarch was executed at Constantinople in 1821. In the largest single massacre of Greeks, some three thousand were murdered with the Turkish capture of the island of Chios in April 1822. George Jarvis, an American volunteer with the Greeks who visited the island in May, described the scene of carnage: wheat grew in the fields, but corpses lay on the ground, with clothing and housewares scattered about.[11]

The Greek War of Independence was a starting point for one early form of ethnic cleansing. Greek nationalism was still young,

and only intervention by European powers sympathetic to Greece
ensured a Greek victory. But the war foreshadowed a future in
which violence would lead to national and ethnic homogeneity in
countries that had previously been part of a multiethnic empire.
War remade Greece's population as it would again elsewhere in Europe. Turks no longer lived in the Morea in the Greek Kingdom created by war.[12] This cleansing proceeded without the action of a powerful state. There was in fact no Greek state or anything that closely
resembled one. In the Morea we see the key ingredients that would
reappear in future episodes of ethnic cleansing: the breakdown of
imperial power on the edge of empire in a region with a divided
population.

The aftermath of the rebellions in Greece and Serbia was as
important to the future of ethnic cleansing as the uprisings themselves. Nationalist writers and politicians, Greeks and Serbs, did not
portray the early-nineteenth-century uprisings as the beginning of
national struggle. Rather, they viewed these rebellions as chapters
within a much longer story of generations of Turkish oppression.
In 1844 the Greek prime minister Ioannis Kolletis, speaking to the
Greek Constitutional Assembly, described a centuries-long national
campaign against Turks, a struggle that "began the day after the
fall of Constantinople; fighters were not simply those of 1821;
fighters were and are always those continuing the struggle against
the crescent for 400 years."[13] Complete victory over Turks would
bring the "Great Idea" or *Megali*, the unity of all Greeks in a single Greek state. Both Greeks and Serbs made hatred of the Turks a
major nationalist theme. Vuk Karadžić, an early Serb linguist who
collected Serb folk songs about the medieval Battle of Kosovo, used
the term "cleanse" (očistiti) to describe the killing of Muslims in
Belgrade in 1806. Petar Petrović-Njegoš, the prince-bishop of Montenegro, glorified past killings of converts to Islam.[14] Such sentiments by themselves did not make ethnic cleansing inevitable, but
the drumbeat of hatred of the Turks created the potential for future violence in much of the Balkans where Turks still lived alongside Serbs and Greeks.

Imperial Arson

Another type of early ethnic cleansing developed under very different conditions when the Russian Empire pressed south toward the Black Sea and the Caucasus Mountains in the eighteenth and nineteenth centuries, into the region now held by the Russian Federation to the north of the Caucasus, and by Georgia, Armenia, and Azerbaijan to the south of the high mountain chain. This was a highly complex political and cultural border zone, a region of dozens of languages and many religions, including Muslims, both Shia and Sunni, and Christians, both Orthodox and Armenians. It was also a region of competing empires: the Ottoman and Russian empires met on the Black Sea, and the Ottoman, Persian, and Russian empires all sought power in the Caucasus.[15] The Caucasus was also home to numerous smaller autonomous and semi-autonomous states under local Muslim rulers, as well as remote mountain regions that were beyond the control of any government.

Russian expansion during the seventeenth and eighteenth centuries established a precedent for moving populations for military reasons, but this was a far cry from ethnic cleansing. Russian authorities pursued resettlement as a means to defend new borders rather than as a tool of nation-building. Russia colonized border zones with subjects chosen for their presumed loyalty, such as Cossacks, and relocated other groups during war for their presumed disloyalty. In the late eighteenth century, for example, Russia periodically moved Muslim Crimean Tatars away from the front lines in time of war.[16]

Russia advanced only very slowly into the Caucasus, especially in the mountains of the North Caucasus that today mark the southern border of the Russian Republic. Russia gained control over the Black Sea by the late eighteenth century but did not establish firm control over the north edge of the Caucasus until the mid-nineteenth century. There Russian forces struggled for decades to pacify remote mountain regions inhabited by Muslim tribes in the northwest and northeast Caucasus. These included Circassians and Abkhazians in the northwest and the mountain tribes of Chechnya and Daghestan in the northeast.

These residents of the North Caucasus, commonly described as "mountaineers," were resolute, accustomed to fighting, and led by charismatic commanders, most notably the imam Shamil. Russian forces fought against Shamil for some thirty years. Besieged in 1832 by Russian troops in a mountain village, Shamil escaped through one of the incredible physical feats that made him famous. According to one report, he jumped over Russian soldiers, cut down several, pulled a bayonet from his chest, struck down another soldier, took another leap over a wall, and was gone. In 1839 Russian forces again almost captured Shamil when they cornered him in his mountain stronghold. After a long siege, Russian troops received Shamil's son as a hostage and then stormed the mountain village, but the imam escaped again and in the early 1840s built an even stronger and more effective fighting force. Russians finally took Shamil captive in 1859. By then they accorded him considerable respect: he was taken to meet the tsar.[17]

In a pattern of war that foreshadowed the bitter conflict between Russians and Chechens that ravaged Chechnya in the 1990s, Russian forces asserted their power in the lowlands but failed to take control of the highlands. Russian commanders built forts such as Grozny, the future Chechen capital that was largely destroyed by Russian armies in the 1990s, but their advance stalled when they dispatched columns into the forests and mountains. For years Russian columns accomplished little more than burning highland villages, known as auls. Participants in the Russian campaigns wrote matter-of-factly about arson. Russian General Tornau, describing an 1832 expedition through Chechen forests, wrote, "The auouls blaze, the crops are mown down . . . again the wounded are brought in and the dead."[18] Sometimes Russian forces barely escaped from their arson expeditions.

The violence of imperial war in the Caucasus left its mark on Russian literature. Pushkin, Lermontov, and Tolstoy all described the wars against the mountaineers. In *The Cossacks*, one of his lesser-known novels, Tolstoy, who joined the army in the Caucasus in 1851, made war and violent raids the backdrop to his plot about a young Russian's experiences in the empire's remote border zone. In a "mountain song," Tolstoy provides a sense of the violent cycle of raids and retribution: "The young brave took his plunder from the village into the mountain; the Russians came, burnt the village, killed all the men, and took all the women prisoners."[19]

Frustrated by continued resistance, in the late 1840s Russian commanders tried something different. In place of expeditions into the forests and mountains, they adopted a more systematic policy of shifting populations. Even if they could not capture Shamil, they could move his people. During the second half of the 1840s, Russian soldiers under the command of General Vorontsov cut down trees, built roads, and destroyed villages with the aim of moving mountaineers out of Shamil's territory. Strictly speaking, this was not ethnic cleansing because Vorontsov actually tried to push people *into* territory now under Russian control, rather than drive them from the empire. But many of Shamil's followers responded by moving south. This Russian strategy of clearing forests continued until the Crimean War of 1854–1856.[20]

After the Crimean War, Russia began selected ethnic cleansing, but in the northwest rather than the northeast Caucasus. After Shamil's capture in 1859, Russian commanders in the Caucasus, including Prince Bariatinskii, sought a longer-term cure for the chronic cycle of resistance in the Caucasus. They dedicated themselves to crushing the resistance of Muslim Circassians in the northwest and along the Black Sea coast. Instead of simply mounting another campaign against mountain villages, they devised a strategy to move restive mountaineers and replace them with loyal Russian subjects. In 1860 the Imperial War Council accepted a plan to drive the mountaineers out of the western Caucasus and replace them with Russians.[21]

To empty out the auls, Russian forces embarked on a campaign of burning and killing. "The mountain auls were burned by the hundred . . . ," one Russian observed. "If we managed to catch the inhabitants of the auls unawares they were immediately led away under military escort to the shores of the Black Sea and then sent to Turkey."[22] By 1864 the clearing out of Circassians was complete. Between one and one and a half million Circassians were gone, and much of the landscape was emptied of inhabitants. As one observer described the scene, "there was not a soul to be seen anywhere."[23] The expulsions created a Circassian diaspora. Circassians today live in Jordan, Turkey, Syria, and the United States as well as in Russia.

Under Russian power, the Muslim population of the Crimean peninsula also fell as Crimean Tatars left the Russian Empire in large numbers after the Crimean War. This was not ethnic cleansing: there was no equivalent in the Crimea to the organized terror directed by Russia against Circassians in the northwest Caucasus. But suspicion that Tatars somehow shared the blame for Russian defeat bred hostility to the Crimea's largest Muslim population. Tsar Alexander II, for example, made it known that "this voluntary emigration should be considered as a beneficial action calculated to free the territory from this unwanted population," and Russian officials in Crimean towns made the tsar's sentiments known to the public. The fate of the Circassians provided Crimean Tatars with additional cause to flee: many feared they would suffer similar violence if they stayed. At the same time the idea of religious migration or *hijra* to land under Muslim rule provided an additional motive to leave. Only after some 200,000 Crimean Tatars had departed did Russian authorities, worried by the economic damage caused by mass migration, cease giving out passports to Muslims.[24]

In these examples of campaigns against Muslim peoples in Russia's new south, imperial commanders pioneered a second type of ethnic cleansing. Much more so than in Turkey in Europe, early forms of ethnic cleansing in Russia's southern border zone derived from state power. Russian expulsions followed on military traditions of arson and strategic resettlement, but only after the Crimean War did Russian commanders move an entire people. None of the particulars of the Russian campaign in the northwest Caucasus—burned villages or massacres—was new, but the scale of violence employed by military leaders with the deliberate intent of reshaping demographic boundaries created a new ethnic landscape, one largely emptied of Circassians.

The violence directed by Russian commanders foreshadowed modern ethnic cleansing, but Russian policy remained inconsistent. Even in Russia's southern border regions there was no general policy of ethnic cleansing. The chief motive was primarily strategic rather than the pursuit of ethnic or religious purity. Along Russia's southern border, Russian authorities did not seek to expel or deport *all* Muslim peoples. Indeed, the Russian Empire was in many respects a hospitable home for Muslims, and Russia retained a large Muslim population.[25]

Bulgarian Horrors

Through the mid-nineteenth century, Russian imperial expansion and Ottoman retreat produced the two types of early ethnic cleansing so far described. In the 1870s these trends intersected in Bulgaria, which at the time was not a state but a region within the Ottoman Empire. Bounded on the north by the Danube River, except near the Black Sea, Bulgaria was cut almost in half by the Balkan Mountains. The Balkan range rises to the north of the present-day capital of Sofia and continues east for more than five hundred kilometers. Bulgaria's southeast formed the Ottoman province of Eastern Rumelia. The population, as in most of the Ottoman Empire, was mixed. Orthodox Christians, primarily Bulgarian speakers, made up the majority. (Many Bulgarians also lived outside Bulgaria.) Muslims made up less than 40 percent of the total population of Bulgaria. Contemporary observers of Bulgarian events often referred interchangeably to Turks and Muslims, but in addition to Turkish speakers, Bulgaria's Muslims also included Bulgarian-speaking Muslims known as Pomaks and Circassians, resettled after their flight and migration from Russia. Other smaller minorities included Jews.

The very notion that Bulgarians made up the majority in Bulgaria reflected the growing influence of nationalism on the Ottoman

Empire's millet system. Through most of the nineteenth century, Bulgarians were classified by religion as members of the same Orthodox millet that comprised all of the empire's Orthodox believers, including Greeks. Indeed, the first generations of Bulgarian intellectuals spoke and wrote in Greek, but in the 1830s and 1840s Bulgarians began to protest Greek control of the Orthodox millet. Austen Henry Layard, for example, observed in 1844 that the appointment of Greek priests "caused great dissatisfaction to the Bulgarians, who demanded that these appointments should be given to men of their own race, with whom they could communicate."[26] Bulgarian resentment against Greek religious power intensified by the 1860s to the point where Bulgarian merchants at Constantinople campaigned for an Orthodox church separate from the Greek patriarchate. Ottoman authorities granted this request in 1870, creating an autonomous church called the Bulgarian Exarchate.

Hostile toward Greeks, Bulgarian nationalist pioneers also developed a national historical narrative that depicted Bulgaria's victimization by Turks. The pioneers of Bulgarian nationalism did not yet have a state, many of them did not live in Bulgaria, and many of them had only recently begun to identify themselves as Bulgarian rather than as Greek intellectuals—but they knew that they hated Turks, and they called for their destruction. In a poem from 1866, the Bulgarian nationalist writer and journalist Georgi Stoikov Rakovski portrayed a nation suffering from four hundred years of foreign rule. "The Turkish yoke, four centuries endured, let us smash heroically," he exhorted. Rakovski encouraged a violent revenge: "Let Turkish heads roll, and their corpses become playthings. Let us sweep away Ottoman power." The poet and journalist Hristo Botev, another leading Bulgarian nationalist, also foresaw a future filled with blood. "The Balkan Peninsula," he declared in 1875, "will turn into a slaughter house."[27]

By the 1870s the Bulgarian nationalist movement had taken a violent turn, though not yet on the scale imagined by Bulgarian nationalists. Armed bands known as Chetas crossed over from Romanian principalities to instigate unsuccessful uprisings in Bulgaria. In 1872, Vasil Levski, the leading Bulgarian nationalist revolutionary, was executed for seeking to organize a rebellion within Bulgaria. In April 1876 Bulgarian nationalists tried again, staging an uprising concentrated in the towns and villages of the Balkan mountain range. Hristo Botev, excited by the news, predicted "a terrific and repulsive slaughter with, countless victims on each side," and Turkish defeat. Only in the first prediction was he correct, at least in the short run. Bulgarian revolutionaries failed to mount an effective military campaign in 1876 but nonetheless killed Muslims.[28] Botev himself arrived in Bulgaria with a small force of some two hundred men after the rebellion had already been suppressed and died fighting Turkish forces to the north of Sofia.

The Bulgarian rebellion soon became synonymous with fields of skulls and bones. By the summer of 1876, reports emerged of atrocities, of "Bulgarian horrors," carried out by Ottoman irregular forces to suppress the revolt and in retaliation against Bulgarians. The American journalist Januarius MacGahan, then reporting for the London *Daily News*, provided gruesome details. For his efforts in publicizing Bulgaria's plight, he became known as the "Liberator of Bulgaria"— a statue dedicated to him now stands in his hometown of New Lexington, Ohio. In 1876 he toured towns and villages in the Balkan Mountains and to the south with American Consul General Eugene Schuyler, collecting accounts of massacres in dozens of villages. Most horrific was his visit to Batak, a village in the Rhodope Mountains of southern Bulgaria. There MacGahan found "a heap of skulls, intermingled with bones from all parts of the human body. . . ." Near the town's church and school, the ground was "covered . . . with skeletons." The church itself was full of "partly burnt" corpses. The survivors, some women and children, told of a massacre carried out by Bashi-Bazouks, the term used to describe Turkish irregulars. Much like witnesses of later ethnic violence, survivors of Batak also said that they knew their attackers. Bulgarians interviewed later that year by a British relief worker recounted how Achmet Aga, the commander of Turkish irregulars, convinced them of the sincerity of his promise of protection: "he had lived thirty years their neighbor and had eaten bread and salt with them."[29]

The reports of atrocities caused a political sensation in Britain, where there was already great interest in the fate of the empires of Eastern Europe and Western Asia—an issue referred to at the time as the "Eastern Question." Incensed by the news from Bulgaria, William Gladstone, Britain's former prime minister and the leader of Liberal opposition to his Conservative rival Prime Minister Benjamin Disraeli, excoriated the Turks and condemned British policy in the region. For years Britain had sided with Turkey in order to counter Russian ambitions. Gladstone decried what he termed the "Bulgarian horrors." In a pamphlet on the subject, he called for the Turks to "now carry away their abuses in the only possible manner, namely by carrying off themselves. . . . one and all, bag and baggage." It's likely Gladstone, who listed the various categories of Turkish police and officials he wanted to see leave, was only calling for an end to Turkish administration in Bosnia Herzegovina and Bulgaria, but his use of the phrase "bag and baggage" soon became synonymous with calling for the expulsion of the Turks.[30]

Defenders of Turkey tried to turn the debate into an argument about numbers: they claimed that the reports of deaths were exaggerated. In 1877 Layard, who after his early travels through the Ottoman Empire had gained fame as an archaeologist and was now British ambassador to the sultan's government at Constantinople, rejected the key claims about the Bulgarian atrocities. In reality, Layard countered, some 3,500 people, including Christians and Turks, had been killed in Bulgaria instead of the 60,000 Christians alleged to have perished in the "horrors." With this argument Layard set up something of a straw man. MacGahan himself stressed the difficulty in determining the number of deaths, noting that estimates ranged all the way from 15,000 to 40,000 or even 100,000 deaths. But, he wrote, "fifteen thousand is enough."[31]

Exodus from Bulgaria

Throughout the late nineteenth century, the Ottoman Empire proved it was still capable of defeating uprisings across the Balkans.

In 1875 its forces suppressed a rebellion in Bosnia Herzegovina, and in 1876 the Kingdom of Serbia was quickly defeated when it declared war on the empire. In the spring of 1877, however, Ottoman authorities faced a far more formidable enemy than rebel groups or new Balkan states: the Russian Empire. For generations the tsars had waged war against the Ottomans along the southern borders of the Russian Empire. More often than not, Russia had emerged victorious, though the most recent Russian-Ottoman conflict, the Crimean War in which British and French forces backed Turkey, was an exception. In April 1877, with the consent of local Romanian authorities, Russian forces moved into the Romanian provinces and massed north of the Danube to prepare for an offensive to the south. Bad weather and high water delayed the invasion, but in late June the Russian army finally launched its long-expected invasion across the Danube. Moving south into Bulgaria, Russians reported Christian enthusiasm, with shouts of "Hurrah!" and "Bravo!" at the town of Tirnova.[32] The Russo-Turkish War of 1877–1878 had begun. Although this war has been largely forgotten outside Bulgaria, it created the foundation for the modern Bulgarian state. It also foreshadowed many of the ethnic conflicts of the next century.

In the first phase of war, Russian forces swept through northern central Bulgaria to the Balkan Mountains, then crossed the mountains into Bulgaria's south, led by General Gourko, a veteran of war in the Caucasus. But the bulk of Russian forces remained in the north, and by August 1877 the war entered a second phase. Turkish resistance stiffened and Russian armies retreated back across the Balkan Mountains. Both sides became involved in protracted struggles in northeast Bulgaria and for the fortress of Plevna to the northwest of Sofia. In the war's third and final phase, the Russians took Plevna on December 10, 1877, and once again pressed south. The war ended in 1878 with Russian forces near Constantinople.

Journalists who followed Russian troops across the Danube into northern central Bulgaria found towns emptied, except for Christian Bulgarians. Recasting Gladstone's words of the previous year, the British war correspondent Archibald Forbes observed, "Now the

whole region was Bulgarian pure and simple, since the Turkish inhabitants with rare exceptions had gone away bag and baggage."
Muslims had almost entirely disappeared from the towns. Their
shops, houses, and mosques were smashed and ransacked. Their
Christian neighbors protected their own houses, marking their doors
with chalked crosses, and looted Muslims' abandoned homes. That
was the scene at the town of Tirnova. In the town's Turkish quarter,
now emptied of Turks, the journalist Frederick Boyle observed "an
honest Bulgar working . . . his family around him. With the ener-
getic aid of his wife he was unscrewing hinges and locks whilst the
children . . . loaded themselves with the window sashes."[33]

Turks abandoning their homes in 1877 left with everything they
could carry, or, as a correspondent for the London *Daily News* put it,
with "wives, children, effects, flocks and herds, from before the advancing Russian."[34] Turks took their bedding, clothes, pots and pans,
and rugs, all piled atop carts, and animals walked alongside. Their
flight began as an exodus not only of people but of sheep, oxen, and
even fowls, though many of these animals died or ended up in the
possession of Christians.

For the most part, Turks fled east or south. Many went east toward
the Black Sea coast and the port of Varna, a region still held by Ottoman forces. A British diplomat at Varna reported that "the roads are
crowded by Turkish families flying from their homes." Thousands of
families camped in fields in eastern Bulgaria. In August 1877 a journalist put the number of "semi-starved" Turkish families in one town
at sixty thousand. Others turned southward across the Balkan mountain passes. Some reached Adrianople, the original Ottoman capital in
Europe, while others traveled all the way to Constantinople.[35]

The Russo-Turkish War was one of the first to feature what
would become a common element of ethnic cleansing: civilians who
expect to be attacked because of their identity. This fear of attack, in
addition or apart from actual violence, remains a major cause of
flight in ethnic cleansing. From Kazanlak, a center of the rose trade
on the southern flank of the Balkan Mountains, British Consul
Blunt described the pervasive fear. "The Bulgarians are afraid," he

wrote, "that the Turks, if successful, will massacre them, while the Turks attribute the same intention to the Bulgarians should the Russians be victorious."[36] Depending on which army was approaching, Muslims and Bulgarians hurriedly packed up their belongings and abandoned their homes.

Each phase of the war led to flight. Muslims fled first during the initial Russian offensive, but Bulgarians in turn fled when Russian forces retreated in the war's second phase. As Turkish forces returned to towns along the southern edge of the Balkan Mountains, many Bulgarian Christians packed their possessions and left. Some made their way south to the comparative safety of larger towns and cities such as Adrianople; others went north following the Russian army. The countryside north of the mountains swarmed with refugees. A correspondent for the *Daily News* suggested that the "whole population of the southern slope of the Balkans have crossed the ridge, and are now drifting slowly down the northern slope." Meanwhile some Muslims returned to their homes. A British officer serving in the Ottoman army, Valentine Baker, recalled that "the people gained heart, and pushing onward . . . re-occupied the villages which they had originally quitted."[37]

By late 1877 it had become clear how civilians would react to the two armies' advances and retreats. Thus in the war's third and final phase, Ottoman defenses collapsed, and Muslims poured out of Bulgaria and Eastern Rumelia. The mood in Sofia was grim as large numbers of Muslims and Jews prepared to leave the town. Among all the region's non-Muslims, Jews enjoyed the most comfortable relations with Muslims, and they shared Muslim fears when Russia won the war. On December 20, Captain Fife, a British military attaché, observed "the feeling of alarm amongst the inhabitants, and the daily departure of large numbers of them from the town." The mood soon turned still blacker. By December 28 a relief worker saw women and children begging government officials for carts for the journey south.[38]

Panicked Muslims tried to make their way out of Bulgaria despite bitter winter weather. Wreckage and castoff belongings

marked their path. Traveling in southern Bulgaria, Archibald Forbes
found a thirty-mile-long trail of "corpses, dead animals, broken
arabas [carts], piles of rags and stray tatters of cast-off clothing."
Others made their way out of Bulgaria by train. Refugees lined the
road to the railway station at the town of Tatar Bazardjik, southeast
of Sofia, and burned their carts for fuel while they waited. They
fought to get a place on a train, including some that did not yet have
an engine. Colonel Noel Allix, an English officer and aide to Baker
Pasha in the Turkish army, reported that the refugees filled every
available space on board the trains: ". . . they clambered onto the
tops of the snow-covered carriages, crowded onto the side boards and
even on the buffers." The severely overloaded trains crept toward
the Ottoman capital—the journey from Adrianople to Constantinople alone could take between four and eight days. Refugees who finally reached Constantinople crowded the roads outside the city. In
the city, refugees camped out at the Hagia Sophia, the mosque created out of the great Byzantine cathedral.[39]

Something that approached what we now call ethnic cleansing
was one result of the Russo-Turkish War of 1877–1878. Turks were
gone, it seemed, "bag and baggage," condemned to flight across Bulgaria. Like the Greek War of Independence, one outcome of the
Russo-Turkish War was greater national purity. War accelerated the
transition from the diverse society of Ottoman subjects—who came
from varied ethnic backgrounds, spoke many different languages,
and practiced different religions—toward new, more homogenous,
ethnically distinct states. At a minimum, hundreds of thousands of
people fled Eastern Rumelia and Bulgaria. Estimates of the total
number of Muslim refugees vary enormously, from 150,000 to 1 million or even 1.5 million. Whatever the exact figure, Bulgaria became
increasingly Bulgarian. Between 1878 and 1913, the Muslim community fell from 26 percent to 14 percent of Bulgaria's population.[40]

In one respect, however, the terror and flight of refugees during
the Russo-Turkish War fell short of fully developed ethnic cleansing
as we define it based on twentieth-century events: the extent of expulsion. This was not yet the complete expulsion found in some cases

of twentieth-century ethnic cleansing. The new Bulgaria created by the Treaty of Berlin in 1878 comprised a principality north of the Balkan Mountains and a separate semi-autonomous region of Eastern Rumelia to the south, and it was not exclusively Bulgarian. Tens of thousands of Muslims returned, though many left again after suffering intimidation, harassment, and invasion of their property.[41]

While some Turks remained in Bulgaria despite massive flight, the language employed by contemporaries described the events of 1877–1878 as something far worse than what we now term ethnic cleansing. Without recourse to a ready-made vocabulary of atrocity—of words such as "ethnic cleansing" or "genocide"—they saw expulsion as tantamount to extermination, with the ultimate goal of getting rid of Muslims. Layard reported in July 1877 that both Muslim civilians and the Turkish government now believed that Russia intended "either to exterminate the Mussulman population by the sword, or to drive it out of the country." There was similar talk of extermination of Bulgarians. Finding no Bulgarian men in September 1877 in the town of Carlova on the southern slope of the Balkans, the British diplomat J. Henry Fawcett suggested that some were probably hiding in the mountains or with the Russians, but he feared worse. "As to the men," he informed Layard, "I can only think that the authorities have come to the conclusion that they will exterminate the Bulgarian race in these parts." Watching repeated waves of violence sweep across Bulgaria, some observers feared a general war of extermination of both Bulgarians and Turks. British Consul Blunt, gathering information in Adrianople, lamented in early August 1877 that the conflict just to the north was becoming "a war of mutual extermination."[42]

Grassroots Ethnic Cleansing

Observers of the Russo-Turkish War asked who should be blamed for forcing entire groups of civilians out of their homes—a question without an easy answer. No commissions were formed to investigate events in Bulgaria, and many observers alleged that reports from

Bulgaria were exaggerated. *Punch* described rival atrocity campaigns in 1877:

> When Tartar meets Turk,
> With their mutual ferocities,
> Then—horrible work!—
> Comes the tug of atrocities.[43]

No source of information escaped criticism. The long record of British support for Turkey on the Eastern Question raised doubts about the objectivity of British diplomats, but diplomats such as Ambassador Layard accused journalists of hunting for atrocities and bidding for bodies to sell papers. Correspondents, in turn, accused political authorities of attempting to influence coverage. According to the journalist Wentworth Huyshe, a "political commission"— actually Turkish censors—blocked damaging stories but "invited" correspondents to cover a violent attack on Turkish villagers.[44]

Only one issue was little disputed: the chief responsibility for violent attacks on Bulgarians. Most observers blamed Bashi-Bazouks, the Turkish irregulars, along with Circassians. There were a few skeptics: the journalist Frederick Boyle, who accompanied Russian forces, mocked reports of Bashi-Bazouk activity, suggesting that they tended to disappear like a "Snark or a Boojum," the fantasy creations of Lewis Carroll. But most believed the reports. The Bashi-Bazouks terrorized towns like Carlova, south of the Balkan Mountains, where a British diplomat found thousands of refugees, mainly women and children, fearful of plunder and sexual assault. From his position as a commander in the Ottoman army, Valentine Baker admitted that misdeeds attributed to Circassians and irregulars were real. Even the Turkish commander, Suleiman Pasha, complained that "he thought that his government had committed a great mistake in calling out Bashi-Bazouks and other irregulars."[45]

Bashi-Bazouks earned general opprobrium, but there was no such consensus about who was to blame for Muslim flight. For Ottoman sources, the Russian campaign to drive Turks out of Turkey in Europe explained the persecution of Turks. Many British diplomats, perhaps influenced by Britain's long-term policy to support the Ottoman Empire as a counterweight to Russia, echoed Ottoman accusations of a Russian plan to expel Muslims. Describing the damage along a 150-mile belt of towns and villages on the southern edge of the Balkan Mountains, British Consul General Fawcett asked in September 1877 "what horde of savages has passed over this smiling land; have Attila and his Huns come to life again? The answer is, that all that has happened has been the presence for three short weeks of a detachment of the great army of . . . the Tzar of Holy Russia." Ambassador Layard gradually reached a similar conclusion. At first he was hesitant to accuse Russia's government or generals of pursuing the destruction of Bulgaria's Muslims, but by the war's end his opinion had changed. As Muslim refugees fled toward Constantinople in January 1878, he declared, "It seems but too probable that the Russians are seeking to exterminate or drive out the Mahommedan population."[46]

The Russians, however, denied any intent to empty Bulgaria of Muslims. Tsar Alexander cast the war as a campaign to protect Christians, but he offered at least some assurance to Muslims: those guilty of crimes would face punishment, but the innocent would not lose their property or wealth.[47] Within the Russian leadership, General Ignatiev spoke most extensively on Russian war aims. In 1875, before the war, Ignatiev, who was then ambassador to the Ottoman Empire, told a *Times* correspondent that Russia planned no advance on Constantinople. The very same nationalist forces that posed a threat to Ottoman rule over Europe would also impede the Russian government. Russia, whatever its wishes, before the "instinct of nationality and love of local self-government spread even among the less advanced races, would now, for its own sake, shrink from the responsibility of subjecting to its sway twenty millions of subjects of various race, creed, and language." Once war began, Ignatiev denied any Russian intent to drive away Muslim civilians. According to one British correspondent, Ignatiev "spoke of the Mahommedan exodus with vexation."[48]

Not everyone took Ignatiev at his word, but there were more fundamental problems with blaming the Russians for Muslim flight.

For one thing, there was no direct evidence of any Russian policy to cleanse Bulgaria of Turks. As war approached, the Russian government took great pains to instruct its soldiers in the laws of war. Also, the Russians lacked any obvious motive for ethnic cleansing. We know today, for example, that in the early 1990s Bosnian Serb paramilitary forces wished to create pure Serb enclaves in Bosnia, but it seems doubtful that Russian forces in 1877 had an equivalent plan. It should not have mattered to the Russians, as masters of a vast multiethnic empire, if Muslims remained in an independent Bulgaria. Russia had encouraged large-scale Muslim migration from the Caucasus in the 1860s, but that was only after years of war and stiff resistance, and even then Russian authorities had not sought to expel Muslims from all regions of the Caucasus. Applying the policies of the Caucasus to Bulgaria might have explained Russian attacks against colonies of Circassians who had been recently resettled in the Ottoman Empire, but it would not have inevitably led to across-the-board efforts to expel Muslim peasants and urban residents. Russian authorities did single out Circassians during the Russo-Turkish War, banning them from returning to their new homes in Bulgaria, but this policy did not extend to other Muslims. Russia actually cared for Muslim refugees at Adrianople and encouraged them to return to their homes. Finally, the very same Russian army that had been condemned for inciting atrocities received accolades for its professionalism. The London *Daily News* expressed disbelief in July 1877 "that in Bulgaria there has been a single instance of personal maltreatment of a Turkish civilian at the hands of Russian soldiers."[49]

If the Russian army had behaved so well, why were so many Turkish houses empty and looted? The blame, several reporters charged, lay squarely with the Bulgarians. Bulgarians, Boyle asserted in July 1877, "are capable of any outrage. . . . I know that they have murdered great numbers of Turks." Others arrived at similar conclusions. Francis Stanley, another special war correspondent, declared, after visiting a village in northern Bulgaria, that "all the ruin was caused by the Bulgars."[50]

The debate over whether Russians or Bulgarians caused Turks to flee is much more than a long-forgotten dispute about responsibility for crimes in obscure towns and villages. The controversy concerns a key issue in ethnic cleansing: who is responsible—state and military authorities, or ordinary people? If perpetrators in Bulgaria in 1877 were chiefly Russians, then the Russian state, acting through its military, initiated and organized Muslim flight, which would support the hypothesis that ethnic cleansing is a crime carried out by states. But if the perpetrators were chiefly local Bulgarians, this would confirm the view that ethnic cleansing rises from society's grass roots.

Detailed eyewitness reports collected by British diplomats revealed a more complex pattern of attack in which both Russian Cossacks and local Bulgarians drove out Bulgarian Muslims. One of the most striking examples came from Balvan, a village in north central Bulgaria. British Vice Consul Edmund Calvert collected much of the evidence about Balvan from Muslim refugees who escaped to the south. The war reached Balvan when Cossacks arrived on July 7 and demanded that residents surrender their arms. The villagers complied, but the next day two more squadrons of Cossacks arrived, this time accompanied by two thousand to three thousand Bulgarians from nearby villages, armed with hatchets, clubs, and guns. The mob plundered the village, taking away cattle and seizing valuables. "They then set the village on fire," driving those who tried to escape ". . . back into the flames." All the while, "the Cossacks, who formed an outer cordon around the village, looked on quietly."[51]

The attack on Balvan was not unique. Similar attacks were made on villages both north and south of the Balkan mountain range. One such massacre took place to the south of the eastern edge of the Balkan Mountains, at the mixed Turkish-Bulgarian village of Büklümük. Occupation ended in late July with a massacre carried out by both Cossacks and Bulgarians. As Cossacks surrounded the village, Bulgarians took the men to a barn, which they set on fire, shooting at those who tried to escape. On July 29, only days before Turkish troops recaptured the village, Bulgarians and Cossacks set fire to houses containing the village's women and children. They shot and killed those who tried to escape, including the two-and-a-half-year-old daughter of one of the refugees who recounted the village's destruction to British Vice Consul Calvert.[52]

Despite doubts raised about possible exaggeration in tales of atrocities from the Russo-Turkish War, survivors' stories rang true. First, diplomats like Calvert looked for innocent stories from reliable witnesses. Second, survivors who fled to different places told consistent stories; other survivors of the attacks on both Balvan and Büklümük gave similar accounts to other British diplomats. Finally, there was the direct physical evidence. When the reporter Frederick Boyle passed through Balvan in late July, he found the village in ruins. All that remained of Turkish houses were "charred posts, black rafters, heaps of ashes. . . ." Bulgarians alone had escaped destruction: their "huts were unharmed of course."[53] Such evidence of selective destruction is remarkably similar to ethnic cleansing more than a century later in Yugoslavia and the Caucasus.

The role of Bulgarian Christians in driving out Muslim neighbors was the most striking aspect of the survivors' accounts. Much like witnesses to ethnic cleansing in Yugoslavia in the 1990s, who described attacks by their friends and neighbors—people they had drunk coffee with, grown up with, or at least knew as acquaintances—Muslims who fled villages in Bulgaria in 1877 often said that they knew their assailants. Asked whether he recognized any of the Bulgarian attackers at Balvan, one Muslim refugee from the village answered, "Oh yes; a good many. They were from the villages in our vicinity." Fleeing Büklümük, Mehmedoglu Ahmed, age twenty-two, encountered a local Bulgarian grocer brandishing a knife. In this war of neighbors, Ahmed asked, "Do not strike me, have we ever quarreled?" When Calvert met Ahmed, he was wounded on his right arm.[54] Similar accounts of neighbors turning on neighbors were related by refugees from other villages south of the Balkan Mountains.

Eyewitness accounts of terror indicated that ordinary Bulgarians were not simply pawns of Russians but active participants in terror. Russian forces—witnesses most often mentioned Cossacks—helped to create the conditions for it. But a significant number of Christian

Bulgarians (an exact percentage is not possible) attacked their Muslim neighbors and acquaintances. Far from being the exclusive invention of military or political leaders, ethnic cleansing began in part as a grassroots movement in time of war.

Although Muslims were the chief victims of Bulgarian Christians in 1877, Bulgarians also attacked Jews. A Jewish merchant who fled Kazanlak described repeated plunder as well as the murder of Jews by Cossacks and Bulgarians. At Eski-Zaghra, another town just south of the Balkan Mountains, it was not the town's Bulgarian residents but Bulgarians from nearby villages who plundered the homes and stores of Jews and Turks, and who tore up copies of the Koran and the Torah.[55]

The most difficult thing to understand in this, as in any other case of ethnic cleansing by ordinary people, is why Bulgarians attacked their neighbors. Plunder was one obvious motive: Bulgarians took both animals and property. Turkish refugees from one village near the Balkan range complained of Bulgarians who left "nothing but the bare walls and floors."[56] Undoubtedly there were many such crimes of opportunity, but it is difficult to see mere greed as the root cause of the extraordinary violence and cruelty of 1877. Some foreign observers sensed an underlying motive deeper than opportunism: a growing Bulgarian antipathy toward Turks. We could call this antipathy nationalism, but this would present another problem: explaining how peasants acquired a sense of Bulgarian national identity. Key institutions, such as schools, the press, and military conscription, that encouraged nationalism among peasants in Western Europe developed much more slowly in Europe's East.

Nonetheless there were several avenues for the spread of Bulgarian nationalism. The first was education: literacy rates were low, but new schools had been established in many of the larger villages by the time of the 1876 uprising, and several accounts of the revolt referred to the role of schoolmasters.[57] Second, nationalism built upon preexisting identities such as religion or, in the case of Bulgarians, the newly formed separate Bulgarian branch of the Orthodox church. Third, personal experiences—none of which required reading—also reinforced national boundaries. It is a mistake to assume that only lessons from a schoolmaster or a drill sergeant can convert a peasant to nationalism. Revenge, in particular, provided a different kind of schooling in nationalism and national struggle. Cycles of massacre and flight were more than personal calamities. They were collective experiences that strengthened national identity and built a desire for revenge. In Bulgaria the cycle of revenge that began in 1876 carried over into the Russo-Turkish War of 1877–1878. When Balvan's Muslims, for example, asked for protection against Bulgarian plundering, one Russian told them the attack was retaliation for the burning of a monastery during the previous year's rebellion. The same refugee who told this story to a British diplomat also saw the violence at Balvan as revenge, but he differed on the details. The monastery had been burnt by troops, but only after Bulgarian Christians first attacked Muslims in 1876.[58] In this case there is little chance of getting to the truth: the key point is that contemporaries increasingly attributed local violence between Christians and Muslims to cycles of revenge.

"As Bitter Against the Greek as the Armenian Is Bitter Against the Turk"

Except perhaps in the number of refugees it produced, the ethnic violence that shook Bulgaria in the 1870s was not unique. In the 1890s an uprising against imperial power again led to ethnic cleansing on the borders of Turkey in Europe, this time on the island of Crete. The Greek Kingdom founded after the Greek War of Independence made up only a small part of the territory of modern-day Greece. The small boundaries prompted Greek nationalists to pursue the idea of *Megali*, a greater Greek state that would unify all Greeks. That meant acquiring more territory, including Thessaly and Macedonia to the north as well as Crete. But because neither Macedonia nor Crete was exclusively Greek, such nationalist goals raised the threat of ethnic and religious violence between Greeks and those neighbors who did not wish to be a part of Greece, especially Muslims.

Greece obtained Thessaly most easily. In 1881 Greece gained the region through a convention with Turkey that followed the 1878 Berlin Congress. The transfer caused alarm among Muslims, and some left for Smyrna. In May 1882 a British diplomatic report described the "continued emigration" of Thessaly's Muslims. Numbered at some forty thousand in 1881, Thessaly's Muslim population continued to drop sharply until it reached three thousand or fewer by 1911.[59]

Gaining Crete proved far more difficult for Greece, even as maintaining order on the island challenged distant Ottoman authorities in Constantinople. Crete today may seem obviously Greek, but that was not always the case. Crete was, in many respects, the nineteenth-century Cyprus, a large Mediterranean island settled by both Greek Christians and Muslims who fell into intractable conflict. The pattern of settlement was similar to that in the Morea before the Greek War of Independence in that Christians predominated in the countryside while Muslims were concentrated in towns.

Throughout the late nineteenth century Greeks on Crete who favored *enosis*—the term for union with Greece—staged rebellions. These uprisings and the Turkish retaliation that followed claimed numerous victims. Thousands fled, for example, during the insurrection of 1866–1868. William Stillman, the American consul in the town of Canea in western Crete, observed how the entry of Muslims into towns "was the signal for a panic with the Christians and a frantic exodus commenced. The Lloyd steamers were overcrowded every trip." Attacking a monastery at Arkadi, Ottoman forces carried out what Stillman referred to as a "Holocaust," reportedly killing "all who fell into their hands" until a priest blew up the magazine.[60] Thousands ultimately left for the Greek mainland where they received aid from foreign benefactors including Samuel Gridley Howe, an American supporter of Greece. Other uprisings followed: a rebellion in 1878 and yet another uprising in 1889.

By 1895 Crete was again ripe for violence. Ottoman authority had now greatly weakened. Elections early in the year passed with less violence than some had feared, but political killings resumed by

June. The mounting violence encouraged the formation of Epitropi, Greek committees of reform that soon turned to military action. Christians threw support behind the Epitropi while Muslims in the countryside began to flee their homes for coastal towns. After months of mounting tension, violence exploded on May 24, 1896, at Canea in western Crete. Fighting between Christians and Muslims came to a halt with an August 1896 agreement, but the familiar cycle of violence and panic soon resumed. In early February 1897 fire destroyed the Christian quarter at Canea, and almost all of Canea's remaining Christians fled, either to Greek islands, or to ships from an international squadron of European powers that arrived at the town in midmonth. Through the spring months, Muslim refugees poured into the port towns emptied of Christian residents.[61]

As in the Russo-Turkish War of 1877–1878, the massive flight of civilians on Crete in the 1890s cannot be explained primarily as a crime of states, because the power of both Greece and the Ottoman Empire was so obviously limited on Crete. Ottoman forces struggled to pacify the island, and the Kingdom of Greece intervened directly only in the last months of the conflict. Crete's own Greek rebels presented a far greater threat to the island's Muslims than did the relatively small contingent of fifteen hundred Greek troops who arrived in February 1897. The rebels' Cretan Committee warned in February 1897 that the island's Muslims would pay a heavy price if Crete did not gain union with Greece. If Greeks were to conclude that Muslims had prevented union, "we should see a war of extermination waged between Christians and Turks."[62]

In a war in which neither Greek nor Ottoman forces controlled large parts of Crete, much of the pressure for ethnic cleansing came from the grass roots. This was especially true when Muslims fled. In inland districts, Christians robbed Muslims and held them hostage, allegedly to prevent further killings of Christians. Muslim losses in rural Crete were measured in the island's chief commodity, its olive trees and olive oil. West of Canea, British Consul Biliotti reported in January 1897 that Christians had robbed Muslims of their "olive oil, wearing apparel, even a few head of cattle." Peasants who abandoned their "olive crops," he predicted, "are not likely . . . to go back."[63]

Many of the reports of violence came from rural districts far from any independent witnesses, but Consul Biliotti caught a firsthand glimpse of Christian desire to expel Muslims. In March 1897 he traveled with an international force dispatched from Canea to evacuate Turks from Candanos in southwestern Crete. Biliotti held talks with local Christian leaders to arrange for a peaceful evacuation of Muslims. As Muslims gathered to leave, Greeks prepared to loot their every possession. Biliotti saw how "armed Christians rushed down from the surrounding heights by hundreds." They raced for plunder. Those arriving first got the best: "beasts of burden, bullocks, sheep, and goats." Those who came next gained "household utensil and wearing apparel." Stragglers settled for "anything else which was not good enough for those who had preceded them." With only "the clothes on their backs," the Muslims of Candanos set off by road for the coast, but first they had to run a gantlet of "Christians . . . standing or following on both sides of the road."[64] In all, some 1,570 Muslims from Candanos left their homes, along with a few hundred Turkish troops.

Aside from the looting witnessed by Consul Biliotti, growing national animosity provided a second motive for ethnic cleansing on Crete. At first glance any national distinction between the island's Christians and Muslims was slight: they spoke the same language and lived near each other. But cycles of revenge had driven them apart into increasingly distinct nations. Cretans attacked neighbors to avenge attacks on their fellows in other locations. This was vengeance carried out not just in the name of one's friends, relatives, or acquaintances but in the name of the nation. The targets of such revenge suffered attack because of their national identity as well as their own supposed misdeeds. In 1897, British Rear Admiral Harris, for example, noted the danger of revenge by Muslims who learned of killings carried out by Christians. In one case he received reports of "a dangerous feeling among the native Mussulmans . . . to rise and slaughter the Christians in the town in return for the brutalities practised on their co-religionists at Candanos."[65]

War for Crete also signaled an important trend in the future of ethnic cleansing in the key part played by refugees in building fear and hatred of national enemies. Refugees' stories of suffering and atrocities accentuated a national divide between the island's two major communities. From his headquarters at Suda Bay, Admiral Harris noted the explosive effect of refugees in Crete. "The contin ual arrival of refugees escaped from Candanos and the Selinos district, some mutilated and other with reports of horrors," he observed, ". . . has worked them up to a high pitch of excitement."[66] Violence also convinced many refugees that they were fundamentally unlike the group that had caused them to flee. Many of Crete's Muslims concluded that they could no longer live alongside Crete's Greeks. This was what Consul Biliotti learned from the Muslim refugees he accompanied out of Candanos. The refugees, he reported, were "so convinced of the impossibility of living in the future alongside of the Selinos Christians, that they wish to emigrate to Smyrna."[67] Exact figures are scarce, but many left Crete. As late as 1881 the population of Crete included 73,234 Muslims, or 27 percent of the population, but by 1900 the island's Muslim population had declined to 33,281.

The refugees brought their stories of national suffering to their new homes in different lands, where their experiences remained a foundation of nationalist feeling for decades after the war. Violence, flight, and the loss of their land radicalized them. Anger became a prominent element of their identity. Years later the Turkish writer Halidé Edib wrote, "No Moslem hates the Greek as a Cretan. Having suffered from the Greek oppression in Crete and having seen frequent Moslem massacres, the Cretan is as bitter against the Greek as the Armenian is bitter against the Turk."[68]

Greek Fear

The 1897 contest for Crete was resolved not on the island itself but to the north, when Greece and the Ottoman Empire went to war. Colonel Vassos's landing in Crete heightened nationalist excitement in Athens, but war began only in April 1897 soon after Greek nationalists intent on making Macedonia Greek staged incursions across the frontier.[69] Turkish forces won a series of swift victories, and combat ended with an armistice on May 20.

The short Greek-Turkish War is very much a footnote in European history, but it revealed the intensity of Greek fear of Turks. Revenge cycles and hatred of national enemies created new rules of motion. Ordinary civilians lived in a world where fear of extermination at the hands of national enemies brought behavior that struck some foreign observers as irrational. Like the Bulgarians and Muslims in 1877–1878, Greeks displayed an extraordinary readiness to flee their homes in 1897. Thus the Greek retreat after an initial defeat in Thessaly was a withdrawal not just of the army but of many civilians. Greeks made clear what they feared. A Reuters correspondent saw a crowd fleeing southeast by road to the port of Volo, who showed "what they expected at the hands of the Turks by drawing their hands across their throats."[70]

Greek civilians fled south any way they could: on foot or by train or ship. Crowds gathered at the railway station at the town of Larissa seeking a place on a southbound train. A later visit to the station by Sir Ellis Ashmead-Bartlett, who accompanied the advancing Turkish army, revealed the Greeks' abandoned possessions. Ashmead-Bartlett saw "the wreck of innumerable trunks, bags, boxes, baskets, and every kind of baggage," all the things the fleeing Greeks could not fit into a crowded train. News of a decisive Greek defeat at Velestino in Thessaly in early May provoked a new surge of flight. Peasants from the surrounding countryside crowded Volo, pressing into ships to get out of Thessaly. Stephen Crane, author of the *Red Badge of Courage*, then working as a war correspondent, placed the number of refugees on one ship at fifteen hundred.[71] Tens of thousands of refugees were forced to camp out in the countryside.

Greek civilians may have exaggerated the dangers presented by the Turkish army. Past failed rebellions against Ottoman rule had led to harsh reprisals against civilians, but Ottoman authorities already recognized Greek sovereignty over Thessaly. Some correspondents traveling with the Turkish army testified to the good behavior of Turkish soldiers. Ashmead-Bartlett, a visitor so friendly to the Turks that he dedicated his book on the war to the Ottoman army, joined several foreign correspondents in sending a telegram to the British ambassador in Constantinople testifying to the "admirable conduct of the Ottoman soldiers."[72] Ashmead-Bartlett met Greek peasants, however, who complained of being plundered by Albanians and by Vlachs, a mountain people of herdsmen with a language related to Romanian.

Not surprisingly, the war looked very different to Turks than to Greeks. The same troops whose approach drove Greeks to flee Thessaly were sometimes men returning to their old hometowns. Entering Larissa with the Turkish army, a British correspondent "met more than one Turkish soldier who had been born in Larissa and lived there all his life" before being driven north by "the persecution of their Greek neighbors" to places like Salonica.[73]

Victory proved anticlimactic for Turks. Larissa remained a foreign town for them because the peace settlement of September 1897 made only very small border adjustments in Turkey's favor. There was no immediate Greek union with Crete. Instead, Greece accepted the European powers' position that Crete be granted autonomy, and in November 1898 Prince George of Greece became governor of the island. Crete finally declared union with Greece in 1908, and Cretans entered the Greek Assembly in 1912.

Pogroms

Whether in Crete, Bulgaria, the North Caucasus, the Morea, or elsewhere, the mass flight of particular ethnic and religious groups during and after war was the most important early form of ethnic cleansing, but much of Europe also experienced another brutal form of ethnic and religious violence during the nineteenth century: the pogrom. A term derived from the Russian word for riot, a pogrom is a mob attack against an ethnic or religious group. Its features typically include beatings, looting, arson, destruction of property, and often murder. The prototypical pogroms were mob attacks against Jews in the late Russian Empire, but even more violent attacks occurred against Armenians in the Ottoman Empire in the 1890s, and waves of massacres and attacks characterized the early-twentieth-century conflict between Armenians and Azerbaijanis, then called Tatars, in the Caucasus.

Pogroms and ethnic cleansing share similar features, but they differ in intent and scale. In most pogroms there is no effort to expel an entire ethnic or religious population, and the violence is usually shorter-lived or more sporadic than in ethnic cleansing.[74] On a spectrum of violence against ethnic and religious groups, where genocide or extermination lies at the extreme end and ethnic cleansing lies in the middle, pogroms are a comparatively more limited form.

Despite these differences, the history of ethnic cleansing cannot be fully understood in isolation from pogroms. Pogroms did not make future, more comprehensive violence inevitable, but the same groups that endured pogroms in the decades before World War I also suffered later attacks, and typically the level of violence increased over time. Pogroms against Jews in the Russian Empire were followed by far more violent pogroms and massacres during the Russian Civil War and by a wave of pogroms during the early days of the Holocaust in 1941. After facing massacres during the 1890s, Armenians became the victims of genocide in 1915. Violence between Armenians and Azerbaijanis in the early 1900s was followed by ethnic war after World War I and by ethnic cleansing when the Soviet Union broke apart in the late 1980s and early 1990s.

Pogroms also occur during ethnic cleansing and genocide. By their very nature, they provide a vehicle for popular participation in ethnic and religious violence. Almost from the start, pogroms in the nineteenth and early twentieth centuries raised suspicion of official complicity. It was hard to believe that mobs roamed the streets without some kind of encouragement by state authorities. But while public authorities may have done little to stop pogroms, this kind of violence typically reveals a breakdown of law and order rather than deliberate state instigation and direction. Mobs and vigilantes kill during pogroms, and through such mob attacks some European peoples have established traditions of attacking minority communities.

Pogroms first drew wide attention when Jews were attacked in the Russian Empire in the decades before World War I. At the time, Jews lived in significant numbers in several countries throughout the Continent, but the largest populations were found in Central and Eastern Europe: in the German Empire, the Austro-Hungarian Empire, Romania, and especially in Russia. Russia's Jews lived chiefly in two large regions: in the areas acquired from Poland in the late eighteenth century when Poland was divided up by Russia, Austria, and Prussia; and in a belt of provinces in western Russia known as the Pale of Settlement.

As the Dreyfus Affair in France indicated, anti-Semitism was scarcely unique to Eastern Europe, but there the persecution of Jews was especially intense and widespread. While religious and economic tensions between Jews and their neighbors were longstanding, nationalism presented a new threat to Eastern European Jews. Nationalism and anti-Semitism were not inevitably linked, but by the close of the nineteenth century nationalism in Eastern Europe had become highly anti-Semitic. In Romania, for example, leading intellectuals endorsed the definition of Jews as a people outside the Romanian nation. Mihai Eminescu, probably the most influential Romanian writer of the nineteenth century, asserted that "the Jews are not—cannot be Romanians."[75] And Polish nationalists, most notably the National Democratic movement, or Endecja, and its leaders, including Roman Dmowski, adopted anti-Semitism by the 1890s.

Official state discrimination against Jews was also pervasive in Eastern Europe. In Russia and in Romania a growing list of civil and economic restrictions targeted Jews. Known as the "Jewish disabilities," such measures specified where Jews could live, how they could make a living, and what their status was as subjects or citizens. In Russia, for example, Jews outside the Polish provinces were largely confined to the Pale of Settlement.

By many measures, official discrimination was even more severe in Romania. Almost from its origins, the modern Romanian state was inextricably bound up with anti-Semitism. Establishing the United Principalities of Moldavia and Wallachia with the Convention of Paris in 1858, the European great powers included the condition that "all Moldavans and Wallachians shall be equal in the eye of the law." This appeared to end legal discrimination against Jews, who made up some 7 percent of the population. But the principalities' leaders circumvented this requirement by simply declaring that Jews were not Moldavans and Wallachians. In 1878 Romania gained full independence from the Ottoman Empire through the Treaty of Berlin, which specifically mandated that Romania protect its Jewish population. Once again Romania's political class excluded most Jews from the nation. After revisions of Romania's constitution, a Jew in Romania could become a citizen only by having served as a soldier in wars of liberation or through special legislation on an individual basis. Between 1866 and 1904 a grand total of some 2,000 Jews gained Romanian citizenship. Professional discrimination was pervasive, and thousands of Jews, especially in the Moldavian region, were driven off the land. Many Romanian Jews, for their part, saw good reason to leave, and between 1881 and 1910 some 68,000 Jews, about one-quarter of Romania's Jewish population, emigrated to the United States.[76]

In addition to legal discrimination and nationalist suspicion, Eastern European Jews also endured periodic mob attacks. Russia became most infamous as a center of anti-Jewish violence with the wave of pogroms that followed the assassination of Tsar Alexander II in March 1881. Rumors spread swiftly that Jews were to blame for the tsar's murder, and other common talk claimed that the new tsar supported popular vengeance against Russia's Jews. In fact there was no particular connection between the empire's Jews and the assassination, but the first pogrom took place in Elizavetgrad in southern Russia on April 15, 1881. More than two hundred other pogroms followed before year's end, most in southwestern Russia. Mobs, often led by workers—though peasants also joined in the mayhem—attacked Jewish homes and businesses. These pogroms left tens of thousands homeless, and more followed in 1882.[77]

It is unlikely that the Russian government itself prompted pogroms. Pioneering Jewish historians blamed the Russian government for the violence, but despite intense suspicion to the contrary, these pogroms do not appear to have been engineered by Russia's central authorities. The Russian government did, however, accept the supposition that Jewish exploitation of Russians had fed the pogromists' anger.[78] As a remedy, the government enacted new anti-Semitic measures, the May Laws of 1882. These created new state sanctions for official discrimination against Jews. In the last decades of the Russian Empire, these laws restricted the ability of Jews to settle outside towns and buy property in the countryside, and prevented Jews from serving in government, even in the Pale of Settlement.

After mob violence against Russia's Jews subsided in the 1890s, it exploded again in the early 1900s, beginning first in Bessarabia, a region then in Russia's southwest, on the border with Romania. With a name that sounds remote and exotic, with its chance suggestion of Arabia, Bessarabia is difficult to find or locate on most maps. Historically its status shifted repeatedly—it was a territory of Romania, Russia, then again Romania, the USSR, and finally Ukraine and Moldava. In this particular case, history becomes personal: my grandfather and his entire family left Bessarabia before World War I, after their neighbors robbed and tried to kill them. My grandfather and a brother hid in a chimney. Their older sister Minnie, my grandfather recalled many years later at her funeral, "saved father's life when a peasant was going to hit him with an ax. You were then maybe only about eleven or twelve years old. You grabbed the peasant by his shoulders and put your knee on his back and stopped the ax from descending on father's head."[79] Another sister was seized and held by a priest.

The chain of anti-Semitic violence that engulfed my grandfather's family began in 1903 in Kishinev, Bessarabia's largest city with 147,000 residents, including 50,000 Jews. In 1903 a local anti-Semitic newspaper, *Bessarabets*, incited a hatred of Jews, claiming that a boy found dead in a nearby town had been the victim of a

Jewish ritual murder. On April 19, which happened to be Easter as well as the last day of Passover, boys and adult laborers began attacks on Jewish businesses and homes. Attempts at Jewish self-defense failed to halt the violence, and by day's end twelve Jews had been killed. The next day, as local Russian authorities stood by without intervening, peasants and men from nearby towns and villages came to Kishinev to join in the mob, which comprised as many as 2,000 people, moving across the entire city. After attacking property, the mob turned to beatings and murders. Some fifty-one people, all but two of them Jews, died, and hundreds of houses were burned.[80]

From Kishinev the pogroms soon spread beyond Bessarabia. A pogrom followed at the city of Gomel, to the east of Minsk. On September 14, several days after a quarrel between a Jew and a peasant led to a brawl at Gomel's market, between four hundred and five hundred railway workers attacked Gomel's Jewish quarter. In the violence at Gomel could be found another common feature of early-twentieth-century pogroms: Jewish self-defense.[81] Jews formed self-defense committees in many cities and towns, often with the participation of political groups, including a Jewish Socialist labor group, the Bund, as well as Bolsheviks and Mensheviks.

The Russo-Japanese War of 1904–1905 marked a new height in the Russian violence against Jews. Multiple pogroms occurred in 1904 as Russia mobilized for war against Japan, and even more in 1905 after the empire's defeat. The Kishinev pogrom of 1903 had drawn on traditional forms of anti-Semitism, such as the libel of Jewish ritual murder, but during the war nationalism provided a new motive for attacking Jews. Anti-Semitic newspapers and pamphlets charged Jews with not doing their fair share for Russia in the war against Japan, and made bizarre and groundless claims of Jewish treason and collaboration. Anti-Semites seized on reports that Jacob Schiff, a New York banker, helped to issue bonds for Japan. Schiff was not Russian, and other foreign Jewish bankers in fact worked with the Russian government. Still, claims of Jewish culpability proved especially explosive in towns and cities where Russian reservists awaited transport to the war zone in the east.[82]

Nationalists blamed Jews both for Russia's defeat and for the revolution that followed. In 1905 a monarchy on the defensive faced pressure for reforms. Following a general strike, the tsarist government issued the October Manifesto of 1905, which promised a Duma, or parliament, with significant legislative power, elected on the basis of an expanded franchise. The manifesto appeared to confirm victory for reformers, but it immediately sparked a backlash among many nationalists and imperial loyalists who frequently blamed Jews for political liberalization. A wave of exceptionally violent pogroms followed. Nationalist groups known as the Black Hundreds blended extreme anti-Semitism, nationalism, and counterrevolution. As A. Dubrovin, a leader of one of Russia's most vehement anti-Semitic political organizations, the Union of Russian People (URP), told a meeting in Odessa, "The Holy Russian cause is the extermination of the rebels. You know who they are and where to find them. . . . Death to the rebels and the Jews." Throughout Russia the pogromists repeatedly identified themselves with nationalism and national symbols. They sang the Russian national anthem, displayed the national flag, and carried the tsar's picture.[83]

The sequence of events at Kishinev was typical of the 1905 pogroms that swept through Bessarabia. The pogrom began with a demonstration of self-styled "patriots" assembled to counter demonstrations in favor of political reform. The patriots' leaders stirred up the crowds by calling out, "Down with the Jews! Hit the Jews! We want Jewish blood! We will show you what freedom is!" "Hooligans," the term commonly used in Russia to identify young toughs, plundered Jewish homes and clashed with Jewish self-defense groups. In all, an estimated twenty-nine people died. Outside of Kishinev, pogroms occurred throughout Bessarabia. At the town of Akkerman, Russian laborers plundered Jewish homes and held a "dance entertainment" in the house of one Jew. Hundreds of Jews fled to safety to a nearby colony of ethnic Germans, who belonged to another of Bessarabia's minority groups. At one mostly Jewish town surrounded by Moldovan villages, Russian hooligans arrived by train from Kishinev, and Moldovans from the surrounding countryside joined in arson, looting, and murder, leaving at least dozens dead, more than two hundred houses burnt, and two synagogues destroyed.[84]

In the days after news of the October Manifesto, pogroms followed a similar course in southern Russia and through much of the Pale of Settlement. One of the largest struck Odessa, a Black Sea port where 138,000 Jews lived alongside Russians, Ukrainians, and others in a city of nearly half a million. Economic tensions and religious friction among Greeks, Russians, and Jews during the Holy Week had sparked earlier pogroms. Economic and political tensions also ran high in 1905: in June the city experienced a severe economic slump as well as clashes between workers and government forces. The violence began on October 18 with a typical sequence of demonstrations and counterdemonstrations: Jews celebrated news of the October Manifesto, Jews and Russian workers clashed, and Russians rioted against Jews. On October 19 patriots rallied, shouting, "Down with the Jews" and "The Jews need a beating." Shots—it was not clear who fired first, patriots, revolutionaries, or Jews in self-defense—led quickly to violence. Shouting "Beat the Kikes" and "Death to the Kikes," the patriots became pogromists.[85] Between four hundred and eight hundred Jews died, and many more were wounded before the pogrom ended on October 24.

The Russian pogromists of 1905 did not literally attempt to kill or expel all Jews, but they damaged and burned houses, synagogues, and shops, and beat and killed many Jews. Self-defense forces attempted to counter the mob violence but were especially likely to suffer serious injury and death at the hands of both the pogromists and the police. Marauding mobs randomly attacked and killed pedestrians and passengers on streetcars. Victims included men, women, children, and, in some cases, entire families.

The Russian leadership welcomed this turn of events. Certainly Tsar Nicholas II was pleased by the pogroms as an expression of opposition to revolution, despite the threat that such disorder might pose to his government. "The people," he wrote in a letter to his mother soon after signing the October Manifesto, "became enraged by the insolence and audacity of the revolutionaries and socialists;

and because nine-tenths of them are Yids, the people's whole wrath has turned against them." But the tsar was also surprised by the spread of the pogroms: "It is amazing with what unanimity and suddenness they took place in all the towns of Russia and Siberia."[86] If the central government did not actually organize the pogroms, local police forces typically abetted the violence by doing little, if anything, to stop them. On the other hand, most Russians did not participate in the attacks, and some Jews were saved by their neighbors.

Merely living in the empire made life risky for Jews, and more and more of them decided to leave their homes and seek new lives in what they saw as a new world. Many left to find economic opportunity, but they also left to escape violent attacks. More than 90,000 Jews left Russia for the United States in 1905, and the numbers rose to well over 100,000 in each of the following two years.

The Armenian Massacres

Even as Jews endured waves of pogroms in the last decades of the Russian Empire, Armenians suffered even more violent pogroms under the Ottoman Empire. Identified through their language, culture, and religious heritage from an independent Christian church dating back to A.D. 303, Armenians had developed thriving communities across much of Western Asia and Eastern Europe in Persia, Russia, and the Ottoman Empire. Armenians in the Ottoman Empire lived in Constantinople and Smyrna, but they were concentrated in eastern Turkey, in cities and towns including Erzerum, Diyarbekir, and Van, where their neighbors were Turks and Kurds.

Ottoman loss of territory in the west, in Greece, and in Bulgaria paradoxically created both opportunity and danger for Armenians living in the empire's capital, Constantinople, and in its east. New laws pressed on the Ottomans by the European powers established greater equality between Ottoman subjects of different religions, but Ottoman defeats also heightened the government's antagonism toward Christian minorities living in the empire, most notably Armenians. At the same time Armenian revolutionary parties, led chiefly by Armenians abroad, hoped to bring about European intervention by mounting insurrection against Ottoman rule. There were two main parties: the Hunchakists and Dashnaks.

Beginning in the autumn of 1895, an explosion of violence shook the Ottoman Empire's Armenian subjects. The immediate spark lay in events in Constantinople. On September 30, 1895, some two thousand to four thousand Armenians marched toward the sultan's government in the Ottoman capital to present a petition protesting attacks during the preceding year on Armenian villages in the highland region of Sassoun. The protesters also raised demands that could easily be interpreted as infringing on Ottoman sovereignty: they demanded reorganization of the Armenian eastern provinces along "homogenous ethnographical divisions," and called for a new post of governor general for these provinces to be filled by a European. Security at the Ottoman court, however, prevented delivery of the petition, and after a brief altercation between protesters and gendarmes, the rally ended in a riot. Mobs then attacked Armenians in the streets of Constantinople. As the British ambassador Philip Currie reported, based on information he received from a "trustworthy eye-witness," Softas (Muslim students of theology) and Turks "supplied with clubs, set on the Armenians in the streets and beat many of them to death under the very eyes of the police."[87]

A wave of violence followed that decimated Armenians as massacres struck town after town in eastern Anatolia. British Vice Consul Telford Waugh at Diyarbekir recalled that the Armenians "talked of massacre, much as in England we discuss the weather." At Trebizond on the Black Sea coast, for example, tension rose in early October amid reports of assassination attempts against Turkish officials. On October 4 thousands of armed Muslims swept through the streets as Christians took refuge. A full-scale massacre of Armenians, chiefly of men, followed on October 8. The British vice consul at Trebizond reported that "hundreds of armed Turks filled the streets, rushing madly about, and slaughtering every Armenian they could meet."[88] He estimated that five hundred were killed before the massacre ended.

Many more massacres took place at towns and villages in eastern Anatolia. Mobs repeatedly looted and burned houses and shops, and murdered Armenians. Much as in the pogroms against Jews, Armenians fought back. At Erzerum, the scene of a slaughter on October 30, self-defense forces, probably Hunchakists, fired on Turkish soldiers. But the violence ended only after the city's bazaar had been destroyed. In all, more than a thousand shops were ruined. British Acting Consul Henry Cumberbatch saw 309 bodies buried in a single grave after the massacre. Similar attacks in hundreds if not thousands of villages throughout the countryside extended to other Christian minorities, including Syrians, Chaldeans, and Jacobites. From Erzerum, Cumberbatch reported that Kurds and Muslim villagers raided "all the Armenian villages, with very few exceptions" throughout several eastern districts.[89]

The number of massacres declined after November, but the violence did not end. During the massacre at Urfa near Syria on December 28–29, a cathedral crowded with Armenians seeking shelter was burned. An account by an American missionary reported that soldiers broke into the cathedral, and "then entering, they began a butchery, which became a great holocaust. . . . For two days the air of the city was unendurable."[90]

The worst violence of 1896 occurred in June in the city of Van, near Turkey's eastern border. Following a clash involving Turkish gendarmes and soldiers and a group whose identity was never established, mobs of Muslim civilians and Turkish forces attacked Armenians. Defenders, organized by the Armenian political parties, fought off a military assault for days before being slaughtered en route out of the country, despite having received a promise of safe passage.

In sum, the massacres of Armenians amounted to massive collective punishment for the activities of Armenian political parties. Responding to British complaints about harsh treatment of Armenians in 1894, Sultan Abdul Hamid II had already established that he personally supported a policy of sweeping reprisals for Armenian rebellion. It is difficult to trace the transmission of a policy of massacre from central authorities to the local level, but reports of massacres indicated that these attacks against Armenians were coordinated. On several occasions killing began with a signal from a bugle or gun. According to a report from Marsovan, a town south of the Black Sea, the massacre of Armenians began on November 15, 1895, after Muslims left mosques, and "at the same time, just as if a signal had been given, the villagers swarmed into the town from the surrounding country."[91] As the American missionary George E. White (who stayed in Turkey long enough to witness the genocide of 1915) later recalled, "the storm burst with the noon call to prayer from the minarets."

The response of ordinary Muslims varied. Some took part in violence and theft. Indeed, the attacks may have been organized by gender: men and women sometimes carried out different tasks. The British diplomat Robert Graves, for example, learned from his temporary replacement as consul at Erzerum, Henry Cumberbatch, that "hundreds of Turkish women flocked into town carrying sacks in which to remove the loot of the Armenian quarter."[92] Massacres then targeted Armenian men, though some Armenians were rescued by their Muslim neighbors.

Despite the violent attacks of the 1890s, the Armenians of the Ottoman Empire survived as an important group at the end of the nineteenth century. In that sense they were not yet cleansed from the empire, though estimates of those killed ranged from a few tens of thousands to upward of 100,000. Still, Armenians now found themselves in an extremely precarious position. The Ottoman Armenians had become an ethnic minority who faced special risk. Even the memory of earlier massacres did not prepare them for what would befall them some twenty years later.

Baku, City of Blood

Nowhere did Armenians face as much violence as in the Ottoman Empire, but they were also involved in interethnic and religious conflict along the Russian Empire's border to the south of the Caucasus

Mountains, a region known as the Transcaucasus or Transcaucasia. The peoples of the Transcaucasus spoke many languages and practiced many religions, a diversity that created new tensions in an age of emerging nationalism. Georgians and Armenians mistrusted each other, and Armenians and Azerbaijanis (then known as Tatars) viewed each other with increasing suspicion. The Armenian and Tatar populations were often closely intermingled, especially in towns and cities such as Baku, the oil city on the Caspian Sea, in the regions of Nakichevan and Zangezur near the Russian border with Persia, and in the Karabakh highlands.

Like their counterparts in the Ottoman Empire, Russian authorities saw nationalism, in particular Armenian nationalism, as a potential threat to imperial power, but their efforts to dampen nationalist passions badly misfired. Russia in the early 1900s did not follow the approach that the Ottoman sultan Abdul Hamid had adopted only years before. There was no equivalent to the massacres that had swept eastern Anatolia in the 1890s, but Russian authorities took over control of Armenian church property in 1903 and arrested Armenians, and in turn Armenian revolutionaries assassinated Russian officials and wounded the general governor.[93]

Defeat in the Russo-Japanese War and the revolution of 1905 coincided with pogroms in Transcaucasia. Baku, the city dubbed by J. D. Henry, editor of *Petroleum World*, "the greatest blood spot in the mysterious, rebellious and blood-stained Caucasus," became the flash point for violence in 1905. Baku was new, diverse, and extremely tense. Driven by the late-nineteenth-century oil boom, the old town had become a new urban center, growing from a population of 14,000 in 1863 to 206,000 in 1903. It was a mixed city of Muslims, Armenians, Russians, and others, often living in distinct neighborhoods. When violence broke out between Baku's Armenians and Tatars in February 1905, the exact cause was difficult to determine. Both sides told of murders that precipitated days of violence, but Henry, noting the many conflicting versions of events, called Baku "the hot-bed of wild theories, misrepresentations and lies."[94] As in other Russian pogroms, some of the participants, in this case Tatars, came from outlying villages on the city's edge. Several days of fighting left hundreds, perhaps even thousands, dead. Fighting again broke out in September, this time in the oil fields, leaving destruction and still hundreds more dead.

From Baku, ethnic warfare spread across much of Transcaucasia. At the town of Shusha in the highlands of Karabakh in August, Tatars and Armenians engaged in arson attacks. Combat followed, leaving extensive damage and hundreds dead. Nakichevan experienced more of the same. The Italian traveler Luigi Villari, touring the region in the fall of 1905, found Armenians and Tatars ready to blame each other for the bloodshed and destruction. At one mixed village, "the Armenian quarter had been looted even down to the doors and window-frames."[95] Villari's tour of the Araks River valley along the Persian border reminded him of another region then infamous for ethnic violence: Macedonia. All told, between 3,100 and 10,000, including both Armenians and Tatars, lost their lives across the region.

Ethnic Cleansing Before Ethnic Cleansing

By the early twentieth century, emerging forms of ethnic cleansing were already reshaping the ethnic and religious map of Europe. Targeted attacks against specific ethnic and religious groups had swept away many communities from Russian and Ottoman borderlands. Circassians were gone from the northwest Caucasus. The Muslim share of the total population dropped sharply across much of Turkey in Europe—in the Morea, parts of Bulgaria, and Crete. Flight created new refugee communities. As the Turkish writer Şevket Süreyya Aydemir, born in 1897, recalled of his childhood in a refugee settlement on the edge of Adrianople, "Ours was a refugee neighborhood. The flotsam of torrents of refugees torn by wars and massacres from the Crimea, Dobruja, and the banks of the Danube, had been pushed back here." The shift in population distribution was less striking in the case of pogroms—this was one of the factors that distinguished pogroms from early forms of ethnic cleansing—though mob violence nonetheless motivated Jews to leave the Russian Empire.[96]

Sofia was one of many towns affected. This small Ottoman town had become the capital of a Bulgarian nation-state. At first it did not seem suitable for its new role. One British visitor in 1879 described the new capital as a "straggling town," without pavement, gas, even drains. "The Prince's palace would be a very third-rate inn in England." Yet the transition to Bulgarian rule was already under way. Two mosques had been made over into "store-houses." By 1912 Sofia impressed the British war correspondent Reginald Rankin: "Fifteen years ago Sofia was a collection of adobe buildings on the usual Turkish plan. . . . Now it is a modern city, with spacious boulevards and well planted squares."[97]

Early forms of ethnic cleansing across Eastern Europe and Western Asia began both as government policy and as a grassroots phenomenon. Russian conquests of the North Caucasus demonstrated the power of state authorities to remake the map by deliberately moving entire peoples. But much of the pressure to expel neighbors of a different ethnic or religious identity emerged at the local level. A populist path toward ethnic cleansing was most evident in Ottoman regions. Violence and mass flight most often took place when Ottoman authority either broke down or confronted major threats, whether in the Morea during the early years of the Greek War of Independence, in Bulgaria in 1877, or in Crete in 1896–1897. Numerous eyewitnesses to massacres in the wars for Turkey in Europe reported how strikingly ready so many ordinary people were to attack their neighbors, to steal their property, to burn their homes, even to kill them—and to drive away any survivors.[98] Ethnic cleansing was not simply something that bad states did to good people.

The motives for these early forms of ethnic cleansing were varied. Russia moved people to pacify newly conquered border zones, and individuals may have joined in attacks to gain loot. But neither of these motives explains why significant numbers of people attacked their neighbors. The mere fact that ordinary people so often looted does not demonstrate that they drove out neighbors or people much like themselves solely or chiefly for purposes of theft. Nationalism was a vital ingredient of ethnic cleansing. Across Eastern Europe, the pioneers of nationalism sharpened antagonism between intermingled ethnic and religious communities. Publicists, poets, and writers helped build modern national identity, and on the ground floor they placed hatred of neighbors of a different nation. Intellectuals crafted new national ideas and stories, but personal experiences helped spread these ideas far beyond the circles of educated elites. Although literacy was often low, the peoples of Eastern Europe and Western Asia did not learn about nationalism only through books, newspapers, and school: cycles of revenge killings, the experience of flight, and the tales of refugees provided a different kind of schooling in nationalism.

The emergence of ethnic cleansing and pogroms in Turkey in Europe and the southern Russian Empire created potential for still further violence. Victories emboldened nationalists to call for further gains; defeats fed the desire for revenge. The loss of territory provided new episodes in an ever-lengthening story of Turkish victimization, and the arrival of destitute refugees in Constantinople placed a visible symbol of humiliation in the heart of the Ottoman Empire. No single episode of mass flight or massacre made future ethnic violence inevitable, but much of this landscape became the site of further violence, and several of the groups already subjected to attacks suffered future assaults. Where violence had flared in Macedonia and Thrace, entire populations would soon experience ethnic terror, and many of those who survived would flee for good. Where Armenians had endured massacres in eastern Anatolia, they would very soon suffer genocide. Where Jews had suffered pogroms in regions such as Bessarabia and Ukraine, they would later experience far more devastating attacks.

By the early twentieth century, a history of violence and nationalist animosity had already begun to divide many of the intermingled ethnic and religious groups of Eastern Europe and Western Asia, though relations between such groups often remained peaceful and even cordial. Nineteenth-century Serbian, Greek, and Bulgarian nationalist writers and publicists decried Turkish hegemony even as many ordinary Serbs, Greeks, and Bulgarians lived peacefully close to Turks or Muslims. By the turn of the century, Balkan nationalists also increasingly turned against each other, though peasants were less interested in their presumed national identity. The lack of interest in the national question displayed by Macedonian villagers frustrated both Bulgarian and Greek national activists.[99] Partly, differences in the rate at which nationalism spread accounted for this contradiction between images of peaceful peasants and accounts of neighbors who looted and killed longtime acquaintances. But the paradox also revealed a type of cognitive dissonance. While new stories of age-old nationalist hatred constructed by intellectuals, along with the personal experiences of revenge killing and flight, cast entire peoples as national enemies, on an individual level those who were identified as members of an enemy nation might simultaneously be seen as harmless acquaintances or neighbors. This same paradox would remain a key element of ethnic cleansing through the end of the twentieth century.

Farewell to Salonica

THE BALKANS, 1912–1913

O n the northern end of the Aegean Sea lies the city now known as Thessaloniki, Greece's second largest. But in its long and colorful history the city has had many names. Until almost the end of the Ottoman Empire it was not part of Greece and was called Salonica. Leon Sciaky, a Sephardic Jew who grew up in Salonica and left in 1915, recalled a city of many languages, cultures, and religions. In a memoir suffused with nostalgia for the lost world of his childhood, he wrote of growing up in a house that had once belonged to a Turkish official, in a city filled with Greeks, Bulgarians, Gypsies, Kurds, Armenians, and Jews. Salonica's Sephardic Jews, the descendants of refugees who had fled Spain during the Spanish Inquisition, made up the city's single largest ethnic group. As late as the early twentieth century, most still spoke a dialect of Spanish, though some of them, a group known as the dönme, had converted to Islam. By 1912, however, Salonica's days of diversity were numbered. This chief city of Balkan Sephardic Jews, the Selanik of Turks, and the Solun of Slavs was about to become a Greek city.[1]

The transformation of Salonica was part of a broader shift in populations that began with a new pulse of ethnic cleansing during two now largely forgotten wars that preceded World War I: the First and Second Balkan Wars of 1912–1913. The Balkan Wars resembled the Russo-Turkish War of 1877–1878 and the uprisings on Crete: they were not just the wars of armies—villages were burned and entire communities fled.

The Balkan Wars had their roots in the continuing struggle for Ottoman territory in Europe. By the dawn of the twentieth century, the once vast Ottoman European domain had been reduced to a belt of land across the southern Balkan peninsula, from Albania on the west to the city of Constantinople in the east. New nation-states had gained control of the rest of Turkey in Europe, but Balkan nationalists along the borders of the remaining Ottoman possessions hoped to carve out still larger nation-states from what remained. They described compatriots who still lived under Ottoman rule as "unredeemed," and they dreamed of ending Turkish power—or, as many put it, the "Turkish yoke"—to build a larger Bulgaria, a larger Greece, a larger Serbia.

The struggle for the remnants of Ottoman Europe pitted Balkan nationalists not only against Ottoman authority but against each other. Kosovo was one of the key contested zones. Ottoman Kosovo was larger than present-day Kosovo, extending into what is now southwestern Serbia and northwestern Macedonia. Then, as now, Kosovo had an Albanian majority, but Serb nationalists still claimed the region. They viewed Albanians with a disdain that reflected the influence of new racist thinking. From a Serbian "person of some education," W. D. Peckham, British vice-consul in Uskub, had previously heard of the "first steps of the ladder of life, as: first, man; second, gorilla; third, Albanian."[2] But the core of the Serb case for Kosovo rested on history. Serbs mythologized the 1389 battle of Kosovo between Serbs and Ottoman Turks in which the Turks were said to have defeated a Serb force under Prince Lazar. For Serbs, this history and the region's monasteries made Kosovo "Old Serbia," and they demanded that "Old Serbia" be redeemed or returned to Serbian rule.

To the south and east of Kosovo, rival nationalists also disputed the future of Macedonia. This was an Ottoman region that is today divided between Greece, Serbia, Bulgaria, and the Republic of

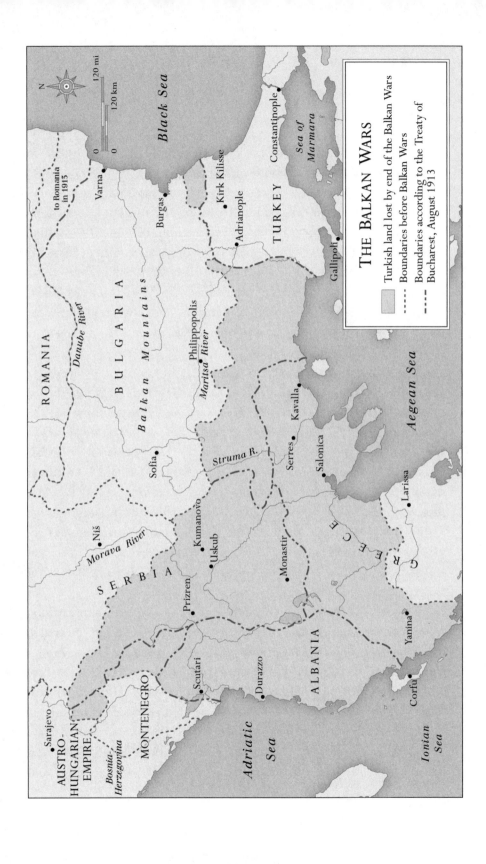

THE BALKAN WARS

Turkish land lost by end of the Balkan Wars

Boundaries before Balkan Wars

Boundaries according to the Treaty of Bucharest, August 1913

Macedonia. Salonica was the chief city of southern Macedonia. As recently as the 1990s, ownership of the name Macedonia caused dispute between Greece and the Republic of Macedonia—one of the states that emerged from the breakup of Yugoslavia. The contest for Macedonia was, if anything, even more complex in the late nineteenth and early twentieth centuries because so many groups regarded themselves as Macedonia's owners. In England, Gladstone had called for "Macedonia for the Macedonians," but the British journalist G. W. Steevens noted in 1897 that "there are at least six kinds of Macedonians. Each insists that it is the true and only heir, and must enter into the whole inheritance."[3] A Macedonian could be a Turk, an Albanian, a Serb, a Bulgarian, a Greek, a Vlach—and there were even some who saw themselves as members of a separate and distinct Macedonian nation.

The antagonism between Bulgarians and Greeks in Macedonia was especially sharp. According to the British traveler Edith Durham, "the hatred between the Greek and Bulgar churches . . . was so intense that no one from West Europe who has not lived in the land with it, can possibly realize it."[4] Rival nationalists subsidized rural schools, and some moved to armed struggle. The International Macedonian Revolutionary Organization (VMRO) was the most powerful of these movements until it led an uprising against Turkey that was suppressed in 1903. Even after the uprising's defeat, violence continued between Bulgarians and Greeks. Durham told of Bulgarians seeking poison to kill Greeks and of Greeks betraying Bulgarian irregulars to Turkish authorities.

The crisis in Macedonia destabilized the entire Ottoman Empire. Army officers stationed at Salonica threw their support behind a Turkish revolutionary movement, the Young Turks, and its umbrella organization, the Committee of Union and Progress (CUP).[5] In July 1908 these officers rebelled against Sultan Abdul Hamid, who in 1909 was deposed by parliament after a failed counterrevolution.

Leon Sciaky, returning to Salonica in 1908 after a year in New York, remembered the excitement of revolution. Muslim "*hodjas, softas*, and dervishes walked arm in arm with Orthodox priests and

Jewish rabbis," and irregulars "still in their mountain garb, sat at the same café tables with Turkish army officers . . . to celebrate the spirit of amity and comradeship."[6] But their optimism soon faded. The Young Turks vowed to modernize and strengthen the empire, but their very successes brought further crisis to Ottoman possessions in Europe. As CUP introduced more efficient tax collection and military conscription, these reforms sparked a series of rebellions in Albania and Kosovo. Albanians on the empire's periphery did not want a stronger, more effective government if that meant conscription and higher taxes. Albanian rebels swept across Kosovo in the spring and summer of 1912. Amidst continuing resistance to reforms, the optimism of 1908 soon faded.

"Let Them Burn!"

Facing an obviously weakened enemy, Balkan leaders joined together to form a Balkan League to take what remained of Turkey in Europe, and in October 1912 Bulgaria, Greece, Serbia, and Montenegro struck. As a military affair, the First Balkan War, at least at its start, was a near rout. Although Ottoman armies had defeated Serbia in 1876, put up stiff resistance to Russia in 1877, and defeated Greece as recently as 1897, the Ottoman military suffered swift and massive defeat in 1912. Turkish defenses in Kosovo and Macedonia collapsed almost as soon as the war began. Morale had been poor and desertion common among Turkish units in Macedonia even before the start of war, and the forces defending Ottoman Europe were badly outnumbered. The combined armies of the Balkan League exceeded their Turkish foes by a ratio of roughly two to one. Foreign observers were struck by the poor condition of the retreating Turkish units. A British diplomat in northwestern Macedonia noted in November 1912 that many of the Turkish soldiers were "without rifles. Knapsacks and greatcoats, and, in most cases, the whole personal equipment, have vanished."[7] Facing an often ill-equipped, outnumbered, and depleted enemy, the Balkan allies rapidly scored one victory after another. Serbs swept into Kosovo and northwestern Macedonia. Greek forces pushed north, entering Salonica. Bulgarian forces pressed south into Thrace.

As the Balkan allies moved on Turkey, dozens of war correspondents from Europe and North America hurried to the scene. Reports on Eastern wars had become a staple for journalists, and many hoped to write books on this new Balkan War. As a group they endured disappointment and frustration: it proved surprisingly difficult to gain access to the front. Military authorities, especially in Bulgaria, sharply limited access to the fighting. Many of the correspondents complained that this marked the end of an era. Instead of traveling to battlefields, they spent hours and days waiting at railway stations in towns behind the front. The Italian journalist Filippo Tommaso Marinetti, one of many correspondents waiting for another train at Novi Zagora, a town south of Bulgaria's Balkan range, tried to amuse his fellow reporters. Best known as the author of the "Futurist Manifesto" of 1909 (which had set forth the goals of one of Europe's most provocative artistic and literary movements), Marinetti cheered onlookers, both foreign correspondents and Bulgarians in the area, by singing, dancing, and reciting his poem "The Automobile." Philip Gibbs, a special correspondent for the *London Graphic*, recounted that the "first recitation of the master Futurist in Novi Zagora was an immense success."[8]

Some of the war correspondents, frustrated by their inability to get close to combat, found another story. Balkan leaders attempted to portray the war as a noble cause, a crusade, a war of liberation, and revenge for Turkish oppression. But journalists, travelers, and diplomats discovered that this was also a war of terror against Muslim civilians, a fact confirmed by an International Commission of Inquiry created by the Carnegie Endowment for Peace. Much like later wars of ethnic cleansing in Yugoslavia in the 1990s, the First Balkan War was a conflict by and against civilians.

On the northwestern edge of the war zone, Serbian and Montenegrin advances brought devastation to Albanians in Kosovo and northwestern Macedonia. Albanians made up one of the most distinct of all Balkan populations. In contrast to some of their neighbors, religion was not the key factor in Albanian identity. So while Serbs were Orthodox, Albanians could be Muslim (the majority), Orthodox, or Catholic. (The most famous of all Albanians of the late twentieth century was the Roman Catholic nun Mother Teresa.) Albanians spoke a language unrelated to Slavic languages, and this distinct tongue, along with their culture and clan affiliation, especially in highland areas, gave them a strong sense of separate Albanian identity.

One of the foreign observers closest to the war in Albania was Edith Durham, the English traveler who possessed a voluminous knowledge of Albania as well as a passionate dedication to Albanian interests. By the time of the first Balkan War, Durham had been traveling to Albania for twelve years. She had become a celebrated figure among Albanians, who sometimes asked her to adopt children and referred to her as the "queen of the mountains." Given her long commitment to Albania, it was scarcely surprising that she issued a passionate indictment of Montenegrin and Serbian conduct. Durham described burned villages and desperate refugees, some of whom were reduced to living in outhouses. She told of visiting more than a thousand families burned out of their homes, and described the hatred of Montenegrin civilians toward Albanians. As villages burned an old woman exclaimed, "Burn! Let them burn! I am very glad."[9]

Leon Trotsky, then working as a war correspondent, also reported on the terror against Albanians. Trotsky was not at the battlefield, but he put together a disturbing account based on his conversations with Serbs. One witness, a Serb friend of Trotsky's, told of "horrors" in Macedonia. The darkening sky at night revealed that "burning was going on all around us. Entire Albanian villages had been turned into pillars of fire." Such arson destroyed not only the homes but the accumulated wealth of Albanian victims. Irregular forces broke into houses of Turks and Albanians to plunder and kill, and Trotsky's friend met a corporal then stationed in Kosovo who, when asked what he was doing, replied, "Roasting chickens and killing Arnauts [Albanians]. But we're tired of it."[10]

Were these accounts accurate? Rebecca West, author of the classic traveler's account of Yugoslavia, *Black Lamb and Grey Falcon*, later depicted Durham as naive, mocking her in particular for her supposed credulity in believing one 1912 report (false, as it turned out) of the castration of the Austrian consul in Prizren by Serbs.[11] West herself has been accused of favoring Serbs in her account. But Durham was an eyewitness to the war, and the Serbs whom Trotsky interviewed had no obvious motive for wishing to put their own fellow countrymen and soldiers in a bad light. Durham, Trotsky, and others provided remarkably consistent accounts confirmed by other sources, including officials of the Catholic church, who also told of extensive massacres. The death toll at Pristina, the present-day capital of Kosovo, alone numbered some five thousand.

To the south and east of Albanian regions, the advance of the Balkan allies also brought terror for civilians living in Macedonia and Thrace. For decades Macedonia had been notorious for brigands, rebellions, reprisals, and waves of assassination, but that history did not prepare Macedonia's residents for the violence of the First Balkan War. Some of the most detailed evidence of killings of Muslims collected by the Carnegie Commission described a reign of terror at Strumnitza, a town in the southeast of the present-day Republic of Macedonia. In 1912 Strumnitza stood at the very edge of Bulgarian and Serbian front lines. Soon after Turkish troops evacuated, Bulgarian and Serbian forces entered the town and irregulars began looting, but even worse followed after Bulgarian forces withdrew. A commission, a sort of martial court presided over by the Serbian commander, summoned Muslims one by one. In each case, one survivor recalled, the Serbian commander asked, "What kind of man is this?" It took only the word of "one member" of the commission to condemn a suspect. More than 590 Muslims were sentenced to death. The victims were marched to an abattoir, bayoneted, and buried.[12]

In 1912 Salonica was a city surrounded by terror as Greek and Bulgarian forces advanced through central Macedonia. The Carnegie Commission found that "even in the immediate neighborhood of Salonica, Moslem villages were burned by the Greek troops." Accounts of the Bulgarian advance painted an even grimmer picture: nearly all reports collected by British diplomats and by the Carnegie Commission told of repeated massacres and arson. At the town of Serres, northeast of Salonica, local Christian and Muslim leaders actually pledged to protect both their communities, but a slaughter of Turks took place once Bulgarian irregulars and troops arrived—estimates of the death toll ranged from 150 to 600. The path of destruction extended to villages along the Struma and Vardar rivers, and the violence reached close to Salonica. Bulgarian bands burned villages some 25 miles north of Salonica. Reportedly they burned people too: a Catholic priest told how a Bulgarian band drove men into a mosque, set fire to the building, and shot those who tried to escape.[13]

The Bulgarian terror campaign against Muslims extended east along the Aegean coast into Thrace, a fertile agricultural region inhabited chiefly by Muslims, Greeks, and Bulgarians. From Kavalla, a port in the center of Western Thrace's tobacco region, Acting British Vice Consul James Morgan tracked the violence. In the war's early days, Kavalla's Christians feared massacres, but with Bulgarian victory, irregulars arrested and killed "a considerable number of Moslems." News from outlying villages was harder to come by, but Morgan also heard of murders carried out to the town's east and west. By December he concluded that the carnage was even greater than initially feared—in many Turkish villages "scores of males have been massacred, in others, rape and pillage have taken place."[14]

Terror in the First Balkan War was broad-based. Muslims of Ottoman Europe faced an onslaught both from invading armies and from their own neighbors. British Vice Consul Wilkie Young, who traveled extensively through the war zone, reported "the wholesale destruction of villages" by Bulgarian forces that faced little or no military opposition. But Muslims discovered that soldiers were not their only enemies. With the advance of the armies of the Balkan League, local residents also participated in attacks. "In many districts," the Carnegie Commission noted, "the Moslem villages were systematically burned by their Christian neighbors." That was the fate of one village outside Salonica. Most of the villagers fled to the larger city, leaving a small detachment of men. Then, a Muslim village leader recounted, "Greek soldiers came, together with people from the neighboring Greek villages. They killed fifteen Moslems," then took all the sheep, goats, cattle, and grain, and finally burned the village. Elsewhere, Bulgarian villagers looted and burned down the houses of neighboring Muslims.[15]

Of all the agents of terror, bands of irregulars prompted the greatest fear during the First Balkan War. Such bands remained a nearly constant feature of Balkan ethnic warfare for well over a century. In the nineteenth century the Bashi-Bazouks, or Turkish irregulars; the Komitadjis, as Bulgarian or Macedonian irregulars were known; and Greek bands of irregulars had spread violence and fear across the Balkans, and the wars of the early twentieth century were no different. Indeed, this pattern of paramilitary violence continued through the 1990s wars for the former Yugoslavia.

In the First Balkan War, bands of irregulars had strong connections both to military authorities and local communities. Concern for international opinion ultimately led Bulgaria to convene some courts-martial, but most observers concluded that the irregulars acted in close cooperation with the Bulgarian army. The British newspaper correspondent Crawfurd Price described the terror as nothing less than a "system" in which Bulgarian columns passed through villages, disarmed Muslims, and armed Bulgarians. The British diplomat Wilkie Young actually saw noted Komitadjis openly meet with Bulgarian authorities. Visiting Serres in late January 1913, he found the chief hotel "full of komitajis." They "were constantly to be seen *tête-à-tête* with Bulgarian officers." At the same time irregular bands were also an important link between the invading Balkan armies and native Christian populations. Sometimes irregular forces were simply local residents with a cache of weapons. The Carnegie Commission found that "a priest and a war-like grocer" led one of the bands that terrorized Muslims west of Kavalla.[16]

The accounts tell us that ordinary people played a major part in the terror of 1912, but they do not tell us why. Theft seems one obvious motive. The evidence came in the form of things taken: grain, animals, and people. Harry Lamb, the British consul at Salonica, reported that looting of animals near the Vardar River was so extensive that in one district sheep and goats were sold for "one third of their normal value." He also learned of survivors of a massacre, girls and younger children, taken to a Christian village.[17]

Local villagers who attacked their neighbors often stole, but theft was not necessarily their chief motivation. Did ordinary people attack their neighbors and acquaintances and breach all established norms of behavior simply to steal some goats? A few criminals can be found in every society, but for a broad cross section of the population to burn and steal, something else is required: a sense that those under attack do not deserve the protection afforded by conventional rules of conduct, and perhaps a conviction that the violence is just or deserved.

National animosity provided another motive for joining in the terror campaign. We have direct evidence of this form of nationalist sentiment, closely tied to revenge. Volunteers with the Macedonian Legion, for example, killed in the name of the nation: one volunteer told the Carnegie Commission how the Legion's men, angered by seeing the bodies of murdered Bulgarians, "retaliated by shooting all the Turkish villagers or disbanded soldiers whom they met next day on their march." From Macedonia to Thrace, revenge cycles sharpened national antagonisms. The ensuing fear was almost palpable. In the war's early days, the British vice consul at Monastir observed the Muslims' growing dread: "They are now in terror of the treatment which, they conceive, may await them if the town is occupied. . . ." Most of all, more than any enemy army or irregular force, "they dread the reprisals of the Christians of the town itself." The currents of revenge and opportunism that poisoned relations between Greeks and Bulgarians and Muslims were not distinct but melded. Wilkie Young, investigating the war zone in December, found that many Muslims executed at Kavalla in November 1912 "seem to have been denounced by Greeks who had a personal grudge against them," though in his opinion extortion was the chief motive for terror.[18]

"Universal Exodus"

Assaults by Balkan armies, irregulars, and local residents prompted Muslims to flee. The entire war zone was a region in flux. Villages and houses went up in smoke, and everywhere civilian refugees were on the move. The outpouring was apparent in areas conquered by the Greeks and Serbs, but the Bulgarian advances in Macedonia and Thrace probably propelled the greatest torrent of refugees. Noel Buxton, a British Member of Parliament and one of the foreign observers most sympathetic to the Bulgarian cause, admitted that "a universal exodus took place from Turkish villages."[19]

Some of those who fled had experienced terror firsthand, but others left their homes before they actually encountered enemy soldiers or irregulars. As the Carnegie Commission established, the burning of homes and villages often persuaded those who could see the fires to abandon their own homes. Fire was both a warning and a signal. "The population, warned by the glow from these fires, fled in all haste," the Commission reported.[20]

Then there was history. History did not make terror or the mass exodus of civilians inevitable, but the news of violence reinforced national animosities and fears that had developed over decades. The Carnegie Commission noted that this culture of fear predated the Balkan Wars. "Since the population of the countries about to be occupied knew, by tradition, instinct and experience, what they had to expect from the armies of the enemy and from the neighboring countries to which these armies belonged, they did not await their arrival, but fled."[21] Civilians feared attack not because of their own actions or their sympathies but because of the past history of nationalist violence.

Muslims fled in multiple directions across a broad swath of Macedonia. Along the Vardar River and the upper Strumica River, thousands tried to reach Salonica, which demanded a dangerous journey across a landscape infested by marauding bands. Some turned back only to be massacred along the way. Even as Muslims fled south through Macedonia, away from Serbian and Bulgarian forces, others fled north and east away from advancing Greeks. On the Greek-Turkish front, the movement of civilians during the campaign of 1912 presented a mirror image of 1897. Then, Greek civilians had fled in panic. Now it was Muslims, and this time refugees would not be saved by the terms of a final peace. As Turkish forces retreated after defeat to the west of Salonica, the reporter Crawfurd Price witnessed families fleeing. He saw "a troop of barefooted Moslem peasants leading donkeys upon which were piled mattress and quilt and coffee-pot, all they had saved in the rush." Others, wealthier families, hauled their goods, including prayer rugs and copper pots, away in wagons pulled by oxen. Some of the refugees begged Crawfurd Price for bread.[22]

No place was completely safe, but Muslims in 1912 sought comparative security in towns or cities. They lacked food and shelter, and many depended for their sustenance on charitable organizations such as the Balkan War Relief Fund. Thousands of refugees who fled north before the Greek advance in search of a safe haven in Salonica met thousands more fleeing south from the Serbian and Bulgarian advance into northern Macedonia. The first to arrive gained shelter in mosques and schools, but there was no way to house all the refugees who pressed into the city. [23]

In Thrace, increasingly terrified Turks fled south from Bulgarian forces. They traveled with wagons piled high with household goods. Eager to reach Constantinople as quickly as possible, they tried to cram into already overloaded trains, abandoning possessions they had dragged with the greatest difficulty along bad roads. The peasants left standing at one station let out "a great wail of grief, of infinite despair."[24]

Ellis Ashmead-Bartlett and his brother Seabury, sons of one of England's chief admirers of the Turks, Sir Ellis Ashmead-Bartlett, were two witnesses of the 1912 exodus through Thrace. In 1897, Ellis had traveled with his father to view the Greek-Turkish War. Then he had seen towns emptied of much of their Greek population as panicked civilians fled before the Turkish army. Now, in 1912, he saw Muslims abandoning their homes as the Bulgarians approached. Twenty miles from Lüle Burgas, a major Turkish fortress west of

Constantinople, journalists saw a line they first mistook for a retreating army, but which they soon made out to be a procession of "women and children, tramping across country with all their worldly goods packed in bullock wagons." The line of refugees continued all day long. Some sixty miles west of Constantinople, Ellis saw still more refugees on the road, and trains so crowded "that men, women, and children preferred to sit on the bare roofs of the carriages . . . rather than risk being left behind."[25]

Ellis's brother Seabury provided a grim account of the flight back to Constantinople. Refugees traveled slowly. Trains, "festooned with humanity," with civilians and soldiers clutching onto the engines and crowds on the roofs, crept along the tracks, and a day's march on clogged roads yielded only ten miles' progress. Those refugees who reached Constantinople found at best only modest improvement in their condition. They took shelter in mosques, including the Hagia Sophia. They slept in streets; some, barred from entering the city, took up residence in outlying graveyards. Food was scarce and disease rampant. Meanwhile, others sought to profit from the chaos and panic of defeat. A second, much smaller throng, traveled to Constantinople at the same time as the refugees. Seabury discovered the city had become a mecca for art dealers, hoping to find bargains from those eager to sell in the event that Constantinople fell. The dealers "hoped that the priceless heirlooms contained in the Museum," including "heaps of unknown but suspected jewels . . . would fall into the hands of the looters, who, in turn, would be only too pleased to part with them for a tenth of their value for cash down."[26]

The Ashmead-Bartlett brothers and others struggled to find language to vivify the extent of the flight and the degree of fear to readers far from the Balkans. One British reporter asked his readers to imagine that "the entire agricultural population of England from as far north as York were to pour, panic-stricken, down every highway and byway leading to London." It was actually quite difficult to determine how many were fleeing; there was no completely reliable overall figure. By 1913 there may have been 200,000 or more refugees in larger towns and cities outside of Constantinople. According to Serbian statistics, 239,825 Turks over the age of six left Serbia and occupied territories for Turkey between November 1912 and March 1914. By another count more than 240,000 Muslims migrated through Salonica to Turkey, but this figure did not include total Muslim flight, for many left by other routes. All attempts to arrive at a single accurate estimate of refugees were complicated by the fact that some Muslims returned to their original homes.[27]

Salonica itself was undergoing a transformation. The greatest violence during the First Balkan War occurred in outlying towns and villages, and the new Greek police managed to preserve order within Salonica. Its character was nonetheless significantly altered. Leon Sciaky described how prosperous Turkish families fled east to Constantinople or Anatolia. The writing on shops and streets soon changed. "Arabic characters had vanished from shop fronts and from posters on the walls of corner houses, and Greek ones had taken their place." Former Byzantine churches made into Muslim sites at the time of Ottoman conquest were returned to the Orthodox faith. Salonica's Jews on the whole preferred Ottoman to Greek rule, and Sciaky and his friends talked of leaving the new Greek city. They spoke of Spain, Paris, Lausanne, Vienna, and Canada.[28] There was a strong sense of a world slowly coming to an end—not destroyed, but ebbing away.

The Second Balkan War

The First Balkan War was a disaster for Turkey and a catastrophe for the Muslims of Macedonia and Thrace, but the Bulgarians never conquered Constantinople; instead they were stopped some thirty miles west of the city. In early December 1912 the Bulgarians and Serbs, but not the Greeks, agreed to an armistice with Turkey. War resumed, however, in February 1913 after a January coup staged by the Young Turks. The change in government did not lead to immediate Turkish revival. The Greeks won further victories, and Bulgarian forces besieged Adrianople until it fell on March 26. The war concluded with the Treaty of London on May 30, 1913, which marked all but the end of Turkey in Europe. From its former position as sovereign state over much of the southern Balkans, Turkey was reduced to holding a sliver of eastern Thrace, just beyond the outskirts of Constantinople.

The alliance between the Balkan states was always fragile, and they began to quarrel even before Turkey's final defeat in the First Balkan War. Relations between Greek and Bulgarian troops grew tense in the streets and cafés of Salonica. Sciaky, observing the breakdown of the accord between the former "brothers-in-arms," described how "dark, muttered threats, followed vehemently denied insults or alleged provocations." Greek forces also discovered that many of the people they thought of as Greeks turned out to be Bulgarians or Macedonians. Chiding Bulgarians who did not accept that they were Greeks, frustrated Greek gendarmes at one village in March 1913 declared, "We have freed you. The voice of Alexander the Great calls to you from the tomb; do you not hear it? You sleep on and go on calling yourselves Bulgarians!"[29]

Almost as soon as the First Balkan War ended, the second one arrived. On June 1, 1913, Serbia and Greece formed an alliance, and General Savov of the Bulgarian army, eager to gain more of Macedonia, ordered an attack that began on the night of June 29. The Second Balkan War proved to be a military and political debacle for Bulgaria. Struggling to contain the advance of Serbian and Greek forces, Bulgarians simultaneously faced offensives from Turkey in the south and Romania in the north. Turkey joined the war to regain some of the territory it had lost the preceding year, and Romania aimed to extend its power over the Black Sea coast south into the disputed region of Dobruja.

The Second Balkan War was fought on much of the same terrain as the First, but it was a new kind of war. This was now a postimperial conflict. Most Ottoman possessions in Europe were gone for good. Yet victory over Turkey did not satisfy the victorious Balkan nation-states. Bulgarian, Greek, and Serb nationalists all saw their goal of unification as incomplete: there were still—or so the respective nationalist camps firmly believed—Greeks living outside of Greece, Serbs living beyond Serbia, and Bulgarians outside of Bulgaria.

With the Second Balkan War, former allies became bitter enemies—reports of the fighting showed no trace of lingering solidarity from the joint campaign against Turkey. The campaigns of the Second Balkan War were difficult to follow because rivals told contradictory stories. Bulgarians and Serbs, for example, accused each other of mutilation and atrocities on the battlefield. Serbs described villages burnt during the Bulgarian retreat and brought foreign diplomats to see soldiers said to have been mutilated by Bulgarians. Bulgarian refugees, for their part, told of a terror campaign east of the Vardar River in which Serbian troops plundered and burned villages while Serbs and Turks killed Bulgarian men and women.

Bulgarians and Greeks similarly accused each other of arson and massacres. A dispute over events at the town of Serres was symptomatic of the mutually exclusive war stories publicized by the combatants. One thing was clear: much of the town was heavily damaged by a fire on July 11. Some reports held Bulgarian troops responsible for the damage, but Bulgarians described a reign of terror by Greek militia. One Bulgarian told of being imprisoned along with two hundred other Bulgarians in the girls' gymnasium. "Every evening from ten to fifteen were taken to the floor above and butchered."[30]

In Salonica, Greek authorities placed the small contingent of Bulgarian soldiers there under arrest almost immediately after the war's start. Bulgarians remaining in Salonica, and those mistaken for them, faced mounting terror. Many were robbed and imprisoned, and those murdered included Archimandrite Eulogius of the Bulgarian archbishopric, reportedly thrown into the water to drown and then shot.

The dispute over responsibility for fires and massacres in the Second Balkan War also caused tension between the Carnegie Commission and Greek authorities. The Commission's report remains an indispensable source for the history of the Balkan Wars, but the body did not gain equal access to all sides. Bulgarian authorities cooperated with the Commission to a greater extent than Greek authorities, who charged that the Commission's members were too friendly to Bulgaria. Members did not absolve Bulgarian forces, but they declined to accept Greek charges that retreating Bulgarian units "followed a general policy of devastation and massacre."[31]

Greek soldiers and irregulars carried out especially violent attacks against Bulgarians in smaller towns and villages. Throughout southeastern Macedonia, Bulgarians told of massacres and arson carried out by Greek forces and irregulars. British Vice Consul Heard concluded that "the wholesale extermination of the Bulgarian population has been carried out on a systematic plan by the Greek troops, with the assistance of organised bands of Antartes [irregulars]." The Carnegie Commission estimated that at least forty Bulgarian villages were burned in the area north of Salonica. One of the centers for violence was the town of Kukush. Soon after the Greeks captured it, Leon Sciaky's grandfather took him for a ride in the countryside north of Salonica, where he had done business for many years, to see what had happened. They passed through an almost deserted landscape. The villages were vacant: "doors stood ajar, yards and sheds were empty." The few Turkish families who remained cowered behind their doors; they did not know where the other Turks had gone, and the animals were nowhere to be seen. Kukush itself was destroyed, "a mass of charred timbers and smoking wreckage." There was, in short, next to nothing left. "We're going back to the city tomorrow," Sciaky's grandfather said. He added, "There is nothing we can do here. They're all gone."[32]

As in 1912, both direct encounters with enemy soldiers or irregulars and the sight of burning villages prompted peasants, on this occasion Bulgarians, to flee. Thousands departed for Bulgaria's capital, Sofia. Vice-Consul Heard spoke of refugees "swarming over the frontiers" of Bulgaria. By August 1913 estimates of the total reached 150,000.[33]

More than in either the First Balkan War or in the Russo-Turkish War, the Second Balkan War produced evidence of official intent to expel civilians. Mail from Greek soldiers, captured by Bulgaria and handed over to the Carnegie Commission, described an organized campaign of attack against all Bulgarians. Analysis of the letters, including the language used, the handwriting, and the addresses, convinced the Commission they were real. The tone of the letters varied greatly. Some depicted the campaign in chilling language. A corporal named Georges wrote, "Everywhere we pass, not even the cats escape. We have burnt all the Bulgarian villages that we have traversed." Another soldier wrote of marching through Bulgarian villages where "everyone has fled. Those who remain are 'eaten' by the Mannlicher rifle and we have also burnt a few villages."[34]

Other soldiers defended atrocities as a necessary part of a national war of vengeance. One Spiliotopoulos Philippos, though referring to the war as "painful," also wrote, "We have burnt all the villages abandoned by the Bulgarians. They burn the Greek villages and we the Bulgarian. They massacre, we massacre, and against all those of that dishonest nation, who fell into our hands, the Mannlicher rifle has done its work." In one of the most aggressive letters, one soldier informed his parents, "Wherever there was a Bulgarian village, we set fire to it and burned it, so that this dirty race of Bulgars couldn't spring up again."[35]

But some of the Greek soldiers expressed guilt. One sergeant, describing how his division had killed Komitadjis and burned villages and homes, concluded, "All this was done without pity or mercy, executed with a cruel heart, and with a condemnation still more cruel." Another soldier, telling of massacres and the burning of villages, wrote, "God only knows what will come of it."[36]

How was it possible for ordinary soldiers to take part in a deliberate terror campaign against peasants who lived in much the same fashion as many of their own families? The Carnegie Commission was puzzled by the extreme violence between fellow Christians, Greeks and Bulgarians. Hostility between the rival Greek and Bulgarian branches of the Orthodox church had its roots in the nineteenth century, and political violence between Greek and Bulgarian bands in Macedonia was still a recent memory, but Bulgarians and Greeks had been allies in the First Balkan War. How could onetime allies turn to arson and massacre of each other in less than a year? The Carnegie Commission looked for an answer in the Greek press and in propaganda. "In talk and in print, one phrase summed up the general feeling of the Greeks toward the Bulgarians, 'Dhen einai anthropoi' (They are not human beings)." One poster, seen by commission members in Salonica, was entitled the Bulgar-eater. It included the verses:

> The sea of fire which boils in my breast
> And calls for vengeance with the savage waves of my soul,
> Will be quenched when the monsters of Sofia are still,
> And thy life blood extinguishes my hate.[37]

Turkish Revival and Revenge

A disaster for Bulgarians, the Second Balkan War brought military gains for Turkey. As Bulgarian forces collapsed, the Turkish army advanced into Eastern Thrace, retaking territory all the way to the old Ottoman capital of Adrianople. Some Turks took the opportunity to return to their villages. Those who had abandoned their villages east of Adrianople during the First Balkan War returned after the Second War, though many of their houses had been destroyed during Bulgarian occupation.[38]

Turks returned to Thrace with a new attitude: after the humiliation of the First Balkan War, Turkish nationalism had grown more radical, and Turks wanted revenge. More so than any previous war, the First Balkan War brought Turkey to fear that its European neighbors sought nothing less than Turkey's complete destruction. This shift was especially significant for the Young Turks and the Committee of Union and Progress. During their years of opposition to Sultan Abdul Hamid, the Young Turks had forged alliances with political leaders of other ethnic and religious groups. Now, leading CUP members increasingly viewed all such groups associated with

Christian nations as suspect and committed themselves to an exclusively Turkish nationalism.[39] The first result of this shift was a wave of vengeance and reprisals against non-Turks in 1913.

The return of Turkish authority to Eastern Thrace frightened Bulgarians; just the previous autumn they had seen vast trains of Muslims fleeing toward Constantinople, but now they witnessed the rapid withdrawal of Bulgarian forces. Bulgarian houses as well as churches were burned when Turks returned. Bulgarian refugees who reached Constantinople reported murders carried out by advancing Turkish troops as well as by "Arabs," or cavalry units, though the Carnegie Commission did not report that these forces were actually from Arabia. One refugee recounted events in his village: "It was night and the village slept. All at once the Turks arrived. . . . They asked for money. They killed many people."[40]

Turks also attacked Greeks in Eastern Thrace. Greek reports received by the Carnegie Commission outlined a campaign of arson, looting, and murder by soldiers, irregulars, and civilians. Malgara, a town in southern Thrace, was one of the towns hardest hit by the Turkish campaign. It suffered massive fire damage, though the cause was disputed: inadequate firefighting equipment, munitions left by the Bulgarians or hidden Christian residents, or arson by Turkish forces. A Greek account charged that "Wagons full of cans of kerosene oil circulated all night in the streets of the city, and the soldiers joined in with the Bashibouzouks . . . encouraging the spread of the flames."[41]

Returning to Thrace, Turkish forces also targeted Armenians as traitors, even though they had not been members of the alliance against Turkey in the First Balkan War. Some Armenian volunteers had fought in Bulgaria's Macedonian Legion, but Armenians had also served in the Turkish army, reflecting the policy of the Young Turks to extend the draft beyond Muslims. Malgara provided striking evidence of the rising Turkish nationalist fury against Armenians. According to a report of events compiled by the Armenian patriarchate, Turkish commanders had accused the town's Armenians of betraying their country and called Armenian leaders "Armenian

traitors." Once fire broke out, soldiers and local Muslim residents attacked Armenians. "The soldiers and the Mussulman population
forced their way into the Armenian houses, situated on the outskirts
of the town, and sacked them." Turkish forces also attacked Armenians and Greeks at other towns such as Rodosto, a small port on the
northern coast of the Sea of Mamara.[10]

"From This Day On You Are Bulgarians"

The Second War's end brought a halt to ethnic cleansing, but not to
efforts by the victors to create more homogenous nation-states. The
goal of crafting a unified nation was easiest to achieve where ethnic
cleansing had proceeded farthest. A town devoid of Muslims could
more easily become Bulgarian, just as a village emptied of Bulgarians could more easily become Greek. Elsewhere, where ethnic
cleansing was incomplete, victors pressured civilians to adopt a new
national identity. They typically began by harassing local leaders—
most often priests and teachers. Those with the wrong national loyalty lost their jobs and in many cases were deported.

The Pomaks, Bulgarian-speaking Muslims, were one of the first
groups pressured to change their identity during the Balkan Wars. For
Pomaks living under Bulgarian rule, conversion from Islam to the
Bulgarian branch of the Orthodox church came at the barrel of the
gun. In the eastern Macedonian town of Xanthi, Pomaks begged
the traveling British diplomat Wilkie Young in early 1913 "to protect
them from the violent measures which their conquerors were adopting to force them into Christianity." Pomaks recounted beatings and
the imprisonment of their imams. In one petition to foreign diplomats, Pomaks from a village to the north of Serres recounted how
Bulgarians, including priests, destroyed mosques, killed local Muslim
leaders, and then began the work of conversion. They assigned Bulgarian names to the remaining villagers, "made us Christians, and
said, 'From this day on you are Bulgarians.'"[43]

Greece and Serbia also pursued forced assimilation. During and
after the Second Balkan War, the Kingdom of Greece wanted Bul-

garians and Macedonians living within Greece's new borders to declare themselves Greek. Once again a victorious Balkan state began
the work of molding national identity with an assault on priests and
teachers. At the town of Edhessa, west of Salonica, Greek authorities arrested priests and teachers and urged remaining Bulgarians to
sign a statement that attributed their previous Bulgarian identity to
propaganda and Komitadji terror and ended with a confession of
"our Hellenic nationality."[44]

Ethnic cleansing of Bulgarians under Serbian rule was unlikely
because Serbian authorities regarded the Slavic population of Macedonia as Serbs. The challenge for Serb nationalists lay in convincing
Bulgarians of this. One "declaration," published in a Serbian newspaper, asked "Slavs" to state "That we are familiar from history that we
have been Servians since ancient times . . ." and concluded, "we will
work in the future, shoulder to shoulder, to strengthen our country—
Greater Servia."[45] Those who refused to accept Serbian identity faced
what the Carnegie Commission described as "assimilation through
terror." The Serbian government harassed the archbishops of the Bulgarian church in Macedonia and ultimately drove them out of Serbian Macedonia. Serbian bands and officials also carried out mass arrests of teachers. Many who refused to declare themselves Serbian
were expelled.

Muslims in the new regions of Serbia faced similar if not
greater intimidation and violence. Serbian policy encouraged Muslims to leave and Serbs to move in. Serbia placed special high tax
rates on Muslim property and forced local residents to make housing
available for new Serb settlers.[46] In Kosovo the fulfillment of the
Serb nationalist dream of vengeance for the battle of 1389 placed
Serb authority, in the form of military rule, over a suspicious and re-
sentful population, angered by the massacres of the First Balkan
War. An Albanian uprising in September 1913 in Kosovo provided
the opportunity for violent reprisals by Serb forces and irregulars in
the area of the Liouma River.

The campaigns against Albanians in Kosovo did not qualify as
full-scale ethnic cleansing, though Serbia employed many of the

methods typical of the practice. The chief difference was in results: Kosovo remained primarily Albanian, and a large Albanian population remained in northwest Macedonia. Because Albanians made up the vast majority of the population, to conceive of, let alone carry out, the immediate expulsion of such a majority would require vast ambition and extraordinary organization coupled with almost boundless inhumanity. This combination of capabilities was not yet in place, though in 1999 a much later Serbian campaign did seek to empty large parts of Kosovo of Albanians.

The new rulers of Macedonia and Western Thrace sought to remake not just present-day national boundaries, but also past history. They attacked the region's Muslim cultural and religious legacy. As much as possible, advancing armies and bands attempted to erase the evidence of a Muslim society by looting and destroying mosques and vandalizing Muslim cemeteries. Observing smashed gravestones in Turkish cemeteries during a trip through Macedonia, Richard von Mach, a German foreign correspondent with decades of experience in the Balkans, suggested that "every trace of the Turk must be erased." Destruction in Bulgarian-occupied Macedonia in 1913 distressed British diplomat Wilkie Young. He observed that "everywhere one of the most childish features of the occupation is the wanton damage which has been done to cemeteries, mosques, and ancient shrines."[47] Here again the Balkan Wars foreshadowed much of what was to come decades later in the 1990s in Yugoslavia, when hundreds and thousands of mosques and churches would be destroyed.

The Legacy of the Balkan Wars

By the end of the Balkan Wars, the demographics of Macedonia had been changed forever. At a minimum, several hundred thousand people fled their homes, and many never returned. For some this was not the first experience of flight: Muslims who had moved to Salonica as refugees now faced the task of once again finding a new home.

For Salonica, the Balkan Wars marked the beginning of the decline of the diverse society forged during many centuries of Ottoman rule. In 1913 there were still more Jews and Muslims than Greeks in Salonica, but the city entered a new chapter in its history as a Greek city. The victorious Greek state set about making Salonica Greek by posting officials to the city. Its streets acquired new Greek names. A large Jewish population survived in Salonica until the Holocaust, but Salonica's Jews suffered a major blow in 1917 when a fire destroyed old Jewish neighborhoods.[48] Muslims remained in large numbers through the early 1920s, but the Balkan Wars also marked a turning point in Salonica's history as a Turkish city. This can be seen in the life of Mustafa Kemal, who was born in Salonica in 1881 and later became famous as the founder of modern Turkey under the name Kemal Atatürk. His mother and sister were among the Muslim refugees who left Salonica after the Balkan Wars, and Mustafa Kemal never returned to his birthplace once it became a Greek city.

By late-twentieth-century standards, the Balkan Wars brought only partial ethnic cleansing because significant minority populations remained within the Balkan states; but contemporary witnesses often viewed the wars' consequences as something worse than what we now call ethnic cleansing. They spoke of extermination. Trotsky, for example, asked, "did not the facts" lead to ". . . the conclusion that the Bulgars in Macedonia, the Serbs in Old Serbia, in their national endeavor to correct data in the enthnographical statistics that are not quite favorable to them, are engaged quite simply in systematic extermination of the Muslim population . . . ?" Crawfurd Price saw a "systematic attempt to exterminate the Moslems." And the Carnegie Commission, after the Second War, remarked that "the object of these armed conflicts . . . was the complete extermination of an alien population."[49] Such statements may strike modern readers, accustomed to hearing of genocide, as exaggeration, but in a time before genocide in Europe, driving out an entire community was seen as extermination.

For many observers of the Balkan Wars, the ultimate causes of all the terror, mass flight, and violence lay in what they saw as the primitiveness of Balkan life. Western travelers were already accustomed to describing the Balkans as backward, and the Balkan Wars reinforced a commonly held notion of a stark contrast between Europe's civilized West and its rudimentary Balkan frontier. To observers from the West the behavior of armies, irregular bands, and civilians seemed to be a trait peculiar to Balkan peoples. As the veteran foreign correspondent Richard von Mach contended, war was different in the Balkans than in Europe. "In Europe," armies moved while peasants stayed put, but in the Balkans, "war is a migration of peoples" in which civilians immediately followed retreating soldiers out of the war zone.[50]

Such interpretations of Balkan violence as primitive were simple and persuasive, but wrong. Accounts of atrocities, a longtime staple of Western reporting on wars in Europe's East, depicted the Balkans as backward. But ethnic cleansing emerged just as Eastern Europe and Western Asia were modernizing. The borderlands of the region were indeed more rural than Western Europe. Balkan capitals often struck foreign observers as poor, rough, and provincial, and it is true that Sofia and Bucharest were not Paris, London, or Berlin. But it was not economic or technical backwardness that generated terror and ethnic cleansing. It was a newer phenomena: the rise of nationalism and the emergence of modern states. Nationalist desires and myths helped fuel the Balkan Wars. The idea of the nation had sunk roots in the Balkans. Poets had compiled vivid national epics. Cartographers had produced maps showing the outlines of the nation. Teachers had taught national history, and personal experiences of flight and revenge had anchored individuals within national communities. Now with war, those who did not fit into this nationalist picture were at risk. At best, those on the "wrong" side of a national boundary found themselves subjected to harassment, particularly of their teachers and religious leaders. At worst, they were driven out or murdered. It did not matter that people had lived side by side, or in nearby communities, for decades. Neighbors of another nation had become by definition enemies, and ordinary people came to learn the new rules of motion: when to stay and when to pack up and flee.

The Balkan Wars provided both a general model and a specific cause for future ethnic war and ethnic cleansing. The Second War, in particular, suggested a future with continued strife because the defeat of the old imperial government left Balkan nationalists still unsatisfied. On gaining victory over the Ottoman Empire, the new Balkan states turned immediately to crafting more perfect nation-states through forced assimilation or expulsion. This close connection between national liberation and intolerance foreshadowed the future. Ethnic cleansing would spread even more broadly across the borderlands of Europe when other empires fell or broke apart.

Within remaining Ottoman territories, the experience of the Balkan Wars bred fear and a thirst for vengeance. Where Europe met Asia, refugee populations provided a living reminder of the past. In Turkey these refugees created an economic burden for a struggling state, and the sight of refugees in city streets and graveyards fueled a desire for vengeance against the new masters of most of what had been Turkey in Europe. The catastrophic defeats in Europe made victimization a key component of nascent Turkish national identity. Anger, desire for retribution, fear of further territorial losses, and a search for scapegoats helped make ethnic cleansing and genocide not just possible but likely during World War I.

CHAPTER THREE

"How Much Worse It Is Than Massacre!"

Elâziğ is a small city in eastern Turkey of several hundred thousand inhabitants, situated near a series of lakes created by a dam on the Euphrates River. Today its residents are mostly Turks and Kurds, but as late as the spring of 1915 it was also very much an Armenian town. In 1915 Armenians called it Kharpert while Turks referred to it as Harput. It had been an Armenian center for many centuries and was actually two linked towns. The old town was perched on a mountain some one thousand feet above a high plateau and was the site of a college established by American Protestant missionaries. Down below lay a newer town, known as Mezreh, which grew considerably during the nineteenth century. Beyond the city hundreds of agricultural villages were spread out over a plateau.[1] By the autumn of 1915 the city and its surrounding plain would be changed forever. Armenian Harput was about to be destroyed.

The end of Armenian Harput was part of a new wave of ethnic cleansing and related violence during World War I.[2] In the United States and Western Europe, this war, the so-called Great War, the "war to end all wars," brings to mind images of foxholes, trench warfare, mustard gas, and shell-shocked veterans limping home from the western front. But on the eastern front it was also a war of mass flight, deportations, ethnic cleansing, and genocide. In southeastern Europe, where memories of the Balkan Wars remained fresh, civilians were ready to flee their homes at the first hint of an approaching enemy army. In Russia, the scene of recent pogroms, Jews and Germans faced deportation during World War I. In the Ottoman Empire the war introduced the twentieth century's most heinous new crime as ethnic cleansing gave rise to genocide.

The massacres of the Great War and the columns of refugees produced by it illustrated both the past and future of ethnic conflict and terror. The victimization of Jews and Armenians built on a base of violence and discrimination that preceded the war. But war also brought something new: increasingly ambitious plans to purify nations. These projects of expulsion and killing took place in old empires, but were also early examples of an emerging wave of nationalist violence that continued through the end of World War II.

Fear of defeat brought radical consequences in empires that had recently suffered major losses. For military and political leaders who already saw their states as victims, new losses intensified their obsessions with those on whom they would place blame. In both the Ottoman and Russian empires, powerful figures blamed internal traitors as well as external foes, and plotted vengeance.

Balkan Wars in the Great War

World War I, which began with a crisis caused by the assassination of the Archduke Franz Ferdinand in Sarajevo in Bosnia, was a general European war but also a Balkan war. The killing of the archduke still shapes popular memory of the war, yet much about the struggle that followed has been largely forgotten: the crisis in Bosnia that precipitated war on the western front also sparked a new war for the Balkan peninsula. This Balkan war had two dimensions: it was a war by Austria and its ally Germany against Serbia, and it was yet another war in which the countries that had emerged from the

wreckage of the Ottoman Empire sought vengeance for past disap-
pointments and pursued their conflicting national aspirations. In
this way World War I can also be seen as a Third Balkan War. In Serbia, Bulgaria, and Greece, Balkan nationalists had made up national
maps that included regions lying well beyond the existing boundaries of their countries. In 1912 and 1913 the Balkan states had gone
to war to make good on these claims. The war that broke out in 1914
gave them yet another chance to adjust national boundaries and
drive out civilians they considered undesirable.

During World War I visitors to the Balkans found that nationalist passions still ran hot. This was immediately apparent to the
American journalist John Reed, who would soon gain fame as a
chronicler of revolution in Russia. Visiting Serbia in 1915, he observed, "The secret dream of every Serb is the uniting of all the Serbian peoples in one great empire." In Romania he learned that "national aspirations" included Bessarabia and Bukovina, two border
regions then held by Russia and Austria-Hungary respectively, as
well as Transylvania, a high plateau separated from Romania by the
Carpathian Mountains. Reed saw one map that showed even Macedonia as properly belonging to Romania. In Bulgaria he learned that
Bulgarian national aspirations were also "practically boundless,"
and of his visit to Greece he wrote that "The Greeks hated the Serbians normally, but when they spoke of the Bulgars it was in term
of torture and burning alive."[3] All conditions appeared ripe for a
new Balkan war of arson, plunder, massacres, and mass flight.

Where the war in 1912 had been most devastating for Turks, and
in 1913 for Bulgarians, this new war in the Balkans proved most catastrophic for the Serbs. Serbia repelled two Austrian invasions in
1914 and advanced into Albania in 1915, but these victories came at
high cost. Austrian forces—chiefly Hungarians, according to
Reed—seized thousands of civilians at border towns "and drove
them into Austria-Hungary." After Serb forces regained the upper
hand, the countryside bore the familiar marks of Balkan war:
burned and looted villages, and refugees on the move.[4] Food short-
ages and typhus outbreaks caused many deaths.

In 1915 alliance politics and nationalist vengeance culminated in Serbia's dismemberment. Austria, supported by its ally Germany, launched a third invasion of Serbia, and this time Bulgaria joined in the attack. Bulgaria's motive was simple: reclaiming as much territory as possible from regions recently lost in the Second Balkan War. Both major wartime alliances, the Entente allies of France and Britain, and the Central Powers, Austria and Germany, cultivated Bulgaria, but the Central Powers won the bidding contest, promising Bulgaria Macedonia as well as territory in Greece and Romania if those countries entered the war. Both would eventually do so. Outnumbered, exhausted from previous fighting and the typhus epidemic, Serb forces were ill prepared to stop simultaneous invasions in October 1915 by Austrian-German forces and by Bulgaria. This campaign quickly became a rout as Serb forces retreated on both fronts.

War in Serbia in 1915 did not produce full-scale ethnic cleansing (the country was not emptied of Serbs), but it is clear that Serbian civilians saw war as a conflict of peoples as well as armies. Like Muslims in 1912 and Bulgarians in 1913, large numbers of Serbs fled their homes in the fall of 1915. The scenes of Serb families in retreat were familiar: long lines of wagons piled high with belongings clogged the roads. In eastern Serbia whole towns were deserted as Bulgarians approached. The earlier Austrian invasion had left the town of Nis in southeastern Serbia crowded with refugees, but the town emptied out as the Bulgarians neared. When Alice and Claude Askew, two English writers, entered Nis, they found that "most of the inhabitants had already taken to flight."[5] Thousands joined Serbian military units south of Nis in a calamitous retreat as wagons stuck in the mud.

Driven out of the north and east, the Serb retreat ended up in Kosovo in November 1915. This new addition to Serbia, the scene of nationalist triumph only three years earlier, was not hospitable ground for the fleeing Serbs. A large majority of the population was made up of Albanians—in Pristina, the Askews said, "you might just as well be in Albania"—and these Albanians lived with the

memory of suppressed rebellions and recent massacres carried out
by Serbs during the Balkan Wars.[6] Given this legacy, it was scarcely
surprising that Kosovo's Serbs lived in fear of a new Albanian uprising.

Fortier Jones, an American relief worker who accompanied the
soldiers and refugees moving into central Kosovo, was a witness to
disaster there in November 1915. Jones had traveled south amid
thousands of carts, automobiles, and peasants on foot, all intermingled with the retreating Serbian army. Peasant women led children
by the hand and carried babies on their backs while old men carried
heavy packs. The refugees making their way south toward Pristina
were already tired, wet, and exhausted when the weather took a turn
for the worse. On November 17 the temperature fell, a blizzard
struck, wet clothes froze solid, and icicles formed on the oxen. The
refugees tried to speed up but quickly became exhausted. Within
two hours the animals pulling their carts began to die. Those who
had automobiles abandoned them to continue on foot. Jones and his
companions began to pass families who "were losing strength fast.
The children, hundreds of them, were all crying. Mothers with infants on their backs staggered, fell, rose, and fell again." Rifles cast
off by struggling soldiers—some were boys who had only recently
been given guns, piled up on the road. "Soon it seemed as if the
snow had turned to firearms," Jones wrote.[7] Those who survived the
blizzard marched on through the famous field of the 1389 Battle of
Kosovo to reach Pristina, already crowded with thousands of
refugees. Many continued on to Prizren in southeastern Kosovo,
close to Albania. From there the remnants of the Serbian army labored over mountain passes—along a route similar to that later followed by Kosovo Albanian refugees in 1999—into Albania, where
they were later evacuated to the island of Corfu and then shipped to
help support an allied force that had opened up a new front at Thessaloniki.

The Serbian flight of 1915 formed an important link in a chain
connecting past and future ethnic cleansing. The behavior of civilian refugees makes sense only when seen as a response to earlier

Balkan wars of ethnic cleansing. Struggling to understand why families packed up their belongings and set out in carts in late autumn, Fortier Jones thought the refugees might have heard about the fate of Belgium, where Germans were said to have carried out atrocities. But he was perceptive enough to add, "many had seen what the Bulgarians were capable of doing."[8] For many Serbs—the exact number of refugees was never firmly established, though observers spoke of thousands, tens of thousands, and even hundreds of thousands of Serbs on the move—this almost palpable fear outweighed all considerations about protecting homes and fields. Serbian civilians knew that entire populations of ordinary people had recently been treated as enemy combatants, subject to theft, expulsion, and massacre, and many would not wait to find out if this would be their fate in a conquered Serbia.

The Serb catastrophe in Kosovo and Albania in 1915 also shaped future versions of Serb history. It provided the most current episode in a national story of victimization and defeat in which tragedy always struck in Kosovo. The drama of 1915 now took its place alongside the battle of 1389. The Serb novelist Dobrica Cosic later memorialized the catastrophe of 1915 in historical novels. This story of national suffering—with new elements added during World War II—would play a powerful role in propelling Serbia toward ethnic war in the 1980s and 1990s.[9]

Many Serbian fears came true under Austrian and Bulgarian occupation. Between 150,000 and 180,000 people were deported, most of them to camps in Hungary, and others to Austria. Occupying authorities attacked the core roots of Serbian identity, shutting down the University of Belgrade and banning the Cyrillic alphabet in schools. Bulgaria pursued similar and even harsher policies in eastern Kosovo and Macedonia, confiscating property of those who had fled the country and seeking to end the use of Serbian names. The human toll exacted by war and occupation was immense. Famine, disease, and war caused soaring mortality: by war's end the Serbian government estimated that the country had lost one-quarter of its prewar population.

Bulgarian Aegean

The new round of war between the former Balkan allies of 1912 also brought conflict between Bulgaria and Greece, though this developed more slowly than the war between Bulgaria and Serbia. While Germany and Austria courted Bulgaria with promises of territory, including Macedonia, and persuaded Bulgaria to enter the war on the side of the Central Powers, Greece's political leaders were deeply divided on whether to remain neutral or join the Allies. War in Greece actually began before Greece officially entered the war. In October 1915 France and Britain opened a new front at Thessaloniki. War also split the Greek government. Eleutherios Venizelos, the prominent Greek-Cretan politician who had championed *enosis* or union between Greece and Crete, favored the Allies and established a provisional government. The Greek government finally entered the war on the Allied side in June 1917 after King Constantine abdicated.

As in the Second Balkan War, a new Bulgarian-Greek War brought terror to Macedonia. Where in 1913 Bulgarians had fled Greeks, in 1916 thousands of Greeks now fled Bulgarians. What followed under Bulgarian occupation was not full-scale ethnic cleansing but targeted terror and general intimidation. Rather than driving out the entire Greek population, Bulgarian authorities at first deported professionals, priests, and teachers to Bulgaria. A 1919 report on Bulgarian occupation by an Inter-Allied Commission comprising representatives from Britain, France, Belgium, Greece, and Serbia noted, "The Bulgarian command hastened to hunt out the leaders of Greek sentiment." The Bulgarian occupation also provided an early example of what would become one of the twentieth century's most notorious human rights abuses: disappearance. Many of those arrested vanished, never to be heard from again.[10] The remaining population was subjected to forced labor.

The terror campaign intensified in 1917 when Greece entered the war on the Allied side. Moving closer to full-scale ethnic cleansing, Bulgarian authorities began to treat all Greek men as enemy combatants subject to deportation. The Inter-Allied Commission described a general Bulgarian policy of sending men between the ages of eighteen and fifty-five to labor in Bulgaria. Estimates of the numbers deported ranged from 42,000 to 100,000 or more. The Greek men traveled to Bulgaria in closed cattle or freight cars, arrived at what the Inter-Allied Commission described as a "concentration camp," and were sent from there to other work sites in Bulgaria. Epidemics, forced labor for up to twelve to fifteen hours a day, and a meager ration of as little as "250 to 500 grams of bread and a very unsubstantial broth" led to extremely high mortality.[11]

Meanwhile, famine exacted an ever-higher toll on Greek civilians who remained in Macedonia. Famine itself was a Bulgarian instrument of war against the Greek population, according to the Inter-Allied Commission. For its part, the Bulgarian delegation to the peace conference rejected all charges of violations of law during the occupation of Macedonia. If food had been short, it was not Bulgaria's fault: the Bulgarian Red Cross had distributed relief during a time of general shortage in Bulgaria.[12] Bulgaria's expansion came to an abrupt conclusion at the end of the war. Defeated by a combined offensive of Allied forces, Serbians, and Greeks, Bulgaria signed an armistice on September 30, 1918. Occupied Greek and Serbian territory was evacuated. With the final peace in November 1919, the Treaty of Neuilly, Bulgaria lost still more territory. No part of the Aegean coast remained Bulgarian.

Between Two Plagues: Jews on the Eastern Front

Where the Ottoman Empire had receded, World War I led to flight and deportation that fell just short of ethnic cleansing. Where empires survived, however, war brought massive deportation and outright ethnic cleansing. This may seem counterintuitive—after all, the old empires of Eastern Europe and Western Asia were still multiethnic states where an emperor or a sultan was sovereign to people of many languages and creeds. But with the old idea of empire fading, war endangered the ethnic and religious minorities accused of treason in each empire. In what remained of the Ottoman

Empire, that meant Armenians and Greeks, and in the Russian Empire, that meant Jews and Germans.

War in a multiethnic state like Russia provided an opportunity to redefine nations. The prospect of war had always challenged rulers to recruit and maintain armies, but the era of nationalism raised new questions: which groups could be trusted to fight for the tsar and for Russia, and conversely, which could not because they sympathized with rival nations?[13] The issue of whether Jews could fight for the Russian Empire had first surfaced in the early nineteenth century when Tsar Nicholas I had enlisted Jews in the military under harsh conditions: boys as young as twelve were conscripted. But Nicholas's successor, Alexander II (whose assassination had set off pogroms in 1881), doubted that Jews were suitable for service.

Once World War I began, Russia's Jews were unable to convince the Russian military of their loyalty. In the war's early days some Jews took part in patriotic processions. S. Ansky, a Jewish writer best known for his play *The Dybbuk*, recalled "a brief moment of half-genuine, half-bogus Jewish patriotism for Russia."[14] But almost immediately Russia suffered defeats that triggered a wave of anti-Semitic extremism. Military setbacks reawakened a nationalist hatred of Russia's Jews left over from the period of the Russo-Japanese War. Although Russia's Jews had caused neither Russia's defeat by Japan in 1904–1905, nor its losses to Germany in 1914 and 1915, the logic that had earlier justified pogroms was now repeated. In this vision of history, Jews were a disloyal people who had betrayed Russia before and now betrayed her again.

From the war's beginning, commanders at Stavka, the Russian headquarters on the Polish front, suspected Poland's Jews of supporting the German cause. They accused Jews of any number of acts of treason, ranging from sending signals to German forces to shooting at Russian soldiers. "Every commander and every colonel who made a mistake," Ansky asserted, "had found a way to justify his crime, his incompetence, his carelessness. He could make everything kosher by blaming his failures on a Jewish spy."[15]

The resulting pogroms of 1914 and 1915, however, were different from those in 1904–1905 in two key ways. First, the role of the military was much greater. In 1905 Russian political and military authorities took comfort in anti-Semitic violence but did not organize or direct the attacks against Jews. But in 1915 Russia's military leaders on the front, most notably the commander-in-chief of army headquarters, General Nikolai Nikolaevich Ianushkevich, took the initiative in persecuting Jews.[16] The second distinction was geographic: in 1904–1905 Jews lived nowhere near the main theater of combat, but in 1914 and 1915 Jewish communities were spread across the war zone.

What happened next, forgotten for decades, was the forced evacuation of Jews and other civilians. Russian officers began to move Jews out of the war zone in 1914. Expulsions of Jews from Polish towns began as early as September. Ansky witnessed the impact of these early expulsions in Warsaw in November and December. "Each day brought thousands of additional refugees, most of them on foot, robbed, naked, starving, shaken, and helpless." He estimated the number of Jewish refugees in Warsaw at more than fifty thousand.[17]

Mostly the war went badly for Russia, but even when the Russian army won its battles they attacked Jews. That was the fate of the Jews of the Austrian border region of Galicia, occupied by Russia in an early offensive. Visiting Brody, a town just within Austria to the east of Lvov, Ansky found nearly half the town burnt—"several hundred exclusively Jewish houses." The rationale for arson—the lie that a Jewish girl had fired at Russian troops—became "the standard pretext for all the pogroms and violence against Jews." Galician Jews were distinctive in that they were more likely to own land than Jews in many other regions of Eastern Europe, and Russian forces singled out Jewish landholders for especially harsh treatment. Russian troops stole their money, livestock, and food, and, according to Ansky, "killed a lot of them or deported them to Russia."[18]

In 1915 the Russian military's persecution of the Jews of the western Russian Empire intensified. In January the Russian command expelled some 100,000 Jews from towns near Warsaw. They drove from their homes even the families of Jewish men serving in the Russian army. The shortest journey without shelter or secure supply of food became arduous. The Bund, the Jewish socialist party, lamented that "children die on the road."[19]

In April 1915 even larger deportations followed a major Russian defeat at the hands of Germany and Austria. In its scale, this phase of Russian military policy toward Jews began more closely to resemble ethnic cleansing: in some regions the goal really was to clear out *all* Jews. In a move that foreshadowed the more draconian expulsions later organized by Stalin against supposedly disloyal ethnic minorities in World War II, between 500,000 and a million Jews were forced out.[20] Most received only twenty-four to thirty-six hours' notice of their forced evacuation. From Poland through the Baltic, Jews were pushed east.

Pogroms were a consistent feature of Jewish life on Russia's western front. Ansky, crossing back in 1915 from Galicia into Russia, spoke of Jews "waiting for two plagues: a pogrom and a mass expulsion." Everywhere he went, Ansky heard about pogroms. Russian forces on the defensive attacked Jews in Poland, and Russian soldiers on the offensive attacked Jews in Galicia inside of Austria's borders. At Sokal, a Galician town north of Lvov, a Jewish hotel owner told Ansky of days of destruction during a pogrom: "They destroyed Sokal. They spent the whole week looting, smashing, beating." A Cossack, she added, had chopped off her daughter's arm. John Reed heard similar stories in Galicia. Where Russian forces, especially Cossacks, led, local residents followed. A survivor of a pogrom at the small Jewish shtetl of Yuzefow in Lublin province told of local Christians who took the pogrom as an opportunity for looting: bands of peasants—men and women, young and old—came to town, joined soldiers in attacking Jews, and left with baskets filled with loot.[21]

The Russian command's forced evacuation led to the expulsion of as many as one-fifth of all the empire's Jews, but in the end Russia's political authorities would not countenance a policy of total ethnic cleansing. Forced evacuation had created a bizarre paradox for Jewish refugees. The Russian military pushed Jews east out of Poland and the Pale of Settlement into regions of Russia where Jews could not legally reside. Protests within Russia against the forced evacuations eventually reached the country's Council of Ministers. The Council's deliberations revealed both humanitarian concerns and an exaggerated sense of the influence that Jews living abroad exerted on world opinion. Breaking with the military, the Council of Ministers in August 1915 published a circular allowing Jews to reside in most of Russia's capital cities, with the exceptions of Petrograd (changed in 1914 from St. Petersburg because it sounded too German) and Moscow. Some two-fifths of Jewish refugees ultimately moved to places where they could not have legally lived before this notice.[22]

Even where the war on the eastern front did not lead to forced mass evacuation, it provided vivid reminders that Jews remained a minority at risk. Romania, already infamous for withholding citizenship from most Jews, was a prime example. Romania did not enter the war until August 1916 when it invaded Transylvania, which was then in Hungary's possession, but it suffered defeats that by 1917 left most of Romania occupied. At every stage of the war, anti-Semitism remained intense. Upon Romania's entrance into the war, recalled the American envoy Charles J. Vopicka, "many Jews were charged with being German spies, and many were arrested and interned and their property confiscated."[23] Vopicka took pride in persuading the Romania government to free many of these Jews. As the war came to an end, Vopicka heard rumors of planned pogroms and warned the government that such actions would harm Romania at the peace conference.

Russian Germans in the Great War

Beyond Germany's own borders, ethnic Germans were another minority to suffer wartime persecution on or near the eastern front. Although it may be difficult to imagine today, when German persecution of the Jews so marks twentieth-century history, ethnic Germans living in Russia during World War I actually suffered fates similar to the empire's Jews.

Germans, like Jews, made up one of the many minorities in the multiethnic Russian Empire. The Russian Germans, many of them descendants of Germans who had been invited to found agricultural settlements in the eighteenth century, were chiefly concentrated in areas of western Russia, including the Black Sea, and on the Volga River. Others in Volhynia were more recent immigrants from the 1880s. Even into the twentieth century, Russia's ethnic Germans often lived in distinctly German villages in these regions. Others lived in the empire's large cities.

Once war began, their Russian countrymen began to suspect ethnic Germans, like Russia's Jews, of lack of patriotism. Ethnic German deputies in the Russian parliament, the Duma, declared their loyalty, but this pledge meant nothing after Russia lost the battle of Tannenberg to Germany in late August 1914. Instead, ethnic German soldiers were removed from their units in the west and sent to work in labor units in the Caucasus. German civilians sensed the mounting suspicion under which they lived. Gottlob Ensslen, a German farmer who had lived in Bessarabia, recalled years later that "we were stamped enemies of the state during the war."[24]

From the war's early days, many of Russia's Germans were victims of forced evacuation. Several hundred thousand German peasants living near the front in Poland and the Baltic in 1914 were moved hundreds of miles and shifted beyond the Volga, and in early January 1915 Russian authorities also began to deport urban Germans. Defeats in 1915 imperiled still more of Russia's Germans. General Ianushkevich ordered Russian Germans deported from provinces along the empire's western border and moved to the interior. Even in their evacuation the empire's Germans stood out. "You could recognize the Germans' huge solid covered wagons half a mile away . . . ," Ansky observed. "A German strode alongside his wagon, calm and self-assured, his face revealing neither confusion nor despair."[25] Germans of Volhynia, one of the largest groups of German farmers in Russia, received just days to dispose of their assets. Russian peasants picked up tools and farm animals at bargain prices in the resulting fire sale. With the exception of men already sent to fight in the Caucasus, the approximately 200,000 Volhynian Germans ended up on the Volga River or in Siberia, though some managed to hide in the Pripet marshes located on the present-day borders of Ukraine and Belarus. A few, those with a husband or son in the army, received permission to return home during the harvest. Insecurity for ethnic Germans living in cities far from the front also mounted. In May 1915 mobs plundered German shops and apartments in Moscow.

One of the harshest blows for farming people like Russia's Germans was the loss of their land. From 1915 until the Russian Revolution, the Russian government passed a series of complex laws that compelled increasing numbers of ethnic Germans to liquidate their land and any other capital holdings. This first became a reality in February 1915 for many ethnic Germans living within approximately one hundred miles of the German or Austro-Hungarian borders or within approximately sixty-six miles of the Baltic Sea or Black Sea, who were given ten to sixteen months to sell their land. Germans in nearby regions feared the same fate. Gottlob Ensslen recalled that "evacuation hung over us like the sword of Damocles."[26] The liquidation law was extended repeatedly until it covered virtually the entire country by early February 1917—but just then the tsarist government collapsed.

The Russian imperial persecution of ethnic Germans was less consistent than later campaigns against national minorities, including Germans, during the Stalinist era—small consolation to the thousands forced to move or sell their land. Visiting Russia in 1915, John Reed noted the contradictions and absurdities of policies toward Germans. "Preposterous war regulations in Petrograd" made it possible to be fined for speaking German on the telephone or sent to Siberia for speaking German on the street, but Germans "with money" could continue to live there or in Moscow.[27] The policy of deporting Germans from selected areas was difficult to implement because of lack of transportation, lack of housing, and the economic costs of driving away peasants. Still, at no point did the Russian government retreat in principle from its policy of treating ethnic Germans as an alien population, subject to being moved at will, regardless of the fact that most ethnic Germans were Russian subjects.

Although later perfected by Stalin, the punishing of ethnic minorities through forced migration was no invention of the Soviet era. The more complete the forced evacuation and the more distant the site for resettlement, the more closely such measures of an empire at war resembled and foreshadowed later Soviet expulsions of minorities. The Volhynian Germans expelled from their farms, for example, did not know when or if they would ever be able to go back home. Some fifty thousand did return to their heavily damaged farms after the fall of the imperial regime, and some remained until the new era of forced migrations that came with World War II.

Turks and Greeks

In Russia the Great War brought forced evacuation of Jews and Germans, but in Turkey it was Armenians and Greeks who faced the greatest danger. On the eve of their destruction, Turkey's Armenians continued to live chiefly in the east while the country's Greeks resided mainly along the country's coasts and nearby river valleys. The largest number of Greeks lived in the west: in Eastern Thrace, Constantinople, and the western coast of Anatolia. There was also a distinct population of Pontic Greeks, so named after the ancient name for the northeastern coast of Asia Minor or Anatolia. The Pontic Greeks spoke their own dialect and lived in towns and cities along the Black Sea in a community that stretched into Russia.

In 1914 Greeks, Turks, Armenians, and all Ottoman subjects still theoretically lived in one state governed by the sultan, but imperial rule had become all but a fiction. While the sultan and an imperial administration still existed at Constantinople, after multiple revolutions and coups real power now resided with the Young Turks, and in particular with the Ittihad Party or Committee of Union and Progress, the CUP. The party's leaders, most notably Minister of the

Interior Talaat Pasha and Minister of War Enver Pasha, along with Jemal Pasha who held several different high-ranking positions, were the real powers in the empire.

In the Ottoman Empire's core regions, CUP pursued a radical nationalist policy against Armenians and Greeks. All Greek gains in the Balkan Wars placed Ottoman Greeks at greater risk. The loss of Macedonia, a key political base for the Young Turks in their rise to power, personally affected Turkey's new leaders. Convinced that Greece sought Turkey's destruction, the leading Young Turks viewed Greeks in Turkey with suspicion, and the arrival of destitute Muslim refugees from Macedonia and Thrace further fueled nationalist animosity against Greece. So too did a naval arms race with Greece and Greek annexation and occupation of offshore islands. For CUP's leaders, attacking the country's Greeks was a means to purify the core regions of Turkey. Talaat Pasha made clear that this was his intent. When U.S. Ambassador Henry Morgenthau in early 1914 objected to the mistreatment of Greeks, Talaat explained that Turkey had already lost many provinces. "If what was left of Turkey was to survive, added Talaat, he must get rid of these alien peoples. . . . Therefore he proposed to Turkify Smyrna and the adjoining islands."[28]

Persecution of Turkey's Greeks began in the spring of 1914 even before the start of World War I. The first stage was harassment: boycotts, visits by Turkish irregulars, and threats delivered either by letters or by graffiti on walls. The second stage was actual terror: thefts, attacks on homes, and killings. Armed bands, sometimes made up of recent Turkish refugees from the Balkan Wars, attacked Greek villages in Eastern Thrace and on the west coast of Anatolia. One of the largest massacres occurred at the town of Phocaea (Foca), northwest of Smyrna, where some fifty Greeks were killed. The German correspondent Harry Stuermer, a reporter usually sympathetic to Turkish authorities, later saw the town's "smoking ruins."[29]

Living in a climate of fear, Greeks began to flee their homes. Some departed for the comparative security of the larger Greek community of Smyrna. Others left Turkey altogether for islands recently occupied by Greece. Tens of thousands of Greeks sailed from the coastal town of Cesme, west of Smyrna, for the nearby Aegean island of Chios, and newly arrived Muslim refugees of the Balkan Wars moved into the departed Greeks' houses, even taking their clothes.[30] Other Greeks sought more distant refuge: "Whenever we passed the Greek consulate," Ambassador Morgenthau recalled, "we could see a throng of excited Greeks besieging its doors in an effort to get passports to leave the country."

At the same time Turkey began to deport Greeks from much of the coast of Asia Minor. This did not yet amount to a campaign of full-scale ethnic cleansing, but some 150,000 Ottoman Greeks were forced out of Turkey to the Greek islands or mainland, and tens of thousands of others were sent to the interior of Anatolia. George Horton, the American consul at Smyrna, distinguished between the treatment of those who held Greek citizenship, who did not suffer "extreme persecution," and the Ottoman Greeks who "were massacred, robbed, driven out of their homes, ravished," or drafted and sent to forced labor without "food or clothing, until many of them died of starvation or exposure."[31] Probably the fact that an independent country could intercede on their behalf afforded Greek citizens greater security than Ottoman Greeks.

The Turkish campaign against Greeks only intensified with the war. Turkey entered the conflict in late October 1914, and the intimidation of Greeks reached a new level in 1915 after the Allied landing at the Gallipoli peninsula. As Turkish and Allied forces fought for control of the strategic land above the narrow Dardanelles straits, Turkey deported Greeks from villages in the surrounding region and from islands in the Sea of Marmara.

One of the Greek communities deported in 1915 was that of the island of Marmara. On June 5, 1915, the local governor told Greek councillors that Greek residents of Marmara were to be sent to Asia Minor. An account by one resident who later escaped to Athens depicted swift and complete expulsion. The order to leave came quickly: on midnight of the following day, local authorities knocked on doors, telling Greeks to prepare to depart. The Greeks had little time to pack, but that did not matter, since local authorities did not permit them to take much more than some bedding. Everything else was handed over to the government.[32] The first steamer left on June 7. The island's Greeks were not formally expelled en masse from Turkey but driven from their homes and removed of most of their possessions with little hope of return.

As the war continued, the Turkish campaign against Greek civilians expanded to include the Pontic Greeks who lived on the Black Sea. The road to persecution here was quite similar to that elsewhere on the war's eastern fronts. Military threats and setbacks—in this case defeats by Russia—convinced Turkey's leaders to begin a campaign against a civilian population accused of treason. This was either a preemptive strike against Black Sea Greeks or a harsh response to military activity by Greek bands, but in either case Turkey deported Greeks as Russian forces advanced into eastern Anatolia.

Greek diplomatic reports told of deportations and growing dread in the region of Trebizond, site of a port of the same name founded by ancient Greek colonists, and an adjoining strip of land bounded by high mountains to the south. Pontic Greeks from villages near Trebizond ordered into the interior in April 1916 feared they would be slaughtered like the Armenians. So instead they "took refuge in the woods, hoping that they would be saved by a quick advance of the Russian army." The Turkish campaign against Pontic Greeks also focused on areas farther from the front, including Samsun, another Black Sea port more than 150 miles to the west of Trebizond. A new wave of violence peaked late in 1917, which the Austrian consul general Kwiatowksi attributed to an attack by a Greek band on a Turkish village near the town of Baffra, northwest of Samsun. Turks retaliated by driving out the residents of nearby Greek villages. In all, Kwiatowksi estimated some 70,000 Greeks were deported from villages along more than 100 miles of Black Sea coast.[33]

Subject to state-sponsored terror despite their status as Ottoman subjects, during World War I Turkey's Greeks experienced persecution just short of full-scale ethnic cleansing. Deportations and expulsions of Greeks were not complete, but they were very nearly so in

some regions of Turkey. Ambassador Morgenthau, the most prominent critic of wartime Turkish persecution of civilians, estimated
that between 200,000 and 1,000,000 Greeks were transported to the
interior of Asia Minor, where they "suffered great privations, but
they were not submitted to general massacre as were the Armenians."[34] He attributed this difference in treatment to the existence of
a Greek government, and to the concern of Turkey's ally Germany
that Greece might enter the war.

From Ethnic Cleansing to Genocide

World War I brought misery and insecurity for Serbs, for Ottoman
Greeks, and for Jews and Germans in Russia, but no people suffered
a worse fate than Turkey's Armenians. In 1914 Armenians still made
up a large minority within Turkey, living predominantly in eastern
Anatolia and in Cilicia on Turkey's southwest Mediterranean coast.
But these communities would not survive the war. Unlike many Ottoman Greeks, Armenians were not deported to the interior of Asia
Minor or to islands. Instead they were either massacred or driven
into the desert where many more were slaughtered or left to die
from hunger and thirst.

The genocide of 1915 was very different in scale and intent from
the recent persecution of Armenians under Sultan Abdul Hamid. The
massacres of Armenians in the 1890s had been so severe that Europeans took to calling the Ottoman monarch the "Red Sultan." But
Turkey's new leaders, the Committee on Union and Progress, were
not simply waiting for an opportunity to wipe out the country's Armenians. The Young Turks were not initially committed to driving non-
Turks out of the Ottoman Empire. Shortly after their 1908 revolution,
one of their leaders, a young officer named Enver Bey, told a crowd in
Salonica, "There are no longer Bulgarians, Greeks, Serbs, Romanians,
Jews, Muslims—under the same blue sky we are all equal, we are all
proud to be Ottomans!" Indeed, Young Turks spoke of creating a
"union of peoples," though members of CUP, including the sociolo-
gist Ziya Gökalp, also championed Turkish nationalism.[35]

A powerful sense of victimization, nurtured by recent defeats in the Balkan Wars and reinforced by setbacks in World War I, played a key role in propelling CUP's leaders toward a policy of expelling and exterminating Armenians. Russian and British offensives awakened fears that the Great War would continue a long sequence of Ottoman defeats, this time perhaps resulting in the empire's full destruction. For their predicament the leading Young Turks blamed not just enemy armies but also Turkey's Armenian population. This vision of Armenians as a traitorous people provided the central rationale for genocide.

After initial successes, Turkey's war took a sharp turn for the worse. In the first days of January 1915, Minister of War Enver Pasha (as Enver Bey was now known), who had led a Turkish campaign into the Caucasus, suffered a decisive and shattering defeat by Russia at the Battle of Sarikamish. Much of the Ottoman Third Army was destroyed. Far behind the front, badly wounded soldiers filled the mission hospital at Harput. "Frozen feet and hands," Henry Riggs, an American missionary at Harput recalled, "were common, and amputation was inevitable as often as not." Yet CUP blamed not Enver Pasha but Armenians, in particular the Armenian volunteers who had aided Russian forces, even though many Armenians served with Turkish forces. One Armenian refugee, recounting the effects of the battle in eastern Anatolia, reported that a Turkish officer returning from Sarikamish told an Armenian bishop, "Many of our soldiers were shot by Armenians."[36]

The systematic persecution of Turkey's Armenians began soon after Sarikamish with the disarming in February 1915 of Armenian soldiers serving in the Turkish army. Armenians had only recently entered the Ottoman military. Their removal marked the final failure of any attempt to create a broad national identity in Turkey and reduced the Armenian capacity to resist deportations later in the year. Armenian soldiers were stripped of their weapons and sent to forced labor; many were murdered. Recounting the fate of several thousand missing Armenian soldiers, Leslie Davis, the American consul at Harput and Mezreh, wrote that "it finally appeared that all of them were shot by the gendarmes who accompanied them."[37]

In a climate of fear and intensifying persecution, violence between Turks and Armenians broke out in the spring of 1915 in the
eastern town of Van. Turkish authorities described this as a rebellion, the climax of months of attacks against Muslims. But Armenians, American missionaries, and Ambassador Morgenthau countered
that the conflict broke out only when Djevdet Bey, governor general
of the district of Van and the brother-in-law of Enver Pasha, demanded that Van's Armenians supply some four thousand soldiers.
Armenians saw this order as tantamount to a death warrant. The
American missionary physician Clarence Ussher, a resident of Van
for several years, described a tense city ready to explode amidst rumors of massacres and reports of murders of disarmed Armenian
soldiers. Even in Ussher's presence, Djevdet Bey gave orders to destroy a nearby community. It was small wonder, then, that when Bey
demanded four thousand Armenian men, Armenians "felt certain
he intended to put the four thousand to death." On April 19, according to Ussher, Turkish units stationed in villages around Van received the order that "the Armenians must be exterminated."[38] The
next day fighting erupted between Turkish soldiers and Armenians
inside the city's walls.

Although Ussher was a missionary and sympathetic to Armenians, he did not describe them as entirely innocent of aggression. He
noted that Armenian political parties had prepared their defenses,
and he described Armenian revenge in Van after Turkish forces
withdrew at the approach of Russians. "They burned and murdered;
the spirit of loot took possession of them."[39] The Russian offensive
took Van in May, but by the end of July 1915 the Russians were
preparing to retreat. Many of the surviving Armenians fled east, and
so too did Ussher, whose wife had died of typhus only weeks before.

Turkish authorities claimed that the uprising at Van justified the
deportations of Armenians. CUP leaders maintained that they had
taken justified defensive measures against Armenian rebels. Minister
of War Enver Pasha told Ambassador Morgenthau that the Armenians had rebelled at Van even as Turkey defended the Dardanelles,
and added: ". . . we cannot permit people in our own country to at-

tack us in the back." Talaat told German diplomats of weapons and bombs found at Erzerum and asserted that deportations would protect the "Armenians from worse, namely from massacres." Charging the Armenians with aiding the Russians, Talaat told Morgenthau of the need to cleanse Turkey of Armenians. "There is only one way in which we can defend ourselves against them in the future, and that is just to deport them."[40] If there were no Armenians in Turkey, they could not pose a threat.

Objectively there was little evidence that Armenians as a whole represented a real military threat to Turkey, but Van looked different to men who saw it as part of a recent history of defeat and betrayal. Years of Ottoman defeats had created a sense that Turkey was beset by external and internal enemies, and Sarikamish and the British landing on April 25, 1915, at Gallipoli added to the Turkish sense of crisis. CUP's leaders were already prepared to see Armenians as traitors, and they took Van as proof that Armenians could be trusted only if they were destroyed.

Far from the east, CUP launched an assault on Armenian intellectual, political, and religious leaders. On April 24 and April 25, 1915, two hundred and fifty leading Armenians—physicians, pharmacists, journalists, writers, newspaper editors, professors, politicians, and religious figures—were arrested at Constantinople and within days deported to the interior of Turkey. For this reason, April 24 is now the date that commemorates the Armenian Genocide. Hundreds if not thousands more suffered the same fate in the following weeks as the campaign against Armenian leaders quickly spread to towns across Anatolia. At Harput, Armenian professors from Euphrates College were imprisoned with other prominent Armenians and tortured to extract confessions about supposed plots.[41]

The Final Days of Turkish Armenia

The disarming of Armenian soldiers and the arrests of Armenian leaders dismayed Turkey's Armenians, but few imagined the horrors that would follow. The exact date that the CUP leadership decided to deport all Armenians is unknown. An emergency law authorizing deportations was announced on May 27, 1915. But evidence from trials carried out just after World War I and from other sources indicates that the decision to expel Turkey's Armenians had already been reached in governing circles.[42] Limited deportations had in fact already begun in the high country of Cilicia.

The magnitude of the deportations increased rapidly in late spring and into the summer of 1915 in the towns of eastern Anatolia. At Erzerum on the Western Euphrates River, vivid accounts of deportations were provided by Germans. Because the Germans were Turkish allies, they proved to be key witnesses—far less likely to be credibly accused of slander. The German consul Max Erwin von Scheubner-Richter described a campaign of deportations that began in mid-May in the villages north of Erzerum. Armenian villagers received as little as a few hours' notice before being forced to leave their homes. Lieutenant Colonel Stange of the German military mission at Erzerum reported that Turkish irregulars carried out killings "with the toleration" and even the assistance of military escorts. Refugees, many of them women and children, camped out in Erzerum, but the attacks did not end with the clearing of outlying villages.[43] By early June the Armenians of Erzerum themselves faced imminent deportation—no one knew precisely to where, though a destination far to the south in Syria was rumored. By late June the order came from the "commander in chief" to expel *all* Erzerum's Armenians.

To the north, the summer of deportations also swept away Armenians living on or near the Black Sea. At the port of Trebizond, Armenians learned on June 26 that they were to leave within five days. The German consul, concerned about the "justified criticism" that deportation of women and children south without food or shelter might raise, claimed to have persuaded local authorities to make initial exceptions for children under ten, widows, orphans, and women on their own; but the Austrian Consul reported that such "promises were not kept." Instead Trebizond's Armenians handed over their possessions to the authorities and prepared to leave. Employees of Anatolia College, another institution founded by American missionaries, witnessed the deportations from Marsovan, an interior town south of the Black Sea. As in many other towns, the Armenian men were massacred first. George E. White, president of Anatolia College, heard that Armenian men arrested on June 26 were taken in "groups of 100 to 200" and killed by peasants under government supervision. Marsovan's remaining Armenians—women, children, and elderly men—received the order in early July to prepare to leave, and sold their goods for a pittance. Awaiting exile, they feared the worst. White recalled, "The people felt that the government was determined to exterminate the Armenian race, and they were powerless to resist."[44] Within weeks the town was nearly empty of Armenians.

The massive deportations made it difficult for even Turkey's allies to defend the campaign as a protective measure against an Armenian revolutionary threat. There were two problems with CUP's rationale: the scale of deportations and the spread of deportations to more and more regions. Even in eastern Anatolia, Germans on the ground rejected claims that deportations were a response to a general Armenian revolutionary threat. Von Scheubner-Richter described Anatolia's Armenians as "Jews of the East," most of whom were "not active revolutionaries." The extension of deportations toward the west also sewed doubts in German circles. The German ambassador Baron Hans von Wangenheim, who was charged with passivity or worse in the genocide, observed on July 7, 1915, that the "expulsion and resettlement of the Armenian population," previously limited to the eastern front and Cilicia, had now extended to provinces that did not face imminent threat of invasion. "This circumstance and the way in which the resettlement is being carried out," he concluded, "shows, that the government really pursues the purpose of annihilating the Armenian race in the Turkish empire."[45]

Harput was one of many towns engulfed by the terror spreading outside the immediate war zone. The sequence of events here was typical: first came the arrest, torture, and imprisonment of Armenian leaders, followed by the order to leave—announced on June 26 by the town crier walking through the streets. With only days to place their affairs in order, Armenians hurried to close their businesses and sell their possessions. What followed next was the equivalent of a townwide fire sale as Harput was suddenly flooded with all manner of goods. Anyone remaining in Harput and the neighboring town of Mezreh, that is to say mainly Turks (Kurds were more likely to live outside of town), could acquire virtually any item for a fraction of its normal cost. "The streets," recalled Leslie Davis, the American consul, "were full of Turkish women, as well as men, who were seeking bargains." There were plenty of these to be found. Clothes, furniture, rugs, musical instruments, sewing machines, and more—everything was for sale, and many took the opportunity to buy. "You could not look out of the window," remarked the American missionary Henry Riggs, "without seeing someone walking down the street carrying some sort of a load of booty, bought or stolen from Armenian houses."[46]

Facing exile, some sought to hide. Others approached Consul Davis, claiming American citizenship, in most cases with no strong evidence, though some women's husbands had lived in the United States. There were strong connections, for example, between Harput and the American city of Worcester, Massachusetts, where for years Armenians from Harput had found work. Harput's Armenians implored Americans to take their savings for safekeeping, and they swarmed the mission hospital, begging the American missionary physician Herbert Atkinson and his wife to take in their children.[47] In the end, dozens hid at the American consulate, and a tiny minority survived as hospital workers. But most of Harput's Armenians, predominantly women and children, set out south for the desert; many of the men had already been murdered.

By August, deportations extended to towns across Turkey. Everywhere Armenians were driven from their homes with the partial exception of those living in Constantinople and Smyrna. At Constantinople, Turkish authorities chiefly targeted Armenian men who had moved to the city without their families, but in nearby towns they carried out general deportations. South of Constantinople, across the Sea of Marmara in Bursa, deportations of Armenians (though not of Protestants) began on August 18. The local government gathered up ox carts from nearby villages and then sent some 1,800 Armenians to the railway station, from where they were to be sent by train to Konia, a town some 150 miles south of Ankara. CUP members bought Armenians' houses at steep discounts or for nothing. Armenians who reached Konia told the missionary and physician William Dodd that even the "bag of coin" given to them as payment for their property had been taken away, "to be used for the next sale."[48]

Deportations ultimately reached all the way to Turkey's western border at Adrianople in Thrace. On October 27, 1915, police appeared at the homes of prosperous Armenians there and gave them a half-hour to leave. Everything—houses, shops, and possessions—had to be left behind by the deported, who could expect to find themselves sent all the way to Mosul, a town on the Tigris River in Mesopotamia (now Iraq). It was a strange night of both despair and festivity. In a joint report, the diplomatic representatives of Austria and Bulgaria described how Turkish police entered the empty houses to celebrate, eat whatever food had been left behind, and even play the piano.[49]

Solving the Armenian Question

That the deported Armenians would almost certainly die was predictable. In order to charge Turkey with genocide, it is essential to establish that this was true and that Turkish officials knew it. There are always those who would deny or minimize genocide, but in no other case have their arguments won so much influence. To this day many American newspapers feel compelled to balance any reference to the Armenian genocide by also referring to Turkish denials that it ever took place, a practice they would never employ in referring to the Holocaust or to the Cambodian or Rwandan genocides. This false balance has crept into the work of the most influential historians.

The deportations filled Armenians with terror and observers with dread. Across Turkey, onlookers feared the worst for Armenians expelled in the summer and fall of 1915. Could they actually reach Syria or Mesopotamia or some other distant desert destination to the south? At Erzerum, the German consul von Scheubner-Richter was extremely pessimistic. Already, by June 18, he had heard of the murder of deported Armenians, and the sheer distance to be traveled over mountains and desert left little hope for any who escaped massacre. Resettlement to Deir ez Zor, a town on the Euphrates River in eastern Syria that was reportedly one destination, he viewed as "equal to massacre." This, he soon concluded, was no accident. Armenians were meant to die, if not by massacre then through "deprivation on the long journey to Mesopotamia and the unaccustomed climate there. . . . This solution to the Armenian question appears to be ideal for the hard-liners, to which almost all military and government civil servants belong."[50] Most remarkable about this statement, with its ominous foreshadowing of genocide, was that it came from a diplomat who repeatedly insisted that Erzerum's Armenians had fared better than those living elsewhere.

On the Black Sea, expert observers also saw deportation as tantamount to death. For Trebizond's Armenians, the supposed destination was Mosul. But to reach Mosul, they first had to cross a mountain range to the town's immediate south. Then, without water, food, or shelter, they had to travel over hundreds of miles of further mountains as well as desert—and there were already rumors of murders en route. The Austrian consul Kwiatowski predicted that most would die. A journey over this distance without food and shelter "equals . . . a death sentence," he informed the Austrian embassy. It was necessary to look far back in history, he added, to find such a "violent attempt at the annihilation of a people."[51]

Harput was farther south, so the Armenians' journey to the desert was shorter, but here too residents equated deportation with death. Leslie Davis feared the worst for the exiled. He expected few of the deported Armenians to make it to Urfa, about seventy-five miles to the south, let alone to Mesopotamia, which he believed might be their final destination. "Much of the way was over the desert . . . it was summer. . . . It was certain that most of them would perish on the way." Turkish authorities counted on precisely that outcome. Just before deportations began from Harput, one Young Turk Member of Parliament, Hadji Mehmet Effendi, told Henry Riggs, "The Armenians know what massacre is, and think they can bear that. But let them wait and see what deportation is. . . . They will soon learn how much worse it is than massacre!"[52]

As so many observers—missionaries, physicians, diplomats, soldiers, Americans, Germans, and Austrians—predicted, expulsion meant death for most Armenians. The death toll mounted quickly. From the west, many deported Armenians first passed through Konia, either by railway or on foot. Many thousands camped out without shelter in fields around the railway station, and the continuing deaths, observed William Dodd, an American missionary at Konia, "kept a priest and several sets of grave diggers in the cemetery from dawn to sunset burying the bodies that were brought in in constant procession." From the east of Anatolia, Armenians made their way south to the deserts of Mesopotamia and Syria, but many never reached this destination. They died from disease and hunger—one German sergeant met Armenian women so hungry that they "ate grass."[53] Some died by their own hand, and vast numbers were massacred.

The chances of even reaching the desert were slimmest from departure points farthest north, near the Black Sea. Some Armenians in those areas never even began the journey south. At Trebizond, witnesses spoke of Armenians placed on boats and drowned in the Black Sea or in a nearby river, while those who started south were murdered. From Erzerum, Lieutenant Colonel Stange of the German military mission reported that Trebizond's Armenian men were murdered in the mountains "with the assistance of the military."[54]

The journey south was almost as long for Erzerum's Armenians. Doctor Ida Stapleton, an American physician and missionary who had lived in Erzerum for years, learned of the fate of one group of Armenians from a letter from an Armenian woman. After a few nights on the road, "a motley crowd of Kurds, Turks, soldier police began to attack the caravan with guns, swords, scythes, clubs, fists. . . . All the men were killed outright except one." Armenians arriving in Harput from Erzerum in early July similarly told of the murder of their men by Kurds, and still more died in massacres south of Harput.[55]

The actual killers of Armenians came from several groups. An organization formed by CUP known as the Special Organization or Teskilat-1 Mahsusa oversaw and carried out many massacres. The Special Organization recruited from among released convicts, Kurds, and Muslim immigrants and refugees. In 1914 the armed bands created by the Special Organization had begun attacks on Armenian communities along the borders with Russia and Persia; in 1915 they played a key role in carrying out genocide.[56]

The actions of the Special Organization appear to foreshadow the first phase of the Holocaust in 1941, when Nazi mobile killing units called Einsatzgruppen murdered Jews in the Soviet Union.[57] But it would be a mistake therefore to conclude that highly trained or specialized death squads spearheaded the murder campaign against Turkey's Armenians in 1915. Reports by foreigners and accounts by Armenians who survived the march south noted some killing by gendarmes and at times by military units, but irregular forces and tribes, including Kurds, carried out a great deal of the killing. In one long diplomatic report from August 1915, von Scheubner-Richter enclosed an account by an Armenian who described an attack by "Camel drivers, emigrants, and irregulars."[58]

By the fall of 1915 the physical evidence of slaughter marked the landscape. Roads and rivers were filled with dead bodies. For weeks corpses, many tied back to back, floated down the Euphrates River into what is now northern Syria. The Euphrates briefly cleared, then corpses reappeared, if anything in still larger numbers. This time the dead were "chiefly women and children." Travelers on the roads of eastern Turkey also saw the dead everywhere. A journey outside Harput in November revealed hands and feet sticking out of the ground, and decomposing bodies: the missionary Mary

Riggs wrote, "The Land was polluted." In early November, von Scheubner-Richter saw corpses while traveling south to Mosul, even though such evidence of killing had presumably been removed before the Germans' arrival. The consul and his traveling companion told an American missionary "that in one place . . . the Vali [governor] had sent men on ahead to cover the bodies along the road."[59]

Some of the most shocking evidence of slaughter came from a lake near Harput. In late September, Leslie Davis rode out some five hours to Lake Golcuk. In happier times, Harput's American missionaries had gone to Lake Golcuk for vacation, but in 1915 Davis found evidence of butchery so massive that even today local residents recall it, despite all official Turkish denials of genocide. As one sixty-five-year-old woman, Tahire Cakirbay, told a reporter in 2000, "They took the Armenians up there and killed them. . . . My parents told me."[60] In September 1915 Davis saw dead bodies all along his route, many only partly covered in shallow graves. Then he reached the lake itself. "In most of these valleys there were dead bodies and from the tops of the cliffs which extended between them we saw hundreds of bodies and many bones in the water below." He returned in October with the missionary physician Dr. Atkinson, who estimated the number of dead bodies surrounding the lake at "between five and ten thousand," mostly women and children. Amidst the slaughter, at least one woman survived. Dr. Ruth Parmelee, yet another of the American missionaries at Harput, met a woman exiled from a town near Erzerum and sent to Lake Golcuk with her children. Wounded in her head and falling unconscious, she awoke "among the many dead bodies of her fellow Armenians, no living being in sight."[61]

For those who escaped massacre and survived the trek across Anatolia's mountain ranges, arrival at the desert brought new misery. The common cry of Armenians making their way through the desert was for bread. Few men arrived—most had already been murdered—and many young women had already been abducted. Refugees, mainly women and children, who arrived in Syria were so depleted by their journey that they continued to die in large numbers. At Mosul the German consul observed that "women and children die daily from hunger."[62] At Urfa, near the modern Turkish-Syrian border, the temperature reached 56 degrees Celsius (133 degrees Fahrenheit). Surviving Armenian women and children who reached Urfa were exhausted and often ill, and many collapsed. The refugees were so desperate that women and children could be purchased for modest sums.

Urfa was also the site of a major Armenian uprising. The town's Armenian residents escaped mass deportation in the summer of 1915, but tensions increased in August when a mob killed some two hundred Armenians and Syrian Christians in revenge for the killings of police who were searching for Armenian weapons. With the announcement in September of their imminent deportation, Urfa's Armenians prepared to fight. Some two thousand Armenian men began an uprising in October against Turkish authorities. The rebellion was crushed by October 16, though individuals continued to hold out into November. In all, some three hundred to four hundred Armenians and fifty Turks died during the uprising. The men who surrendered were slaughtered, and "women and children" were deported south.[63] One group was forced back and forth across the desert repeatedly between Tell-Abiad, just south of the modern Syrian border, and Rakka on the Euphrates.

"They Are Practically All Dead Now . . ."

In an era of many forced evacuations, Turkey's Armenians suffered the most massive ethnic cleansing, so severe that it crossed the line to genocide. Earlier episodes of mass flight in the Balkan Wars and in the wars of the nineteenth century had caused many deaths, but the end results fell short of extermination. Refugees from Macedonia, Bulgaria, and Crete had fled to a sympathetic if severely overburdened Ottoman Empire. In 1915, by contrast, there was no Armenia for Armenians to reach even if they could escape. Some escaped to regions of Russia with large Armenian populations, or even to Greece, but most were sent south where no real refuge awaited them.

Although the term "genocide" did not exist at the time, contemporaries saw the Armenian deportations as tantamount to extermination. Ambassador Morgenthau charged that Turkish authorities "knew that the great majority would never reach their destination." Morgenthau was well known for his condemnation of Turkey's Armenian policy, but the evidence was so overwhelming that even Turkey's allies conceded that the Turkish government had sought to exterminate the country's Armenian population. At Constantinople, the Austrian ambassador Johann Margrave Pallavicini, though determined to extend every possible sympathy to the Turkish government, admitted that Armenians from regions as far north as the Black Sea had little chance of surviving deportation. Pallavicini's colleague, the Austrian chargé d'affaires Karl Graf von und zu Trauttmansdorff-Weinsberg, was even more direct. The mass of evidence, not only from Armenian sources but from bankers, German officers, consuls, and other witnesses, led him to conclude in late September that the Turks, whatever their motives—and Trauttmansdorff was ready to charge many Armenians with treason—carried out the "extermination of the Armenian race."[64]

Ultimate responsibility for the destruction of Turkey's Armenians lay with the leadership of the Committee of Union and Progress. When Morgenthau, trying a different approach in his dealings with Turkish leaders, tried to please Minister of War Enver Pasha by suggesting that the government, and in particular the Young Turk leaders, were "not to blame for massacres," Enver was "offended." Calling Morgenthau "mistaken," he countered, "I am entirely willing to accept the responsibility myself for everything that has taken place. The cabinet itself has ordered the deportations." Of all CUP's leaders, Talaat Pasha was probably most direct in discussing his government's intentions toward the country's Armenian population. Although he claimed that the deportations would protect the Armenians, Talaat made no secret of his desire to rid Turkey of its Armenians and Greeks. In June he informed a German diplomat that Turkey's government "wanted to use the world war, in order to thoroughly clear away their internal enemies (the indigenous Christian)."[65]

Oddly enough, Talaat became increasingly candid in telling Morgenthau what had actually become of Turkey's Armenians. Speaking with the American ambassador in early August 1915, Talaat again accused Armenians of aiding the Russians, but he added that something more was also at stake. Observing that many of the chief towns in eastern Anatolia were already emptied of Armenians, Talaat said, "The hatred between the Turks and the Armenians is now so intense that we have got to finish with them. If we don't, they will plan their revenge." What did it mean to "finish" with the Armenians? Talaat, in one conversation, revealed that he knew that most had died. Indeed, he tried to profit from this knowledge by collecting their life insurance policies for the Turkish government. Making a request that astonished and enraged Morgenthau, Talaat asked the ambassador to have U.S. life insurance companies send a list of Armenian policyholders. As Talaat explained, "They are practically all dead now and have left no heirs to collect the money. It of course all escheats to the state."[66] Morgenthau refused.

From Constantinople, CUP's leaders transmitted orders to local officials, typically through the apparatus of their political party or through the Special Organization. Dr. Bahaeddin Sakir of the Special Organization coordinated much of the work of deporting and killing Armenians. The official channels of government seem to have been less central to carrying out the genocide. Some official Ottoman documents even called for secure transport of Armenians.[67] But such statements did not correspond to reality: repeated predictions of death and repeated death. The documents may provide evidence of divisions within the Turkish government, or they may simply reflect an effort at subterfuge.

The response of ordinary Turks to the deportations was mixed. Many Turks and Kurds aided Armenians, but eyewitnesses, on the whole, described a Turkish population balanced between opportunism and passive complicity. CUP officials themselves certainly profited directly from the deportations by seizing Armenians' assets, and Turkish civilians also repeatedly took advantage of conditions to acquire their Armenian neighbors' property at virtually no cost.[68] In many cases, Turkish or Kurdish men also took young Armenian women or girls. Indeed, the seizure of Armenian women and girls forms a major theme in accounts of the Armenian genocide. Exploitation, whether economic or sexual, was a mass phenomenon.

A legal claim filed against the Turkish government in 1920 by Nafina Chilinguirian, the grandmother of the Armenian-American author Peter Balakian, detailed the immense losses suffered by one Armenian family. Nafina's husband had died "of violent sufferings" (the young widow would soon marry Balakian's grandfather Bedros Aroosian). Her father, mother, brothers, sisters, and other relatives, including young nieces and nephews, had been killed. The goods stolen from her husband's store in Diyarbekir included large quantities of sugar, coffee, and rice as well as money. Her claim also listed textiles taken from a brother's shop, and the theft of sheep, jewels, and money. The total claim for damages amounted to $124,666.66.[69]

There are parallels between the Turkish looting of Armenians and the gains of many Germans under Nazi rule who acquired property and businesses formerly owned by Jews in the late 1930s in a process known as Aryanization.[70] The opportunity to win personal profit on the eve of genocide was even more immediate and direct in 1915 in Turkey. The chief phase of Aryanization occurred several years before the Holocaust, but Turks acquired Armenians' property just as the genocide began. The proportion of Turks to profit directly from the Armenian genocide was also probably higher than the percentage of Germans who gained wealth from Aryanization, because Armenians made up a larger minority in Turkey's east than did Jews in most of Germany. If Aryanization gave Germans cause to look the other way as deportations of Jews began, the massive opportunistic looting of Armenians gave Turks reason to adopt a passive stance toward deportation.

Witnesses to the destruction of Turkey's Armenians were, if anything, more curious about the possible role of Turkey's allies, Germany and Austria-Hungary, than they were about the roles of ordinary Turks. From early on in the terror campaign, Ambassador Henry Morgenthau of the United States, still a neutral country in the war until 1917, sought to stem the escalating violence, both through his personal contacts with Turkish authorities and through discussions with German and Austrian diplomats. This was not easy work. German and Austrian diplomats were sympathetic to Turkey, and they seemed to regard their American colleague Morgenthau as, at best, a pest. In late April when he suggested that Austrian Ambassador Pallavicini intercede with the Ottoman government, Pallavicini assured his superiors in Vienna, "I do not intend to do that under any circumstances." A few weeks later Morgenthau was still trying to persuade Pallavicini to take an interest in the Armenians, and the Austrian ambassador was still explaining that he was not in a position "to do something." Through late June he counseled doing nothing. Asked by the Austrian consul in Trebizond what position to take regarding Catholic Armenians, Pallavicini informed Vienna that he had told him to remain "completely passive."[71]

The German embassy shared much the same passive stance toward the threat facing Armenians. The German consul in Erzerum, von Scheubner-Richter, for example, assured the German ambassador in May of his commitment to this policy: "As far as the position of the local consulate in the Armenian question is concerned, I have avoided a direct intervention on behalf of the Armenians, in accord with the instructions of your Excellency. I have also turned down all pleas directed to me on the part of the Armenians." Such sentiments caused a particular crisis for Johannes Lepsius, a German pastor and ardent friend of Armenians, who compiled a collection of German diplomatic records on the genocide. Lepsius deleted those sentences most damaging to Germany from his collection, leaving instead only von Scheubner-Richter's statement that he had countered the "idea of a 'settling of scores.'" This was no accident. The destruction of Erzerum's Armenians horrified von Scheubner-Richter. In August he had remarked that "it was known to me, and also complied with the instructions to me from your Excellency that we do not possess a right to stand up for innocent Armenians affected by the expulsion."[72] Once again Lepsius deleted the consul's reference to the German ambassador's instructions.

War, Ethnic Cleansing, and Memory

Following immediately after the Balkan Wars, the Great War continued to remake the ethnic and religious map of the European and Asian borderlands. As in the past, war triggered targeted mass flight and expulsion, but this time the effects were far more devastating and far-reaching. Ethnic cleansing in the Balkan Wars was only partial, but World War I permanently eradicated the historic Armenian communities of eastern Turkey. A small portion of Turkey's prewar Armenian population clung to existence for a few more years in Constantinople and Smyrna, but the Armenian communities of most of Turkey never returned. The cities and towns where Armenians once lived in large numbers became Turkish and eventually, especially in Turkey's southeast, also Kurdish. Along with much of their homeland, Armenians also lost many of their key national symbols, from historic monasteries to Mount Ararat.

Harput was one of many towns to experience this shocking rupture with an Armenian past. By 1915 Armenian Harput had almost entirely disappeared. Some refugees, mainly women and children, managed to stay, but the Armenian town was literally taken apart. The deserted houses of Armenians were removed of everything of value, including windows and doors. Even roofs were removed, and houses were dismantled for firewood. Below Harput, the Armenian villages of the plateau lay in ruins, with churches destroyed. The lower town of Mezreh became the center of a Turkish city, but the old town of Harput was never rebuilt. The Armenian districts of the old town atop the mountain have since fallen into ruins.[73]

The destruction of Harput and most of the other communities of Turkish Armenia marked a new stage in the development of ethnic cleansing. Many of the details of carnage so shocking to eyewitnesses were not new to Ottoman borderlands, but the deportation and expulsion of Armenians was ethnic cleansing of unprecedented intensity. In part, the central role of Turkey's political leaders accounted for this new level of violence. Never before had a government in power set out to destroy a core population of one of Europe's

old empires. Never before had an empire's leaders been so determined to eliminate a "traitor people." The leaders of the Committee of Union and Progress built on a prewar legacy of growing mistrust toward populations accused of insufficient loyalty, and war
brought a heightened obsession with the threat of internal treason.
Under the new nationalist logic, treason was not a crime of individuals or even of organizations but of entire populations, and the only
remedy lay in their complete removal or destruction. On Russia's
western front, the military adopted similar logic in its campaign to
deport Jews and Germans; in contrast to Turkey, however, the tsarist
government ultimately withdrew from the most radical anti-
Semitic course.

Long after the Great War ended, mass flight, deportation, and
genocide shaped the identities of survivors and their descendants.
The Serb catastrophe of 1915 formed a major theme in images of
Serb victimization through the late twentieth century. Genocide, of
course, became a central event in Armenian identity. Even as survivors concentrated on making new lives for themselves, commemoration of genocide developed as one of the major goals of Armenian civic life, both in the Soviet Republic of Armenia and in the
huge diaspora of Armenians abroad. Along with the survival of
their people and culture, Armenians remember what is missing and
lost: the dead, the towns and cities, and the national symbols that
now stand in the Republic of Turkey. Many Armenians also remembered Turks as destroyers.

Conversely, denial of genocide became a key element in Turkish
efforts to present Turkey's history to the world. It is possible to sym-
pathize with Turks angered by the speed with which the fate of
Muslim victims of ethnic cleansing has faded into near oblivion. It
is also useful to understand how past ethnic cleansing radicalized
Turkish nationalist opinion in the early twentieth century. For that
very same reason, however, it is long past time for all historians to
accept the reality of the Armenian genocide.

Paradoxically, the same horrors that have remained so central to
national identity were soon forgotten by the wider world. The Great

War confirmed the connection between war and ethnic cleansing in modern Europe, but this lesson was almost immediately lost. The trek of Serbians west across Kosovo in 1915 has become a minor footnote to the war's history. That is also true of the forced evacuations of Jews, Germans, and other minorities from Russia's west. Today, few recall these episodes, possibly because of more violent or more recent examples of ethnic cleansing and genocide.

CHAPTER FOUR

Ethnic Cleansing Between the World Wars

The Ottoman city of Smyrna lay on a deep bay edged with mountains on the west coast of Anatolia or Asia Minor. Smyrna had been settled since antiquity: it was the site of a Hittite settlement as well as later Greek, Roman, and Byzantine towns. Under Ottoman rule it became a major port for trade with European merchants, and the city grew rapidly in the late Ottoman period. A French company built a new quay, which became the site for hotels, consulates, and a theater. By the early twentieth century, Smyrna was a cosmopolitan city of more than a quarter-million people, including Armenians, Jews, Turks, and Europeans, the last group known as Levantines or Franks. But most of all, Smyrna was a Greek city. Greeks made up its largest single ethnic group into the early twentieth century. By 1923 this Smyrna was gone. The Greeks had left, either in flight or as part of a population exchange, and the district where they had once lived lay in ashes.

War continued across much of Eastern Europe and Western Asia for years after the end of World War I, and one of these wars destroyed the core of Greek Smyrna. The Russian Empire did not survive the Great War, and the Ottoman Empire survived only in a shattered and short-lived form. The end of empires generated new wars. Imperial collapse created a power vacuum, and varied states and nationalist and revolutionary movements struggled to replace the old empires. Warfare in the former Ottoman and Russian lands involved irregulars and armed bands, combatants who were overburdened and sometimes desperate, and conditions often verged on anarchy.

These wars generated a wide range of ethnic and religious violence. Nationalists fought to carve nation-states out of old imperial lands, and rival nationalist movements that coveted the same land engaged in ethnic war. In the Ottoman Empire, war between Greeks and Turks led to massacres, ethnic cleansing, and population exchange. In Transcaucasia, Armenians faced off in an ethnic and religious war with Turks and Tatars. In Russian borderlands in Ukraine, the death toll in new pogroms during the years of the Russian civil war exceeded that of all the pogroms of recent decades combined.

Ottoman Half-life and Greek Nationalism

In Turkey the immediate postwar years were a period of Ottoman half-life. The leaders of the Committee of Union and Progress who had dominated Turkey during the Great War lost power. A 1919 trial of former cabinet ministers, conducted under Allied pressure, found Talaat and Enver Pasha guilty of murder and sentenced them to death in absentia. Their sentences were never carried out, but Talaat was assassinated in Berlin in 1921 by Soghomon Tehlirian, a young Armenian. The jury at Tehlirian's trial in Berlin acquitted him after hearing harrowing testimony from survivors of genocide. Enver died fighting the Soviets in Central Asia in 1922.[1]

The demise of the CUP did not, however, restore the imperial government to health. A sultan remained at Constantinople, but the sultan's government mattered less and less. The sultinate did not even control its own capital city: in December 1918 the Allies established a military administration in Constantinople. Three high commissioners, one each from Britain, France, and Italy, oversaw the Allied administration.* The Allied hold over the city tightened in 1920 when British troops led an Allied military occupation of Constantinople. Meanwhile the decaying imperial government faced a Turkish rival for power, the Turkish Nationalists led by Mustafa Kemal (Kemal Atatürk). In 1920 the Nationalists staked their claim to power by setting up a provisional government at Ankara.ª

As the longtime "sick man" of Europe entered a terminal phase, the European powers and Greece carved up Ottoman territories. The Treaty of Sèvres, signed by the sultan's government in August 1920 but never recognized by the Turkish Nationalists, parceled out much of the empire. The treaty gave Thrace and the remaining Turkish Aegean Islands to Greece and the Isle of Rhodes to Italy. France received a mandate over Syria; Britain received mandates in Palestine and Mesopotamia.

Ottoman defeat brought particular excitement to Greece. From its founding, the Greek Kingdom had never been home to all Greeks. Greeks outside of Greece lived in merchant communities across Europe, but in Greek nationalist terminology the largest number, those under Turkish rule, were known as the "unredeemed Greeks." Over the course of nearly a century, Greece's boundaries expanded to include Greek populations living in Thessaly, Epirus, Southern Macedonia, and Crete. Following its victories in the Balkan Wars, Greece's borders on the European mainland came to closely resemble its present borders in all regions except Thrace. But Greek nationalists wanted more. In particular they eyed lands in the Ottoman Empire where more than a million unredeemed Greeks still lived.

---

* The title "high commissioner" had earlier been used by Britain. After the end of World War I, it was employed for several purposes in Turkey and in the Near East and the Caucasus. High commissioners oversaw Allied military administration in Constantinople and nearby waters, but the United States also appointed a high commissioner, Admiral Mark Bristol, as its diplomatic representative in Turkey. Britain also named a high commissioner as diplomatic envoy to the Transcaucasus, and U.S. Colonel William Haskell oversaw relief work as allied high commissioner to Armenia.

The Great War and its end created both the need and the opportunity to rescue the unredeemed Greeks. Never before had their plight been so desperate—Turkey had deported hundreds of thousands of Greeks from their homes during the war. Greek nationalists believed, however, that they could now guarantee the safety of Ottoman Greeks. As recently as 1897, Ottoman armies had easily defeated Greece, but in the aftermath of World War I Greece confronted a vanquished empire on the verge of collapse. There had never been a better time to fulfill the idea of Megali, to unite all Greeks, including the Greeks of nearby Asia Minor, under Greek rule. Greek Prime Minister Eleutherios Venizelos aimed to gain the region around Smyrna, but he was more cautious about Constantinople. Venizelos suggested making the Ottoman capital into an international territory, a step he hoped would lead to the city gradually becoming Greek; but the most ardent champions of Megali called for making it the capital of an expanded Greek state. Victory would be complete when the Orthodox liturgy was resumed in the great church of Hagia Sophia.

The concept of Megali exemplified the problems inherent in matching political boundaries and national boundaries. In the Balkans, victors in recent wars struggled to integrate populations with the "wrong" national identity. The Albanians of Kosovo, for example, provided an extreme example of a people whose national identity diverged from the national identity of their new rulers in Yugoslavia. But the Greeks who sought to expand the Greek state into Asia Minor faced even greater challenges than Yugoslavia confronted in Kosovo. The Yugoslav state, founded in 1918, ended at Albania and Greece, but there were no clear geographic or political boundaries to mark a new Greek frontier in Turkey.

"Greeks and Turks Are Killing One Another"

In May 1919 British Prime Minister Lloyd George, eager to counter Italian interest in Turkey, encouraged Greek occupation of Smyrna (the present-day Izmir), and Greek troops landed there on May 15.

Violence followed immediately. Greek civilians and some soldiers attacked Turkish soldiers who had been taken as prisoners, and newly
emboldened local Greeks in nearby villages attacked and looted
their Turkish neighbors. The new Greek governor of Smyrna soon
imposed order in Smyrna itself, but insecurity persisted outside the
city. Harold Armstrong, a British military attaché at Constantinople,
recalled that the "Greeks pushed out, massacring, burning, pillaging, and raping as they went in the ordinary manner of the Balkan
peoples at war." Turks condemned a chain of destruction and killing
by Greek troops at towns including Bergama, the site of ancient
Pergamon, and an Inter-Allied Commission formed to investigate
the occupation of Smyrna and adjacent territories found that "entire
villages have had to be abandoned."[3]

The Greek occupation humiliated the Turks. The Greeks, reported Captain Hadkinson, a British relief officer attached to the
High Commission, were "doing their level best to make themselves
obnoxious, unpopular, and hated by the Turks." Greeks celebrated
their triumph by flaunting Greek nationalist symbols. Flags, portraits of the Greek prime minister Venizelos, and Greek patriotic
songs "cannot but create ill-feeling, and a wider breach between
these two races." Greeks also celebrated a victory for Orthodox
Christianity over Islam. Greek troops arriving at Smyrna sang, "Now
that we have taken Smyrna, let us fly to Aghia Sofia. The mosques
will be razed to the ground, and the Cross will be erected thereon."[4]

Unsurprisingly, the Greek advance into Anatolia catalyzed Turkish anger and political activity. Turkish anti-annexation societies
and leagues formed to protest the Greek ambitions and held demonstrations in Constantinople and other towns and cities.[5] These events
were the most obvious manifestation of a Turkish nationalist awak-
ening, but it was not just the urban elites who resented Greek rule.
Cycles of revenge killing spread beyond Turkey's cities as Greeks
and Turks engaged in tit-for-tat attacks and counterattacks in
smaller towns and villages.

Aidin, southeast of Smyrna, was one of those towns. Greek and
Turkish forces fought there from May through early July 1919. Soon

after Greek forces entered the town they arrested local Turkish leaders. Orders for non-Muslims to wear hats and for Greek and Armenian shopkeepers to put up signs in Greek helped ensure that only Turks would be persecuted. In late June, Greek troops preparing to retreat set fire to Turkish houses. Captain Hadkinson reported that "All the Turks who tried to escape from the flames were shot with machine guns and rifles by the Greek soldiers and civilians to whom rifles had been distributed." When Turkish irregulars retook the town, it was their turn for revenge: they burned houses and robbed and killed Greeks. By the time Greek forces returned in early July, much of the town had been destroyed and most of the Turkish population had taken flight.[6] It was very difficult to get to the truth of what was happening at Aidin. As British Admiral Richard Webb wrote from Constantinople on June 28, 1919, "Greeks and Turks are killing one another wholesale in the Aidin Vilayet." The shifting terror foreshadowed much of the fighting in the new Greek-Turkish War: repeated cycles of violence and flight in which both Greek and Turkish civilians suffered.

The Greek advance into Anatolia was especially shocking to Turks because it seemed to complete a century-old process of dismantling Ottoman domains. The cumulative loss of territories—the Morea, Bulgaria, Thessaly, Crete, Macedonia, and part of Thrace—had significantly shrunk the Ottoman Empire. The Greek invasion in 1919 put the very survival of any Turkish state in question. Greeks, Serbs, and Bulgarians had gained their own countries from the wreckage of the Ottoman Empire in Europe, but would the Turks be left with any state of their own? With the Greek invasion there was no obvious end in sight, no boundary to fall back on, and no security for a new Turkey. Many Turks saw their nation threatened by nothing less than extermination.

The threat of extinction radicalized Turkish opinion. A summary by Admiral Webb of the findings of the military control officer at Akhissar, east of Smyrna, depicted Turks united in their determination to fight Greece. The Turks he met, "military leaders, civilian notables, irregular troops and civilian peasants," interpreted the Greek occupation not simply as an opportunistic invasion but as the final step in a long history of Greek aggression. "Now the Turks say . . . Thinking little of their lives, they would sooner be exterminated fighting against the Greeks, than have their country a second Macedonia."[7]

After consolidating their grasp on the regions of Smyrna and Aidin, the Greeks expanded their area of occupation. In 1920 they advanced farther east into Anatolia and also took Eastern Thrace and the Ismid peninsula near Constantinople. Rear Admiral Mark Bristol, U.S. high commissioner in Constantinople and the senior American representative both with Turkey and the occupying Allies in Constantinople, told the State Department: "The Greek advance in Asia Minor is like a drowning man grasping a straw." Bristol noted that some "predicted that Venezelos . . . may turn out to be the greatest enemy Greece has ever had. This may be the time of his downfall."[8] Venizelos in fact fell; his government was defeated in elections in November 1920. It made no difference. The new royalist government of King Constantine continued the Greek thrust into Turkey.

Greek victories created new conflicts. War pitted refugees against each other. During World War I the Turkish government had deported Greeks, and Muslim refugees from the Balkans had moved into Greek houses. Now these same Muslims faced the prospect of moving again. The Inter-Allied Commission that investigated Greek occupation in 1919 learned from a Venizelos telegram that "occupation was partly intended to enable refugees living in Greece to be repatriated." Not all Greeks who had left Turkey during the war wished to return, but more than 100,000 Greeks did go back home—though not for long.[9]

Where Muslims did not flee during the initial Greek advance, Greek forces typically persecuted local leaders. The British historian Arnold Toynbee referred to a "policy of striking at the Turkish upper class." In probably the best-known account of Greek occupation of western Anatolia, Toynbee, who had only recently helped compile a study detailing the mistreatment of Armenians, turned his attention to the plight of Turks. He described a pattern of atrocities carried out by Greek soldiers or irregular forces in 1921 with the frequent "murder of rich men and subsequent seizure of their property." Toynbee himself observed Greek soldiers burning houses and boats in June 1921, and a Commission of Enquiry for the Ismid Peninsula came to similar findings: Greek troops "raped women, and robberies and acts of violence have been committed."[10]

As Turkish irregulars fought back, much of western Turkey fell into warfare between Greek and Turkish armed bands. Harold Armstrong described a war of neighbors caught up in a cycle of cruelty and vengeance. He saw burned houses, corpses in ditches, and emptied villages. Turkey had become a country of fear: "The people were afraid of the brigands. . . . They were afraid of the gendarmes and police. . . . They were afraid of their neighbors."[11]

By 1921 some Greek leaders increasingly viewed the Greek adventure in Asia Minor as misguided. Early victories paradoxically demonstrated Greece's weakness. John Metaxas, a general who had opposed Venizelos during World War I (and later became something close to a dictator before World War II), questioned the viability of the attempt to occupy large parts of Turkey. In April 1921 he observed that the Greeks made up only "an ethnological minority even in the area round Smyrna." In the interior the Greek population was "minute." Under these conditions, the Greek policy might succeed if the Turks "had no national feeling. . . . " But the opposite was true. The Turks "realize that Asia Minor is their country and that we are invaders."[12] Metaxas did not use the term "empire," but his comments suggested that Greece was seeking to create a new kind of empire in Turkey. Unlike the Ottoman Empire of old, however, this new empire purported to represent a single nation, and that Greek nation made up only a minority in Turkey.

Pontic Catastrophe

Greek forces in Turkey faced their greatest threat not from the dying imperial government in Constantinople or even from Turkish irregulars but from the new Turkish nationalist government led by

Mustafa Kemal Pasha. Born in Salonica, Mustafa Kemal gained renown as a Turkish commander at Gallipoli in 1915 and four years later took a leading role in organizing the new Turkish Nationalist movement in 1919. By April 1920 the Nationalists had broken completely with the sultan, creating a new government under Kemal at the central Turkish town of Ankara.

The rise of the Nationalists gave the Turks hope but placed Turkey's Greeks in peril. Ottoman Greeks had suffered persecution during World War I even before Greece had entered the war. Now with Greece directly involved in war in Anatolia, they feared worse: a radical Turkish Nationalist campaign to purify Turkey. Most of Turkey's vast interior remained free of Greek troops, and Greeks began to move out very early in the Greek-Turkish War. In November 1919 British Admiral de Robeck referred to "a strong and growing tendency on the part of all Christians in the interior to make for the sea-coast, where they arrive destitute and homeless."[13]

Far from Greek forces, the Pontic Greeks who lived near the Black Sea made up the first large Greek population to experience the Turkish Nationalist backlash. Despite forced evacuations during World War I, Pontic Greek communities had survived, and some new Pontic Greeks actually left Russia for Turkey during the Russian civil war. But this refuge proved to be highly insecure. Turkish Nationalists began to expel Pontic Greeks in 1920 and intensified the process after a Greek warship shelled a Black Sea village in June 1921.

British Lieutenant Colonel A. Rawlinson was one of the few witnesses to the destruction of the Pontic Greeks. Rawlinson had been sympathetic to the Turks, but when he traveled as a prisoner to Trebizond on the Black Sea he saw "that the coast range and its fertile valleys, hitherto intensively cultivated by the Greeks, was at this time everywhere deserted, the villages being abandoned." He saw gangs of Greek prisoners marching to the interior to replace Armenian forced laborers, most of whom were already dead. The Turkish Nationalists cleansed the coastal towns of Greeks. By May 1922 Herbert Adams Gibbons of the *Christian Science Monitor* found Trebizond almost entirely emptied of Greek men. Two years earlier, he estimated, there had been 25,000 Greeks at Trebizond. "To-day, be-tween the ages of 80 and 14, the male population numbers 6 priests and 10 civilians."[14]

The most telling evidence of the deportation of the Pontic Greeks came from Turkish Nationalists as they responded to queries about treatment of Greeks from Allied commissioners at Constantinople. Their explanation echoed the Committee of Union and Progress during the Great War: Pontic Greeks were now labeled a traitor people, much as the Armenians had been in 1915. Nationalist Minister of Foreign Affairs Youssouf Kemal claimed that the threat posed by Greek secret societies and bands justified immediate deportations and transfers to the interior to prevent spying and a possible Greek landing on the Black Sea coast. Those affected included foreign Greeks and, noted British High Commissioner Horace Rumbold, summarizing a telegram from Youssouf Kemal, "all capable of bearing arms and consequently of actively assisting the Hellenic forces in the event of a landing."[15] Women were relocated into the interior only if "proved guilty of participation in secret societies." In theory, then, elderly men and boys along with women of unquestioned political reliability could escape deportation. Yet at this point full-scale ethnic cleansing was not far off. The Pontic Greeks, Turkish Nationalists concluded, had stabbed them in the back, and there was no place for them in the new Turkey.

"Laying Waste the Country"

The Greek-Turkish War reached its decisive stage in summer 1921 when the Greek army attacked along the Sakarya River toward the Nationalist capital of Ankara. In late June the Greek military gathered forces for the offensive by moving troops out of Ismid, leaving a looted city in flames. News of the Greek pullout caused panic among Armenian and Greek refugees who had found safe haven in Ismid. Now they sought a way out. Dr. Mabel Elliott, an American physician working for American Women's Hospitals at Ismid, described Armenians pushing onto a ship, "filling it to overflowing,

crowding the decks to the limit of standing-room, even pushing up-
wards and clinging to the masts."[16] Greek residents left too, whether
because of complicity in atrocities during the Greek occupation, as
Alfred Toynbee maintained, or because they feared sweeping, general Turkish revenge.

Turkish Nationalists depicted every stage of the Greek offensive
as a terror campaign. A series of pamphlets produced by the general
staff of the Turkish Nationalist army on the western front detailed
Greek atrocities. The Greek advance east in August 1921 brought re-
lentless pillage and theft of everything of value that villagers possessed: sheep, cows, donkeys, chickens, butter, wheat, barley, cheese,
lentils, furniture, carpets, and carts. Wherever there was a town
large enough to have its own mosque and school, these went up in
flames. Greeks subjected men to forced labor and assaulted women.
After their offensive stalled in the dry country west of Ankara, they
retreated, systematically burning villages along the way.[17]

The Turkish general staff placed the blame for the destruction
squarely on Greek commanders and in particular on Prince Andrew
of Greece, probably best known today as the father of Queen Elizabeth II's husband Prince Philip. A member of a royal family with
Danish ancestry, Andrew had served in the Balkan Wars, but in 1917
Venizelos dismissed him from the army. When Venizelos lost the election of 1920, Andrew returned to Greece and commanded the Second Army Corps during the 1921 Sakarya offensive. There, according
to the Nationalists' general staff, he ordered the burning of villages,
though statements by Greek prisoners of war, cited in Nationalist
publicity, differed on whether the prince had issued orders or simply
knew of arson. An especially lurid account described Prince Andrew
watching fires "like Nero," warning that he would come back and
burn other places if Kemal did not make peace.[18] These charges appear to have made little impression on Andrew himself, who made no
mention of them in his memoir about the campaign, though he defended his military decisions from criticism.

Whatever Prince Andrew's precise role, there was ample evidence of destruction during the Greek retreat. Harold Armstrong,

working as a supervisor of Turkish gendarmes, remarked that the retreating Greek forces "killed every Turk who was foolish enough to be still there, and for 200 miles behind them left desolation and the villages flat with the ground." Even the Greek delegation at the Lausanne Peace Conference later acknowledged that Greek forces burned villages during the Sakarya retreat, though only because of "purely military exigencies." By present-day standards, the Greek army did not carry out full-scale ethnic cleansing. No one described a Greek policy of trying to expel all Turkish civilians. On the other hand, Turkish Nationalists perceived something even worse. Thus the preface to one of the Nationalist pamphlets on the Sakarya campaign drew readers' attention to a Greek "policy of extermination."[19]

Greek Exodus

Demoralized and depleted of supplies, in 1922 the Greek army in Turkey almost seemed to be awaiting the Turkish Nationalists' final blow. On August 26 the Nationalists launched an offensive, and the Greek army began its retreat out of Asia Minor. Both soldiers and civilians poured west toward the coast. The scenes of flight resembled those of the Balkan Wars. Families traveled with wagons packed with their belongings, but they left much along the way. The roads were soon littered with abandoned carts, discarded property, and dead animals.[20]

The dominant theme of 1922 was Greek catastrophe, but Turks told a very different story. According to Turks, the Greek army's retreat was marked by burned villages, destroyed olive and fig orchards, and corpses. At the town of Salihli, some fifty miles east of Smyrna, the Turkish writer Halidé Edib found most of the buildings destroyed. Even the Greek delegation at Lausanne conceded Greek misdeeds during the retreat.[21]

The Greek adventure in Turkey ended back where it had started, in Smyrna. A little more than three years after Greeks there had greeted the arrival of Greek troops, the tattered remnants of the

Greek army returned, accompanied by a multitude of Ottoman Greeks seeking refuge in Smyrna. Ismet Inönü, one of the Turkish commanders, later suggested that the Greek civilians had little choice but to flee to the west. At Lausanne he said he "pitied the unfortunate people who, having been driven by the aggressor to take part in the fighting, had naturally had to follow the invading army in its retreat." Thousands of Greeks arrived daily in Smyrna, doubling the number of people in the city to 700,000 in less than two weeks. Greek soldiers passed by on their way to the Aegean Islands, but most of the civilians had no place else to go. Thousands sought protection at the American consulate, and tens of thousands scrambled to get out of the city before it fell. They climbed aboard every available boat in the harbor, but there was no room for most.[22]

On September 9 the Turkish Nationalist army entered a city waiting in dread. Some of the city's residents suffered exactly what they feared: pillaging and killing. T. Roy Treloar, an Englishman in the carpet business, "saw a house-to-house search for Armenians . . . thousands of Armenians were slaughtered."[23] The most notorious single murder was the killing of Greek Archbishop Chrysostom, handed over by Turkish commander Nureddin Pasha to a mob and then mutilated and murdered.

Mustafa Kemal himself gave mixed signals about the fate of Smyrna. He told John Clayton of the *Chicago Tribune* that there had been "no massacres." He did concede some "pillaging and killing" but described these as the "inevitable" result of desire for revenge for Greek atrocities. "When an army enters a city, after marching 450 kilometres through their own land, which has been burned and sacked, seen its parents and relatives slaughtered, it is difficult to control," he said. Turkish soldiers, the Nationalist leader implied, had every reason to exact a terrible punishment on Smyrna as a payback for Greek sins against Turks. Yet Mustafa Kemal assured order. He told Clayton, "We are not here to regulate past accounts."[24]

The Turks nonetheless settled past accounts on September 13 when Smyrna burned. Eyewitnesses, including Minnie Mills, head of the American Collegiate Institute, testified to seeing Turkish soldiers at work setting and spreading fires, though Turkish Nationalists later maintained that Armenians or Greeks were responsible. Fire in the Armenian quarter spread to the Greek and Levantine quarters and burned most of Christian Smyrna. As the city went up in flames, residents and refugees crowded the harbor. A throng of tens of thousands gathered on the quay, trapped between the fire, the sea, and Turkish soldiers. Some jumped into the water seeking to escape the flames, described as "an un-broken wall of fire, two miles long."[25] Some swam out to American warships, which had been dispatched to Smyrna to protect Americans. At the water's edge, American sailors held the crowd at bay and picked out those with papers that proved claims of American citizenship.

The fire marked the beginning of the end of Greek Smyrna. In the rubble, John Clayton observed, "The problem of the minorities is here solved for all time."[26] There was no longer any question about Turkish Nationalists' views on the future of Greeks and surviving Armenians. The Turkish Nationalists classified all Greek and Armenian men between the ages of eighteen and forty-five as enemy combatants and prisoners of war. They had until the end of September to leave or face deportation to the interior.

The fire at Smyrna signalled many of Turkey's remaining Greeks to flee. The Greeks of Constantinople, which was still occupied by Allied troops, were divided on whether to stay or go. But Greek flight was nearly universal in parts of Eastern Thrace, due under the terms of an October 1922 Allied-Turkish agreement to return to Turkey. Refugees once again abandoned their homes, packed their goods on wagons or on occasion—this was new—into cars, and crowded onto trains. But the intensity of Greek fear impressed observers more than all the physical details of flight. Reporting on a twenty-mile-long column of refugees crossing the Maritza River (the present-day boundary of Greece and Turkey) in October 1922, Ernest Hemingway, then a correspondent for the *Toronto Daily Star*, wrote, "They don't know where they are going. They left their farms, villages and ripe, brown fields . . . when they heard the Turk was coming." Another reporter declared that "every single Greek and Armenian in Thrace believes that to be found here then would be equivalent to a sentence of death."[27]

Refugees from western Anatolia and Eastern Thrace made their way to Greece. Thousands a day arrived at Thessaloniki until nearly all available buildings, including churches, mosques, and schools, were crowded with refugees. Others reached Athens with virtually nothing in hand. Some had lost the fruits of a life's labor. At Athens's port of Piraeus, an American reporter met a sixty two year old Greek refugee named George Leopolous who had built a business in Smyrna from the profits he had earned running a candy store in Worcester, Massachusetts. Having lost all his wealth, Leopolous said, "I shall have to go back to America and start another candy store."[28]

With its defeat by the Turkish Nationalists, Greece again assumed a major role in modern European ethnic cleansing. In the nineteenth century the rise of Greece had served to initiate ethnic cleansing in a previously multiethnic region. Greek independence brought the flight of Turks from core regions of the new Greek nation-state. With the collapse of Greek power in Turkey in 1922, Greeks became the victims of a new type of ethnic cleansing, one generated not by the dissolution of an old multiethnic empire but by the yearning of a state to expand into a new kind of nationalist empire. Pushing Greek boundaries east into Anatolia, where Greeks made up only a minority, doomed the ancient Hellenic communities of Turkey. Instead of realizing the Megali idea of uniting Greeks through the expansion of the Greek state, Greek nationalists achieved quite the opposite: the union of Greeks through the expulsion and transfer of Greek communities on the eastern coast of the Aegean and the southern coast of the Black Sea. Building a nationalist empire in the age of nationalism ultimately endangered the very nation whose interests generals and political leaders claimed to represent.

"Two Blacks Do Not Make a White"

Far to the east of Smyrna, the collapse of empires also brought ethnic war to Transcaucasia, the region south of the Caucasus that stretched from the Black Sea to the Caspian Sea along the borders of the Russian and Turkish empires. This was another region ripe for ethnic violence. The Great War had created large numbers of refugees, many of them eager for revenge. And several new national movements, including those of Georgians, Armenians, and Azerbaijanis, a Turkish people then commonly known as Tatars, competed to replace the old empires.

The wars for Transcaucasia fell into three phases. In the first, the Russian and Ottoman empires and their respective allies contended for power. In the second phase, the collapse of the Russian and Ottoman empires inaugurated a struggle by new states and local military strongmen to carve out new boundaries and fill the power vacuum. In the final phase, resurgent Turkish and Russian power— in the form of the Turkish Nationalists and Soviets—brought an end to the war.

The wars for Transcaucasia produced a wide range of ethnic violence, from pogroms to partial ethnic cleansing. All combatants agreed that the conflicts brought intense suffering, but there was no consensus as to who was primarily responsible—Armenians or Azerbaijanis and Turks. Rather, each side engaged in publicity campaigns, seeking to win over foreign opinion through reports of atrocities. Much of the fighting took place far from independent observers, and the flow of atrocity stories, seldom verifiable by any except the narrators, caused no small measure of frustration. Thus Admiral Mark Bristol, the U.S. high commissioner in Constantinople, complained in November 1920: "it is almost impossible to take news in this part of the country from native sources at its face value. . . . I have not yet been able to get the true facts in regard to the situation in Armenia."[29]

There were two chief narratives or versions of the events that occurred in the first phase of war in Transcaucasia. For Turkish and Azerbaijani sources the pattern was simple: Armenians took any opportunity to massacre Turks and Azerbaijanis. This was the story that Turkish authorities worked hard to get out. As Turkish forces advanced eastward in 1918 after the Russian Revolution, the Turkish military publicized recent Armenian atrocities. Lieutenant General

Mehmet Vehip, commander of the Ottoman Caucasian Armies, reported massacres committed by Armenians, and the Turkish military published photos of corpses and made available accounts of Armenian atrocities that came from Russian officers. The war journal and notes of Twerdo Khlebof, identified as a Russian artillery officer, recounted a reign of terror by Armenians against Turks at Erzerum in eastern Turkey in February 1918. "The Armenians," the account claimed, "congratulated themselves on having massacred that evening three thousand persons."[30]

Where Turks depicted Armenian atrocities, Armenians described a final Turkish effort, aided and abetted by Tatar allies, to exterminate Armenians once and for all. As the Russian army withered away, Ottoman forces pushed east far beyond the former Russian-Turkish border, deep into Transcaucasia, sending refugees flying. The Russian surrender of Kars, a fortress long contested by Russia and Turkey, produced the panicked flight of thousands of Armenians before the first Turkish troops arrived on April 25, 1918.[31]

Visitors to the war zone echoed the divergent Turkish and Armenian narratives. In 1919 two American travelers engaged in relief work, Captain Emory Niles and Arthur Sutherland, painted a picture of Armenian-generated terror in eastern Anatolia. They charged that "the Armenians committed upon the Turks all the crimes and outrages which were committed in other regions by Turks upon Armenians." But an Austrian, Stephan Steiner, who traveled in Anatolia and Transcaucasia from April through July 1918 at the invitation of Turkish headquarters, found both sides guilty. Turkish officials, he recounted, worked diligently to persuade him and a German reporter "that the Armenians are the greatest criminals in the whole world and the Turks are the innocent victims of Armenian barbarism." The efforts of Steiner's Turkish handlers were only partly successful. He agreed that Armenian troops "treated the Turkish population that fell into their hands just as the Turks once did the Armenians," though the smaller number of Turks who remained behind kept the death toll well below that of the Armenians in 1915. But when the Turks advanced, Steiner added, "they took cruel revenge."[32] Several districts were almost void of Armenians except for those who had hidden in the mountains.

As the Russian and Ottoman empires suffered collapse or defeat, the war for Transcaucasia gradually entered a second phase in which armed bands and new national armies fought from the Caspian Sea to the disputed former Russian-Ottoman border. "Every race, nation, tribe, and clan," the British freelance journalist C. E. Bechhofer noted, "had been clamouring, intriguing, and fighting to assert its independence and humble the pretensions of its neighbors and rivals."[33] Now they had their chance. The chief battlegrounds included the new republics of Armenia and Azerbaijan, along with a series of hotly contested ethnically mixed regions. These included Karabakh, a mountainous enclave within western Azerbaijan, and Nakhichevan and Zangezur along the Persian border.

Centered in towns previously part of the Russian Empire, the Armenian Republic took advantage of Ottoman defeat in late 1918 to establish itself within larger borders. Armenian nationalists also coveted territory that stretched into Turkey. The new Armenian state struggled with the burden of caring for hundreds of thousands of refugees, but in 1919 Armenian forces pushed out from the Armenian capital of Yerevan. Few doubted that the Armenian campaign brought acts of vengeance. But charging something more sinister than local war between rival Armenian and Tatar bands, Turkish officers accused Armenians of undertaking an organized campaign to clear out Turks and Tatars. In August 1919 Turkish General Kazim Karabekir referred to a decision to "exterminate all Moslems" in several contested regions and provinces.[34]

British Lieutenant Colonel A. Rawlinson, posted to Transcaucasia on an intelligence mission, attempted to find out if Turks were correct in their claims. On at least one occasion, Rawlinson saw a group of Muslim refugees, a "miserable column," said to be fleeing an Armenian disarmament campaign. He reported that both Armenians and their rivals talked about revenge killings and massacres in a matter-of-fact way. Meeting Armenian generals at Kars in July 1919, Rawlinson heard them reject Turkish accusations with their own "counter-charges against the Turks," but the Armenian commanders described violence against Muslims as predictable. Holding territory assigned to Armenia required disarming the Tatars. "It obviously led to fighting; and fighting, as between Moslem and Armenian, of necessity led to massacre and atrocities of all kinds," Rawlinson wrote. On the other side, Kurdish chiefs, men who impressed Rawlinson with their height, demeanor, and riding skills, expressed their own desire for revenge against Armenians. The Kurds refused to live under Armenian rule. One Kurdish chief, Rawlinson recounted, warned that he "would cut the throat of every Armenian who came within his reach."[35]

Conversations with Kurds and General Karabekir, and his own travels, left Rawlinson increasingly critical of Armenian policy, so much so that he advised by telegram: "the Armenians should not be left in independent command of the Moslem population." Under the undisciplined Armenian troops, "atrocities were constantly being committed." Rawlinson's position greatly pleased Karabekir. "Rawlinson," he informed the Ottoman Ministry of Defense on June 27, 1919, "seems to realize at last the fact that we are maintaining our moderation and silence, contending with protesting Armenian violence."[36]

Visitors to the Republic of Armenia saw a country scarred by ethnic and religious war. Oliver Wardrop, appointed British high commissioner for Transcaucasia, briefly traveled through Armenia in October 1919. He found sickness and destruction. At Yerevan, Wardrop observed, "nearly everybody is suffering or recovering from disease." Elsewhere, ethnic war had emptied the landscape. For some twenty miles along Lake Sevan, Armenia's largest lake, deserted houses lay "in ruins from internecine conflicts between Armenian and Tatars." By April 1920, C. E. Bechhofer described a country exhausted by war with a landscape of ruined villages.[37]

War in the Republic of Armenia highlighted one of the most unsettling aspects of ethnic violence: how easily perpetrators and victims could change places. Narratives of ethnic cleansing and genocide often depict groups as either victims or perpetrators. From the Holocaust and the Armenian genocide we remember Jews and Armenians as people victimized and destroyed. But no single ethnic or religious group has a fixed identity as either aggressor or victim. Germans and Turks are not by nature predisposed to be genocidal, and a group victimized once may later become the victimizer. Advocates of ethnic cleansing and related violence frequently claim they are acting defensively, but so too do their victims come to believe in cleansing as a form of defense. Precisely because of the extermination of Armenians in Turkey, Armenians in the Republic of Armenia moved toward more extreme violence to protect themselves. Perpetrators became victims and victims became perpetrators as various groups in the old Ottoman-Russian borderland established legacies of ethnic cleansing and pogroms. All sides—the Turkish Nationalists, Armenian forces, and Azerbaijani or Tatar forces—carried out either regional or local ethnic cleansing.

Bechhofer's evidence of Armenian defensive violence carried particular weight because he was highly sympathetic to Armenia. Bechhofer insisted that the Tatars bore the chief blame for devastation, but he conceded that both sides were guilty of violence. His description of actions by Armenians was very similar to ethnic cleansing. When Armenians retook ground, "they naturally preferred to drive out the men, rather than ruin their own country by destroying villages." And when Armenians destroyed Tatar villages, they did so out of revenge for the destruction of their own homes. Even Bechhofer, touched by the Armenians' plight, recoiled at the policies of the Dashnaks, the leading political party in Armenia. The men in power in Yerevan shaped an Armenian government that "retaliated upon Turk and Tatar aggression with methods as violent as its enemies'," Bechhofer lamented. "You cannot persuade a party of frenzied nationalists that two blacks do not make a white." The consequences of endless ethnic war included daily "complaints from both sides . . . of unprovoked attacks, murders, village burnings, and the like."[38]

In Baku, the capital city of Azerbaijan to Armenia's east and the site of pogroms in 1905, ethnic rivalry intersected with political conflict over the fate of the Russian Revolution. A local Soviet government known as the Baku Commune formed during the revolution. In March 1918 a showdown over the Soviet's demands for the disarming of Muslim troops ended with a two-day-long rampage through Muslim neighborhoods by Armenian soldiers allied with the Soviet, during which the soldiers set fire to a large part of the city and killed thousands.[39] In September, Azerbaijanis enacted revenge. An advancing Turkish army drove to the edge of Baku but held off from entering the city until Azerbaijanis massacred between nine thousand and thirty thousand Armenians. This was the largest single death toll, but daily attacks against Baku's Armenians continued through 1920. The chief motive, according to Colonel William Haskell, the American who served as Allied high commissioner to Armenia and oversaw relief work, was anger at the Tatar-Armenian conflict in disputed regions to the west of Baku. Haskell feared "that Armenian inhabitants of Baku face extermination."[40]

Much of the most hotly contested territory in the wars for Transcaucasia lay in a belt of disputed regions with mixed populations— Nakichevan, Zangezur, and Karabakh—that circled around southern Armenia. As in the much later war at the end of the Soviet era, Karabakh, a mountainous region southeast of Armenia, formed a chief battleground between Azerbaijanis and Armenians. This struggle pitted the Azerbaijani governor, Sultanov, against Armenians including Dashnak bands. According to Colonel J. C. Rhea, acting Allied high commissioner, Sultanov "countenanced a polity of extermination of the Armenians." These attacks culminated in June 1919 with the massacre of some six hundred Armenians at the town of Shusha (Shushi) and neighboring villages. In 1920 Dashnak bands tried to fight their way into Karabakh, but a March revolt by Armenians in Shusha met with failure. In revenge, Azerbaijanis carried out a massacre and burned some two thousand buildings.[41]

Years later, much of the city was still in ruins. In Shusha the great Soviet poet Osip Mandelstam wrote in 1931:

I tasted terrors
that the soul knows too well.

Forty thousand dead windows

stare out from all directions, there. . . .

Of their trip, Mandelstam's wife Nadezhda recalled that "the scene of disaster and massacre was terrifyingly vivid. We walked in the streets, and it was the same everywhere—two rows of houses without roofs, windows, doors. Through the windows we saw empty rooms, bare walls with shreds of wallpaper, semi-destroyed stoves, and broken furniture."[42] Some of this damage was still visible in the 1960s.

The third and final phase of the war for Transcaucasia ended with resurgent Turkish and Russian military power under new political leadership—the Turkish Nationalist movement of Mustafa Kemal, and the Bolsheviks. For Armenia this brought disaster and then a very meager salvation. Armenians faced catastrophe when Turkish Nationalist forces crossed the old Turkish-Russian border into territory claimed by the Armenian Republic. After genocide in Anatolia and years of ethnic war in Transcaucasia, the Turkish military advance meant one thing and one thing only to Armenians: a signal to leave. The absolute panic of Armenians at the Turkish approach made a strong impression on relief workers in the old Russian stronghold of Kars. Edward Fox of Near East Relief watched as terror gripped the city's Armenians. A falling shell marked the Turkish approach. Within five minutes "the entire population of the city poured into the streets with all the luggage they could carry on their backs, on ox-carts, and on animals of every description, and started out." Some refugees, blocked by corpses, dead animals, and carts, turned back, but thousands fled east to the shrinking territory still under Armenian control.[43]

Defeated, reduced in size, and swollen with refugees, independent Armenia had been crushed. It was powerless to resist Turkey. Armenia turned instead in early December 1920 to the Soviet Union. A last uprising, this time in 1921 against Soviet power, failed. Armenia survived, but only as a republic within the Soviet Union until that empire collapsed seven decades later.

"We Are After Jews"

As Greeks, Turks, Armenians, and Azerbaijanis learned, the decay and collapse of the great empires that once knit together Eastern Europe and Western Asia brought ethnic and religious violence. Similar conflicts erupted in the west of Russia between 1917 and 1920, during the years of revolution and civil war. Here those most at risk were Jews who suffered renewed pogroms. In Ukraine alone between 50,000 and 200,000 Jews—as much as 10 percent of Ukraine's Jews—were killed by the time the pogroms ended. There is no appropriate term in the standard vocabulary of ethnic and religious violence to describe such slaughter. This was not planned genocide or full-scale ethnic cleansing, but the death toll far exceeded that of all earlier pogroms combined.

Ukraine at the end of the Russian Empire was not a country but a region long ruled by Russia's tsars. It comprised nine provinces in the western Russian Empire, where Ukrainians predominated. They spoke a Slavic language related to Russian but used a different Cyrillic alphabet. In the late nineteenth century they made up more than 70 percent of the population of predominantly Ukrainian provinces, but the several other populations in Ukraine included Jews, Russians, Poles, and Germans. Poles and Jews lived chiefly in western Ukraine while Russians were more concentrated in the east. Ukrainian national identity was still in an early stage of development, and it was often difficult to distinguish between Ukrainians and Poles in the west, or between Ukrainians and Russians in the east. But there were sharp differences between the populations living in the countryside and those in the towns and cities. Few Ukrainians lived in towns—most worked on the land; but some four of five Jews lived in towns and cities. The Dnieper River formed a rough dividing line: Jews made up a large proportion of the urban population to the west of the Dnieper while Russians made up a large part toward the river's east.

The collapse of state power during the Russian civil war was the prelude to pogroms in Ukraine. In simplest terms, the Bolsheviks (Communists) or Reds fought foes known collectively as Whites, but the war was far more complex in many regions, including Ukraine.

From 1917 through late 1919, the Bolsheviks' rivals for power in Ukraine included varied Ukrainian nationalists, a German-backed government, a major White or anti-Bolshevik army, and diverse bands of armed men, including myriad bandits and even anarchists. For three years governments rose and fell as armies, armed bands, and criminals swept back and forth across Ukraine. First, after the February 1917 revolution that toppled the last tsar came the rise of a Ukrainian national movement led by the Ukrainian Central Rada or Council. The Rada chose independence in January 1918, retreated from Ukraine's chief city Kiev under Bolshevik attack in early 1918, and then regained Kiev with German help. In April 1918 a German-sponsored coup produced a second government under General Pavlo Skoropadskyi, who took the title Hetman. The Hetman's regime lasted all of seven months until November 13, 1918, when it was displaced by a third new Ukrainian government known as the Directory and led by Simon Petliura, a journalist and nationalist politician.

Petliura, in turn, spent the next year fighting the Bolsheviks and competing for power with other forces, including an anti-Bolshevik Volunteer Army under the command of the former tsarist officer Anton Denikin. The remnants of the Directory left Ukraine in late 1919 just as the Bolsheviks finally defeated the Volunteer Army.[44]

With the partial exception of the Bolsheviks, the varied forces fighting for Ukraine shared an eagerness to attack Jews. Earlier anti-Semitism was one obvious cause of the pogroms, but the Bolshevik Revolution and the Russian civil war magnified the violence. The civil war brought a general insecurity and disorder: there was often no authority to restore order once a pogrom started. But there was also a widespread belief that Jews and Bolsheviks were one and the same. Jews as a group were not Communists, but some Jews did serve as commissars or Communist political officers in Ukraine's cities, where Jews made up a large segment of the urban population. The actual number of Jewish Communists counted for less than a sense that the Bolshevik Revolution brought an undeserved improvement in the status of Jews. This resentment—the claim that a people accused of not doing their share in the Great War now profited from Communist rule—helped trigger the massive pogroms of the civil war years.

Pogroms in Ukraine began around the time of the Bolshevik Revolution. Roughly as many as sixty occurred in November and December 1917. Pogroms resumed in March 1918 before ending temporarily with the Hetman's coup in April, but a proclamation issued by German occupying authorities charged Jews with "agitating" against the government. Soon after the Directory and Petliura took power from the Hetman, Ukraine's Jews suffered an unprecedented wave of violence. These pogroms began in January 1919 west of Kiev and continued during a February retreat by Directory forces. A March counteroffensive brought still more pogroms against Jews accused of having supported Bolsheviks, and the town of Zhitomir was the site for a second pogrom in less than three months. By now Zhitomir's Jews knew they would bear the brunt of blame and punishment for Bolshevik occupation, and many left as Soviet troops retreated. This was a wise decision: almost as soon as they reentered the town on March 22, Directory soldiers and local residents began killing Jews. Over the next five days, 317 Jews died in Zhitomir and nearby villages.[45]

Of all the pogroms carried out by the Directory's forces, none became more infamous than the pogrom at Proskurov, now Khmelnytskyy, a town of 20,000 or more people some 175 miles west and south of Kiev. In February 1919 Directory troops under the command of Otaman Semesenko occupied Proskurov. Semesenko and his men began a pogrom on February 15 after a failed uprising by local Communists and two mutinous Directory regiments. Semesenko called upon his troops to massacre Jews whom he blamed for the uprising. Remarkably, he expressly banned looting: murder was his chief aim. One captain reportedly refused to allow his soldiers to kill civilians and was sent out of town, but the rest followed Semesenko's orders. That afternoon Cossacks burst into the houses of Jews, many of them asleep after eating their Sabbath meal, and according to a report compiled by the Committee of Jewish Delegations, "killed alike old men, women, children and even infants in arms." Jews unfortunate enough to arrive by railway in Proskurov that afternoon were also attacked. Some Ukrainians tried to stop the killing, but one witness recounted that when he asked neighbors for help with the wounded, "one peasant woman only was willing to help, all the others refused." Semesenko finally stopped the massacre at 6:30 after receiving a telegram from his commander, but scattered murders of Jews continued for several days, and Cossacks carried out another pogrom in the nearby town of Felshtin. Estimates of those killed or wounded at Proskurov ranged from 1,500 to 4,000.[46]

The extent to which these pogroms reflected Directory policy is a matter of controversy. Samuel Schwartzbard, a Bessarabian Jew who declared himself to be avenging the pogroms, assassinated Petliura in Paris in May 1926 and then was acquitted at his 1927 trial there. The Directory government could actually claim to have been sympathetic to Ukraine's Jews: the new government maintained a

Ministry of Jewish Affairs which collected some of the evidence about the pogroms of 1919. But the Directory's policies toward Jews did not correspond to its actions. Many of its soldiers looted and killed Jews, and when it issued directives against attacks on Jews, the Directory came close to adopting anti-Semitic logic, in particular the idea that Jews were connected to bolshevism. Thus the first such Directory order in January 1919 called on Jews "to fight energetically those individual Bolshevik-anarchist members of the Jewish nation who behave as enemies of the working people of the Ukraine and of the state."[47]

With the Directory close to defeat, irregular forces and gangs of bandits roamed the countryside in the spring and summer of 1919, attacking and killing Jews. The bands led by a warlord named Grigoriev carried out especially violent pogroms. Jews who survived the Grigoriev attacks consistently told of being attacked as Communists. Soldiers bursting into one house at Cherkassy, southeast of Kiev, shouted, "Communists, Jews, just such little fellows were on the front yesterday." Another survivor told of the murder of her husband and younger son, and of a soldier who cried out "you are a communist; you want a commune" as he killed her older son, a fifteen-year-old boy. The pogromists also declared that they simply wanted to kill Jews. When one victim protested that he and his neighbors were not Communists, soldiers responded, "We aren't after Communists, we are after Jews." They then separated the men from the women, took away the men, and murdered them.[48]

The Grigoriev bands, though especially violent, were by no means unique. The anarchist Nestor Makhno, who had Grigoriev killed in late July 1919, banned pogroms, but his soldiers nonetheless attacked Jews. A British diplomat, seeking to explain the logic of anarchist banditry in Ukraine, recounted the Makhno slogan: "Down with all authority; kill the lords, for they own the land; kill the Jews, for they own the money; kill the generals; kill the Communists, and then the country will deal with the towns, and will say what the towns must give in return for food."[49] Other bands simply stole for the sake of stealing. The Struk bands near Chernobyl, for example, stopped ships on the Dnieper River, robbed Jewish passengers, and sometimes threw them overboard into the river.

By late summer 1919 the Volunteer Army of the White commander Anton Denikin took the lead in pursuing pogroms in Ukraine. First based in the northern Caucasus, the Volunteer Army advanced rapidly through Ukraine in June 1919. Virulent hatred of Jews permeated the army. John Hodgson, an English journalist who visited the Volunteer Army, observed that "The officers and the men of the army laid practically all the blame for their country's troubles on the Hebrew." Denikin and his colleagues removed Jewish officers from the army, banned Jews from buying land on the Black Sea, and forced Jewish municipal officials out of their posts in occupied territory; and by August, Denikin's army was engaging in frequent pogroms. The White Army's pogroms combined methodical looting with extreme violence. It killed hundreds of Jews at Kiev, for example, after taking the city from the Bolsheviks, even though Denikin, perhaps considering his image abroad, told his troops in Kiev in October 1919 to halt attacks on Jews. The Volunteer Army's advance soon stalled, and Denikin's soldiers engaged in still more pogroms when they retreated in November and December 1919. The peak of the violence passed with the defeat of the Volunteer Army, but Jews living in Ukraine and neighboring regions continued to suffer intermittent violent attacks in 1920. The effects of the terror remained visible after the war. Visiting a hospital for children in Kiev, the exiled American anarchist Emma Goldman learned that children who in some cases had seen their own families killed still woke with nightmares.[50]

As the pogroms continued and intensified, increasing numbers of Ukraine's Jews recognized that the Bolsheviks offered comparatively more security than did their rivals for power. This did not mean that Bolsheviks were free from anti-Semitism—Red Army forces occasionally engaged in pogroms—but as a practical matter, gains by Bolshevik forces usually reduced the chances of pogroms in any given area. Jews, in some respects, were in a position similar to Armenians in the Caucasus. Both groups found a far better chance of survival under the Bolsheviks than under alternative rulers during the civil war years.

The violence in Ukraine demonstrated that Jews remained very much at risk after World War I. The tsarist autocracy had been notorious for pogroms, but Jews met with even harsher treatment in the anarchic conditions of the civil war. As subjects of an imperial state, Jews experienced insecurity; absent that state they suffered even more. If the pogroms of the civil war era did not amount to a clear campaign of ethnic cleansing, they nonetheless reached an entirely new scale. Over forty years, pogroms in western and southwestern Russia and Ukraine had escalated from beatings with scattered killings, committed by loosely organized groups, to massacres with hundreds and even thousands of victims that ultimately brought tens of thousands of deaths.

Varied Ukrainian and anti-Bolshevik forces carried out the bulk of pogroms during the Russian civil war, but in the region of Galicia, formerly on the northeastern edge of Austria-Hungary, Poles also carried out pogroms against Jews. Both Polish and Ukrainian nationalists in Galicia wished to build new nation-states from the wreckage of empire, both coveted the ethnically mixed city of Lvov, and both suspected Jews of taking the other side. As Austrian power collapsed at the end of the war, Poles and Ukrainians fought for Lvov. In November 1918 Ukrainians briefly gained control of most of Lvov, but Polish forces soon counterattacked, retaking the city by November 22. In victory, Poles took revenge. They exacted punishment for Jewish neutrality during the struggle for Lvov. Militia, soldiers, convicts released from prison, and local residents attacked Jews for three days.[51]

The New Europe

By the early 1920s the first long wave of modern European ethnic cleansing ended with the final collapse of the empires of Central and Eastern Europe and Western Asia. The wars that followed World War I made several old imperial lands less diverse than ever.

The shift was most pronounced in Greece and Turkey, where war permanently changed the ethnic and religious makeup of many cities and towns. The rupture with the past was especially striking in Smyrna. That city of Greeks, Turks, Armenians, and Levantines had become the Turkish city of Izmir. Visitors found they could not recapture the city's past. The Greek writer and diplomat George Seferis, who was born in Smyrna, returned for a visit to Izmir when he was posted to the Greek embassy in Ankara in 1950. "My God, what am I doing here!" Seferis wrote in his journal as he approached the city. He searched for his childhood house but found nothing. He also went to the coastal village where his family had owned a home. Returning to Izmir a few months later, Seferis looked for the outline or, as he put it, "cloak" of the old city. "Except that the whole center has been burned," he remarked, "the outskirts remain. . . . " Nearly three decades after the destruction of Greek Smyrna there were still traces of the disaster: "You still pass by the burned debris. . . . " Seferis decided that if he were to live in the city again he would be overwhelmed by memories, "a constant, almost nightmarish piling up of images." Visiting Ephesus, he wrote that the catastrophe of Greek Asia Minor was more than a war; it was the end of a way of life, or, as he put it, "the sudden extermination of a fully alive world."[52]

Ethnic cleansing and pogroms left the people of Eastern Europe and Western Asia with widely divergent memories. Turks and Greeks had lived alongside each other for centuries, but they now constructed parallel, alternate histories of the recent past. Where Turks celebrated triumph after years of failure, Greeks felt a powerful sense of loss. Turkish heroes were Greek villains. Turks revered Mustafa Kemal (Atatürk) and General Karabekir as national heroes. Greeks and Armenians decried the very same men for ending Hellenism in Anatolia and further devastating Armenians. Meanwhile Turks and Azerbaijanis recalled the Dashnak heroes of Armenia as killers. War for the borderlands of the western Russian empire created similar divisions. Unlike Greeks and Turks, Jews, Poles, and Ukrainians still lived in the same countries, but they held very different memories of the civil war years. Petliura, for example, remained a hero for Ukrainian nationalists, but Jews remembered him as a murderous villain. These neighbors also attached different memories to places. For both Poles and Ukrainians, the mixed city of Lvov in eastern Poland was a symbol of national struggle during World War I, but Jews remembered the pogrom that struck Lvov in 1918.[53]

The collapse of the Ottoman, Russian, and Austro-Hungarian empires emboldened nationalists throughout Central and Eastern Europe. In place of empires, postwar treaties created a series of new states, all purporting to represent national groups. The states that succeeded Austria-Hungary included Czechoslovakia, Austria, and Hungary, though Hungary, deprived of more than half its prewar territories, was one of the chief losers of the postwar settlement. Yugoslavia, the new state of the south Slavs, included Serbia along with other territories once held by the Ottoman Empire and Austria-Hungary. Poland, restored after more than a century, now included territories regained from three empires: Germany, Austria-Hungary, and Russia. To the far north lay the new Baltic states: Lithuania, Latvia, and Estonia.

The end of the Ottoman Empire also remade the map of Western Asia. The new states carved out of the Ottoman Empire included the Turkish Republic, Syria, Lebanon, Palestine, Mesopotamia, and much of Arabia. Britain received mandates from the newly formed League of Nations to govern Palestine and Mesopotamia (which became known as Iraq) while France received mandates for Lebanon and Syria. Meanwhile a power struggle for Arabia ended with the founding of the kingdom that became known as Saudi Arabia.

The new map of Europe and Western Asia appeared to mark the triumph of United States President Woodrow Wilson's vision of self-determination, but the rise of nation-states also generated a new wave of ethnic cleansing. Both old empires and the nation-states that replaced them were unstable. Each empire comprised many ethnic groups at a time when nationalists demanded that each national group have its own state. But the new nation-states were fictions.[54] If a state or country can be conceived of as a building, the old empires of Europe and Western Asia were dilapidated mansions in which many different ethnic groups lived in different wings or adjoining rooms. A nation-state, by contrast, is home to a single national group. In the new Europe, homeowners resented the fact that they had to share rooms with people outside their national family, and many ethnic groups lacked their own house. Thus the Polish state was not an exclusively Polish house: Poles lived alongside Jews, Ukrainians, and Germans. Similarly the Romanian state was home not to a single national family but to Romanians, Jews, and Hungarians; and Czechoslovakia was home to many Germans along with Czechs and Slovaks.

Some left new states in which they did not feel at home. The collapse of Austria-Hungary and the defeat of the German Empire, for example, left many Germans and Hungarians stranded in new states that were neither German nor Hungarian. Hungarians were not driven en masse out of the states that succeeded Austria-Hungary, but many left afterward. From 1918 to 1920, between 350,000 and 426,000 Hungarians moved from the successor states.[55] Germans migrated in large numbers from Poland and the Baltic states. By 1922 between 500,000 and 800,000 ethnic Germans moved from former German provinces assigned to Poland, and others left Russia for Germany.

European politicians and diplomats identified two chief solutions to ethnic conflict in new nation-states: population exchanges and minority rights treaties. The first approach, which had previously been attempted on a small scale between Bulgaria and Turkey in 1913, pursued peace by removing minorities. The second protected minorities. Even after the Greek-Turkish War there were still significant numbers of Greeks in Turkey and Turks in Greece. Their fate emerged as a key issue at the 1922–1923 Peace Conference at Lausanne, presided over by the British diplomat Lord Curzon. As recently as March 1922, Curzon had expressed doubts about a Turkish Nationalist proposal to exchange the entire Greek and Muslim populations. "The populations in question were too large," he thought, and many would not wish to go.[56] But his objections faded during the conference, and the final Turkish-Greek agreement of 1923 provided for the exchange of populations, making a partial exception only for the Greeks of Istanbul.

The population exchange marked the end of Muslim Thessaloniki. Nearly 20,000 Muslims still lived in Thessaloniki in 1923, but by November the city's Muslims as well as those from the surrounding countryside began to leave—thousands every week. More than 100,000 were gone by year's end, and by December 1924 the population exchange was complete. With Muslims gone, the city soon set to work to erase the most obvious traces of their presence by destroying minarets.[57]

This particular population exchange placed immense strain on both the refugees and on the Turkish and Greek governments. Greece, only just defeated in war, had suddenly to find room for more than a million new citizens. In the late 1920s refugees from Turkey made up more than 1.25 million of a total Greek population of less than 5 million. The move was difficult for all refugees but especially for those whose prior identity did not quite fit the label of either Greek or Turk. Muslims from former European possessions of Turkey had become identified as "Turks" regardless of their relation to the part of the former Ottoman domain that became Turkey. For many Muslims from Greece, only their religion identified them as Turks—they actually spoke Greek dialects. As a diplomat in Turkey after World War II, George Seferis heard Greek, including the Greek of Crete, spoken by Muslims who were now Turkish citizens. The owners of a restaurant in Izmir, he wrote, spoke "wonderful Greek; they feel great nostalgia for their island."[58] He found a pastry shop in central Turkey run by a proprietor who had left Macedonia before the Balkan Wars. Similarly, some of the Greeks from the interior of Turkey who moved to Greece were Orthodox Christians, but they did not speak or read Greek. Now all became simply Greeks or Turks.

A smaller population exchange took place between Greece and Bulgaria. The Convention of Neuilly-sur-Seine of November 27, 1919, provided for the voluntary resettlement of Bulgarians from

Greece and Greeks from Bulgaria. Tens of thousands from each group moved, though not always voluntarily. Greece expelled Bulgarians to encourage further departures, and the Bulgarian Red Cross charged that Greece "was trying to get rid of her Bulgarian population at any cost." From the summer of 1923 to the end of 1924, more than forty thousand refugees left Greece for Bulgaria. Many of the refugees crowded into Sofia, which beginning in 1913 had already received multiple waves of refugees.[59]

Creating treaties to protect minority rights provided a second, less radical solution to ethnic conflict. The Paris Peace Conference established a series of minority-rights treaties to apply to the new states of Eastern and Central Europe. The first such treaty concerned Poland. Jewish delegations to the Paris Peace Conference lobbied for protections for Poland's Jews. Their proposals ranged from guarantees for Jews' rights to calls by Zionists for a special parliament for Polish Jews. To receive international recognition, the new Polish state pledged to protect minority rights of citizenship and religious freedom.[60] Other minority rights treaties and declarations established under the authority of the League of Nations had similar terms. Minorities could raise complaints about breaches of the treaties to the League of Nations, which could then refer these cases to the Permanent Court of International Justice in the Hague. By 1938 hundreds of complaints had been raised.

Alongside the new nation-states there remained one large multiethnic empire in Eastern Europe, the Soviet Union. Here there was no wholesale redrawing of the map to create new nation-states, except on the western fringe of the former Russian empire. The Soviet Union was not in name an empire, but it functioned as a kind of new Communist multinational empire in place of the old imperial state of the tsars. Before World War II, ethnic minorities of the Soviet Union were both better off and worse off than their counterparts who lived elsewhere. Writers who later publicized the abuses of Stalinism portrayed the Soviet Union as a kind of prison for nations. The British poet Robert Conquest, who wrote a series of books detailing Soviet terror, entitled one of his works, *Stalin: Breaker of*

Nations. But the Soviet Union, especially in its early years, also provided ethnic minorities with opportunities for cultural and linguistic development. In the 1920s Soviet authorities created dozens of national republics and administrative territories, hundreds of national regions, and thousands of national townships where ethnic minorities could enjoy their own cultural institutions and often be schooled in their own languages.[61]

"We Believed in Them"

In much of Central and Eastern Europe, the new remedies for resolving ethnic conflict broke down during the period between the World Wars. The interwar states proved to be efficient incubators of nationalist hatred. Ethnic and religious tensions that had previously caused disputes in large empires proved even more explosive within the much smaller confines of Europe's new states. In the past, rulers of the large multiethnic empires had never expected that all imperial subjects would adopt a single national identity. But after World War I, nationalists hoped to achieve much greater homogeneity in the states that succeeded empires. They resented large minority groups in the new states, and they were especially concerned about the potential power of minorities in areas where they actually made up the majority. Thus Germans in Czechoslovakia made up the majority in the Sudetenland, along the northern borders of Bohemia and Moravia; Ukrainians made up the majority in many rural districts of eastern Poland; and Albanians made up the majority in Kosovo.

Almost every one of the new nation-states had its own story of internal ethnic and religious conflict. Polish authorities placed limits on German education, and land reform consistently targeted German landowners, especially in Poland's west. In eastern Poland authorities carried out periodic campaigns of repression against Ukrainian nationalists, and the already tense relationship between Poles and Ukrainians grew worse after the death in 1935 of Poland's authoritarian leader Jozef Pilsudski.[62]

Like Poland, Czechoslovakia had a German problem. From the early days of the new state of Czechoslovakia, Czech nationalists portrayed Germans as interlopers who had seized Czech lands in 1620 during the Thirty Years' War. Relations between Czechs and Germans grew even worse during the economic crisis that hit industrial regions of Bohemia in the 1930s, and disputes over such symbolic issues as place and street names embittered Germans who perceived their culture under attack.[63] In politics, the division found expression in growing support by ethnic Germans in the region of the Sudetenland for a new movement known as the Sudeten German party. By September 1938 the Sudeten Germans supported the removal of the Sudetenland from Czechoslovakia.

Within the Balkans, ethnic conflict was probably most complex in Yugoslavia. The new union of the south Slavs foundered amid deteriorating relations between Croats and Serbs.[64] These two ethnic groups shared a common language but were divided by religion and history. Croats were Catholics who had long lived under Hapsburg rule; while Serbs were Orthodox Christians who had lived under Ottoman rule until the nineteenth century. Instead of creating a common bond, participating in a shared political system increased tension between the south Slavs, and political violence soon followed. The prominent Croatian political leader Stjepan Radić died from injuries he suffered when he was shot in the Parliament in 1928 by a Montenegrin deputy. Yugoslavia's King Alexander tried to end political conflict by creating a royal dictatorship in 1929, but in 1934 a Macedonian revolutionary assassinated Alexander in Marseilles. The real hand behind the killing, rumors suggested, was Ante Pavelic, an exiled Croatian fascist who had found refuge in Mussolini's Italy.

Discrimination against Jews intensified in most countries of Central and Eastern Europe between the wars. Older religious forms of anti-Semitism fused with economic resentment and nationalist anger at Jews who, for the most part, did not see themselves as members of any of Eastern Europe's national groups. Discriminatory measures and, in the case of Hungary, laws that capped Jewish entrance into the professions. Discrimination against Jews and anti-Semitic harassment intensified in Poland after Pilsudski's death in 1935. Nationalist parties in Poland, including the National Democrats (Endeks) promoted boycotts of Jews. The Endeks called for taking away Jews' right to vote, and they also sought to push Jews out of commerce and business, replacing them with Poles.[65]

Despite widespread discrimination and ethnic and religious tension, many people experienced a different reality in their daily lives. Interaction across ethnic and religious boundaries actually improved in some places. In Poland more Jews than ever before obtained a good knowledge of Polish. In Romania, a hothouse of anti-Semitism, Jews played a prominent role in intellectual life into the late 1930s. Survivors of World War II recalled the ordinary quality of their prewar relations with neighbors of a different ethnic and religious identity. One such witness, Waldemar Lotnik, a Pole who fought against Ukrainians during World War II, remembered a childhood spent with Ukrainians. Ukrainians resented the Polish presence in eastern Poland, he recalled, "But it was with Ukrainians that I spent most of my childhood, learnt to read and write, skated on frozen lakes in winter, and discovered shards of Russian and German ammunition, left over from the First World War." Rivka Lozansky-Bogomolnaya, a Jewish Holocaust survivor from Lithuania, had similar memories. She decried the widespread looting and killing of Jews during World War II by Lithuanians, her "good neighbors," but she also recalled a different world before these catastrophes. "Nearby, Lithuanian neighbors in the village were friendly with the Jews. Many of them spoke fluent Yiddish, even using Hebrew words just like the Jews. That was why they were trusted and we believed in them."[66]

Toward Ethnic Cleansing

By the late 1930s persistent conflict gave rise to a new interest in ethnic cleansing. Nationalists looked for methods to perfect or build nation-states. Ethnic cleansing wasn't always their first choice, but enthusiasm grew among many of them for plans to separate major ethnic and religious groups. In Germany, for example, political economists hoped to remove selected populations, namely Jews, in order to strengthen Eastern Europe's agrarian economy. Political movements of the far right—both those in power like the Nazis, and opposition movements—developed the most ambitious schemes for expulsion. In Romania, for example, Colonel Corneliu Zelea Codreanu, leader of a Romanian fascist movement called the Iron Guard, demanded that Jews leave Romania. Speaking with a journalist in January 1938, he exclaimed: "The essential thing is that the Jews must go. Every single Jew must leave this country. You ask where they should go? That is not my business."[67]

Public discussion in several European countries of the possibility of sending Jews to the island of Madagascar indicated the growing interest in mass resettlement. In January 1937 the French colonial minister, Marius Moutet, caused great excitement in Poland when he seemed to tell a newspaper that Jews could go to the French island of Madagascar off the coast of East Africa. Moutet's remarks had probably been misconstrued—French authorities soon explained that they were considering only modest immigration, and not exclusively by Jews. But Poles seized on the possibility of shipping Jews to Madagascar, the same island identified only a few years later by Nazi Germany as a fit destination for European Jews. At the Lodz city council in Poland, the National Democrats exchanged their usual cry, "To Palestine!" for the new demand, "Jews to Madagascar," and a Polish delegation actually traveled to Madagascar in 1937 to investigate resolving Poland's "Jewish question" by resettling Polish Jews there. Like their Polish counterparts, Romanian politicians considered sending their country's Jews to Madagascar. In January 1938, Octavian Goga, prime minister of a short-lived government, mentioned Madagascar as a suitable destination for Romania's Jews.[68]

Some of the most violent plans for resettlement emerged in Yugoslavia, where Serb nationalists saw Albanians as their chief enemy. Serbian intellectuals called for programs to rid Kosovo of its

Albanian population. In 1937 the historian Vaso Cubrilovic, once a terrorist, advised, "The law must be enforced to the letter, to make staying intolerable for the Albanians." This could include harsh punishment, refusal to recognize land deeds, religious persecution, and "secretly burning down Albanian villages and city quarters."[69] Such a policy would have amounted to ethnic cleansing in all but name.

Even nationalists without states voiced their interest in forcing out their ethnic rivals. Radical Ukrainian nationalists, for example, hoped to remake eastern Poland into part of a Ukrainian nation-state. The most extremist Ukrainian nationalist movement, the Organization of Ukrainian Nationalists (OUN), operated in exile. From its founding, the OUN called for a pure Ukraine for Ukrainians. The OUN's First Congress, held in Vienna in 1929, demanded "the complete removal of all occupants from Ukrainian lands, which will follow in the course of a national revolution." The OUN's Second Congress, held in Rome in August 1939, promised a violent campaign to remake Ukraine: "We will not leave one inch of Ukrainian land in the hands of enemies and foreigners. . . . Only blood and iron will decide between us and our enemies."[70]

The fact that Nazis, fascists, and anti-Semites had already contemplated ethnic cleansing before World War II is not particularly surprising. But interest in less violent forms of population transfer was extraordinarily broad. There were signs of an emerging consensus in favor of remaking Europe through forced migration. Liberals, socialists, and even Communists discussed moving ethnic and religious groups as a means to resolve national and ethnic conflict. Czech President Eduard Beneš, the last democratically elected leader in Central and Eastern Europe in the 1930s, considered population transfers as a way to reduce his country's German population. In September 1938, as Hitler pressed for the Sudetenland, Beneš first raised the possibility of a policy of border corrections to diminish the number of Germans in Czechoslovakia. A proposal in a communication to the French government suggested that Czechoslovakia would transfer three border regions with some 800,000 to

900,000 Germans to Germany if Germany would also accept another 1 million Germans.[71]

In the 1930s even the Soviet Union began to move ethnic and religious groups. At first glance the USSR, unlike other states of Eastern Europe, had adopted a multiethnic structure. But in the 1930s, when Stalin unleashed a terror campaign against "class enemies," he often targeted members of ethnic groups suspected of insufficient loyalty to the Soviet Union. Soviet policy took on an ethnic quality with the most tragic consequences in Ukraine during the famine that killed millions in 1932–1933. In other cases, Soviet authorities began to deport suspect peoples, usually from ethnic groups that lived both within and outside the borders of the USSR, including Germans, Poles, Finns, and, in the far east of Siberia, Koreans.[72]

Conflict over the future of Palestine also indicated the growing interest in large-scale population transfer. In Palestine the Zionist project of creating a Jewish nation-state encountered opposition from local Arabs. If Zionists achieved their goal, some Arabs would end up living within a Jewish state, and ongoing Zionist land purchases radicalized Arab opinion. In 1920 and 1921 Arabs attacked Jews in several areas of Palestine. Violence subsided during most of the 1920s, but in 1929 Arab attacks on Jews in towns including Tel Aviv convinced the Zionists of the need to build a strong militia. The years before World War II brought the most intense violence yet: a major Arab rebellion in 1936, the launching of more aggressive Zionist fighting forces, and terror by both Arabs and Jews. The Arab rebellion ended only in 1939.[73]

The basic incompatibility between Arab and Jewish visions of the future persuaded some Zionists to consider population transfer. Zionists advocated other options for creating a state with a sizable Jewish majority, but transfer represented one of several strands of Zionist thinking. By themselves, the leaders of the Yishuv, Palestine's Jewish community, could not resettle Palestine's Arabs, but in 1937 a British investigation into the causes of recent "disturbances" provided a key test of support for population exchange. The Peel Commission, led by Lord William Robert Peel, visited Palestine and submitted a report in July 1937 that recommended partition or division of Palestine between Arabs and Jews. To ensure that the new Jewish state contained a distinct Jewish majority, the Peel Report also called for a population exchange or transfer of 225,000 Arabs and 1,250 Jews. In August, David Ben-Gurion, a labor union leader and prominent Zionist who later became first prime minister of Israel, spoke in Zurich to the Twentieth Zionist Congress about the Peel Commission report and transfer of Arabs. "Transfer . . . is what will make possible a comprehensive settlement program," Ben-Gurion told the Congress. It was fortunate, he added, that "the Arab people have vast, empty areas."[74] The Congress decided to support the Peel recommendations, but transfer soon disappeared from the negotiating table when the British government backed away from the Peel Report.

From Palestine to Poland, proposals for forced migration attracted widespread attention by the late 1930s. The upheaval caused by the Greek-Turkish population exchange had not discredited the forced relocation of entire communities. To the contrary, the idea was more popular than ever. Some political leaders saw population transfer as just one of several options for resolving nationalist conflict, but a number of nationalist extremists in Central and Eastern Europe were eager to purify or create national homelands by forcing out unwanted ethnic groups. Their ambitions did not make violence inevitable, but a war would allow them the opportunity to achieve their goals. For many decades, war in the borderlands once ruled by the empires of Central and Eastern Europe had generated mass flight and ethnic cleansing. Now, with an increased interest in schemes for mass settlement, war was more likely than ever to serve as a catalyst for the violent redrawing of ethnic and religious boundaries. Europe in 1939 was primed for ethnic cleansing.

CHAPTER FIVE

"There Was No One Left for Me"

With a population of 350,000, Lvov was the chief city of the region of Galicia in Eastern Poland in 1939, but it was a city of Jews, Ukrainians, Germans, and Russians as well as Poles. For Poles it was Lvov (Lwów), for Ukrainians Lviv, for Germans Lemberg. Jews who spoke Yiddish knew it as Lemberg or Lemberik, though most of Lvov's Jews also knew Polish, and many also spoke German. More than half the residents of Lvov were Poles, and more than a quarter were Jews. But more than two-thirds of the residents of the towns and countryside surrounding the city were Ukrainians. Such diversity was typical for a region that had developed within a multi-ethnic empire. Lvov had been part of Austria for two centuries when it came under Polish control in 1919.

Recent German expansion and the threat of war created anxiety in Lvov in 1939, but few expected the catastrophes that would soon beset the city. Dr. Samuel Drix, then a young Jewish physician working in Lvov, recalled a March 1939 breakfast conversation in a hospital cafeteria in which another physician had warned of a grim future. "My dear gentlemen," said Drix's colleague, "we are living in historical times, and this is our disaster."[1] At the time Drix found

159

this view too pessimistic. There was reason for concern, "but he seemed to be overly alarmed. Indeed, none of the rest of us took the current situation so tragically."

But multiple disasters did strike Lvov during the next six years, and this diverse city of many nations and religions disappeared during World War II. The Holocaust destroyed the city's Jewish population; the Jews of Lvov were massacred in pogroms and killed in far larger numbers at the death camp of Belzec, not far away. But although the Holocaust killed the greatest number of Lvov's residents, there was more to the old city's demise. The city and surrounding countryside changed forever because World War II on the eastern front developed into a widespread ethnic war.

In many respects the Holocaust was unique, but in other ways it was part of the broader process of ethnic violence that occurred during and after the war. Hitler's most powerful associates, the leaders of the SS, conceived of this "Final Solution" of the "Jewish question" as one key step in a larger program to move and remove entire peoples. They wanted to get rid of Jews, but they also wished to redraw the ethnic and religious map of Europe all the way to the Ural Mountains in central Russia. In its methodology the Holocaust pioneered new models of industrialized mass murder with death camps, but the early phases of the Holocaust were less distinctive. They began in 1941 with both pogroms and the ethnic cleansing of Jews, before the killing shifted in 1942 to such factories of death as Auschwitz and Belzec.

The German assault on Eastern Europe was the first and prime cause of this war of ethnic cleansing in Europe. Invading Poland in September 1939 and the Soviet Union in June 1941, the Nazi leadership pushed current nationalist ideas to their limit. For decades European nationalists had dreamed of uniting the members of their respective nations by building larger nation-states, and they had increasingly viewed nations in racial terms. With war, Nazi Germany's leaders planned to unify Germans, as an "Aryan" race, into a single state. Hitler and his associates dreamed of so vast a German state that they burst the logical boundaries of any nation-state or national

OCCUPIED CENTRAL AND EASTERN EUROPE, JANUARY 1943

300 mi

300 km

Allies

Germany, including annexed territories

German allies

Occupied by Germany

Occupied by Italy

Neutral

SOVIET UNION

Stalingrad

Moscow

Rostov

Kursk

Kharkov

Smolensk

Leningrad

Helsinki

Riga

OSTLAND

Vilna

Minsk

Kaunas

Königsberg

UKRAINE

Kiev

Lvov

Transnistria

Odessa

Black Sea

Bucharest

Istanbul

Ankara

TURKEY

Smyrna

Stockholm

Baltic Sea

Danzig

Bialystok

Warsaw

General Government

Cracow

Lodz

SLOVAKIA

Budapest

HUNGARY

ROMANIA

Belgrade

SERBIA

Sofia

BULGARIA

GREECE

Athens

SWEDEN

Oslo

NORWAY

Copenhagen

DENMARK

Berlin

GERMANY

Prague

SWITZERLAND

Zagreb

CROATIA

Istria

Sarajevo

ALBANIA

Rome

ITALY

North Sea

NETHERLANDS

Amsterdam

Brussels

BELGIUM

Paris

FRANCE

Marseille

Mediterranean Sea

Algiers

Tunis

FRENCH NORTH AFRICA

UNITED KINGDOM

London

IRELAND

Dublin

Atlantic Ocean

Madrid

SPAIN

N

home for Germans. The new Germany would be a racial empire that stretched far into Eastern Europe.

This projected Nazi empire would be vastly different from the old empires whose collapse brought the final phase of the first wave of modern European ethnic cleansing. Germany's leaders and elites never envisioned the Third Reich as a multiethnic empire along the lines of Austria-Hungary: their empire was to be nationalist and racist—German and Aryan. Creating this new empire required massive terror. There was no way to make the east Aryan without changing the nationality or forcibly removing many of the millions of non-Aryans who lived in the space slated for the new German Empire. The result was a series of projects of forced assimilation, deportation, ethnic cleansing, and genocide designed to make people into Germans, remove them, or kill them. Germany's leaders carried out some of these projects; some were only partially realized while others remained on the drawing board.

German aggression launched a war of extermination, and the collapse of German power toward the end of World War II further extended Europe's war of ethnic cleansing. As the tide of war turned, a very different empire—the Soviet Union—deported several ethnic and religious groups living along the borders of the USSR. Stalin punished those ethnic and religious groups that he accused of wartime treason by removing them from their homelands.

It would be all too easy to write the history of ethnic cleansing during World War II as a cautionary tale of the dangers of the kind of immense state power that was amassed by Hitler and Stalin. But that story alone, though true, neglects the other story of pervasive wartime enthusiasm for ethnic cleansing. The conflict also provided a general opportunity for political leaders and movements to realize radical nationalist ambitions. For years, varied governments and political parties had discussed population transfers as a means of removing troublesome minority populations. And for years the most radical nationalist movements had suggested that national homelands could be created and purified through violence. In peacetime many of these grandiose plans had not seemed realistic, but now, in wartime, talk became action. Governments unleashed violent campaigns against ethnic and religious groups they accused of treason. Previously exiled radical nationalists returned home ready to kill or expel those who did not fit into their new national homeland schemes. Ordinary people, men and women, peasants and city dwellers, joined in efforts to force their neighbors out of their homes, to loot their houses, farms, and workshops, and sometimes to kill them. Europe's war of ethnic cleansing during World War II was a war of dictators, a war of radical nationalist movements, and a war of ordinary Europeans.

"All the Way to the Urals"

Mass resettlement and expulsions figured in German plans from the war's start. In the 1920s Hitler had outlined grandiose geopolitical schemes in *Mein Kampf*. A month into the war, he unveiled the idea of a "New Order" that would redistribute nations and ethnic groups throughout Europe's east. Hitler made his goals public in an October 6, 1939, speech to the German Reichstag. "The main task," he declared, "is to create a new ethnographic order; that is, to resettle the nationalities so that in the end, better lines of demarcation exist than is today the case."[2]

Hitler's New Order threatened coercion and violence. His language suggested a program that might resemble the 1923 population exchange of Greeks and Turks. He planned to begin by resettling "splinters" of the German nation, by which term he meant some of the scattered groups of Germans in Eastern Europe. But resettling such "splinters" implied aggression against non-Germans. Finding homes for German settlers would mean forcing out previous residents. In fact Hitler combined German resettlement with attacks on undesired populations. A draft of the same decree from the Führer that instructed SS leader Heinrich Himmler to bring back Germans living abroad also told him "to eliminate the harmful influence of such alien parts of the population, especially in the newly acquired territory, which in their present position constitute a danger to the Reich and the German community."[3]

Planning for the new German east united terror with social science. Himmler, by most accounts the second most powerful figure in Nazi Germany, headed the resettlement project. The head of the SS also held many other posts, including leadership of an agency with the unwieldy name of the Reich Commission for the Strengthening of Germandom, more often termed the RKFDV, and in this capacity he oversaw the resettlement of selected Germans. Reinhard Heydrich, another leader of the Nazi terror apparatus as head of the Security Service (SD), joined in the work of moving people through his supervision of the Central Resettlement Office. Along with SS men, varied experts—economists, political scientists, and historians—took part in planning the new east. They set to work with two goals in mind: making the east German and raising the region's economic productivity. One such expert, Otto Reche, an anthropologist at Leipzig University and a racial scientist, argued in a September 1939 memo that mass expulsions would create space for a future German nation of 150 million people, a total that would more than double Germany's actual population.[4] Reche took the recent Greek-Turkish population exchange as proof that his plans were possible: if Greece could resettle 1.5 million people, surely Germany, a much stronger state, could be far more ambitious.

Plans for building the new German east began with Poland. Soon after Germany and the Soviet Union divided Poland between them on September 28, Germany annexed western Poland. Germany now extended all the way east to the Polish city of Lodz, and indeed practically to Warsaw. But shifting the German border east created a paradox: it allowed more space for Germans, but it also placed 8 million more Poles and 550,000 more Jews inside Germany. This was far too many non-Aryans, so the new masters of the east called for expelling Poles and Jews out of the enlarged Germany and into central Poland, which they had transformed into a German zone of occupation called the General Government.

German plans for a new European ethnic order also involved a belt of land along Germany's new southern borders, including Bohemia, Moravia, and Slovenia. First came annexation: after the Munich Agreement with Britain, France, and Italy, Germany took over the Sudetenland, on the northern edge of Bohemia and Moravia, in October 1938. It occupied most of the rest of Bohemia and Moravia in March 1939, and northern Slovenia in the spring of 1941. The next task, making these regions German, was far more difficult because Bohemia, Moravia, and Slovenia had only German minorities. One possible solution was expulsion: in 1940 Hitler considered expelling Czechs to the east, but they were too valuable as labor to deport en masse at that time, and there was no place to send them. Instead Hitler decided on a long-term program of Germanization—he would gradually make some Czechs into Germans and remove the rest. Heydrich, who added the post of head of the Protectorate of Bohemia and Moravia to his many titles, also held back from full-scale expulsion of Czechs. In 1942, the same year he would be assassinated by Czech partisans, Heydrich pointed to the risk of inciting "revolution." He held out the goal of a "later peaceful evacuation" of that part of the population that could not be made into Germans.[5]

To remake northern Slovenia, German authorities aimed to drive out a large part of the region's Slovenian population. Initial plans called for expelling 260,000 or more, roughly a third of the region's Slovenian population, and Heydrich immediately set up a staff to oversee resettlement. Once again there was no obvious destination for unwanted peoples. The notion of sending hundreds of thousands of Slovenians to Serbia, for example, struck the German military command in occupied Serbia as an extreme burden. Thousands of Slovenians, especially members of the intelligentsia, were deported to Croatia, Serbia, and even to Germany, but as of January 1943 the SS conceded only "moderate success" at Germanization.[6]

Conquests and annexations from 1938 through 1941 propelled planning for a new German east, but the final vision for a nationalist racist empire emerged only with the German invasion of the Soviet Union in 1941. Expelling Poles and Jews from annexed western Poland, driving Slovenians out of Slovenia, making Czechs into Germans—none of these plans, no matter how inhumane, matched the ambition and cruelty of German plans for redrawing the ethnic

map of the Soviet Union. The new program for the east, termed
General Plan East, outlined a vast German empire that would
stretch thousands of miles from the German frontier past Poland,
past Moscow, all the way to the Ural Mountains in central Russia.
But this vast region was filled with tens of millions of non-Germans.
Even with the mass murder of Jews, every German advance added
Slavs and other ethnic groups to the population under German rule.
Making the east truly German would therefore require ethnic
cleansing on a scale exceeding any other example in world history.

The new vision of the east foresaw a Poland virtually without
Poles. A first version of the General Plan produced in late 1941 or
early 1942 spoke of driving out 16 to 20 million Poles. The sheer dimensions of such a project raised doubts about its feasibility. Dr. Erhard Wetzel, a German racial expert who worked for the Ministry of
the East, the civilian occupation authority for much of the Soviet
Union, estimated that transporting 700,000 to 800,000 people per
year might require devoting 100 to 120 trains solely to that purpose
for some 30 years. The magnitude of the task forced the Germans to
look for another solution. Wetzel specifically added that "one can
not solve the Polish question in the sense, that one liquidates the
Poles, like the Jews. . . ." Wetzel did not object to the mass murder of
Jews, but he feared Germans would pay a price for extermination of
Poles. Such a "solution of the Polish question would burden the German nation up until the remote future," and would create fear of a
similar fate among neighboring peoples.[7]

The first version of General Plan East projected a campaign to
reduce the entire Slavic population of Germany's new east. Millions
of Ukrainians and White Russians would join Poles in the east, but
German racial experts struggled with the problem of what to do with
tens of millions of Russians in the western Soviet Union. Wolfgang
Abel, an anthropologist who headed the race science department at
the prestigious Kaiser Wilhelm Institute for Anthropology, Human
Heredity, and Eugenics, studied that very question for the German
army command in Russia. According to Wetzel, Abel saw two options
for dealing with Russia: extermination, or else Germanization of
those Russians with "northern" qualities. Liquidating the Russians,

Wetzel commented, was "barely possible," so the only practical option was to divide up the Russian population. This corresponded closely to Himmler's hopes for the east. By breaking down Russia's population into an "ethnic mush," it would then be possible to filter out those with the necessary racial qualities to become Germans.[8]

A second version of General Plan East completed in June 1942 by Konrad Meyer, head of the planning department for Himmler's office for the Strengthening of Germandom, was more modest, if only by the standards of the first version. It called for creating German settlements in the regions that included the Gulf of Finland and the Crimea, and connecting these settlements to Germany by a chain of thirty-six strategic outposts. This was not enough for Himmler. He approved of the general concept but demanded more Germanization. In September 1942 he spoke of pushing German strategic settlements to the Volga and added, "I hope all the way to the Urals."[9] Even as the German Sixth Army suffered shattering defeat at the Battle of Stalingrad in the winter months of 1942–1943, SS authorities continued to outline goals for uprooting millions of people.

The General Plan East would, if completed, have formed the most extreme example of ethnic cleansing in world history. The entire enterprise reflected a deep-seated commitment to making the east German, whatever the human cost. This goal united key figures from the Nazi leadership, the German military, and academia. Defeat blocked many of these plans, but how far could Germany have gone in realizing General Plan East if the war had ended differently? The General Plan enjoyed support at the highest levels of the same Nazi terror apparatus that carried out almost unimaginable crimes against humanity. Millions of civilians died on the eastern front, and it is likely that many millions more would have died or lost their homes if Germany had won the war.

Moving Poles and Jews

The work of creating a new German east began with Poland. From 1939 through 1941 German authorities pushed Poles and Jews east from annexed western Poland into the General Government. Local deportations began as early as October and November 1939, and the SS then conducted a series of three centrally planned deportations, termed short-term plans. In December 1939 the first short-term plan pushed close to 88,000 people east. The second short-term plan began in April 1940; the third in February 1911.[10]

Germans engaged in the expulsions reported working hard in Germany's new east. Police and reserve police battalions helped with the task of driving Poles out of their homes. In 1940 one such unit, Reserve Police Battalion 101, carried out expulsions "night and day without pause." The battalion made good headway. "On the average some 350 Polish peasant families were evacuated daily," though that figure reached as high as 900 in a day. So busy were the German reservists driving Poles out of their homes that the battalion's "men had the opportunity to sleep only while traveling at night by truck."[11]

Poles lost nearly everything. At Gdynia, a port northwest of Danzig where deportations began on October 16, 1939, Poles were given as few as ten to twenty minutes, at most a few hours, to leave their homes, and they could not take much—hand luggage and ten to twenty reichsmark. Under the logic of German occupation, Poles had no real need to put their affairs in order, for they were stripped of their valuables, tools, and almost all assets before being moved to the east. One woman was also told that "the flat must be swept, the plates and dishes washed and the keys left in the cupboards, so that the Germans who were to live in my house should have no trouble." Poles tried to prepare as best they could when expulsions took place over a longer period. At the city of Poznan, one Polish man who was eventually expelled explained that "it became the habit" for Poles who expected their deportation ". . . to spend the nights ready dressed, waiting for the arrival of the police."[12] Sure enough, the police arrived one night in February and ordered everyone out in minutes.

Crowded onto buses or trains, deprived of most of their money and valuables, Poles faced a grim future. Early expulsions were so poorly planned that some found their own transportation east. In the winter of 1939–1940 they endured days of freezing temperatures and lack of food in railway cars, and many died in transit. Others arrived without any means of support at railway stations in Polish cities. Deported Poles and Jews crowded into Warsaw, a city already heavily damaged by war. The later stages of evacuation saw many Poles sent to labor camps or in some cases to Germany to carry out agricultural labor.[13]

If it was easy to imagine, expelling Poles was hard to accomplish, not for tens of thousands or even a few hundred thousand, but for millions. Indeed, as the experience of the Jews ultimately revealed, it was often easier to kill people than to relocate them. War provided both the chief opportunity for and the chief obstacle to the full-scale ethnic cleansing of Poles. Clearing people out of their homes to make the east German created a series of headaches for the German military and occupation authorities. Military authorities worried that the rage that deportations provoked created more work for occupying forces. As one German unit put it, the resettlement caused "constant worry."[14] There were also economic concerns. No one wanted to pay to house or feed refugees, and where Poles provided vital labor, Nazi authorities did not wish to see their departure. Thus a deputy for Fritz Arlt, the official in charge of Strengthening Germandom in Upper Silesia, referred to the "task" of making the region German by evacuating Poles and Jews, but pointed out in 1941 that "we must have regard to the needs of the armaments industry that is such an important part of our regional economy."[15] For all these reasons, the project of expelling Poles en masse into the General Government came to a halt in early 1941.

Unable to push millions of Poles to the east, German authorities instead ejected Poles from their houses and placed them in camps near factories or sent them to squeeze together in nearby homes. The most violent ejection of Poles carried out in the war's later stages occurred in the region surrounding the town of Zamosc, southeast of Lublin. German authorities forced more than 100,000 Poles out of almost 300 villages between November 1942 and August 1943. Hans

Frank, head of the General Government, complained bitterly about
the problems this created for his occupation regime. In May 1943 he
told Hitler that the panic caused by forcing Poles out of their homes
and dividing up families in camps encouraged "bandit groups" that
made newly settled Germans insecure. Reprisals carried out by the
Order Police against bandits only made the situation worse. "Mass
shootings . . . especially of women and children," encouraged Polish
resistance and provided fodder for Communist propaganda.[16]

Himmler and Heydrich and their allies in the campaign to clear
western Poland of Poles only partly achieved their ethnic cleansing
goals. They uprooted hundreds of thousands, but not millions, of
Poles. Through the end of 1940 as many as 325,000 Poles had been
deported, and between 1941 and 1944 several hundred thousand
more were forced out of their homes and dwellings. Altogether between 750,000 and 1 million or more Poles were deported or ejected
from their houses during the war—some 10 percent of Poles in in-
corporated territories—a total that does not include the forced evacuation of the civilian population of Warsaw late in the war.[17]

To Poland's east, Germans also missed their targets for expelling
Slavs. Germany forced some one million people from Ukraine to
leave for work as forced laborers in Germany, and Himmler carried
out small-scale expulsions and resettlement in Ukraine in late 1942
in villages near the German field headquarters at Hegewald. But he
still failed to meet the ambitious goals outlined in the General
Plan.[18] Even in the Crimea, where Hitler ordered the deportation of
Russians and colonization by Germans, evacuation and resettlement
had to be placed on hold. Occupying authorities and the German
army could ill afford the economic disruption that such population
transfers would create.

As in the case of German efforts to expel Poles, plans to move
Jews east also faced opposition from within the Nazi hierarchy and
from the German military. German leaders quarreled over where to
push the Jews. Himmler and Heydrich wanted to expel Jews east,
but German administrators and the German military authorities
had no interest in accepting more Jews into the General Govern-

ment. Hans Frank objected to plans to deport Jews en masse into the General Government, not because of any humanitarian scruples but because he repeatedly asserted that his administration lacked space and resources to accept large numbers of Jews. There were already 1.5 million Jews in the General Government, and that was more than enough. In an October 1940 meeting he spoke against plans to transfer Jews from Vienna and East Prussia to the General Government on the grounds that "it is unheard of that people are sending such masses of Poles and Jews into the General Government when no facilities are available to accommodate them."[19]

Simultaneous plans to deport Jews and Poles and resettle ethnic Germans also created disputes over priorities.[20] Given limited resources and transportation, which groups should be moved first? There was no simple answer. If reaching racial purity was the key task, then deporting Jews was goal number one, for Jews fell lower than Poles in the Nazi hierarchy of inferior people. But plans for resettling ethnic Germans provided more reason to deport Poles than Jews. Poland's Jews were not farmers, and driving Polish peasants out of their homes was vital if the RKFDV was to find farms for ethnic Germans.

Instead of pushing Jews east en masse, German authorities concentrated and isolated them. Within Germany that meant forcing Jews out of their homes into special houses for Jews, and cutting them off from the rest of the civilian population. In Poland, German occupying forces pushed Jews into ghettos in several Polish cities including Warsaw. To create a ghetto, occupying authorities selected a district, usually old and densely populated. They next forced out any resident Poles and replaced them with Jews driven out of adjacent neighborhoods or forced from their homes in surrounding towns and villages. Ghetto life was often deadly: severe overcrowding and lack of food made residents susceptible to epidemics. The monthly death rate in the Lodz ghetto, for example, increased from 0.09 percent in 1938 to 0.63 percent in 1941 and 1.49 percent in the first half of 1942.[21]

"Home to the Reich"

Driving out Jews, Poles, and various Slavic peoples would make the east more German, but only if Himmler, Heydrich, and their colleagues could also find Germans to replace at least some of those deported and murdered. In the long run, the SS planned to examine people living in the occupied territories for racial qualities that could make them suitable candidates for a program of Germanization; but for a more immediate supply of Germans, the architects of the New Order turned to ethnic Germans living outside of Germany. They began, not with the larger populations of ethnic Germans of the interwar era from the Sudetenland, Hungary, Yugoslavia, or Transylvania, but with smaller communities of ethnic Germans living on the borders of the expanding Soviet Union or under fascist rule in Italy. Both Italy and the USSR were ready to negotiate population transfers with Nazi Germany. Mussolini had become Hitler's closest ally, and the Soviet Union, despite being an object of Nazi contempt, had concluded a nonaggression pact with Germany in 1939.

Nazi Germany had long sought to build ties with Germans living abroad, but the announcement of plans for resettlement nonetheless came as a shock. Some ethnic Germans were eager to move to Germany, but others preferred to stay in their own homes. Enthusiasm faded, for example, among the 200,000 Germans who lived within Italy's borders in the South Tyrol. Italy had gained this mountainous region in the southern Alps from the breakup of Austria-Hungary at the end of World War I. Under an agreement reached with Italy in October 1939, ethnic Germans who chose to leave South Tyrol had until the end of 1942 to actually depart, but many thought better of it. By late 1942, nearly 83,000 Germans had left, but that still amounted to less than half the number who had originally chosen resettlement.[22] South Tyrol, then, was never emptied of Germans, and to this day retains a sizable German-speaking population.

Most of the ethnic Germans brought "home to the Reich" came from territories on the edge of the expanding Soviet Empire. In late September 1939 Germany and the Soviet Union agreed to resettle

Germans living in the Soviet sphere, including eastern Poland, and in September 1940 Soviet and German authorities made similar arrangements for ethnic Germans living in North Bukovina and Bessarabia, border regions taken from Romania by the Soviet Union at the end of June 1940. Perhaps tipped off by German diplomats, some German landowners actually fled Bessarabia before Soviet occupation. On the morning of June 26, 1940, just days before Soviet forces entered Bessarabia, Countess Waldeck, an American citizen born in Berlin, observed the fleeing Germans at Bucharest's Athene Palace Hotel, perhaps the city's chief center of intrigue. There they brought "paintings, silver chandeliers, rosewood café tables, Aubusson carpets"—in short, whatever luxuries they could carry on their way out of Bessarabia and Bukovina.[23]

In comparison to the Germans of the South Tyrol, those who had only recently come under Soviet rule proved eager to resettle in Germany's new lands. Neither severe limits on sales of household goods nor artificially low compensation for the homes and farms they left behind dissuaded Germans from leaving. A former member of the resettlement command for Bessarabia noted that "at no place and time" did Bessarabia's Germans debate whether they should resettle, though they made their decision to leave with "heavy hearts." Fear of life under Stalin after years of Soviet collectivization and terror outweighed their attachment to homes, possessions, and communities. Gottlob Ensslen, a German farmer whose great-grandfather had left the Black Forest in 1806, explained that the Romanian occupation of Bessarabia in February 1918 had "rescued us from Bolshevism." In the fall of 1940 "we escaped so to say with our bare lives." Such dread of Soviet rule was so great that many non-Germans also wished to leave. Indeed, so many wanted to leave Bessarabia that the more than 93,000 people who chose resettlement actually exceeded slightly the region's total population of Germans.[24]

Similar logic governed the choices of Germans from the Baltic and from Volhynia in northwest modern-day Ukraine. Many of the Germans living in Volhynia on the eve of the war had already been evacuated once before during World War I when Russia relocated suspect minorities away from the front. Walter Quiring of the German Foreign Institute, for example, told of meeting a German who had fought for Russia in both the Russo-Japanese War and World War I. Despite his active military service, "his family was sent to Siberia in 1915."[25] He had worked for several years in America after the war to save money to rebuild his farm. Now his future apparently lay in a move west to the newly expanded German Reich.

Resettled Germans followed a long path to their new homes. The presumptive Aryans were first examined to see if indeed they were Aryans: some were found so wanting in Aryan qualities that they were sent back. Some waited in a camp at the city of Gleiwitz in Silesia before their return. Through the beginning of 1942 nearly six thousand of the new settlers had been returned to Romania.[26] Those who made it through racial screening often waited in transit centers and resettlement camps, sometimes for years.

Despite these obstacles and delays, many ethnic Germans gained the ultimate prize of resettlement: the home of a Polish or Jewish family. In the countryside, German settlers typically moved into Polish farms. In an instant they gained homes and land that they had never before seen. Walter Quiring watched as the German settlers arrived at a Polish village, each "family father," carrying the number of the house his family was soon to receive. One ethnic German peasant received two Polish farms from an SS man. The new owners wandered "slowly from room to room."[27] The new settlers also obtained furniture and housewares confiscated from deported Jews and Poles and distributed by a trust company set up by Himmler's agency for Strengthening Germandom.

New homes, furniture, and housewares did not guarantee an easy life for resettled Germans. Their new neighbors were often hostile, and it was not only Poles who viewed the settlers as unwelcome intruders. Local Germans who already lived in Poland resented the special privileges accorded to German newcomers. For their part, German peasants placed on new fields struggled to adapt to a region with different farming conditions. Agricultural methods, Ensslen observed, were very different from those in Bessarabia and "caused me much trouble and headache."[28] Finally, as the war turned against Germany, Polish partisans attacked the resettled Germans.

From Ethnic Cleansing to Genocide

In 1941 Nazi Germany's war of ethnic cleansing gave rise to the single most infamous murder campaign of World War II, the Holocaust. This infamy was part of a broader Nazi effort to remake Eastern Europe, but it proceeded from unusual motives. Since the nineteenth century, people and states that engaged in ethnic cleansing typically saw their victims as rivals for power in disputed border regions. But Germany never faced any political or military threat from the small Jewish minority of less than 1 percent of its population. More so than in other cases of ethnic cleansing, racism, rather than national or ethnic conflict, was the chief motive for Nazi persecution of the Jews. Hitler and the men in charge of the German terror apparatus took it as an article of faith that Jews, by their very presence, tainted and threatened the German nation. In their anti-Semitism, biological racism grounded in pseudo-science played a much more powerful role than nationalism, though the Nazis also claimed that Jews and Communists had betrayed the German nation at the end of World War I.[29]

In its motives, the Nazi campaign against Jews was distinct from earlier ethnic cleansing but it was similar in its goals: Germany's leaders wanted to drive out Germany's Jews. Severe discrimination, including loss of citizenship, persuaded many Jews to leave Germany. By 1938 the country's Jewish population had dropped to 350,000 from 515,000 when Hitler took power in 1933. But German expansion reversed that trend, adding 190,000 Jews with the *Anschluss* (annexation) of Austria in 1938 and still more with the conquest and seizure of western Poland. With a growing Jewish population, Germany's "Jewish problem" was worse by 1939 than it had been in 1933, the year the Nazis took power. Himmler and Heydrich tried to push Jews east into the General Government, but they soon looked for another dumping ground. For a time in 1940, Himmler and German racial experts believed they had found just such a location in the island of Madagascar, the French colony off the coast of southeast Africa. This was a major factor in Himmler's order of July 8, 1940, for "a halt to the evacuation of Jews to the Generalgouvernment."[30]

In hindsight the Nazi plan to ship Jews to Madagascar may seem far-fetched, but was it any more implausible than the program actually implemented from 1941 to 1945: the mass murder of Europe's Jews? Leigh White, who was a young blond "obviously . . . Aryan" American journalist hired by the Overseas News Agency (formerly the Jewish Telegraphic Agency) because he could work in places that a Jewish reporter could not, suggested that Madagascar was not a good destination for Jews because of the likely opposition of the island's four million inhabitants. Plans for making Madagascar Jewish might require *their* extermination, and White thought that mass killing on that scale was impossible even for Germany's leaders. He added, "four million people are too many to exterminate, even for the Nazis, who have thus far failed in their endeavors to exterminate that many Jews in Europe."[31] But Germany's leaders were indeed willing to kill on this scale, and they also discussed the Madagascar plan as a serious option for getting rid of Jews until Germany's defeat in the Battle of Britain in the fall of 1940. At that point continued British naval power blocked any far-ranging German shipping schemes.

With the invasion of the Soviet Union in June 1941, clearing away Jews meant mass murder, not expulsion, although Hitler may already have intended to wipe out Europe's Jews. On January 30, 1939, he had declared in a speech to the German Reichstag: "I want today to be a prophet again: if international finance Jewry inside and outside Europe should succeed in plunging the nations once more into a world war, the result will be . . . the annihilation of the Jewish race in Europe!" But it remains uncertain whether Hitler's "prophecy," as this passage in the speech became known, revealed Hitler's blueprint for the future or a vaguer expression of anti-Semitic rage. Genocide actually began during Operation Barbarossa, the German invasion of the Soviet Union. Much more than just an ambitious military campaign, Operation Barbarossa was also a vast war of extermination that emboldened Nazi leaders and pitted the German army against opponents described as racial enemies of Aryans and as less than human.

There was, of course, no single cause of the Holocaust, but the failure of plans for the forced evacuation of Jews made genocide the most effective option for getting rid of them. Here the connection between expulsion and genocide was more complex than in the case of the Armenian genocide. In that earlier situation, extraordinarily violent ethnic cleansing was carried out with little or no regard for the survival of the deported, and it led to genocide. In the Holocaust, the shift to mass murder was more a product of the frustration of expulsions than of intensified ethnic cleansing. Jews could not be sent to Madagascar. Nazi authorities did not want them living in Germany. German military and political authorities in the General Government did not wish to accept shipments of Jews. Proposals to send Jews still farther east or north, to the deepest reaches of Siberia or to the Arctic Ocean, were tantamount to genocide, and these schemes could be realized only when and if Germany won the war. In the absence of any other plan for emptying Europe of Jews, the Holocaust was a final solution.[32] There was no need to find a destination for Jews if they were simply murdered.

"Death to Muscovite-Jewish Communists"

Often seen as a rupture in human history, the Holocaust, at least at its start, shared much with previous attacks on unwanted ethnic or religious minorities. In 1941 the Holocaust built on the legacy of pogroms on the eastern front at the end of World War I. In western Russia and Poland the most violent pogroms to date had taken place during the Russian civil war of 1918–1920, and with a new war there was another outburst of pogroms in much of the same territory.

The easiest explanation for the new violence was that German forces encouraged pogroms. In retrospect this seems like the most comforting hypothesis: it assigns responsibility for violence to those we already know to be the aggressors. We know Germans unleashed the Holocaust, so we assume they also started pogroms, and there is some evidence for this view. In June 1941, Reinhard Heydrich told commanders of the Einsatzgruppen, German mobile terror units, not to block "self cleansing." But more than German planning catalyzed pogroms. Many began before the arrival of German forces, and at the very least any German efforts to encourage pogroms found a ready and receptive audience: considerable numbers of local residents attacked Jews in such regions as Ukraine, northeastern Poland, Lithuania, and Bessarabia.[33]

Few topics in the history of the Holocaust generate more controversy and even rage than the mention of popular participation by Eastern Europeans in the Holocaust. A typical defense of Poles, Ukrainians, Lithuanians, or any other Eastern European ethnic group asserts that the group in question was itself persecuted, and adds that the very same ethnic group included many individuals who rescued Jews.[34] Such statements provide a broader understanding of World War II and the Holocaust but have no bearing on the extent to which local residents joined in attacking Jews or approved of such assaults. The German campaign in the Soviet Union started a war of extermination, and those who rescued Jews on the eastern front faced particular danger. But if the acts of rescuers truly represented the views of an entire population, it could be said that no ethnic or religious group ever played a significant role in any wave of pogroms or campaign of ethnic cleansing or genocide.

Even before the war, Jews experienced growing anti-Semitism across Eastern Europe, but war and occupation opened up a chasm of mistrust between Jews and the people who lived alongside them. On one level this was surprising because Jews, Poles, Lithuanians, and Ukrainians shared many experiences in the war's early years. They lived through the same deprivations, the same advances of German and Soviet troops, and the same occupation regimes, but these common experiences did not create greater solidarity. The problem, especially within Soviet-occupied regions, lay in divergent perceptions of these events. Jews and their neighbors interpreted war and occupation in radically different ways. In the popular perception, the same events that victimized everyone else gave privileges to Jews.

The first phase in the breakdown of relations between Jews and many of their neighbors came with the start of war. In Eastern Poland, Jews and Poles split in their immediate reaction to Soviet occupation. At Lvov, the chief city in Poland's east, Jews waited with dread as German troops advanced in September 1939. Jews from western Poland poured into the city. Adolf Folkmann, a Jew from Lvov who survived the Holocaust by later fleeing to Sweden, recalled, "Dozens of relatives and friends arrived at my apartment." Some wanted to keep moving east, while others hoped to reach Hungary or Romania. Eventually nearly 30 people, including both Jews and Poles, crowded into Folkmann's house. The surge of refugees raised Lvov's Jewish population from 100,000 to 160,000. News from the front was unrelentingly bad, but the Germans did not arrive. Instead Soviet troops (still Germany's allies) entered Lvov on September 20. For Jews, the Soviet advance offered protection against Germany, and many Ukrainians also initially greeted Soviet forces. Poles, however, saw the Soviet arrival as a final blow against their state. As a poster issued by a Polish commander put it, "The Bolshevists have treacherously stabbed us in the back."[35]

An even sharper division arose between Jews and Lithuanians over the comparative threat posed by Nazi Germany and the Soviet Union. Lithuanians, Jews recalled, preferred Germany to the Soviet Union, whereas Lithuania's Jews feared Nazi Germany as the direst threat to their security. The Soviet Union acquired power over Lithuania in stages: in October 1939 the Soviets gained the right to occupy military positions in Lithuania, and in June 1940 Soviet forces invaded. At first the approach of tanks in June 1940 caused panic among Jews until the tanks came close enough to reveal that they each bore a red star. At that point, one Jewish survivor of the Holocaust, Harry Gordon—then almost fifteen years old—recalled, "our mood changed. Instead of panic, we felt an unnatural joy."[36]

This was a logical reaction because Jewish refugees from Poland had already given Lithuania's Jews a good idea of what they could expect from a German occupation. Young Communists, Jews among them, were even more excited by the Soviet advance.

The second phase in the poisoning of relations between Jews and many non-Jews came with Soviet rule over eastern Poland and the Baltic states. Perceived Jewish gains—real or imagined—from Soviet rule fed popular resentment.[37] We must be careful here not to blame the victims, to charge Jews with culpability for pogroms that followed the collapse of Soviet power in 1941. But we need to understand the depth of animosity against Jews to recognize a key cause for popular violence perpetrated against them in June 1941, even though this perception of Soviet favoritism toward Jews bore only a loose connection to reality. Some Jews joined civilian militias established under Soviet occupation. At Lvov, for example, Adolf Folkmann noted that members of the new militia "were chiefly workers and young Jews." But Jews were not a major force in Soviet terror in eastern Poland. The NKVD or Soviet secret police was not a Jewish institution. Finally, the Soviet occupation regime persecuted Jews along with other populations, and Jews were among those deported to Siberia. Jacob Gerstenfeld, a Jew who had lived in Lvov until 1932 and then returned in 1939, recalled hiding during Soviet deportations in May 1940. For twelve days Gerstenfeld and his wife hid "in an attic above a pigsty."[38] There was a dreadful irony: had they been found, Gerstenfeld's wife, who was sent to the Belzec death camp, might have survived the war. While deportation east was a terrible experience, it sometimes saved lives only because Jews taken to the Soviet east were not in Lvov when the Germans invaded in June 1941.

The third phase in the destruction of relations between Jews and their neighbors came in June 1941 when Germany invaded the Soviet Union. Just before Soviet forces pulled out of eastern Poland, the NKVD killed thousands of prisoners in cities including Lvov. Estimates of those killed ranged as high as twenty thousand to thirty thousand. For Eastern European peoples convinced that Jews had made undeserved gains under Soviet rule, rumors of Jewish complicity in the NKVD killings provided the final proof of Jewish treason. Once again, perception counted for more than reality. There was little evidence that Jews were responsible for the killings—in fact Jews were counted among the dead, though Poles made up the largest number of victims.[39]

Between 1939 and 1941 the rapid sequence of invasion, occupation, and renewed invasion ruptured bonds between Jews and many non-Jews. Before the war, this relationship was strained but complex. Poles, Ukrainians, Lithuanians, and members of other ethnic groups held multiple images of Jews. Anti-Semitism was powerful, but peoples of eastern Poland and the Baltic states knew Jews, and in some communities they had close contacts with them. On an individual level, the same Jew who was part of a mistrusted minority was also an everyday acquaintance. As Samuel Drix later explained, "Personal relations between Ukrainians and Jews were often friendly. . . ." But "hatred toward Jews as a people was great."[40] War upset this uneasy balance. The Soviet advance into eastern Poland and the Baltic radicalized and strengthened a kind of nationalist story line in which Jews always figured as enemies and traitors. An event such as the NKVD killings in June 1941 had an especially powerful effect because it fit so easily into this narrative of Jewish treason. Claims of Jewish responsibility for the crimes seemed to confirm all the most negative images of Jews. For many non-Jews—and we cannot quantify the numbers—this image of Jews as traitors who victimized other nations proved more powerful than memories of ordinary contacts with Jews in everyday situations before the war.

The wave of pogroms in Lvov and adjacent regions of Galicia began in June and continued into July 1941. At Lvov local militias, encouraged and assisted by the public, carried out one of the largest pogroms. As David Kahane, one survivor who later became chief rabbi of the Israeli air force, recalled, "The Polish and Ukrainian populace rendered whole-hearted assistance to the Germans." Near Jacob Gerstenfeld's dwelling a mob tormented Jews at a bomb crater. The crowd beat "old people, children and women" and forced them to dig up and

move paving stones. Gerstenfeld saw the murder of four or five people. His uncle was seized from his house, beaten, and left to die in the
street. The dead numbered in the thousands. Similar killings occurred
in other towns outside Lvov. Seeking refuge in the town of Stryj, south
of Lvov, Samuel Drix learned from a fellow physician about the
killing wave nearby. "In some localities, where the Ukrainians had no
weapons, Jews were clubbed to death." In Stryj itself, Ukrainian militia members sang "Death, death, death to the Lachs [an insult for
Poles], death to Muscovite-Jewish Communists."[41]

A final pulse of pogroms underscored the importance of national vengeance as a motive for attacking Jews. In late July, after
several weeks of German occupation, Ukrainians carried out yet another pogrom. The killings of some two thousand Jews at Lvov between July 25 and 27 were described as "Petliura days." Talk of
Petliura made sense only for Ukrainians who saw the pogrom as part
of a cycle of violence and revenge that dated back to the 1920s.
Simon Petliura had led Ukraine's Directory government, which had
sought and failed to create an independent Ukraine during the Russian civil war. Ukrainians had denied that Petliura, assassinated in
1926 by a Bessarabian Jew in an act of vengeance for pogroms of the
civil war years, bore responsibility for killing Jews, but some
nonetheless chose to honor him in 1941 by killing Jews. "This is for
our hetman [leader] Simon Petlyura," Ukrainian police announced
as they attacked Jews in Lvov in late July 1941.[42]

Ukrainians turned against Jews in much the same way in Volhynia, the setting for more than twenty pogroms in the summer of
1941. Local residents robbed, beat, and killed Jews. In some cases a
pogrom preceded German arrival. At Ludvipol, on the Sluch River,
Germans watched as Ukrainians from the surrounding countryside
attacked Jews. Here, according to one witness, "Peasants stormed
into each Jewish house they took a liking to, dealt atrocious blows
and looted everything they could lay their hands on."[43]

This record of Jews beaten and murdered by Ukrainian militia
and bystanders is difficult to reconcile with the complaint on August
9, 1941, by one of the mobile Einsatzgruppen that efforts to inspire

pogroms as part of Operation Barbarossa "unfortunately did not bring the desired result." Most likely the German complaint revealed the gap between even vicious pogroms and a truly genocidal mentality. As many as ten thousand Jews died in Galicia alone during the July pogroms—a vast number, but small in comparison to what would follow.[44] There were also regional variations: Ukrainians in eastern Ukraine were less likely to take part in pogroms.

Along with Ukraine, Lithuania was a major center for pogroms in the summer of 1941. Despite deportations under Soviet rule, the Jews of Lithuania feared even worse from the Germans. Many Jews fled advancing German forces, but it was difficult to beat them to the border, let alone reach a safe haven, and Germans were not the only threat. Lithuanian gangs also attacked Jews trying to escape. Solly Ganor, a thirteen-year-old trying to make his way to the Soviet border as the Luftwaffe strafed the road, saw armed men kill Jewish refugees, including his history teacher, her husband, and their five-year-old daughter. "My teacher's five-year-old daughter, thumb in mouth, clung to her mother's leg. Before them, dressed in old Lithuanian uniforms, stood a group of *Siauliai* [paramilitaries] with rifles." The first volley killed the adults but left the five-year-old girl standing. Ordered to shoot the girl, the men did not fire, so the "leader, an older man, calmly went up to the girl and hit her over the head with his revolver." Jews who turned back suffered further attack.[45]

Kovno, or Kaunas as Jews called it, a city of 120,000, was a place of particular peril. Lithuanian partisans drove Jews out of an outlying suburb, and residents of Kaunas joined in killing thousands of them after the German army entered the city. The leader of the German Einsatzgruppe A, Walter Stahlecker, later complained that "it was surprisingly not easy at first" to start a pogrom at Kaunas, but survivors recalled a Lithuanian public eager to attack and humiliate the Jews of Kaunas. The pogrom combined festivity with cruelty. Lithuanian partisans shaved off rabbis' beards with "with bits of broken glass." "Groups of Jews were made to dance in front of jeering crowds." Avraham Tory, a young attorney, noted in his diary that "Lithuanians

stood on the sides of the street and mocked the Jewish tragedy." German soldiers meanwhile photographed the proceedings.[46]

To the east, the Jews of Vilna suffered fewer attacks. Vilna,
Lithuania's largest city with 200,000 residents, was only very tenu-
ously Lithuanian. It had been part of Poland for most of the period
between the world wars, and more Poles than Lithuanians lived
there. Vilna experienced no pogrom; instead there was an epidemic
of kidnapping of Jews. Herman Kruk, a refugee from Warsaw who
left one of the most detailed accounts of life in the Vilna ghetto, described the wave of kidnapping or "snatching," as he called it, during the early days of the German invasion. By July 3, he observed,
"the snatching assumed a mass character." The snatchers hunted for
Jews, especially men, everywhere: in apartment buildings, on the
streets, and in courtyards. Consequently, Kruk observed, "You see almost no Jewish men in the streets." Jews made hiding places for
themselves. Kruk built what he called a melina, a thieves' term for
a place for hiding stolen goods. He soon heard of worse crimes than
kidnapping. Many Jews were taken outside of the city and killed in
a nearby forest. From one teenage girl left for dead on September 3
he learned, "All the work was done by the Lithuanians. They were
supervised by one German."[47]

Smaller Lithuanian towns had their own share of massacres and
pogroms. Rivka Lozansky-Bogomolnaya, a Jew from the town of
Butrimonys (Butrimantz) in the Alytus district of southern Lithuania, recalled how her town's non-Jews took part in looting and murder, referring bitterly to "good friends" who exploited and destroyed
the town's Jews. Friends who received Jews' belongings for safekeeping "took every opportunity to turn in the Jews all the sooner. . . . "
Neighbors wrote "Jews live here" in both Lithuanian and German
to mark out the houses to be robbed. Lithuanians, she asserted, "had
no rest until they had satisfied themselves with as much wealth as
possible from their victims," and, led by the local police, they murdered Jews.[48]

In the summer of 1941, attacking Jews was by no means an exclusively Lithuanian or Ukrainian activity. A wave of pogroms against

Jews also occurred in northeastern Poland. Much like Ukrainians and Lithuanians elsewhere, Poles in this region joined in pogroms against their Jewish neighbors. Postwar trials revealed how Poles in the town of Jedwabne joined in the killing. As one witness testified in 1949, "the Polish population bestially massacred the Jews, and Germans only stood to the side and took pictures."[49]

Latvia, too, was the scene of pogroms carried out by local residents. In the chief city, Riga, Boris Kacel, a nineteen-year-old Jew, recalled days of terror carried out by "Latvian vigilante groups." Five of Kacel's relatives were kidnapped and disappeared forever. "The greatest tragedy," he recalled, "was that these crimes were committed not by strange, invading forces but by the local Latvians, who knew their victims by their first names." Such groups were not operating outside the law. Bernhard Press, a Jewish resident of Riga who survived the war, recalled, "The center of the terror in Riga was the police headquarters."[50]

The pace of the killing accelerated as German forces pushed into the Soviet Union. Day after day the Einsatzgruppen killed Jews along with other victims, including commissars or Soviet political officers. At first these mobile killing units attacked mostly men, but by late summer they began to wipe out entire Jewish communities of men, women, and children. In the vast spaces of Ukraine and Russia, the terror units were hard pressed to complete their task, but they received assistance from units of the German army that helped round up Jews and at times took part in the massacres themselves. By the end of 1941 the Germans had emptied much of the western Soviet Union of Jews. The chief distinction from past campaigns of ethnic cleansing lay in the determination to shoot as many Jews as possible rather than relying on massacres and arson to promote flight.

By 1942, mass extermination in the death camps became the chief killing method. This phase of the Holocaust has been so intensively studied and discussed that it cannot be covered in detail here in a broad narrative of European ethnic cleansing.[51] The murder of millions of European Jews at Auschwitz and other death camps in Poland stands apart from other cases of genocide.

It was at Auschwitz that the long history of the Jews of Thessaloniki ended. Thousands of Jews left Thessaloniki in the decades after it fell under Greek rule, but fifty thousand Jews still lived there at the start of World War II. In early 1943, Adolf Eichmann of the SS decided to deport the Jews of Thessaloniki, and on March 15 SS officials began to send them to Auschwitz. The Jews of Thessaloniki who were selected for forced labor rather than for immediate death stood out for their resourcefulness and toughness. They made a powerful impression on Primo Levi, an Italian Jew who wrote a classic account of life in Auschwitz. Levi arrived at Auschwitz in early 1944, by which time the number of Jews from Thessaloniki had dwindled. Still, they dominated the permanent black market at the camp and won the respect of all. Levi described them as "tenacious, thieving, wise, ferocious and united, so determined to live, such pitiless opponents in the struggle for life . . . whom even the Germans respect and the Poles fear."[52]

Auschwitz was both a killing center and an array of labor camps, but several other death camps focused almost exclusively on killing. These included the Operation Reinhard death camps in Poland: Belzec, Treblinka, and Sobibor. These small and secluded camps functioned as factories of death in which most of the Jews of the General Government were killed in 1942. Most of the Jews of Lvov, for example, were murdered in Belzec. At the peak of killing in August 1942, some fifty thousand were murdered in just over two weeks. Frania Drix, the wife of the physician Samuel Drix, was one of the Jews of Lvov killed at Belzec. Jacob Gerstenfeld managed to escape the gas chamber by jumping off of a train bound for Belzec.

"Kill a Third, Expel a Third, Convert a Third"

Nazi Germany launched a war of ethnic cleansing, but it was not only Germans who wished to redraw Europe's ethnic map during World War II. So too did a host of nationalists across Central and Eastern Europe who hoped to rid their countries of undesired ethnic and religious groups. For champions of ethnic and national purity, as of 1939 there was still much to do. The ideal of the nation-state that housed an entire nation and only that nation remained elusive. War, however violent, offered promise for champions of national and racial purity. War gave nationalists the opportunity to clean house by expelling or eliminating undesired minorities from their states. War gave the most radical nationalist movements—often exile or opposition groups—the chance to vie for power. And war was also a time for building larger national homelands. War, however, also had unintended and unexpected consequences: cycles of killing and revenge often led to outcomes almost directly opposite to those desired by many extremist nationalists.

In Yugoslavia, for example, German aggression triggered a war of nations. In April 1941, in a reprise of blitzkrieg, German forces defeated the outmatched Yugoslav army in less than two weeks. German victory was also a success for German allies who had coveted bits and pieces of Yugoslavia. A larger Italy, a larger Hungary, and a larger Bulgaria were all possible now that Yugoslavia was gone. To Italy went much of the west, including coastal areas desired by Italian nationalists since World War I. Bulgaria occupied eastern and central Macedonia, regions long identified as Bulgarian by Bulgarian nationalists, and Hungary occupied land in northern Serbia lost by Hungary after World War I. Germany placed what was left, the remnants of Serbia, under military occupation.[53] In addition, a brand new state, the Independent State of Croatia, also emerged out of the destruction of Yugoslavia. Its head of state was Ante Pavelic, the Paglovnik (the Croatian equivalent for Führer), who returned to Croatia after twelve years of exile.

From the start, Germany terrorized occupied Yugoslavia. In Serbia, German soldiers rather than SS units carried out the bulk of the killing. German forces burned villages and murdered hostages as punishment for attacks on German soldiers. This was a deliberate policy of the German Army High Command, which in September 1941 ordered the execution of 50 to 100 "Communists" for every dead German soldier. A string of massacres made clear that almost anyone was a Communist for the purpose of reprisal killings. For the month of October 1941 the 717th Infantry Division reported more than 5,000 "enemy losses," including 4,300 killed as punishment for German casualties. German soldiers also murdered Jews and Gypsies held in camps. A detailed report from November 1, 1941, by Hans-Dietrich Walther, commander of an infantry company, described the killing of Jews and Gypsies from a camp at Belgrade. "At the beginning," Walther noted, "my soldiers were not impressed. On the second day, however, it was already apparent, that one or the other did not possess the nerves, to carry out an execution for a long time."[54] Serbia's remaining Jews were killed in gas vans in early 1942, and Serbia was declared "free of Jews."

While Yugoslavia's war began with a German invasion, terror was not a specifically German activity. German allies, such as the Croatian Ustasha fascists, took advantage of their good fortune to pursue their own plans for ethnic purity through discrimination, expulsions, and mass killing. The Paglovnik and some three hundred Croatian fascists who returned with him sought to create a pure Croatian nation defined by race and blood. They identified Jews, Serbs, and Gypsies as their chief racial and national enemies. In a February 1942 speech, the Ustasha minister of the interior, Andrija Artuković, who later lived for years in the United States before his extradition to Yugoslavia in 1986, expounded on the Jewish threat to Croatia. "Judeo-communists" wished to destroy Croatia, and Croats therefore had no choice "but to clean off the poisonous damagers and insatiable parasites—Jews, communists and Freemasons from their national and state body." As for Serbs, the Ustasha aimed, according to a widely cited remark by Minister of Education Mile Budak, to "kill a third, expel a third, and convert a third." Ustasha leaders regularly used a term very similar to "ethnic cleansing" to describe their plans for the country. They spoke of the need to "cleanse" (cistimo) the Serbs.[55]

The Ustasha pursued racial and national purity through methods familiar from 1930s Nazi Germany and Eastern Europe. First the Ustasha government isolated racial and national enemies including Jews, Serbs, and Gypsies. Next, the authorities created a regime of systematic economic, professional, and cultural discrimination against Serbs and Jews. Independent Croatia barred Jews from work in the press, radio, theater, or any other profession of cultural life, and confiscated their property. Jews wore the Star of David, Serbs blue armbands. Serbs also lost their vehicles and in some regions their property, and, in a distinctive touch, the Ustasha government banned the use of the Serbian Cyrillic script.[56]

The Paglovnik proved impatient to purify Croatia. Whereas Nazi Germany had employed systematic discrimination for several years before implementing mass terror against non-Aryans, the Ustasha moved quickly to mass killings, ethnic cleansing, and genocide. Ustasha forces carried out a string of massacres of Serbs. In Glina, a mixed town of Croats and Serbs south of Croatia's capital Zagreb, Ustasha men repeatedly killed Serbs in the spring and summer of 1941.[57] In one of the most notorious single massacres, on the night of August 3 Ustasha men killed twelve hundred or more Serbs at a church in Glina. The Ustasha regime also established its own concentration camps, including the Jasenovac camp on the Sava River. Tens of thousands of Serbs died at Jasenovac, and most of Croatia's Jews died on Croatian soil.

The Ustasha extended their terror into Bosnia-Herzegovina, a region annexed by the Croatian state but also divided into German and Italian zones. Serbs died at many of the same places that would again become infamous for violence during the wars that accompanied the breakup of Yugoslavia in the 1990s. At Mostar in Herzegovina, hundreds of Serbs were arrested, brought to the banks of the Neretva River, shot, and pushed into the river. Near Sarajevo, Ustasha forces expelled Serbs from villages, destroyed Orthodox churches, and massacred and shot Serbian peasants. Even Germans claimed to have been shocked by the brutality of the Ustasha terror campaign. An SD report of April 1942 referred to the "senseless slaughter of the Serbian population in Bosnia." But there was a purpose: clearing out Serbs. A German report indicated that the mere "rumor of the proximity of the Ustasha" sufficed to cause flight.[58] Serbs hid in the forests, and some left Bosnia altogether. They crossed the Drina River to the east to seek refuge in German-occupied Serbia. To the west, Serbs as well as Jews sought safety in the Italian occupation zone in Herzegovina. Despite Mussolini's previous patronage of Pavelic, the Italian army in western Yugoslavia recoiled at the Ustasha's massacres.

For decades afterward, the total number of Serbs who died or lost their homes remained disputed. This quarrel was symptomatic of the broader division between Serb and Croat nationalists. Estimates of the number of Serbs killed at Jasenovac range from more than 55,000 to almost certainly exaggerated figures in the hundreds of thousands. As of 1941, Germans reported 300,000 Serbs killed. Pavelic himself estimated that between 1941 and early 1943 the number of Serbs living in Croatia fell from 2 million to 1 million.[59]

Triggered by German aggression and spread by Ustasha violence, the war of nations in the ruins of Yugoslavia escalated as others—Serbs, Bosnian Muslims, and Albanians—joined in the ethnic warfare. The role of Bosnian Muslims in this war was different from the wars of the 1990s. Later both Croats and Serbs saw Bosnian Muslims as a distinct group, but in the 1940s the Ustasha's leaders defined Bosnian Muslims as part of the Croat nation, and Chetniks (Serbian nationalists and monarchists) attacked Muslims as Ustasha allies. Several Chetnik massacres of Bosnian Muslims took place around Foca, a southern Bosnian town that would also become known for ethnic cleansing in the 1990s. Chetniks killed some two thousand Muslims at Foca in August 1942 and thousands more, mostly civilians, at Foca in February 1943. The aim, according to one report from 1943, was to destroy everything and kill everyone: "All Moslem villages have been completely burned. . . . All property has been destroyed, except cattle, corn and hay. During the operations we carried out the complete annihilation of the Moslem inhabitants, without regard to their sex and age. . . . The whole population has been annihilated. The morale of our units was very high."[60]

Much of the controversy over Serbian ethnic warfare during World War II centers on the role of the Chetnik leader, Colonel Draza Mihailovic. Mihailovic had survived the Serbian army's retreat across Albania in 1915 and had witnessed Yugoslavia's dismemberment and occupation in 1941. He first took up arms as a leader of resistance against fascism and later also fought against Communist Partisans. Led by Josip Broz, a veteran of the Austro-Hungarian army in World War I who became a Communist and adopted the name Tito, the Partisans quickly emerged as the most effective resistance force in occupied Yugoslavia. The growing Communist challenge caused Mihailovic to contact the Germans to discuss possible cooperation against the Partisans, and in 1946 he was sentenced to death for collaborating with the Germans. At the same time, the new Yugoslav state founded by the victorious Partisans also charged Mihailovic and his commanders with massacring Muslims. Mihailovic himself denied responsibility for the murders of Muslims and Croats, but he recalled strong Chetnik sentiment for doing exactly that. He described one wartime meeting at which a speaker, identified by Mihailovic as a Muslim, told of three ways to solve the question, the first "to slaughter them all." All those present, according to Mihailovic, "shouted: 'Let us slaughter them!'" And slaughter there had been, Mihailovic stressed, on all sides. "Entire regions were destroyed by Moslems," he told the court, "but this had its repercussions afterwards. The men revenged themselves in battle," and the Drina became a "river of blood."[61]

Bosnia's Muslims also took up arms—on all sides. Despite growing disillusionment with Pavelic and his associates, some joined Ustasha forces, especially in areas where Muslims faced attacks from Serbs. Others became Partisans. Some even cooperated with the Chetniks.[62] Like many of their counterparts in other Balkan regions, Bosnian political leaders also tried to win German support. Overtures for Bosnian autonomy failed to gain German backing, but the SS recruited Muslims into the Handzar Division, a unit that took part in attacks against Serbs. Depending on the time or place, Bosnian military forces fought with the Ustasha, the Chetniks, the Germans, the Partisans, and sometimes simply on their own.

In Kosovo the war was also the occasion for a new round of ethnic violence, revenge, and flight. Here, those most at risk were Serbs who had settled since the founding of Yugoslavia. Albanians had suffered harsh repression under Serbian rule since the end of World War I, and they wanted revenge. Tens of thousands of Serb settlers, perhaps as many as sixty thousand to seventy thousand, fled attacks by Albanians. Those who did not escape risked death. The Italian civil commissioner in Kosovo saw burnt homes throughout the countryside. "Slavs and Albanians, he observed, had burnt down one another's houses, had killed as many people as they could, and had stolen livestock, goods, and tools."[63]

Slovenia, Croatia, Serbia, Bosnia, Kosovo—almost no region of Yugoslavia escaped the war of nations, and that was also true of Macedonia where Bulgaria tried to win advantage from the war. Bulgarian ambitions for Macedonia had been repeatedly frustrated. In the First Balkan War, Bulgaria took much of Macedonia, only to lose many of its gains in the Second Balkan War in 1913. Bulgaria once again took the offensive during World War I, but conceded still more territory at war's end. Now, with a new war, Bulgaria tried to make Macedonia more Bulgarian by driving out the Serbs.

"Everything Back, Everything Back"

Yugoslavia's neighbors, Hungary, Bulgaria, and Romania, all sought to use war to pursue their own nationalist aims. For Hungary and Bulgaria, war offered a chance to satisfy territorial grievances dating back to the treaties that had ended World War I. Hungary had lost numerous territories, including most of Transylvania, and Bulgaria had lost an outlet to the Aegean Sea. All three countries looked to Germany to win favorable border adjustments, but only Bulgaria and Hungary made territorial gains in the war's early years. Romania, in contrast, shrank. Nineteen forty was a very bad year for Romania. In late June the Soviet Union annexed Bessarabia and Northern Bukovina on Romania's eastern border, and on August 30 a German settlement of borders, announced in Vienna, transferred much of Transylvania back to Hungary. Days later, Romania lost the region of southern Dobruja on the Black Sea to Bulgaria.

The new borders satisfied neither Hungarians nor Romanians. The division of Transylvania outraged Romanians but struck Magyars as inadequate, as American journalists reported when they accompanied the Hungarian army into western Transylvania. Hungary had regained many of the lands lost at the end of World War I, but apparently it was still not enough. American journalist Leigh White heard Hungarians, villagers and soldiers alike, chant, "Everything back, everything back."[64] He took their words as a reproach to Germany for not restoring all lands lost to Hungary by the Treaty of Trianon.

In southern Dobruja, Bulgarians too wanted more. The *New York Times* correspondent C. L. Sulzberger heard about Bulgarian goals at a victory parade in September 1940 in the Black Sea town of Balcik. Sulzberger, along with other reporters, was in fact expected to join in the parade, so he marched carrying his typewriter. Balcik's new Bulgarian mayor made clear that Bulgaria's appetite for territory was not yet sated. "Now let us hope," he told the crowd, "that our country will be enriched not only by golden Dobruja but also soon by the level plains of Thrace and the blue Aegean."[65] In 1941 Bulgaria regained an outlet to the Aegean when Bulgaria occupied Western Thrace after the German conquest of Greece.

New borders created a new question: what was to become of populations that suddenly found themselves inside the wrong country? The Bulgarian occupation regime sought to place a Bulgarian stamp on Western Thrace by imprisoning and expelling Greeks and settling Bulgarians. Many Greeks fled, more than 100,000 of them seeking safety in German-occupied Greece.[66] The issue of unwanted peoples was more complicated when Germany's bickering allies had to deal with one another. The possibility of a population exchange with Romania worried at least some Hungarian authorities. At the city of Cluj/Kolozsvar in central Transylvania, Leigh White learned in early October 1941 that some four hundred Romanians had been seized and sent to the last railway station then in Hungarian possession, where they were being held hostage to discourage Romania from expelling Hungarians. A much better plan was to expand Hungary. As a Hungarian commander told White, "We're determined to regain all of Transylvania. As soon as we do, we'll be delighted to deport every last Rumanian to Wallachia. Then see how the Rumanians like it!"[67]

Still, Bulgarians, Hungarians, and Romanians moved with new borders. Some 62,000 Bulgarians left northern Dobruja in a population exchange with Romania, and 160,000 Hungarians left southern Transylvania for Hungary. But Romanians paid the highest price for border changes: some 110,000 left southern Dobruja, and more than 200,000 left Transylvania for Romania. Romanians lined up at railway stations to return to the remaining core of Romania, the region known as the Old Kingdom, and with them, the American journalist Robert Parker reported, came national symbols. Departing Romanian officials packed up "enormous bronze statues of Rumanian national heroes." Refugees also poured into Romania from Bessarabia and North Bukovina. In Bucharest the British journalist Derek Patmore watched the refugees arrive by road and by train. At the Gare du Nord railway station, "the platforms and waiting rooms were crowded with peasants lying about in exhausted heaps after their sudden flight."[68]

A "Huge Anti-Semitic Factory"

Within its borders, Romania unleashed a drive for ethnic purity and Romanian supremacy. The campaign to secure Romania for Romanians included persecution of Magyars and Ukrainians but targeted Jews in particular. Romania subjected hundreds of thousands of Jews in Romania to systematic, comprehensive legal discrimination, and expelled hundreds of thousands of Jews to ghettos and camps where many died.

Romania's drive for ethnic purity unfolded during a complex power struggle between rival authoritarian leaders and nationalist movements. As war approached, Romania's King Carol II attempted to create a royal dictatorship, but his rule proved fragile. After the humiliating loss of Bessarabia and Northern Bukovina, the German decision to transfer territory from Romania to Hungary was the final blow for the king. In early September 1940 a coalition led by General Ion Antonescu and the fascist Iron Guard took over the Romanian government. This partnership ended with a failed Iron Guard revolt in January 1941 that left Antonescu in power.

Amidst border adjustments, population movements, and changes in government, anti-Semitism remained a constant, a sentiment that permeated Romanian society. Mihail Sebastian, a Jewish writer active in Romania's cultural life and author of a very rich diary of life in the fascist years, observed in early June 1940 that "the old Romanian anti-Semitism (with its eternal promise of deliverance) has been expectantly bubbling up." Leigh White, who visited Romania in 1940 and 1941, argued that this very anti-Semitism bound ordinary Romanians to the Iron Guard. "The Jews," he suggested, "were the one bond which linked Rumanians of every class with the Iron Guard revolution. The average Rumanian hated Jews with a fury unapproached in Germany and equaled only in Poland."[69]

Romanian soldiers took vengeance for their humiliation in 1940 by killing Jews. As they withdrew from Bukovina, soldiers from the 16th Infantry Regiment, for example, killed Jews. The murders continued within Romania's new and smaller borders. Corpses of Jews, some of them soldiers, lined the railroad tracks in Moldavia. Romanian soldiers took part in killing Jews during a pogrom in the town of Dorohoi, and Romanian soldiers killed four hundred Jews, who were trying to flee for Soviet territory, at the train station at the Danube River port of Galati.[70] These massacres appalled some Romanians but also inspired celebration and even song. In July 1941, Mihail Sebastian heard Gypsy children singing in the streets of Bucharest of the previous year's massacres:

> The train is leaving Chitila
> Taking Stalin off to Palestine
> The train is pulling out of Galati
> Full of hanged Jews[71]

Romania's Jews suffered pervasive discrimination. Even before the takeover by Antonescu and the Iron Guard, Romania enacted

legislation in August 1940 that mirrored Germany's infamous
Nuremberg Laws. Jews could no longer marry Romanians. The new
Antonescu–Iron Guard regime intensified discrimination. A cam-
paign of Romanization led to widespread seizure of Jewish busi-
nesses, dismissal of Jewish white-collar employees, and purges of
Jews from virtually all professional associations. Meanwhile the Iron
Guard racists beat and killed Jews.[70]

The Iron Guard campaign against Romania's Jews culminated
in January 1941 with an orgy of anti-Semitic violence during a
failed attempt to seize power from the Guard's erstwhile ally Antonescu. Fighting for Bucharest, the Greenshirts, as the Iron Guard
squads were known, sacked and burned synagogues, and began a
pogrom. As Jews' homes and businesses burned, their Christian
neighbors sought to save their own property by posting signs such as
"Christian Property, Romanian House, Romanian Owner," but some
of these houses and shops too were destroyed. In perhaps the most
infamous scene of slaughter, Romanian fascists killed Jews at a
Bucharest slaughterhouse in what Leigh White described as a
"fiendish parody of kosher methods of butchering."[73]

The campaign against Romania's Jews did not end when Antonescu defeated the Iron Guard. In June 1941 Romanian entrance
into the war initiated a new onslaught of anti-Semitic policies. Sebastian caught the tone of the times when he described the Romanian government, in an August 1941 diary entry, as a "huge anti-
Semitic factory." Romanian authorities forced Jews to hand over all
manner of goods: beds, pillows, blankets, sheets, shirts, underpants,
socks, handkerchiefs, towels, suits, and overcoats. In September 1941
the loot piled up in Bucharest's Great Synagogue, which served as a
collection point. In December Jews were ordered to hand in skis.
Discrimination extended to food as well. Jews paid higher prices for
less food. Romania also demanded periodic forced labor from Jews,
but the humiliation of Jews seemed more important than advancing
the war effort by putting Jews to work that was useful. Jews, for example, were forced to form work parties to shovel snow, but if no
snow had fallen recently, they simply moved around piles of snow.

"We shift snow," Sebastian observed in early March 1942, "from one place to another—a completely senseless operation."[74]

Romania's Holy War

Romanian anti-Semitism entered a new phase in June 1941 when Romania joined Nazi Germany to invade the Soviet Union. General Antonescu called the joint Romanian and German invasion a holy war. Holy war was war for lost land: Bessarabia and Northern Bukovina. It was a war against Communists and Jews in which Romanian authorities pledged to execute "fifty Judeo-Communists" in reprisal for each German or Romanian soldier killed.[75] And holy war in Bessarabia and Bukovina was also a war of ethnic cleansing and genocide.

The German mobile killing squads that murdered Jews across Eastern Europe in 1941 were also active on the southern sectors of the eastern front, but Romanian slaughter of Jews had strong local and national roots. This was not simply murder made in Germany. Mass murder of Jews was the radical culmination of mounting Romanian anti-Semitism, but Romanians were also motivated by commonplace nationalist ideas of the period. Much as in Lithuania and eastern Poland, nationalist desire for revenge against Jews who were seen as Soviet supporters fed anti-Semitic violence. Political and military leaders and large segments of the population charged the Jews of Bessarabia and Bukovina with betrayal during the 1940 Soviet takeover of these regions. Once again, claims of Jewish treason had an especially powerful effect because they fit so easily into existing stories that depicted Jews as disloyal outsiders.

Romanians took revenge in June 1941, beginning just across the border from Bessarabia in the Moldavian city of Iasi. During the war's first days Iasi was on the front lines, and Romanians charged that Jews assisted Soviet air raids by acting as spotters. Some even claimed that Iasi's Jews were found on board downed Soviet planes. Posters called for vengeance. A witness recalled one that read, "Romanians! Each kike killed is a dead Communist. The time for revenge is now!" Local security officials, including Police Superintendent Lieutenant-Colonel Chirilovici, found Romanian civilians eager to respond. They "accused the Jews of being the only minority to hide and protect Soviet parachutists and terrorists. When measures were taken by the army against Jews, the Romanian citizens unanimously approved of the mass-executions. They would have liked the executions to be on a larger scale." Romanians, including police, soldiers, and civilians, as well as Germans slaughtered Jews. They killed thousands of Jews in Iasi itself. In one of the most infamous incidents of the entire pogrom, Romanian police and German soldiers packed more than 4,300 Jews, many of them injured, into two trains that became known as "death trains." Traveling without food or water for more than six days in severely overcrowded freight cars without windows, 1,400 Jews died by the time the first train reached Călărasi to the south of Iasi, and nearly 1,200 died in the second train, which traveled slowly to the west of Iasi.[76]

The Iasi pogrom set the tone for Romania's assault on the Jews. Moving back into Bessarabia and Bukovina, Romanian soldiers, sometimes accompanied by German forces, and often joined by local residents, continued their killing. This provided a punishment of sorts for alleged Jewish pleasure at Romanian humiliation in 1940. The Romanian 6th Mountain Rifle Regiment, previously stationed in Bessarabia, for example, saw war as a chance for vengeance. If anything, the regiment's colonel, Maties Ermil, wrote on July 31, 1941, the 6th Regiment was not harsh enough toward Jews. "In my opinion," he asserted, "the methods employed by the regiment, while in compliance with higher orders, were too tame, since the Jews had dared to shoot at the Romanian army, and had dared to carry out sabotage acts against it." Massacres were commonplace across Bessarabia and Bukovina. Upon taking Kishinev, Bessarabia's chief city, on July 18, Romanian and German forces killed thousands of Jews, though this massacre is almost a footnote in the history of the Holocaust.[77] Whereas the 1903 pogrom at Kishinev provoked international outrage, the murder of many more Jews in 1941—in the midst of world war—almost escaped attention.

Massacres, however violent and frequent, made up only the first stage of Romania's war against the Jews of Bessarabia and Buko- vina. Romanian officials used a term almost identical to ethnic cleansing to define their broader goals. They called for "ground cleansing," the clearing out of Jews. Mihai Antonescu, vice presi- dent of Romania's Council of Ministers, called for driving both Jews and Ukrainians from Bessarabia and Bukovina. He was "indifferent if history adjudges us barbarians. . . . This is the most opportune mo- ment in our history. If need be, use machine guns."[78]

Like Himmler and Heydrich in 1939 and 1940, General Atonescu and his associates faced one critical problem in 1941: they had no place to deposit unwanted Jews. Himmler and Heydrich discovered that they could not push all the Jews of annexed western Poland into the Nazi occupation zone of the General Government; Romanian author- ities found that they could not push all the Jews of Bukovina and Bessarabia to the east. In both cases the effort to expel an entire peo- ple clashed with other priorities. Romania wished to drive Jews out of Bessarabia east across the Dniester River, but the German military did not want these Jewish civilians arriving too soon, especially if that re- duced transportation available for the ongoing assault on the Soviet Union. Entire towns and villages of Jews driven from their homes reached the Dniester only to be pushed back into Bessarabia by Ein- satzgruppe D. Jews who could not keep pace were shot.[79]

If Bessarabia's remaining Jews could not be forced beyond the Dniester, they could at least be concentrated and isolated. That was the solution Romania pursued in the summer and early fall of 1941 by forcing tens of thousands of Jews into ghettos in towns and cities, including Kishinev. Jewish refugees in the ghettos of Bessarabia took shelter in looted houses previously abandoned by other Jews now dead or gone. Avigdor Shachan, a young Jew sent with his fam- ily to the ghetto of Secureni in northern Bessarabia, recalled how some twenty thousand Jews crowded into "narrow streets lined by the abandoned homes of Jews."[80]

The only remaining obstacle to a still more radical Romanian campaign against Bessarabian and Bukovinian Jews disappeared in

the late summer of 1941 when Romania received a swath of territory known as Transnistria. Awarded to Romania by Germany on
August 30 and mapped out in September, the borders of this territory stretched east of Bessarabia into southern Ukraine. Romania
now had a place to expel any Jews remaining in Bessarabia, and Romania's leaders maintained that these Jews fully deserved their fate.
Wilhelm Filderman, leader of the Romanian Jewish Community,
pleaded for a halt to deportations, but Antonescu countered on October 19 with familiar claims of Jewish treason during Romania's retreat in 1940. The evidence of Jewish killings of Romanians was
"enough to drive one crazy, how your Jews tortured our tolerant,
generous nation."[81]

From the ghettos of Bessarabia, Jews picked up their meager
possessions—for some, clothing and only as much as a day's food—
and walked, driven all the while by Romanian gendarmes, east to
the Dniester River and across to Transnistria. Some drowned or froze
to death, some were killed, others killed themselves. The dead lined
the roads. Avigdor Shachan estimated that only some three thousand
of his group of five thousand deported from the Secureni ghetto survived the journey. Other Jews, driven out of Dorohoi, a region
within Romania's Old Kingdom that had been attached to Bukovina
only in 1938, arrived by train. Miryam Leib, deported from Dorohoi
as a seventeen-year-old, recalled a three days' journey in a cattle car
during which "many people in the train froze to death." By 1942,
the deportations targeted even selected Jews from Bucharest, supposedly as punishment for missing forced labor assignments, for
careless work, or even for Jews who "cultivated close relations with
Romanians."[82]

Whether crossing Bukovina or Bessarabia or entering Transnistria, Jews encountered an intensely hostile public: soldiers and gendarmes eager to drive them forward and peasants who mocked,
robbed, and attacked them. Palestine, the goal of Zionists, became a
derisive insult for Romanians who knew that Jews driven east were
not headed for a promised land. The word "Palestine," repeated over
and over, filled the air as Romanian soldiers drove Avigdor Shachan

along with his family and other Jews out of the Bessarabian town of Khotin in July 1941. In one village on their journey east, peasants lined the road, "and when we came close to them, an old farmer sounded a bugle." That was the signal for "a hail of rocks and sticks . . . while the farmers all burst into raucous laughter." Peasants robbed Jews and even murdered them. Jews who could not keep up, Miryam Leib recalled, "were killed either by the Romanian gendarmes or by bands of Ukrainian peasants."[83]

The mortality rate for Jews who actually made it across the Dniester River into Transnistria was staggering. With winter the temperature plummeted, snow piled up, and ill-nourished Jewish refugees, short of food and fuel, died in large numbers from typhus. Desperate for food, they sold their clothing despite the cold. Mirjam Korber, a girl expelled from the mountains of Bukovina to Transnistria, reflected on the carnage after surviving the first winter. "And what is simpler," she wrote in her diary, "than to kill one Jew or thousands of helpless Jews." The fact that killing took place in the "civilization of the twentieth century" was most shocking to her.[84] The first winter of exile in Transnistria was the worst, but massacres of Jews continued throughout the war, especially along Transnistria's eastern border on the Bug River, where Germans took the lead in killing. Of some 125,000 to 145,000 Jews who reached Transnistria, approximately 50,000 survived the war. In all, the Romanian war against the Jews claimed at least 250,000 and possibly more victims, or approximately half of all Jews in territory under Romanian control.

As Jews died in Transnistria, the Jews of Bucharest, Romania's capital, feared a general deportation order that never came. Bucharest's Jews knew about the catastrophic conditions for Jews driven from Bessarabia and Bukovina into Transnistria, and they expected to share the same fate. "Everybody is talking about a total solution to the Jewish question in Romania," Dr. Emil Dorian, a Jewish physician and writer, observed in his diary on December 16, 1941—"that is, the deportation of all Jews to Transnistria." Limited deportations from Bucharest in September 1942 terrified the city's

Jews. On September 15, 1942, Dorian noted that "the panic among the Jews is now permanent." Mihail Sebastian's diary entry for September 25, 1942 stated: "The specter of the trains heading for Transnistria haunts me all the time." And yet the Jews sent east from Bucharest to Transnistria remained unfortunate exceptions. Neither Sebastian nor Dorian was deported. Dorian lived until 1956; Sebastian died when he was struck by a truck in May 1945—after surviving both the Holocaust and the war. Nobody knew why the final blow never fell for most of Bucharest's Jews. As Dorian wrote in his diary in October 1942, "No one can figure out the reason for the government's sudden decision to change its position regarding Jewish deportation."[85] Most likely, more did not die because Romania realized that Germany was on a path to defeat. Especially after the Battle of Stalingrad, Romania's leaders began to reconsider their policy against Jews. By late 1943 Romanian authorities permitted some Jews to return from Transnistria.

The relationship between ethnic cleansing and genocide was different in Romania and in Romanian-occupied territory than in most of the rest of Europe during World War II. German mass murder of Jews in the Soviet Union and in Poland provided an alternative "solution" to the "Jewish question" in place of resettlement schemes. But in Bessarabia, Bukovina, and Transnistria extraordinarily violent deportations led directly to genocide. In this respect the Romanian slaughter of Jews resembled the Armenian genocide. In both Romania and Turkey the architects of mass murder accused their victims of disloyalty during war, and in both countries deportation predictably led to extermination. The ethnic cleansing of Armenians from most of Turkey caused great numbers of deaths through massacres, exposure, starvation, and disease, and the same factors killed Jews from Bessarabia and Bukovina, though where Armenians died from heat, Jews died from cold. In both cases a segment of the population under attack escaped mass murder—Jews of Romania's Old Kingdom and Armenians of Turkey's largest western cities, though the percentage of Romanian Jews spared exceeded the proportion of Armenians who escaped deportation.[86]

Cleansing by Studebaker

Through 1942, the German war of extermination and the campaigns of radical nationalists unleashed genocide and ethnic cleansing, but the end of 1942 and the start of 1943 marked a turning point both in the war and in ethnic cleansing. Programs of mass murder and expulsion in the war's early years almost always presumed one outcome for the war. Poles pushed east out of annexed western Poland; Jews sent to Madagascar or the General Government, Transnistria, or simply murdered; Serbs massacred in Croatia; Nazi expulsion of Poles, Ukrainians, and White Russians to Central Asia and Siberia—all these schemes assumed German victory. But what if Germany lost? Any balanced account of ethnic cleansing during World War II must, of course, stress the centrality of crimes committed by Nazi Germany and its allies, but Soviet victory and German retreat brought new episodes of ethnic cleansing and ethnic war.

A new phase of Soviet deportations began even before Germany invaded the USSR. Pushing west in the war's early years into eastern Poland, the Baltic states, and Bessarabia, Soviet authorities soon began expelling suspect individuals. Soviet authorities, in particular NKVD agents, carried out the deportations. They rounded up police and army officers, teachers, civil servants, wealthy farmers, their families, and others deemed guilty of anti-Soviet activities. They also deported Jews. In occupied Poland alone Soviet authorities deported more than half a million people.[87] Many died in transit, especially the elderly and children deported during the winter of 1940. Those who survived the journey east ended up in labor and prison camps.

One of the many witnesses of Soviet terror was Christina Soltan, a young Polish musician, who in 1939 and 1940 traveled extensively in eastern Poland. Soltan had studied in Berlin before the war, managed to get her half-Jewish music teacher out of Germany to Japan, and in 1939 returned to Poland. She fled east after the German invasion, and saw the early stages of Soviet occupation at the town of Buczacz, the birthplace of Simon Wiesenthal. "Every day new names were added to the long list of arrested people: all judges and magistrates . . . all political leaders. . . . Poles, Ukrainians, Jews." She made her way to Lvov where deportations began in early 1940. Soltan described railways crowded with sealed freight trains, "men, women and children" packed within. "We could hear them hammering on the walls . . . ." The trains remained parked for days, and some of the passengers died before their journey east even started. Deportations resumed in the spring: for two nights army trucks "rolled through our streets, stopping before almost every house."[88] Soltan soon left for Lithuania; from there she crossed the entire length of the Soviet Union all the way to China and then to Japan.

Once Germany attacked the USSR the Soviet leadership initiated a new style of forced evacuation. Soviet authorities began to move entire peoples. Those selected for deportation spoke many languages and practiced different religions, but they had one thing in common: in official eyes they did not count as patriots during the Great Patriotic War that Soviet forces fought against Nazi Germany. The continuity with tsarist policy during World War I was striking. Then, Russian military commanders had forced the evacuation of large numbers of ethnic Germans and Jews away from the western frontier on the grounds they might support Germany and Austria-Hungary. In 1941 the most obvious targets for deportation were Russia's ethnic Germans.

Soviet authorities pursued ethnic Germans with greater intensity than did their tsarist predecessors. The forced evacuations of World War I gave way to full-scale ethnic cleansing during World War II. Virtually all Russian Germans, as many as a million or more, were sent east. In a death knell for German communities that in some cases dated back centuries, Germans were driven out of their villages in Volhynia, the Black Sea, the Volga River region, and the north Caucasus. They were sent to labor camps and special settlements in Siberia, Central Asia, and the Urals. Tens of thousands of Germans died, and the death toll may have reached as high as 200,000 to 300,000.[89]

Soviet authorities deported suspect populations in defeat, and deported still more such peoples in victory. Stalin had moved peoples for years, but his choice of whom to deport during the final years of World War II reflected older traditions of mistrust. Several of the peoples relocated as punishment for alleged collaboration with German invaders also had a long prior history of resistance to Russian authorities. In the nineteenth century, tsarist armies had struggled to pacify Muslim peoples of the north Caucasus. Now some eighty years after the final Russian conquest of the Caucasus, Soviet forces drove Muslims out of their homes. They deported Chechens, Ingush, Karachai, Balkars, and Meskhetian Turks, and, for good measure, the Buddhist Kalmyks. Altogether the Soviet leadership forced a million people out of their homes in the Caucasus. Regaining control of the Crimea, Soviet authorities deported the Crimean Tatars, another group that tsarist authorities had mistrusted.

Soviet accusations against these "punished peoples" exaggerated their collaboration while overlooking evidence of loyal service to the Soviet Union. It was true that Germans had sought to enlist restive peoples of the north Caucasus and adjacent steppes against the Soviet Union. A German military intelligence officer, Otto Doll, for example, sought to win over Kalmyk support. But Kalmyks had served in the Red Army and many won military honors.[90] In the Crimea the German regime recruited as many as twenty thousand Tatars, but many came from the ranks of Soviet prisoners of war who risked death if they remained in captivity. Germans used the same methods to mobilize far larger numbers of Russians as auxiliaries.

Of all the ethnic cleansing campaigns during World War II, Soviet deportations in the Caucasus relied least on local allies and grassroots participation. The Soviet state by itself initiated and executed these expulsions. The higher degree of state control led to greater efficiency. In a general war of ethnic cleansing, the speed of Soviet deportation was unmatched. Soviet authorities launched the first of these sudden actions against the Karachai. They began in August and

September 1943 by relocating leaders of rebellious bands and their
relatives, and in October Soviet authorities chose to resettle the entire
Karachai people. On November 2 NKVD troops struck. They surrounded villages and took away all residents in trucks. Almost 69,000
people were sent east. This sequence of collection by NKVD agents or
other security forces—transport to railway stations in Studebaker
trucks obtained from the United States via the Lend Lease program
and travel east by trains—became the model for subsequent Soviet
deportations. Between December 26 and December 30, 1943, Soviet
security personnel carried out exactly the same kind of operation
against the Kalmyks, sweeping them from their homeland.[91]

The swift expulsions of Kalmyks and Karachai in late 1943 were
rehearsals for a still larger effort: the total deportation of Chechens
and Ingushes. On February 20, 1944, Lavrentii Beria, commissar for
internal affairs and head of the NKVD, arrived in Grozny. The agency
employed a clever ruse to round up its victims: Chechens were ordered to gather in public on February 23 to celebrate the Soviet holiday of Red Army Day. The festivities consisted of a public reading
of a decree branding the Chechens as traitors and announcing their
deportation. The work of deportation was swift and easy, as Beria reported at the end of the day: "The deportation is going on under
normal conditions. There are no serious accidents." A snowstorm
caused only minor delays, and by February 25 most of the Chechens
and Ingush had been rounded up. All that remained was mopping
up, hunting for Chechens and Ingushes scattered in different regions
of the Caucasus. The Chechens and Ingushes made up the largest,
but not the last cohort to be expelled from the Caucasus. In March
1944 the Balkars (Balkarians), one of several ethnic groups in the
Autonomous Soviet Socialist Republic of Kabardino-Balkar, a mixed
region in the North Caucasus, traveled east in cattle cars to Kazakhstan and Kyrgystan. The decree for their deportation came on
March 5, the deportations began on March 8, and by the end of the
next day the Balkars were gone.[92]

It took only minutes to drive civilians out of their homes, but
transport east was a long, slow ordeal for the Chechens, Ingushes,

and others traveling east from the Caucasus. The very speed of massive deportations caused chaos on the Soviet rail system. One witness to the transports east saw "an unbelievable sight: an extremely long train, made up of heated freight cars, jammed full of people who looked like Caucasian Mountaineers. They were being taken off somewhere toward the east, women, children, old people, all." Many died en route from frigid weather, lack of food, and disease. "Typhus was widely spread among us," wrote an Ingush who had been a Communist party official. "There was no medical help. During short stops . . . we buried the dead in the snow covered in black soot near the train." Going any farther than five meters away would mean being "shot in place."[93]

Soon after Soviet forces retook the Crimean peninsula in April 1944, they deported Muslim Tatars. On May 17–18, 1944, the entire Tatar population was deported. The order to leave came with shocking swiftness. As one survivor recalled, "At 3:00 in the morning . . . the soldiers came in and demanded that we gather ourselves together and leave in five minutes." The NKVD broke into Tatar homes.[94] Men were separated from women and children and sent to forced labor. The Tatars' journey east to special settlements and collectives in Central Asia took weeks, and many died in transit. Even after all Tatars were gone from the Crimea, Soviet authorities sought to wipe their memory from the map by changing all Tatar as well as Greek and German place names.

Forced from their homelands as a collective punishment, the deported struggled to survive in special settlements in Central Asia and Siberia. The largest number of Chechens ended up in Kazakhstan, and the bulk of Crimean Tatars were sent to Uzbekistan. They worked at hard physical labor in an unfamiliar climate with inadequate food and shelter. Many died—the NKVD listed 144,705 deaths among deported Chechens, Ingushes, Balkarians, and Karachai between 1944 and 1948, and Tatars also died in large numbers during their first few years in Central Asia.[95] Only after Stalin's death did their fortunes slowly improve. Beginning in 1956, Nikita Khrushchev ended the exile of many of the deported people of the

Caucasus, and some regained autonomous regions. The late 1950s saw tens of thousands of Karachai, Balkars, Kalmyks, Chechens, and Ingush return home. But the Crimean Tatars remained in exile for decades longer.

"The Peasants Started to Kill Each Other"

The swift Soviet deportations in the Caucasus and the Crimea offered a terrifying display of state power, but elsewhere on the eastern front a temporary power vacuum also encouraged ethnic cleansing. This was, of course, not the first time that imperial collapse created fertile conditions for ethnic cleansing. Decades earlier the collapse of Europe's old land empires prompted wars to control and purify national homelands. Now, in the last years of World War II, the fall of a new and very short-lived empire, Nazi Germany, also generated ethnic cleansing.

It may seem odd to speak of collapsing state power in a war waged between two of the strongest dictatorships in world history, but between 1942 and 1944 the struggle between Nazi Germany and the USSR created just such conditions in Ukraine. The German hold over Ukraine eroded before the Soviets took over. As German power waned, Ukrainian and Polish bands went to war against each other. Both sides aimed to build a nation-state out of the wreckage of empire: Ukrainians fought to establish a Ukrainian state, Poles fought to revive Poland. In this war within a larger war, both Ukrainian and Polish bands carried out ethnic cleansing. Poles were most vulnerable in the east in Volhynia, where they made up an increasingly isolated minority; the two sides were more evenly matched in the west in Galicia.

As the war turned against Germany, the Organization of Ukrainian Nationalists (OUN) began a war against Poles. Always hostile to Poland, the OUN had grown increasingly radical during the war. It split into two factions identified by their leaders—the OUN-Bandera and the OUN-Melnyk. Despite Stepan Bandera's arrest and imprisonment, and the death of most of its leaders at German hands, the

OUN-Bandera, the most extreme branch of the Ukrainian nationalist movement, overpowered the OUN-Melnyk. The OUN had never
been moderate, but the destruction of an older generation of Ukrainian leaders during occupation, and the violence of a war of extermination in which Ukrainian police worked alongside German forces,
created an OUN-Bandera ready to kill Poles.[96]

Waves of killing in the Polish-Ukrainian borderlands gave ethnic
war a broad base. A long prior history of nationalist activity was apparently not necessary for individuals to join in the carnage. Killing
cycles drew in Poles and Ukrainians desperate for revenge. Jews who
escaped the ghettos and death camps for the countryside were struck
by the ferocity of the Polish-Ukrainian war. Nahum Kohn, a Jewish
partisan, witnessed the breakdown of Polish-Ukrainian relations
while convalescing at Yarmelko, a small town where Poles and
Ukrainians lived alongside each other. "The peasants started to kill
each other; Ukrainians and Poles were burning down each other's
places." Kohn had seen his own friends and comrades killed, but this
sudden shift from close relations to killing shocked him. He described
one Polish village where Poles and Ukrainians "were even guests at
each other's feasts and celebrations. Suddenly, centuries of friendship
were erased and replaced by more than just murder—by a barbarity
and sadism I could never have even imagined." After escaping the
Lvov ghetto, Dr. Samuel Drix observed the war in eastern Galicia in
early 1944. Evening brought "a local mass migration, in opposite directions." Poles and Ukrainians left their homes to take refuge in
their respective strongholds. Those who stayed home after nightfall
risked death.[97]

Waldemar Lotnik, a Polish fighter, similarly recalled a war of
constant revenge that made combatants eager to exterminate their national rival. His memoir provides invaluable insight into the psychol-
ogy of ethnic war and ethnic cleansing because the men who carry out
such violence so seldom provide open and reflective accounts of their
own part in the killing. A turning point for Lotnik came in December
1943 when local Ukrainian fighters killed his uncles. Going to the funeral, his "heart filled with hatred for the Ukrainians and I swore to

avenge my uncles' deaths." In revenge, Lotnik and his comrades killed
sixteen Ukrainians, "including an eight-year-old schoolboy," shot by
accident. Ukrainians responded by "wiping out an entire Polish
colony." Polish fighters, in turn, attacked "an even bigger Ukrainian
village and this time two or three men in our unit killed women and
children." At the time, Lotnik recalled, "I felt no remorse for my part
in what happened: this was war and revenge at last." One Polish
fighter, whom Lotnik called Jackal, "lived only for revenge." His family had been killed in a raid. "He continued to exist solely for the purpose of killing and torturing Ukrainians."[98]

On the Ukrainian side, the OUN-Bandera's Ukrainian Insurgent
Army (UPA) provided the shock troops for the campaign to rid a future Ukraine of Poles. The Ukrainian assault gained the upper hand
in Volhynia. Germans reported that the Ukrainians killed Poles and
burned Polish villages. The cleansing campaign peaked in July 1943.
The UPA carried out 167 attacks on the night of July 11–12. In all,
some forty thousand to sixty thousand Poles died in Volhynia in
1943.[99]

Ukrainian peasants joined the UPA in killing Poles. The UPA
mobilized peasants through a paramilitary organization known as
the Kushch Self-Defense units or SKV. Even survivors who described
Ukrainians as rescuers also told of Ukrainians who killed their Polish neighbors and wanted them dead. When a Polish girl wounded
in the attack on her village in July 1943 asked a Ukrainian neighbor
for bread, she was told, "You Polish brat! Are you still alive?" Germans witnessed the pattern of Ukrainian participation in attacks on
Poles. In June 1943 a high-ranking occupation official for Volhynia
noted, "Many Polish families were wiped out and whole Polish villages burned. . . . It should be stressed that the greater part of the
Ukrainian population take part in this."[100]

Poland and Czechoslovakia Reborn

In much of Eastern and Central Europe, both Nazis and their victims embraced ethnic cleansing. Germans looked to ethnic cleansing

to create racist empire, Ukrainians hoped to build a national homeland, and Poles and Czechs saw ethnic cleansing as a vehicle for national resurrection. In the midst of war, Polish and Czech leaders of diverse political views planned to replace German occupation with purified nation-states. Polish leaders, for example, agreed that a revived Poland should be as exclusively Polish as possible. This meant not Jewish, Ukrainian, or German—all were significant minority populations in the prewar Polish republic. Resolving the Jewish question was perhaps the easiest task. Before the war, Polish politicians had proposed mass Jewish emigration out of the country to Madagascar or some other destination, and even after Poland's defeat, they continued, either in exile or in hiding, to discuss how to create a Poland without Jews. Polish organizations were not responsible for the Holocaust, but the wartime Polish underground press revealed an interest in ridding Poland of Jews. As one underground paper declared in November 1943, "We must strive that after the war Jews do not return to Poland but remain where they are or go to Palestine."[101] As it turned out, almost no action was necessary to accomplish this goal, though pogroms in 1946 discouraged the very small minority of surviving Polish Jews from contemplating a future in Poland.

The main contenders for power in a liberated Poland also favored a future Poland without Germans. Polish exiles in London during the war wanted to move Poland's border west and evict large numbers of ethnic Germans. In December 1942 the Polish Government in Exile called for postwar Poland to receive several regions with large German populations, including East Prussia, Danzig, and much of Upper Silesia. This did not necessarily require expulsion of all Germans: General Sikorski, leader of the Polish Government in Exile, suggested that many residents of East Prussia were members of non-German ethnic minorities with Polish roots. Even so, Sikorski spoke of transferring Germans to protect the security of a new Poland against "Fifth column activities." Polish Communists, for their part, increasingly shared the desire for a future Poland without Germans. On August 28, 1944, Edward Osobka-Morawksi of the Lublin Committee, the Polish government established by the Soviet Union, said, "We will not have a German minority."[102]

Czech leaders similarly contemplated a nation reborn without troublesome minorities. As the controversial case of Czech President Eduard Beneš suggests, their chief concern was with Germans. Beneš believed that the Sudeten Germans had aided the Nazis by acting as a fifth column, and he concluded that a liberated Czechoslovakia had to be free of Germans. We do not know exactly when he came to a definitive decision that Czechoslovakia could have no Germans. For several years he continued to work on proposals for reducing the country's German population through a combination of border adjustments and resettlement. But Beneš's position became increasingly clear by early 1943 as he lobbied for a large-scale postwar transfer. In February 1943 he told C. L. Sulzberger of the *New York Times* that "the minority questions of Central and Eastern Europe should be settled this time radically and definitively." What Beneš had in mind truly was radical. Asked whether this meant expelling all Germans and Hungarians from a new Czechoslovakia, he was unequivocal. "Yes," he told Sulzberger, "surely as many as possible."[103]

Europe's War of Ethnic Cleansing

From Germany to the Caucasus, from Yugoslavia to Poland, World War II in Europe was truly a heyday for ethnic cleansing. Like the Balkan Wars, World War I, and the Greek-Turkish War, World War II remade the ethnic and religious map of Central and Eastern Europe. Where earlier wars had shifted populations most notably in former Ottoman territories, this new war led to the displacement and destruction of peoples across a much broader area from Germany to Russia. The most catastrophic result was the annihilation of Jews, erased from most of Central and Eastern Europe. War also ended the Polish presence in Volhynia.

The cumulative effect of genocide and ethnic cleansing permanently altered the makeup of many towns and cities. In Galicia, for example, the city of Lvov, a city of Poles, Jews, Ukrainians, and Germans, became Lviv—a Ukrainian city. The old city was gone. After hiding in the countryside, Dr. Samuel Drix returned to Lvov in 1944. Only 700 of the 160,000 Jews in Lvov as of 1941 were known to have survived. Through chance Drix learned that his wife Frania was among the dead. One day he ran into an old acquaintance, Rudolf Reder. One of only two Jews known to have survived the death camp at Belzec, Reder was able to tell Drix about Frania's fate because he had traveled to Belzec in August 1942 on the same train as Frania, her mother, and her grandmother. Drix worked in Lvov until he was evacuated in June 1945, but he now saw the city differently. "I was leaving behind Lwow, my beloved city," he recalled. As a child and as a young man he had always looked forward to returning home from vacation: "I was always happy when I was coming back." All that had changed. Now Drix left "the city where I suffered so much, and where there was no one left for me." Jacob Gerstenfeld, who visited Lvov in 1943 disguised as a German soldier, expressed even greater bitterness. For Gerstenfeld, Lvov was the city of his youth: "Here I had been born, gone to school, fallen in love for the first time." But he no longer wanted anything to do with the place. "Now the city only stirred up hate on my part."[104]

Others who left Lvov remembered the old city almost obsessively. The poet Adam Zagajewski left Lvov as a baby along with his family in October 1945. Along with other Poles they moved west into Poland. Zagajewski's family talked continuously of Lvov, and how superior it was to their new hometown, the industrial city of Gliwice, the former Gleiwitz. Zagajewski himself could not remember Lvov, but he soon learned that everything was better there, or, as he put it, "for many years afterward I was told about the extraordinarily beautiful city (Lvov) that my family had to leave."[105]

There were many Lvovs, towns and cities transformed by war; and the violence that remade Central and Eastern Europe had many authors. Nazi leaders stand at the top of any list of those responsible for extermination, but a general acceptance of the legitimacy of ethnic cleansing was one of the few things that united Europeans divided by war. Ethnic cleansing appealed to Germans as a way to reshape most of a continent, to Soviet leaders as an appropriate punishment for those deemed disloyal in the Great Patriotic War, and to a host of Eastern and Central European nationalists as a just revenge against supposed traitor peoples and as a means to build and restore national homelands.

What bound Europeans in this common belief? Obviously it was not simply their politics. True, *genocide* occurred only under the worst of dictatorships, but Nazis, fascists of varied stripes, nationalists, Communists, and even democratic leaders all considered mass expulsion, though not all of them championed extermination. Control over a powerful state was useful for developing and carrying out ethnic cleansing, but the expulsions that drove countless civilians across the wartime landscape did not emanate simply from orders from above. It was not only Europe's leaders who embraced ethnic cleansing. So too did many Europeans, and war only deepened their conviction that removing entire peoples was not only necessary but desirable.

It is impossible to say how many ordinary people took part in ethnic cleansing or in related violence, but the number was great. Looking back at the war, we tend to generalize about killers, but we take pains to search out and catalog examples of uplifting behavior. With the exception of truly famous masters of murder such as Himmler, many of the individuals who carried out extermination remain obscure, but every year brings more books detailing the exploits of rescuers. There is nothing intrinsically wrong with this, but collectively this trend presents a misleading picture in which we know a great deal about the virtuous but relatively little about those who profited from a neighbor's misfortune or even attacked or killed that neighbor. For instance, the Israeli Holocaust Memorial Yad Vashem keeps a listing of people identified as the "Righteous among Nations"—non-Jews "who risked their lives to rescue Jews." This is a fascinating and useful project, but there is no opposite effort to detail all the non-Jews who attacked or killed Jews, let alone all the other Europeans, Poles, Ukrainians, Croats, Serbs, Romanians, and others who took part in massacres or ethnic cleansing during World War II.

In a war in which people of many nationalities took part in attacking and killing Jews, anti-Semitic violence was not a uniquely or even distinctively German activity. Equating the Nazi hatred of Jews with earlier German prejudice also understates the intensity of Nazi anti-Semitism. Suppose, however, for the sake of argument, we accept the notion that German anti-Semitism helped to drive a search for a Final Solution for a people who in no way contested German power. We would still be unable to explain much of the violence of the war. German hatred of Jews did not cause Lithuanians, Poles, Ukrainians, or Romanians to attack Jews, and German anti-Semitism certainly does not explain ethnic wars where the victims were not Jews.

What, then, led many ordinary Europeans to take part in pogroms, ethnic cleansing, or genocide? There was no single cause. Europeans carried out ethnic cleansing for a host of reasons. Sometimes they deported or killed civilians because they were told to do so or because it was their job. Sometimes they looted for personal gain, and sometimes they actually enjoyed violence. But none of these explanations is sufficient in itself. In World War II as in previous European wars looting frequently accompanied ethnic cleansing. Such opportunism may well have dulled responses to suffering, but it does not follow that desire for victims' property was the chief motive for ethnic cleansing. As for following orders, this was undoubtedly a major motive, but even here many common assumptions fall apart. NKVD personnel were doing their job when they rounded up entire peoples in the Caucasus, and the men in Einsatzgruppen were working when they killed. But at least in the case of the Holocaust the Germans who murdered Jews did not face the choice of kill or be killed. Almost everyone who begins to study the Holocaust assumes that those who killed Jews feared death themselves, but there is simply no evidence that any German was executed for failing to murder Jews.[106]

In part, Europeans joined in ethnic cleansing during World War II because they were ready to do so. The ideas of ethnic cleansing

were not new. Examples of mass murder and population exchange
from World War I and its immediate aftermath remained fresh in
memory, and talk of massive programs of resettlement was commonplace among varied nationalist movements in the 1930s. War
provided an opportunity for transforming these ideas into plans and
for realizing them. The scale of violence was shocking, but the
strong desire to move entire populations should not have come as a
surprise.

World War II, like earlier periods of ethnic cleansing, was a
time when powerful currents of nationalism swept across Europe.
The intensity of racism was new, but many of the themes and mo-
tifs of wartime nationalism were older. Nationalist extremists who
seized war as a chance to realize their dreams typically depicted
their own nation as victimized and betrayed. Much like Balkan nationalists during the nineteenth and early twentieth centuries who
told stories of bloodthirsty Turks, or Turkish national extremists
during World War I who told stories of treasonous Armenians, nationalists during World War II were fond of stories of national oppression. They told stories of deceit by Serbs, Poles, Ukrainians,
Germans, and, above all, Jews. The villains in such stories were typically close at hand and, according to the stories, richly deserved
their destruction.

Stories, of course, do not by themselves turn people into thieves
and murderers, but the nationalist stories of Europe's war were powerful because they changed the way many residents of Central and
Eastern Europe looked at people who lived nearby but spoke different languages or practiced another religion. In nationalist stories,
these people were not simply different; they belonged to enemy and
traitor peoples. Once you are convinced that a nearby religious or
ethnic group really does present a long-standing threat to your own
nation, the ordinary acquaintance or neighbor of everyday life no
longer seems ordinary. If you join in looting, pogroms, or massacres,
you are no longer attacking a Jewish, or Polish, or Ukrainian, or Serb
acquaintance or passersby. Instead you are taking part in combat
against the historical enemies of your own nation. Whether these

claims are true or false no longer matters: a persuasive fiction can easily overpower a complex reality.

War and occupation brought the nationalist stories of betrayal and victimization to life. In the case of Jews, claims of treason furnished the key justification for anti-Semitic violence. Stories of betrayal linked the present with a past in which Jews were always an alien enemy people. Many residents of Eastern Europe held back from attacking Jews, and some at great personal risk aided Jews. For others, however, alleged Jewish complicity with Soviet occupiers proved once and for all that Jews were enemies of Romanians, or Poles, or Ukrainians, or Lithuanians.

In other cases, cycles of revenge killing played the key role in convincing Europeans that their neighbors truly were enemies. Before the war it required a leap of faith to accept the manifestos of groups such as the OUN or the Ustasha. Once killing began, revenge offered a new motive for taking part in ethnic cleansing. Each round of killing by Poles, or Ukrainians, or Ustasha, or Chetniks proved that a neighboring nation really was as evil as nationalist extremists had claimed. Such revenge killing was an especially important agent for spreading ethnic war in regions where states collapsed during World War II.

Europe's war of ethnic cleansing and genocide created new memories of suffering. These memories were most likely to contribute to future conflict in regions that were not fully ethnically cleansed. Jews were gone from much of Central and Eastern Europe, and Ukrainians and Poles would never again fight for Volhynia, but conditions were different in both Yugoslavia and the Caucasus. Serbs, Croats, and Muslims remained in close proximity in Yugoslavia, and Chechens and Ingush returned from exile to the North Caucasus, though without fully recovering their former homelands.

Past violence did not make future ethnic cleansing inevitable, but World War II left long-lasting divisions in both Yugoslavia and the North Caucasus. The new Yugoslav regime created by Tito's victorious partisans executed the Chetnik leader Mihailovic and declared all south Slavs to be brothers. But even under Tito, Serbs and

Croats remembered the war very differently. Many residents of the North Caucasus were also divided by memory. Even after returning to the North Caucasus, the Chechen and Ingush remembered life and death in special settlements. They remembered lost land—some of which was never returned. Chechens and Ingush lived close by Russians, especially in towns and cities, but these adjacent communities had drastically different memories of the war. For years these memories of suffering and violence produced little noticeable political effect, but they provided a core of powerful stories for national revival when Communist rule weakened decades later.

CHAPTER SIX

"The Land of the Poles That Is Lost to the Germans"

POLAND, CZECHOSLOVAKIA, ROMANIA, USSR, AND YUGOSLAVIA, 1945–1954

In 1939 the old Baltic port of Danzig was a predominantly German city that between the world wars had belonged to neither Germany nor Poland. The Treaty of Versailles took Danzig away from Germany but did not award the city to Poland. Instead Danzig became a "Free City" with its own government and constitution. Poland had a customs union with Danzig and the right to run a post office in the free city.

In 1939, as he prepared for war against Poland, Adolf Hitler exploited complaints about alleged Polish mistreatment of Danzig's Germans in a propaganda campaign. In negotiations with Britain's ambassador in late August 1939, Hitler demanded Danzig, but the city's status had become little more than a pretext for German aggression. The Führer wanted Danzig, but he wanted much more. The city fell quickly when Germany attacked Poland on September 1, 1939, but of course German troops did not stop with the formerly Free City or with the strip of territory (this so-called Polish Corridor) that had separated the German region of East Prussia from the rest of Germany between the world wars.

Danzig's history before and during World War II provides the backdrop for the most famous work of postwar German literature, Günter Grass's novel *The Tin Drum*. The novel is not autobiography. The Nobel Laureate Grass, unlike his protagonist Oskar Matzerath, did not stunt his growth by throwing himself down the cellar stairs on his third birthday. And Grass, unlike Oskar, was surely unable to break glass with his voice. But clearly Grass did draw on his own family background to create Oskar's family. Grass is the most famous German writer of his generation, but his mother was not German. She, like Oskar's mother, was a member of a Slavic ethnic group called the Kashubians. Grass's mother, like Matzerath's mother, had a favorite cousin, also a Kashubian, who worked at Danzig's Polish post office. (In *The Tin Drum*, Oskar is present at the post office during the attack in which his uncle is taken captive and soon after executed.)

For a few years during World War II, Danzig was part of a vast German empire, but as of 1945 it ceased to be German at all. Germany's defeat in World War II marked the end of a German Danzig. The fictional Oskar Matzerath as well as hundreds of thousands of real Germans left the city for good. "I look for the land of the Poles," Grass writes in *The Tin Drum*, "that is lost to the Germans, for the moment at least."[1]

For the second time in less than three decades, the collapse of empires brought ethnic cleansing. At the end of World War I, the demise of the Ottoman and Russian empires led to pogroms, ethnic wars, and ethnic cleansing, and with the end of World War II, the collapse of the Third Reich generated involuntary mass migration. Large numbers of Hungarians, Poles, Ukrainians, and Italians lost their homes, but this was above all a disaster for Germans. In an inversion of the racial order of the war, the first, the Germans, became last. Just as German advance across Central and Eastern Europe brought ethnic cleansing, so too did German retreat, but with a key distinction: it was Germans who now lost their homes. Millions fled west before the war's end, and soon after Germany's final defeat millions more were forced out of their homes by militia units, by new governing authorities, and even by their neighbors.

GERMANY, 1945

----- Germany in 1937
----- Occupation zones in 1945

Twelve million to fourteen million fled or were transferred, and many died. For years afterward, the flight and forced transfer of these Germans so shaped their identity that they became known as the "expellees."[2]

Germans have always known the story of the expellees, but for many years the flight and expulsion of Germans remained almost unknown outside the directly affected regions. Indeed it was barely taught or even mentioned among historians of Germany in the United States. The reasons for this omission were not mysterious. Other topics, such as the rise of Hitler and the causes of the Holocaust, attracted more attention, and dwelling too much on German suffering might have seemed to be offering an excuse for Germans to avoid coming to terms with their own country's responsibility for war and extermination. But by the numbers, the exodus of Germans at the end of World War II was the largest single population movement in modern European history.

This was not the first time a large part of a European nation lost its homeland following a failed campaign waged in part in their name. The mere hint of a comparison between Nazi Germany and any other country can provoke protest because no other European state matched Nazi Germany's combination of terror and racism. Still, the fate of Turkey's Greeks after World War I could have provided a warning about what was to come for Germans outside Germany. The Greek nationalists who invaded Asia Minor in 1919 (though not fascists) sought to extend the Greek state into regions where Greeks made up only a minority of the population. Their endeavor ended in defeat for Greece and disaster for the Greeks who had lived in Turkey. As World War II ended, the collapse of Nazi attempts to create a German empire in the east led to similar catastrophe for ethnic Germans. Indeed, the outcome was even worse. Not only Germans living beyond prewar German boundaries lost their homes, but also many who had long resided *within* Germany— because much of what had been Germany became Russian or Polish territory. In 1943, Churchill, Roosevelt, and Stalin, meeting at Teheran, had agreed that the Soviet and Polish postwar borders would be shifted west, and in 1945 the Soviets insisted on pushing the new Polish frontier all the way west to the Oder River and the western Neisse River.[3]

"Province on the Roads"

Defeat came as a shock to many Germans. It should not have: the boom of Soviet artillery approaching ever closer signaled German defeat, but German civilians clung to the dream of victory, whether because they believed Nazi claims that secret weapons could win the war, or because they simply could not conceive of defeat. Nothing could prepare some Germans for the truth. When wounded German soldiers warned that the Russians could not be stopped, one German resident of Pillau, a Baltic port east of Danzig, recalled, "Not one of us fundamentally believed it." Even some who had already witnessed Soviet victory professed astonishment at Germany's final de-

feat. Take, for instance, the response to the war's end by Erika Fronius, a German from Romania. Fronius was deported to Ukraine in
January 1945, so she was slow to learn of the war's outcome. When
news reached her in June 1945, she wrote, "We simply can not grasp
the disappointment that Germany has capitulated."[4]

The final shocking recognition of defeat filled Germans with
dread. From the Soviets, Germans expected revenge. Few defeated
nations ever feared their conquerors more than Germans feared the
Soviets in 1944 and 1945. Germans saw their doom in an image of
Soviet soldiers they had formed during Nazi Germany's racial war in
the east. Although Germany had invaded the Soviet Union, many
Germans perceived the war in the east as a defensive struggle to protect Germany, perhaps even European civilization, from communism and Asiatic hordes.[5] Nazi propaganda cast the war as a racial
struggle against Soviet "Mongol" troops, and German civilians in-
ternalized these images. News of killings of Germans at Nemmers-
dorf, an East Prussian village briefly taken by Soviet advance forces
in October 1944, appeared to confirm that terror would arrive with
the Red Army.

Rather than wait to meet their conquerors, many Germans—
some three million to four million or more—fled before the Red
Army arrived. The German exodus took place in several major
pulses. Flight began in the Balkans in autumn 1944 as German defenses crumbled in southeastern Europe, and then intensified in
winter in the historic core of Prussia along the Baltic Sea and in East
Prussia. To the south, another torrent of German refugees started
out from Silesia for points west.

Germans living in the Balkans were the first to face the decision
of whether to stay or go. These Germans included the Siebenbürger
Saxons, descendants of Germans who settled in Transylvania during
the Middle Ages, and the Donau-Schwaben or Danube Swabians who
lived along the Danube River and its tributaries. A majority of Germans stayed after Romania capitulated on August 23, 1944, but thousands began to leave soon afterward, and almost 100,000 ethnic Germans from Romania reached Germany by the war's end.[6] Despite the

news from the east, flight developed gradually in Yugoslavia. German authorities were slow to order evacuation, perhaps because they did not wish to suggest that defeat was inevitable, and they gave German civilians conflicting signals, telling them to leave one day and wait the next. For their part, many of the Danube Swabians wished to stay put. A journey to Germany, whether by land or along mined rivers, was risky, and Germany was not their home. Some decided to leave only at the last moment. One German woman who lived north of Belgrade saw German refugees pass by, but she and her family still did not want to leave. Then, as the front approached, they suddenly changed their minds and left on October 11.[7] Weighing attachment to home against fear of their fate after Germany's defeat, half of Yugoslavia's ethnic Germans—more than 200,000 people—chose to flee.

In late 1944 another stream of German refugees began to flow in regions along the east coast of the Baltic Sea, including the port of Memel. Germany lost Memel under the Treaty of Versailles (Lithuania occupied it in 1923), retook the city in March 1939, and lost it for good in January 1945. German farmers first fled in August 1944, only to return home, but in early October retreating German soldiers told the Germans of Memel that the war's end was near. They "encouraged us to immediate flight," one recalled. Ethnic German refugees from the east coast of the Baltic continued to press into East Prussia throughout the fall of 1944. By year's end as many as 500,000 people fled or were sent west as part of official evacuation.[8]

As Soviet forces began a new offensive into Prussia in January 1945, Germans scattered from their homes. In the countryside outside of Königsberg, the historic German port and chief city of East Prussia, "every road was overfilled as far as the eye could see with refugee wagons, migrating people, and free running animals." The sheer numbers of refugees might have calmed German nationalists long anxious that there were too few Germans in the east—if only Germans had not been leaving. One refugee from East Prussia described a "province on the road." The sound of guns and the sight of Russian planes prompted haste, but the crowds, debris, broken carts, and car wrecks made progress slow. So too did the German military, which ordered civilian refugees off the main roads, whether because commanders thought they could still resist the Soviet advance or because they thought military equipment more important than people. The treks of refugees piled up behind one another, causing hour-long traffic jams. The cold, the roads lined with wrecks, and sheer physical exhaustion combined to make flight a labor of Sisyphus for many. Lore Ehrich, a German from Sensburg East Prussia who started out on a winter's day, found herself trying to pull a child's wagon along in the snow, a task that she recalled brought us to "hopeless despair."[9]

A railway journey promised the fastest way out of East Prussia, and many Germans took trains west from Königsberg. But the heavy traffic soon caused massive delays. By January 21 trains waited for four days. Then the route closed up entirely: Soviet forces punched through German defenses, cut rail lines, and reached the Baltic coast. The news caused despair in towns to the east. Trains crowded with refugees turned back to Königsberg, now the center of a shrinking German island between the Red Army and the Baltic Sea.

The same cold winter that added to refugees' torment brought them one benefit: it froze the Frische Haff, a narrow arm of the sea that separates the coast from a spit of land along the open ocean. Refugees trapped along the East Prussian coast crossed the ice to the port of Pillau on the edge of a peninsula. "Household goods" littered across an ice channel testified to the refugees' desperation. There was enough ice that winter to attempt the crossing, but not enough for safety. The weight of the fleeing Germans and their goods was sometimes too great, and one refugee recalled that "many found death in the ice cold waters."[10] Corpses washed ashore that spring.

Once the Red Army cut off land routes, the last way out for Germans trapped along the coast of East Prussia was by ship. Some two million Germans, including refugees and soldiers, managed to escape by sea, but finding a spot on a ship was itself an ordeal. At Pillau refugees competed to find a place on a ship, and even that did not guarantee escape: some steamers took refugees only as far west as Danzig, leaving them to find a spot on another ship. Danzig teemed with refugees, and many never made it out before advancing Soviet forces surrounded the city. As of March 1945, close to 500,000 Germans remained in the shrinking region still under German control around Danzig, and perhaps only half of these managed to flee before Soviet forces occupied the city on March 30, 1945.[11]

Others fortunate enough to board a westbound steamer faced new perils as the ships traveled waterways laden with mines and patrolled by Allied aircraft and Soviet submarines. On January 30 a Soviet submarine sank a refitted German cruise ship, the *Wilhelm Gustloff*, off the coast of Pomerania. Some nine thousand people died, the highest death toll in any shipping disaster in world history. The sinking of the *Gustloff* forms a central episode in Günter Grass's novel *Crabwalk*, a book whose publication in 2002 contributed to a revival of interest in German flight and expulsion at the end of World War II. A survivor of another maritime tragedy, R. Otto Frisch, a retired teacher from Königsberg stranded at Pillau, managed to board the steamer *Karlsruhe* along with his daughter and two of his grandchildren in April 1945. Aircraft sank the ship, leaving only about 150 survivors, including Frisch and one of his grandchildren, out of the 1,000 passengers on board.[12]

To the south, another vast wave of German refugees passed through Silesia. After the war Silesia made up a region of southwestern Poland along the Upper Oder River, north of the Sudetes Mountains, but in 1945 it had been German or at least Prussian since the victories of Frederick the Great in the eighteenth century, though a part of Upper Silesia had been transferred to Poland in 1921. Many Silesian Germans waited for orders to evacuate, but hundreds of thousands still fled, some only hours before Soviet forces arrived. As in Prussia, refugee columns piled up on the roads. At Silesia's largest city, Breslau, a priest named Paul Peikert watched refugees pour through the town "day and night." Evacuation orders caused panic. Breslau's main railway station was a crush of humanity as the city's residents sought a way out on a westbound train.

Waiting hours and even days for a place on a train, people lost their luggage, and "mothers," Peikert noted, "often lost their children."[13] In all, some 150,000 to 180,000 civilians remained in the city when it fell under a Soviet siege that lasted from February 15 through April 1945.

"Watches, Watches"

In much of the former German east, Soviet victory brought a reign of terror against Germans. These were not simply crimes of opportunity: soldiers of the Red Army wanted to punish Germans. The unparalleled destruction on the eastern front created rage, and Soviet wartime publicity, such as the writings of the war correspondent Ilya Ehrenburg, identified the German people as a whole with Hitler's regime. Diaries, memoirs, and soldiers' letters displayed deep anger toward Germans and a desire for vengeance. As one letter from the field in early 1945 put it, "We march further forward every day through East Prussia. And we take revenge on the Germans."[14]

German women feared and suffered much of the worst treatment. In her memoir of the war's end in Danzig, Lisa Barendt, a twenty-eight-year-old widow with three children, told of her "terrible fear" at seeing a first Russian soldier. Her initial contact with Soviet troops was even worse than she had imagined. Soviet soldiers entered her home, briefly interrogated her to find out that her husband had not been in the SS, dragged her children away, threw her into a side room, and assaulted her. Barendt met thirteen- and fourteen-year-olds who had been raped. Danzig was not unusual. A resident of Pomerania, for example, recalled of the early days of Soviet occupation beginning in late February 1945 that "almost all women were raped."[15]

Soviet occupation also brought a wave of looting: any and all German property was fair game. Germans who encountered Soviet troops in Prussia, Silesia, or elsewhere remembered the near ubiquitous order: "watches, watches." Russians grabbed Lisa Barendt's wedding ring and watch soon after she had been assaulted.[16] In the countryside Soviets also seized farm animals, though their attempts to march cattle west typically left many dead along the sides of roads.

Occupation was not all rape, theft, and killing. After the initial terror wave, Soviet commanders sought to reassert discipline. Especially in the countryside, Russians even emerged as protectors, defending Germans against Poles, or, in a more cynical interpretation, assisting young German women. Germans recalled acts of kindness mixed with brutality: Soviet soldiers stole, but they also handed children food. Egon Buddatsch, a thirteen-year-old boy who lived on the outskirts of Danzig and lost his mother when she was mortally wounded by a Russian shell, witnessed looting and rapes. But Russian soldiers also gave him and his younger brother food. "We found out that Russian soldiers in general were quite friendly toward us children." A former German municipal official from Breslau similarly observed that a "Russian soldier shares his last piece of bread with German children." But Russian soldiers also plundered.[17]

Along with watches and jewelry, the conquerors took Germans themselves for forced labor. Some 400,000 were sent east to work in the Soviet Union. As far south as Romania, ethnic Germans feared transport east for labor. A German photographer from Romania, Hertha Bazant, noted in early January 1945 that her daughter Trudi and her friends already lived in dread of being sent to Russia. The police came repeatedly to their house even as Russian patrols and Romanian police seized "Saxons" off the streets. "Behind the entire action," Bazant claimed, revealing her own anti-Semitism, "was the Jew with cold, lurking eyes."[18] As Bazant had feared, Trudi was soon fetched by the police. Why, Bazant wondered, should her only child be given up into "Russian slavery"? Romania's Saxons were Romanian citizens like Romanians and Hungarians, "only much better." Trudi did not return home for more than four years.

In Bucharest, a pair of Allied intelligence officers witnessed abductions firsthand. They described a "slave hunt." Military and police trucks blocked streets, and detachments that included civilians then went door to door. "When they stopped at a house where a victim lived, the leader would glance at his list and give his men one or more names. . . . If the door was not opened promptly, they brought it crashing down." From their houses, the victims were taken to a train station, placed in boxcars, and shipped east.[19]

Like so many other civilians sent across Europe since 1939, Germans traveled where they did not want to go. Trainloads of Germans, sometimes as many as 120 to a car, were sent to Ukraine, the Urals, Central Asia, and Siberia. German captives did not know their exact destination, but their journey east into the Soviet Union was filled with ill omens. The dressmaker Anna Schwartz, deported from Danzig, recalled how the sight of snow caused "horror . . . Siberia was mentioned."[20] The journey east by rail could last days or weeks, and without adequate food or water many died en route.

Germans worked for up to twelve to fourteen hours a day in labor camps, factories, collectives, and mines. Months, even years, of day-long labor in harsh conditions broke many. Survivors spoke of staggering mortality rates. The mood was grim to the point of despair. In November 1946, Friedrich Wilhelm Göckler, a Siebenburger Saxon who had been taken from his home in Romania, recorded in his diary that his mood was "less than zero."[21] Christmas 1946, his second in the Soviet Union, left him thinking of his past life. "Great and benevolent God," he wrote, "let us not despair and send us once again the fortune, to all come together again with our loved ones." Göckler died on February 21, 1947, at the age of forty-one.

"This Time It Was the Poles Who Arrived"

Soviet terror destroyed many lives and left lasting scars, but the Red Army did not pose the greatest threat to the survival of German communities outside Germany's now-shrunken borders. The war was ending, but ethnic wars continued in new form with local assaults against Germans by Yugoslav partisans, Poles, and Czechs. These new attacks against German civilians after the defeat of German armies were not battles but low-intensity campaigns marked by massacres, executions, and systematic looting. This violence should be understood as a first step toward grassroots ethnic cleansing, in which Czechs and Poles began to force Germans out of their homes before expelling them from their homelands.

Across the ruins of the collapsing German empire, partisans and militias harassed and killed Germans. In Yugoslavia threats scrawled on houses revealed the bitter mood toward remaining Germans. Johann Wann, a German who lived east of Belgrade, recalled graffiti such as "Death for the Swabians" and the words "Here dwells Hitler, he must be struck dead" marked on his own house. These were not empty threats. Shootings began in his village on October 18, 1944, and a People's Liberation Committee soon carried out more killings. Some Serbs protected Germans, but partisans killed large numbers, and the final death toll reached sixty thousand to seventy thousand. Germans were also subjected to the same kinds of indignities once reserved for Jews and Serbs: they had to turn in such possessions as radios, motorcycles, and typewriters.[22]

Across Bohemia and the Sudetenland, Czech soldiers, partisans and militias, sometimes joined by Soviet troops, executed Germans. When a Czech military transport crossed paths on June 18, 1945, in eastern Moravia with a train filled with Germans returning to Slovkia, Lieutenant Karol Pazúr of the Defense Intelligence Service and another officer seized the Germans off the train. By 5 a.m. the next morning they had shot 265 Germans.[23] In other cases Czech forces carried out more elaborate spectacles of public humiliation. Czech partisans and Russian troops conducted a so-called "blood court" at Landskron, east of Prague, on May 17 and 18, 1945. As assembled German men held up their arms in the air for hours, partisans selected individual Germans to appear before a table where a partisan court handed out sentences: beatings of 10 to 100 blows or death by shooting or hanging. In a similar case on June 9 at Komotau, in northwest Bohemia, Czech forces ordered the entire male population—some 5,000 or more men and boys from the ages of 13 to 65—to the town square, then made 100 men remove their clothes, sing the German anthem, and say, "We thank our Führer." The proceedings ended with some 12 to 16 beaten to death. The next day Czechs drove more than 4,000 Germans toward the border, though the Soviets did not let most of them into their occupation zone.[24]

At their core, the Czech and Polish campaigns against Germans were struggles for homes and property. Soon after the Soviet army, newcomers started arriving in many predominantly German communities, including Danzig. In *The Tin Drum*, Grass writes, "This time, strange to say, no Prussians, Swedes, Saxons, or Frenchmen came after the Russians; this time it was the Poles who arrived. The Poles came bag and baggage from Vilna, Bialystok, and Lwow, all looking for living quarters." In Grass's novel the newcomer who moves into the grocery store belonging to the Matzeraths is one Mr. Fajngold, who speaks as if he is surrounded by a large family but is actually by himself. His family has died at Treblinka. A German minister from Danzig-Langfuhr, the same district where Günter Grass lived before he entered the German army, spoke of Poles streaming into the city. He described Danzig as drowning in Poles: "incredible masses of Polish proletarians flooded our city."[25]

Polish newcomers began to take over Germans' homes and land. After armies had crossed and recrossed the east, the contest for Poland often came down to personal street-by-street, apartment-by-apartment, house-by-house, farm-by-farm struggles between Poles and Germans. Poles moved into war-damaged cities and towns where many Germans still lived, and for weeks and even months the two nationalities lived side by side, though Poles often pushed Germans into the least desirable living quarters. Anna Bodschwinna, a refugee herself, was forced in February, along with three other families, out of a tiny one-room apartment in East Prussia into a "stable . . . because the apartment was needed for Poles." The cows were taken away, and the stable's new residents lived there through the rest of winter—visited nightly, Bodschwinna said, by Russian soldiers. Others lost their living space more gradually, like a German family from Posen, pushed into a "small living room" when a Polish family suddenly arrived on May 8, 1945, and took over most of the furniture and clothing.[26]

Silesia was a central arena for the struggle between Germans and Poles. Many Germans there had initially fled the Red Army while Poles arrived from afar, including the region of Lvov now slated to be part of the Soviet Ukraine. In some cases Germans and Poles crowded into the same house, but Poles soon started pushing Germans out. The actual seizure of homes proceeded with astonishing speed. German peasants who returned home one July day after attending market found their village in the Grottkau district of Upper Silesia filled with "Polish peasant wagons." Polish militia accompanying the new settlers gave Germans minutes to leave their homes to the new owners. Those who did not make it by the clock risked a beating, and so, a German witness complained, "it went homestead by homestead."[27]

Very occasionally, Silesian Germans encountered Jews as well as Poles. At Reichenbach, south of Breslau, war's end brought the dissolution of a local concentration camp and the sudden release of surviving Jewish prisoners. One German referred to these Jews as "a great plague for us." Locals began calling Reichenbach "Jew-Brook (Judenbach)." Another German from the Reichenbach district complained that the surviving camp inmates "robbed and plundered."[28] They discarded their prisoners' clothing and occupied apartments.

With the late arrival of Allied troops, the timetable of occupation was more compressed in Czechoslovakia, but here, in similar fashion, Czechs moved into many German homes in the months just after Germany's defeat. Hans Enders, a German secondary school teacher from the town of Saaz, northwest of Prague, complained that Czechs, mostly from the "lower classes," arrived with little luggage but could receive "a farm, a house or at least a German apartment" the next day.[29] Some German families were moved repeatedly to make room for Czechs, and Germans worked as day laborers for the new settlers.

Wild Expulsions

By 1945 a powerful consensus could be found in both Czechoslovakia and Poland in favor of the ethnic cleansing of Germans. Nazi aggression and years of German occupation strengthened the conviction that Germans were a traitor people who could not be part of a new Czechoslovakia or Poland. In Czechoslovakia, for example, war reinforced images of Germans as carpetbaggers and colonists who had taken over Czech lands since the seventeenth century, if not earlier. Even the Communist party spoke of regaining land purportedly seized long ago by Germans in the Thirty Years' War. In this version of history, German betrayal of Czechoslovakia in 1938 and during World War II constituted the final and vital evidence that justified mass expulsion. Czechoslovakia could never be safe unless all Germans, whatever their age or political views, were deported. Describing Czech opinion, a press review prepared by the British Foreign Office noted "a universal and burning hatred of the Germans and Magyars, and a demand that they should go, and go quickly."[30]

In both Czechoslovakia and Poland new political and military leaders favored expelling Germans. Jerzy Ziętek, acting provincial governor of Silesia, for example, declared on February 10, 1945, "We will deal with the German population inhabiting these lands, which have been Polish since before the beginning of time, just as the Germans taught us." In March the Polish military command declared that the "entire German people" shared blame for a "criminal" war.[31] The Polish military hoped to push out Germans in order to create military settlements along Poland's new western border.

Polish and Czech political and military authorities wanted Germans gone, but actual ethnic cleansing of Germans began during a period of chaos, even anarchy. The new Polish and Czech governments formed after years of harsh occupation were fragile and politically divided. A July 1945 report to the Polish state repatriation office spoke of a lack of communication between government authorities and of "chaos." But even without any well-established administration, militia units, police, and ordinary Czechs and Poles acting locally drove Germans out of their homes.[32] These were "wild expulsions," so-called because they occurred without any international organization. The contrast with the most organized expulsions of World War II, the rapid Soviet deportations in the North

Caucasus, was striking. In comparison to Soviet-style deportations, the expulsion of Germans from Czechoslovakia and Poland in the spring and early summer of 1945 was ethnic cleansing from the grass roots.

In Poland, wild expulsions targeted chiefly those Germans living near the new western border along the Oder-Neisse. Polish commanders expressly called for severe treatment of Germans. "We proceed with the Germans," declared the command of the Second Polish Army, "as they did with us." It was necessary "to carry out the task in so harsh and decisive a manner, that the German vermin do not hide in houses, but will flee from us."[33] The general details were familiar from the war, though the victims were now Germans instead of Poles: quick expulsion by small detachments of armed men, with the new refugees permitted to carry only modest luggage—20 kilograms (about 44 pounds) according to a Polish report. The early days of the operation through June 26 saw an average of 40,000 to 45,000 Germans expelled daily. This phase of wild expulsion forced some 300,000 to 400,000 or even more Germans out of Poland, though some managed to return to their homes.

The June expulsions came as a particular shock to Germans in Pomerania and Brandenburg. These were not territories seized by Germany during the war but old core provinces of Prussia. Brandenburg and Prussia had become a single state in 1618, and this state of Brandenburg Prussia had received part of Pomerania in 1648. It made almost no sense for Germans to think of these regions as Polish, and German civilians struggled to comprehend the news that they faced imminent expulsion. Elisabeth Westphal, a peasant from a Pomeranian village east of Stettin, for example, explained that Germans at first could not believe that the village's Germans were soon to be sent beyond the Oder River. Such doubts persisted even when Polish soldiers entered the village on June 22, 1945. Expulsion was so swift in Pomerania and Brandenburg that some Germans remained convinced there had been a mistake. When several families from a village near the Pomeranian town of Dramburg decided to turn around, they soon met acquaintances and relatives from a nearby village who told them, "The Germans are expelled at all places."[34] Just beyond the eastern edge of Pomerania, Germans also faced growing pressure to leave Danzig. Poles first cleared Germans out of individual apartments and from individual streets before beginning expulsions in June.

The improvised quality of early expulsions in Pomerania produced conflicts between Soviet authorities and local Polish militia and police. Such conflicts over expulsion versus other priorities had been common on the German side during the war. Now Poles frequently wanted to push out Germans before receiving Soviet approval. Polish militias announced deportations only to see their orders contradicted by Soviet commanders. Frustrated, the command of the Second Polish Army spoke of confronting the Red Army with "completed facts."[35] Much then depended on local conditions. Despite its extraordinary victory, the Red Army did not occupy every single town or village, and during the early summer of 1945 expulsions proceeded in many Pomeranian villages.

Silesia was yet another center for wild expulsions out of Poland. At the village of Tannenberg, in the Neisse district near the Czech border west of Oppeln, a Polish militia soldier arrived on a motorcycle early on the morning of July 2, 1945, with news that residents had to clear out within a half-hour. Soon a hundred militia soldiers arrived. This speed of expulsion was commonplace. At the town of Guben, perched just on the new Polish border, Germans were expelled on June 20, 1945, "within 10 minutes" from the town's larger eastern half into its smaller district just west of the Neisse.[36] The eastern town became the Polish Gubin while the western section remained German.

The improvised nature of wild expulsions was evident at every stage in Silesia. Armed escorts that accompanied ethnic Germans might simply disappear after a few days' journey. This was the experience, for example, of Germans from the town of Neumarkt, west of Breslau. On the morning of June 26 Polish militia knocked on Germans' doors and told them to prepare to leave within two hours. They then took the Germans on a forced march to Haynau; but after a rest day at Haynau, the Polish escort "vanished."[37] Left to fend for themselves, Germans returned exhausted to Neumarkt, where they found that their homes had been plundered during their absence.

It proved difficult to keep the expelled Germans on the western side of the Oder and Neisse rivers in the Soviet zone of occupation. Thousands of German refugees from Silesia arrived every day at the town of Görlitz. Typhus spread, hundreds of Germans died, and many decided to return to their old homes. One resident of the village of Lauterbach in Lower Silesia, for example, recalled being driven out of his home by Polish soldiers on June 17 and led to the Neisse. But Görlitz was overcrowded, with at least ten refugees in every house. Soviet authorities wished to halt the arrival of more Silesians there in early July 1945, and Poles in the countryside needed German labor. So there were abundant reasons for Germans to leave Görlitz, and much of the German population of Lauterbach actually returned in July 1945, to work without pay in the fields.[38]

South of Germany, wild expulsions drove close to half a million Germans out of Bohemia and Moravia in Czechoslovakia. Expulsion there came as a particular shock because the Sudetenland had been comparatively sheltered from combat throughout most of the war. The desperate plight of refugees from Silesia in 1945 had convinced many Sudeten Germans that it was better to stay home rather than abandon property and possessions. Wild expulsions got off to a quick start in Moravia along the Austrian border and in isolated German communities in the interior. They were so successful along the southern border that the Council of the Moravian National Committee, the newly established provincial government, confirmed on July 3, 1945, that southern Moravia was already largely "cleansed of Germans." By August 1945 some 110,000 Germans were gone from Moravia and Silesia, and even more Germans were driven from Bohemia.[39]

Wild expulsions of Germans from Czechoslovakia followed a common pattern. Only the affiliation of those who drove Germans from their homes varied: soldiers, revolutionary guards, gendarmes, or police showed up at a German town, neighborhood, or village and forced the residents out into the streets. They gave Germans between five minutes and a day to leave and placed limits of fifty to three hundred Reichsmark on the amount of money Germans could take with them, and sixty-six pounds (sometimes more) on the total weight of the refugees' luggage. Theft and expulsion went hand in hand: a German civil engineer from the spa town of Teplitz-Schönau, in the mountains of northwestern Bohemia, described how seven men showed up at his door on June 6, 1945, demanded everything of value, "and gave us with watch in hand 20 minutes to gather our 'luggage.'" Then came the journey out under the escort of militia or perhaps even civilians. One German civil servant from the nearby town of Bilin recalled that his transport was fortunate to be escorted "by Czechs from Bilin with whom we had lived for decades in tolerably good harmony."[40]

Brno (formerly Brünn), the capital of Moravia, was the site for the largest single case of wild expulsion. On May 30–31, forces of the local National Committee drove some twenty thousand Germans from their homes in a column that stretched up to ten miles. In an extraordinary account of what survivors came to call the Brünn death march, Maria Zatschek, a German woman from the town, provided a glimpse into the breakdown of relations between Czechs and Germans. Each saw Brünn's recent past quite differently, and both, according to Zatschek, were guilty of inaccurate or selective memory. When one Czech neighbor, remarking on the German expulsion, said, "so have you done it to the Jews," Zatschek asked which of them had taken pleasure from the pursuit of Jews. Her fellow Germans' memories of the Nazi era, however, struck her as just as incomplete. On all sides, Germans on the forced march out of town cursed the "Hitler system," something that amazed her, because the complaints often came from "enthusiastic supporters of the system." As recently as the preceding winter they had expected victory.[41]

Zatschek captured the central paradoxes of grassroots ethnic cleansing. Local Czechs had come to see their German neighbors as traitors and enemies who deserved their fate, and they were eager to expel them. As Czechs looked on, "their expressions were cheerful like at a festival." At the same time there remained traces of common bonds from a shared past. Young Czechs "carried children on their backs" as the column marched on in the rain. Zatschek and her family ended up at a camp at Pohrlitz, where her eighty-five-year-old father died, before she was finally sent to Austria in late June 1945. German Brünn was no more. The town once known as Brünn and Brno was now simply the Czech town of Brno.

As in Poland, the improvised and hasty wild expulsions from Czechoslovakia often produced chaos. Expulsions could end up back at their starting point. On June 22, 1945, for example, Czech partisans forced Germans out of the northern Moravian town of Jägerndorf, on the border of Silesia. One of the women taken on the forced march recalled an arduous journey during which the partisans yelled "forward you German swine."[42] To speed the trip north, the partisans requisitioned a truck, but when they reached the Polish border the Poles refused to accept the transport, and the Germans were sent marching back into Czechoslovakia to a camp. This was symptomatic of an emerging obstacle to wild expulsions from northern Moravia: the shifting of the Polish border westward. German Silesia was becoming Polish, Poles already had more Germans than they wanted in Silesia, and they wanted no more Germans entering from Czechoslovakia.

Potsdam

The Potsdam Conference among Britain, the United States, and the Soviet Union, held from July 17 through August 2, 1945, at a pleasant Berlin suburb known for its Prussian royal palaces, set the stage for the further expulsion or transfer of Germans. The victorious Allies discussed conditions for peace, Germany's future, and what to do with the large majority of the remaining Germans outside Germany. First, they agreed in Article 13 of the Potsdam Protocol that Germans were to leave Poland, Czechoslovakia, and Hungary. But the Allies called for something other than the wild expulsions that had preceded the Potsdam Conference. In terms that have often been bitterly criticized by German survivors of the expulsions, the United States, the USSR, and Britain agreed "that any transfers that take place should be effected in an orderly and humane manner." Such transfers should await an agreement among the victorious Allies on the distribution of Germans among the different zones of occupied Germany. Meanwhile, the Allies asked the Czech, Polish, and Hungarian governments "to suspend further expulsions."

Were the Allies responsible for the largest ethnic cleansing in European history, or did they strive to make an ongoing process more humane? Certainly they made it easier to expel millions of Germans, but they saw little alternative. They recognized that Poles and Czechs, whether nationalists or Communists, seemed determined to rid their countries of Germans. A memo of July 7, 1945, by British Assistant Undersecretary of State Oliver Charles Harvey, for example, noted that the "Polish, Czechoslovak, and Hungarian governments wish to get rid of the overwhelming majority of the Germans in the territory which they control."[43] The Czech government, for its part, made clear that there was to be no future in Czechoslovakia for Germans or for that matter Hungarians. Just as the Potsdam Conference came to an end, Czech President Beneš issued decrees on August 2 that deprived Germans and Magyars (who had adopted German or Hungarian nationality during the war) of Czech citizenship.

Further details on the transfer of ethnic Germans to Germany came in November with an agreement to resettle 6.65 million Germans in Allied zones of occupation in Germany between December 1945 and July 1946. Some 3.5 million Germans were to be moved from the former German east to the Soviet and British zones. Another 3.15 million Germans were to be transferred, most from Czechoslovakia and Hungary, to the American and Soviet zones—of this total 150,000 Germans were to be sent from Austria to the French zone of occupied Germany. These figures suggest a degree of certainty about the numbers of Germans to be moved that the Allied leaders and their advisers did not in fact possess. They knew neither the exact number of Germans who had already fled nor the number who remained east of the Oder-Neisse boundary and in the Sudetenland.

Limbo

Millions of Germans in Poland and Czechoslovakia spent the months after the Potsdam Conference in a kind of limbo, waiting for their departure. Living conditions varied greatly for Germans in Poland during this period. Those fortunate enough to stay in their own homes typically had to pay rent—a policy calculated to strip them of their assets. Others were sent into the countryside to work on farms taken over by the Polish state; some Germans labored for years on Polish state properties even after most Germans had been expelled from Poland. Other Germans spent their last months in Poland in camps, in some cases even in camps formerly operated by the SS. German survivors, recalling the camps, frequently spoke of concentration camps and sometimes, drawing on the terminology of the Holocaust, even of extermination camps. Conditions were harsh; guards abused, beat, and sometimes murdered prisoners; and thousands died, most often from hunger and disease. Still, the Polish camps were not death camps designed for the extermination of entire peoples.[44]

Germans never knew for certain when they would finally be expelled. By the time that day came, many had already been driven from their homes, then allowed to return. This was a common experience, for example, for Germans from Silesia who in the summer 1945 took part in so-called "Hitler marches." These marches combined Polish desire for vengeance with a yearning to loot. A Hitler march began with orders to evacuate a village for ostensible political purposes. Germans were sent, one recalled, "so that we have time to think about why we elected Adolf Hitler."[45] But the marches were also an opportunity for stealing and revenge. Thus Germans forced out of the village of Kleinröhrsdorf to the east of Görlitz on the morning of June 24, 1945, for an "Adolf Hitler march" that would supposedly lead them over the Neisse River, instead returned to find their houses plundered and damaged.

Even before they left, Poland's Germans sensed the destruction of their culture. The arrival of new Polish settlers and the changeover from German to Polish on street signs and shops swiftly displaced the German language in commerce and daily life. At Danzig, Egon Buddatsch saw Poles move into the city before he left in July 1945 with his younger brother and a German woman who had taken care of them. On their long journey to the new German border they saw new Polish settlers. Many farms and villages were still empty, but others "were already taken possession of by Poles." The red-and-white Polish flags indicated which homes had new owners. Germans noted these changes with a mixture of resentment and resignation. One teacher who left Brandenburg in May 1946 complained that her home "had long become alien to us. Foreign street signs, foreign names, eastern types of people," these were the things she recalled.[46] Polish authorities, for their part, accelerated the cultural shift away from the German past. They ordered the use of Polish names and even destroyed German war monuments.

To the northeast, more than 100,000 Germans stayed in the shattered region surrounding Königsberg, which was captured by the Soviet Union. There they suffered epidemics, hunger, and conditions so grim that reports of cannibalism surfaced in the winter of 1945–1946.[47] Those not imprisoned in NKVD camps were set to work in the countryside in a depopulated region desperately short of labor. The population of the Königsberg region fell from 1.2 million before the war to 170,000, including Germans, in June 1946.

In Czechoslovakia the German experience was broadly similar to that in Poland. German shop names swiftly disappeared. Some Germans were sent to work on farms in the countryside, and others were forced into converted prisons, barracks, or labor camps. By November 1945 the total number of Germans in some 300 camps reached 150,000. Daily rations provided inmates with a meager diet of between 700 and 1,000 calories a day, a level far below any necessary minimum. Lack of food, poor hygiene, and forced labor for up to 12

hours a day made prisoners highly susceptible to disease. At a minimum, between 4,000 and 5,000 people, nearly all German, died in
camps in Bohemia and Moravia in 1945, and the total may well have
been higher. Some Germans endured lengthy imprisonment. Steffi
Gritzmann, a German woman from Moravian Ostrau, a town in a
coal mining region near the Polish border, was sent to hard labor for
almost a year. The yellow band that she and her fellow inmates wore
had to be visible at all times. Czechs cursed the German prisoners
and said Czechs had endured more "in the concentration camps."[48]

Expulsion

Whether interned in a camp, pushed into a shed or barn, or repeatedly sent on Hitler marches, Germans in the new east were almost
invariably expelled. Potsdam briefly slowed but did not halt deportations. On August 15, 1945, Lisa Barendt, for example, learned that
she and her children were to appear at a freight railway station six
days later. She packed the few things the family still owned, and
when it was time to depart she passed through the ruined city to
leave Danzig for the new German border.[49]

Expulsions—or rather "voluntary" departures—of Germans
from Poland continued in the autumn of 1945 even though the organized transfers provided for by Potsdam had yet to begin. A German recalled that Poles in one Pomeranian village said that Germans would have to go after bringing in the harvest, and some
Germans left on their own. Polish authorities encouraged "voluntary" departure by harassing and intimidating Germans. The threat
of placement in camps helped persuade them to leave. In other
cases, such as in the Pomeranian town of Stolp, west of Danzig, a
German pastor recalled that Polish militia simply began to carry out
deportations in October 1945. Before leaving Stolp, Germans were
often forced to sign a statement declaring that they departed voluntarily and held no claims against the Polish state.[50] Thousands also
left Breslau and the surrounding region in transports organized by
local authorities.

Expulsions from Czechoslovakia similarly continued after Potsdam. Czech authorities deported Germans as long as they had somewhere to send them: to Austria in the south and to the Soviet zone of occupation in the north. When Austria reestablished border controls, expulsions to the south dwindled. Despite the Czech army's determination to get on with the job, deportations to the Soviet zone in Germany slowed and finally came to a halt in December 1945 in the face of Soviet objections.[51]

After slowing in late 1945, the pace of expulsions accelerated in 1946. In that year alone some 2 million Germans were expelled from Poland, chiefly from Silesia, eastern Pomerania, and Polish parts of the former East Prussia. By November 1946 more than 1.4 million Germans expelled from Czechoslovakia had reached the U.S. zone of occupation in Germany, and three-quarters of a million had arrived in the Soviet zone once Soviet authorities resumed accepting transports from Czechoslovakia in June 1946.[52]

The organized expulsions or transfers of 1946 were less brutal than the wild expulsions of 1945, but the experience was nonetheless harrowing. The journey west, particularly for those in the countryside, began by wagon or on foot. Germans carried suitcases and sacks, which they often abandoned, and once again bystanders benefited from expulsion. As Germans walked to the town of Grottkau, south of Breslau, Poles followed to snatch up the "thrown-away pieces of luggage." The next stage of the journey to Germany was by train. Transport west took place on crowded freight trains with between thirty-one and thirty-six or more expelled Germans per car. Lack of railway cars in northern Poland led to severe overcrowding—on December 2, 1946, fifteen hundred Germans crammed into nineteen railway cars on one train.[53]

The humanity or lack thereof of these organized expulsions caused immediate debate: did the Allies' treatment of deported Germans match the criteria set out at Potsdam? Pointing to the conditions at reception centers in Germany, the Pulitzer Prize–winning reporter Anne O'Hare McCormick wrote that "the exodus takes place under nightmarish conditions, without any international supervision

or any pretense of humane treatment." Conditions of organized expulsions varied, but in general these transfers were humane only by
a very minimal standard: something better than the treatment the
Nazis and their helpers had meted out to expelled Poles. There was
more than a small element of vengeance in that attitude, and there
were frequent breaches of the rules for transfer. Occupation authorities recorded both gradual improvement and continuing problems.
As a British report of March 1, 1946, on the transport of Germans
from Silesia noted, conditions of the transfers had "significantly improved." The supply of food was now sufficient, but there was not
enough milk for children, not enough German doctors, and a disturbing number of ill Germans on board the westbound trains.[54]

Facing the imminent loss of their homeland, Germans on the
verge of expulsion became increasingly preoccupied with their destination: the eastern or western zones of occupation of Germany. Either was possible, for example, for Germans still inside Czechoslovakia. As one German woman recalled, "The big question now among
us all was where we would probably go." This was a matter of
chance in 1946 for Germans transported from Asch, a textile town
pressed up against the Bohemian border: most were sent to the
American zone while others were sent to the Soviet zone. The first
evidence that a train was bound for the Soviet zone—the sight of
rail cars bearing the hammer and sickle—brought disappointment.
Germans found they had some ability to influence their destination.
Thus if they were to be deported from the Moravian city of Olmütz,
according to Fritz Peter Habel, an economist, Germans could be sent
to the American or Soviet zone depending on where they had relatives. When Germans facing expulsion lacked relatives in the American zone, "they were invented."[55]

After 1946 so many Germans had already fled or been expelled
from Czechoslovakia and Poland that in 1947 the number deported
sank to some 500,000. By that time the Soviet Union had adopted a
policy of expelling the remaining ethnic Germans from its portion
of what had once been East Prussia. In October 1947 Soviet authorities reached a secret decision to resettle the Germans of Kalin-

ingrad, the former Königsberg. The first trains left on October 22, and the last transports west were completed by October 1948.[56]

Poles and Ukrainians

Although they made up the largest single ethnic group to suffer expulsion, Germans were not the only people forced to move in the aftermath of the war. Others, besides Germans, found their fate tied to a country that had suffered defeat. Thus Czechoslovakia's Hungarians or Magyars shared much in common with that country's Germans, including loss of citizenship. In the years following the war, Hungary and Czechoslovakia carried out a population exchange involving tens of thousands of Magyars of Slovakia and Slovaks of Hungary.

Poles too were resettled. Obvious evidence of this came from the many German complaints about Poles arriving to take over apartments, homes, and farms in Silesia, Pomerania, and East Prussia. Many of these Polish settlers came from regions newly assigned to the Soviet Union. Strictly speaking, these Poles were not ethnically cleansed—their departure was in principle voluntary, but local policies toward Poles varied. They could face pressure to stay or to leave. Fear of the Soviet Union and of Ukrainians gave Poles reason to leave the new east for Poland's new wild west. The Polish-Ukrainian conflict had already forced tens of thousands of Poles to flee during the last years of World War II, and it continued to claim victims even into the peace.[57]

The very same Poles whom Germans viewed as a threat did not necessarily like their new homes. In his essay *Two Cities*, the writer Adam Zagajewski tells how his family from Lvov never felt fully at home in their new residence, the Polish industrial city of Gliwice, formerly the German city of Gleiwitz. "What sort of city was it? The worse one of the two. Smaller. Unpretentious. Industrial. Alien."[58]

Despite all German talk of streams, torrents, and floods of Poles, their numbers never fully matched the hopes of the Polish government for a vast reservoir of Poles to replace Germans due for expulsion. Poland's new leaders had envisioned as many as four million Poles leaving new Soviet territory, but repatriation agreements between Poland and the Soviet republics saw only approximately one and a half million Poles move west in 1945 and 1946. Poland tried to make up the gap by putting pressure on people of mixed or indeterminate nationality to declare themselves Poles. Considerable numbers of people with some German roots remained in Silesia, and many later moved to the Federal Republic of Germany.[59]

Ukrainians, for their part, found that the new Poland aimed to end their ethnic presence. Between 1944 and 1946 approximately a half-million Ukrainians moved east. Ukrainians who left often did so by their own choosing, but threats and even killings also persuaded them to leave. By August 1946, when the Soviet Union decided against accepting further Ukrainians from Poland, there were still some 200,000 Ukrainians, many of them from the Lemko ethnic group, living in eastern Poland. They did not remain in their homes for long. In 1947, after a Ukrainian partisan ambush killed Polish General Karol Swierczewski, Poland resorted to a new policy to break up and disperse Ukrainians remaining within Poland's borders. Without Soviet cooperation, ethnic cleansing was no longer possible. Instead Operation Vistula, described by Polish authorities as a military operation against Ukrainian partisans, saw Polish troops force 140,000 Ukrainians out of Poland's east to be resettled, in small groups, in the country's northwest.[60]

Istria

The end of war and the drawing of new borders also led to a major migration by Italians from territory assigned to Yugoslavia, including the peninsula of Istria on the Adriatic Sea. This Istrian exodus was not simply the result of ethnic cleansing. The struggle for Istria was in part an ethnic conflict between Italians and Slavs that dated back at least to the 1920s, when the Italian government sought to erase Slavic language in Trieste and Istria. But cycles of revenge killing from World War II and distaste for Yugoslavia's postwar Communist government also gave some Italians cause to leave. When the Italian fascist government collapsed in September 1943, partisans went on the offensive in Trieste and the surrounding region before German forces regained control in October. Partisans carried out executions, sometimes dumping their victims into the *foibe*, cavernous pits in the limestone region.[61]

Every shift in borders after 1945 led to migration of Italians. The city of Trieste on the Adriatic Sea, east of Venice, remained in Italy, but most of the adjacent Istrian peninsula was transferred in several stages to Yugoslavia. Italians left the Yugoslav zone in 1945, and a further wave of Italians left their homes in 1947 when Yugoslavia received another piece of Istria. The Italian government helped to transport Italians in 1947, but Italy did not cause the migration. Alfred Bowman, senior civil affairs officer with the Allied Military Government, said, "Nothing could be done to stem the departure of these people." The final stage of the Italian exodus took place in 1954 with a border settlement that placed more towns in Yugoslavia, and Italians continued to trickle out of Istria for several years. One was Lidia Bastianich, who gained fame as an Italian-American cook. She left with her family for the United States in 1958 after spending two years in a refugee camp in Trieste. In all, 200,000 to 350,000 Italians left Yugoslavia between the end of World War II and the 1950s, though some Italians remained on the peninsula.[62]

Ethnic Cleansing at War's End

Ethnic cleansing and mass flight at the end of World War II and immediately after the war further transformed the ethnic map of Central and Eastern Europe. The effects were especially dramatic in the lands along the former borders of the German, Russian, and Austro-Hungarian empires. Poland, Bohemia, Moravia, and Ukraine became more homogenous than ever before. German communities all but disappeared from much of Eastern Europe.[63] On the Baltic Sea the old Prussian city of Königsberg became Kaliningrad. With the end of the Soviet Union it became a Russian territory separated from the Russian Republic by former Soviet republics that became independent states. Pillau, where German refugees tried to get out of East Prussia by steamer, became Baltiysk in the district of Kaliningrad. In Silesia, the city of Breslau became Wroclaw. In similar fashion hundreds and thousands of other former German communities large and small across East and West Prussia, Pomerania, Silesia, Bohemia, and Moravia acquired new names.

The rupture with the past transformed Danzig into the Polish city of Gdansk. For years many Germans in their new homes in Germany did not see Gdansk as being really Polish, yet Günter Grass's home city became quintessentially Polish in the eyes of the world. The birthplace of the winner of the 1999 Nobel Prize in Literature became known as the home of one of the most famous Poles of the twentieth century, Lech Walesa, winner of the 1983 Nobel Peace Prize. Born in 1943 in eastern Poland, Walesa became an electrical engineer at the Lenin Shipyards in Gdansk. He was fired in 1976 for his role as a shipyard leader, and in 1978 he joined in forming an independent non-Communist union that became known as Solidarity. Walesa gained international attention during Solidarity's 1980 strike. In a 1981 crackdown the Polish government banned Solidarity, but in 1990 the former shipyard worker was elected Poland's president.

Who was responsible for the end of the old German Danzig and the broader transformation of Eastern and Central Europe? The answer depends in part on when we start. Begin with August 1945 and the transfer of Germans was the result of an Allied decision; look back to the spring of 1945 and it was Poles, Czechs, and Yugoslavs who wanted Germans gone; look further back to winter and fear of the Red Army caused German flight; go back to the war itself and we see how German invasion started a powerful and destructive cycle of revenge. By the end of World War II, the principle that it was necessary and even useful to forcibly relocate entire ethnic groups had gained broad acceptance. We should not, therefore, overstate the importance of any individuals, however powerful, in the flight and expulsion of Germans. It was not just leaders, whether Czech, Polish, or, as some maintain, the war's victors, but many Europeans themselves who wanted their neighbors gone. At the grassroots level, the people of Eastern and Central Europe embraced and accepted the logic of ethnic cleansing, or at least accepted that this was what war brought.

The traumas of ethnic cleansing and population transfer at war's end left divided memories. I experienced this firsthand in 1989 at Marburg, a scenic university town some forty miles north of Frankfurt am Main. On a fall weekend day, a little while before the Berlin Wall came down, I walked into the Elisabethkirche in Marburg. I believe I knew at the time that this church was the resting place of Paul von Hindenburg, the German field marshal who defeated Russia in 1914 at the Battle of Tannenberg. He was also the second and last president of the Weimar Republic, and in that capacity he appointed Hitler Germany's chancellor in January 1933. On his death in 1934, Hindenburg was buried in East Prussia, but his remains were removed in 1945. Walking into the church in 1989 I was surprised to see a large delegation of men and women, most of them white-haired, bearing standards and laying flowers on Hindenburg's tomb. They were members of a chapter of expellees from the former Prussia. I said nothing, but I must have displayed some unease because a woman came over to me and asked why I seemed put off. I explained that I recalled Hindenburg as the man who was re-elected Germany's president in 1932, in large part with the votes of Social Democrats and Catholics, and then placed the very same voters who had supported him under Hitler's government. In response she brought up very different memories of Hindenburg. He was the man who had defended Prussia in 1914, and Prussia was her lost home.

CHAPTER SEVEN

After the Ottomans

ISRAEL, CYPRUS, TURKEY, IRAQ, AND
BULGARIA, 1947–2004

O n the morning of September 7, 1906, David Gruen, a twenty-year-old Jew, arrived in the port of Jaffa, then a town in the Ottoman province of Syria. Gruen, who would later become famous under the name he adopted in 1910, David Ben-Gurion, had traveled from his home town of Plonsk, then in Russian Poland, with the aim of joining the Jewish community in Palestine, then known as the Yishuv. Gruen was not impressed with his first encounter with Jaffa. He arrived in Palestine as a Zionist, but the Zionist dream of building a new land of Israel seemed to be having no visible impact in Jaffa. "To me life in Jaffa is a more grotesque exile than life in Plonsk," Gruen wrote his father. Even "a street with a Hebrew name . . . was full of Arab shopkeepers." Gruen made a rapid departure, leaving that very afternoon for a nearby Jewish settlement.[1]

Ben-Gurion achieved some of his first professional successes in Ottoman lands. He was active in Zionist politics in Palestine, moved to Salonica in 1911 to study Turkish, and in 1912 began his legal studies in Constantinople. He returned to Palestine in late 1914, just after the Ottoman Empire entered World War I. Ben-Gurion urged Jews to become Ottoman citizens, even when Jemal Pasha, one of the leading Young Turks and governor for Syria, ordered the deportation of Jews who were not Ottoman subjects. But Ben-Gurion was himself deported in 1915. He lived in exile in the United States before joining a Jewish battalion in the British Army and returning to Palestine in 1918.[2]

After World War I, Jaffa remained a predominantly Arab city. Most Jews who moved to the region lived just to the north in the new Jewish city of Tel Aviv. Jews had founded Tel Aviv, originally named Ahuzat Bayit, as a new neighborhood on Jaffa's northern edge in 1900, and the city experienced rapid growth between the world wars. The two cities, Jaffa and Tel Aviv, developed as parallel Arab and Jewish communities. Despite outbreaks of violence, the two communities retained ties, and there were even Jews who lived in Jaffa as well as Arabs who dwelled in Tel Aviv. But Jews saw Tel Aviv as modern and different from Jaffa, which they identified as old and Arab. The Israeli poet Chaim Gouri, who was born in Tel Aviv in 1923, recalled Jaffa as an almost alien community with a powerful allure. "As children we were warned not to go there," Gouri said in 2005, "but I experienced it in an extremely sensual way—I loved the restaurants the coffee houses the smells of oranges and sea fish the Middle Eastern music."[3] In 1947 Jaffa remained an Arab city of some 75,000 people while Tel Aviv was a fast-growing Jewish city of more than 200,000. The next year most of the Arabs of Jaffa left, and in 1949 Tel Aviv and Jaffa became a single city: Tel Aviv–Yaffo.

The departure of tens of thousands of Arabs from Jaffa was part of the continuing sequence of mass flight and forced migration in former Ottoman lands. Often the collapse of empire led immediately to bitter disputes over how to carve up old imperial lands into smaller and more homogenous national homelands, but violent ethnic and religious conflicts in former Ottoman lands continued long after the empire's end. In part, the varied pace of nationalist development accounted for the long delay between imperial collapse and ethnic struggle, but in some Ottoman lands imperial rule did not truly end with the empire's fall. The island of Cyprus, for example, came under British rule in 1878 and did not achieve independence until 1960. Several other Ottoman territories did not gain independence when the empire collapsed because they instead became mandates of European powers, including France and Britain. These mandates were not technically colonies, but, in a sense, imperial rule did not end in Palestine until Britain left in 1948.

"A Disputed Question for Years to Come"

Ethnic and religious conflict reached a peak in Palestine soon after World War II. In 1948 the state of Israel gained independence, and in the same year hundreds of thousands of Arabs departed the new Jewish state, leaving hundreds of empty villages. Remarkably, given the many controversies over Arab-Israeli relations, several key facts about 1948 are not in dispute. Arabs insisted there were 900,000 refugees, while Israelis conceded a number slightly more than 500,000. But Israelis and Arabs do agree that hundreds of thousands of Arabs rapidly departed Israel during its first year of existence. In 1948 Arabs emptied out of several urban areas, including Jaffa, and deserted close to four hundred villages.[4] Many of the villages were soon dismantled and replaced with new Israeli settlements. Some villages disappeared without a trace, leaving only trees, grass, cactuses, or sand dunes. Elsewhere signs of the past remained: ruins of walls, stones and rubble, graves, and individual buildings.

This was no by no means a complete sweeping away of all Arabs from the state of Israel (140,000 remained in the Jewish state), but why did so many Arabs leave their homes, and why did so many never return? This basic question has caused controversy from the start.-In December 1948 the well-known American journalist Anne O'Hare McCormick, anticipating future debates, wrote "Why these hapless people left their homes will be a disputed question for years to come."[5]

The struggle for power in Palestine began as one of many nationalist conflicts in old imperial lands, but here there was one distinctive element: there was no equivalent elsewhere to the Zionist

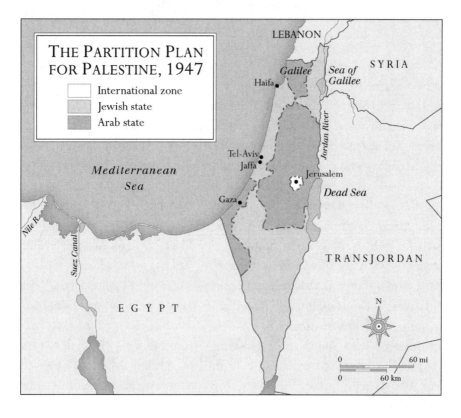

THE PARTITION PLAN
FOR PALESTINE, 1947

International zone
Jewish state
Arab state

LEBANON

Galilee | Sea of SYRIA
Haifa | *Galilee*

Mediterranean
Sea

Tel-Aviv
Jaffa
Jerusalem
Gaza
Dead Sea

Jordan River

Nile R.
Suez Canal

TRANSJORDAN

EGYPT

N

0   60 mi

0   60 km

project of encouraging Jewish immigration to Palestine. Zionists
wanted to create a Jewish nation-state, and Arabs or Palestinians
did not want this to happen. A distinct Palestinian nationalist identity uniting the Arab residents of Palestine emerged gradually, but
the early roots of Arab opposition to Zionism date back to the first
years of the twentieth century.[6] Zionists often spoke of the economic benefits their work brought to all of Palestine's residents,
but such economic development did not address the fundamental
national division. As early as 1919, David Ben-Gurion laid out the
basic problem: "Everybody sees the problem in relations between
the Jews and the Arabs. But not everybody sees that there's no solution to it. There is no solution! . . . The conflict between the interests of the Jews and the interests of the Arabs in Palestine cannot
be resolved by sophisms."[7]

Zionists considered several ways to build a Jewish state in a region with many Arabs. One solution to this problem was to draw up
very careful boundaries or to create a system of cantons, something

like a Jewish-Arab Switzerland in the Middle East. But any boundaries for a prospective Jewish state would still leave a very large Arab
minority, so large indeed that it would be difficult to ensure that the
state would remain Jewish in its politics and identity. The actual
boundaries selected by the United Nations in 1947 promised to leave
the fledgling state with an Arab minority of close to 40 percent of its
population. In a speech on December 13, 1947, Ben-Gurion recognized the dimensions of the problem. "In such composition," he
said, "there cannot even be complete certainty that the government
will be held by a Jewish majority. . . . There can be no stable and
strong Jewish State so long as it has a Jewish majority of only 60 percent, and so long as this majority consists of only 600,000 Jews."[8] In
this speech Ben-Gurion advocated another solution to Israel's demographic problem: immigration. After several decades of Zionist immigration, Jews made up a growing minority. By 1948 Palestine's
population consisted of some 1.25 million Arabs and 650,000 Jews,
and Ben-Gurion aimed to increase the country's Jewish population
to 2 million.

Zionists had a long record of supporting immigration, but they
also discussed some of the same remedies for ethnic conflict that
were considered in other former imperial lands of Eastern Europe
and Western Asia. These included the concept of population transfer, of moving large numbers of Arabs and perhaps Jews to create a
Jewish nation-state. The notion that Zionists considered population
transfers has provoked shock, disbelief, and disputes among specialists in Israeli history as well as a concerted effort to collect statements by Zionist leaders asserting their willingness to live alongside
Arabs. Debates about translations of key documents stand outside
the expertise of this work, but there is no doubt that Zionists spoke
on occasion of transfer. But this is not just an argument about documents.[9] Shocked reaction to the very idea that Zionists seriously considered population transfer casts people like David Ben-Gurion as in
some sense standing outside the history of their times. He would
have had to have been ignorant and naive not to have given this possibility some thought, and no one has ever described him that way.

Even before World War II, Zionists knew full well of the 1923 example of the Greek-Turkish population exchange. They knew of German schemes to resettle ethnic Germans at the start of the war, and they were aware of the population transfer of Germans at the end of the conflict. The war itself brought unthinkable tragedy for European Jews, but by the war's end there was a broad international consensus in favor of population transfers and forced migration. Both the United States and the Soviet Union, for example, accepted the transfer of Germans from Eastern Europe. Zionists knew of all these earlier examples, and they themselves faced what looked like an intractable nationalist conflict over Palestine's future. Given these circumstances, why should anyone express disbelief at the evidence of some Zionist interest in transferring Arabs out of a Jewish state? It would have been far more surprising if the founders of modern Israel had never considered that option.

It is impossible to establish that Ben-Gurion and other leading Zionists were committed to any one plan for resolving the national problem in Palestine. Zionism was not a monolithic movement; Zionists had different opinions about the possibility and desirability of population transfer, and individual Zionists, including Ben-Gurion, made inconsistent statements on whether Arabs should be encouraged to leave a future Jewish state. After all, they had no way of knowing whether such a program would ever be possible. Still, the idea of large-scale transfer was appealing in so far as it provided a remedy for the basic problem of creating a Jewish state in a land with many Arabs.

A kind of civil war between Arab and Jewish forces began after the United Nations voted in November 1947 for a plan that would lead to the partition of Palestine into two states. Arab flight began soon thereafter, especially from towns. The port of Haifa, a city of some 65,000 Jews and 70,000 Arabs, was one important example. Haifa was one of the largest Arab communities in the territory slated to become part of Israel. By late December some 15,000 to 20,000 Arabs had already left the city, according to estimates of the intelligence service of the Haganah, the main Jewish military force in Palestine. There was no evidence of any prior Zionist plan to expel these urban populations. Instead this exodus began with the collapse of local Arab leadership and the departure of many prosperous Arab families as insecurity mounted. Evacuations of the elderly, women, and children contributed to the panic. Anticipating war, the Arab League had previously called on Arab states to accept such groups. Haifa's remaining Arabs were already thoroughly demoralized when the Haganah launched a major offensive on April 21–22, 1948. Rather than accept terms for surrender, the remaining local Arab leadership made the surprising decision on April 22 to evacuate Haifa.[10] Haifa's Jewish mayor asked them to reconsider, to no avail.

Jaffa was another key center for early Arab flight. Under the UN partition plan, Jaffa would have formed an Arab enclave bordered by the Mediterranean and Israel. Arab flight from Jaffa began soon after the outbreak of fighting in late 1947, and a series of Jewish offensives in late April 1948 precipitated the exodus of most of Jaffa's remaining Arabs. In this case it was not the Haganah but a rival Jewish military force, the Irgun or IZL, that launched an attack on April 25, though the Haganah also began an offensive on April 28 against villages to the city's east. Arabs poured out of the city, and by May 8 only five thousand residents remained.[11] When Israel declared independence on May 14, Jaffa was no longer an Arab city.

The cases of Haifa and Jaffa provide some important clues about why Arabs fled in 1948. Some left because their leaders encouraged them to do so, and the flight of many prosperous families also weakened morale, but the actions of the Yishuv and of the state of Israel also led to massive Arab flight. Time and again, Arabs fled towns under attack by Jewish forces. The case of Jaffa was especially instructive for the early stages of Arab flight. Here British forces actually tried to stop the spread of panic, but a British military show of force could not calm Arab fears in the midst of continuing military operations by diverse Jewish forces.[12]

News and rumors of massacres carried out by Jewish forces exacerbated Arab fears. The most notorious such attack took place at

Deir Yassin, a village to the west of Jerusalem. On April 9 the Irgun and forces of the Freedom Fighters of Israel (LHI), commonly known as the Stern Gang, attacked the village. They took the village, though only with help from the Palmach, an elite Haganah commando force, and then blew up houses and executed many villagers. Estimates of the death toll ranged from 100 to more than 250, but the importance of Deir Yassin in prompting further Arab flight did not rest with the exact number of dead.[13] The Arab media may well have exaggerated the extent of killing, but this massacre terrified Arabs living within Israel's future borders because it appeared to confirm their worst fears about the future for Arabs within a Jewish nation-state. This was exactly the same kind of dynamic that had helped to spur mass flight in so many other wars in the old imperial lands of Europe and Asia.

But at the same time, in the spring of 1948 there was no obvious Zionist master plan to expel Arabs. The closest thing to a policy of encouraging Arab flight was the Haganah's Plan Dalet, or Plan D. The Haganah produced this scheme in March 1948, mainly to prepare for an expected invasion by Arab states when the British mandate came to an end in May. Plan D focused on the military threat presented by Arab settlements on or near lines of communication within the new Jewish state. The plan outlined "operations against enemy settlements which are in the rear of, within or near our defense lines, with the aim of preventing their use as bases for an active armed force." Brigade commanders could choose how to achieve this end. Their options included cleansing and destruction.[14] Strictly speaking, Plan D was not a program for ethnic cleansing, but it reflected the fundamental problems with the initial partition plan. Zionists greeted partition because it provided for a Jewish state, but partition also left the future Israel with an enormous Arab minority.

Military operations conducted by the Haganah and by the Israel Defense Forces (as Israel's armed forces became known after independence) produced a massive surge of Arab flight. All told between 250,000 and 300,000 Arabs fled in April and May 1948. The experiences of individual Arab towns and villages varied widely, but this

Arab flight can hardly be seen as voluntary. As in other ethnic wars, Arabs fled when their communities were attacked. And as in so many other ethnic wars, attacks on nearby villages served as signals to flee. Prompting such flight may not have been the first goal of Plan D, but fighters for the Haganah, the IDF, and other forces soon realized that their offensives were driving out large numbers of Arabs. "What do you think about the fact that we are expelling Arabs?" a Palmach commander asked a comrade after heavy fighting in April at a kibbutz near the town of Jenin. His friend answered, "We're not expelling them, they're running away. Maybe they should be expelled, but we're not taking people and expelling them."[15]

Jews, for their part, had reason to fear Arabs. Just as Arabs spoke with dread of Jewish massacres of Arabs, Jews recoiled at the news of Arab killings of Jews. In the most infamous case, Arabs killed 129 Jews after capturing the settlement of Kfar Etzion on May 13, 1948. The war entered a new phase the very next day with Israel's declaration of independence and the invasion of the new state by the armies of Iraq, Syria, Lebanon, Transjordan, and Egypt. Israelis feared what would happen to them if the Arab states won.[16] Led by the Arab Legion, a force that would become Jordan's army, the Arab armies achieved their greatest military success in the Old City of Jerusalem. When the Legion completed its conquest of the Old City on May 28, the district's Jews were expelled into West Jerusalem.

Gradually Israeli forces gained the upper hand, and a series of Israeli offensives generated renewed waves of Arab flight. An offensive between July 9 and 18, known as the Ten Days, led to a new surge of refugees. Officially Israeli forces were told: "Outside the actual time of fighting, it is forbidden . . . to expel Arab inhabitants from villages, neighborhoods and cities, and to uproot inhabitants from their places without special permission or explicit order from the Defence Minister in each specific case." Significant Arab populations, sometimes Christians and Druze, remained in some regions of the north, but it could hardly have come as a surprise to IDF forces that their offensive also prompted further Arab flight. After a truce of several months, further Israeli offensives in October again had the same effect: massive Arab flight. In the north, tens of thousands of Arabs, mostly Muslims, left by the end of Operation Hiram, an Israeli advance at the end of October 1948. General Moshe Carmel, the Israeli commander in the north, wrote of villagers who left in a panic, dropping their belongings along the sides of paths. "Suddenly, every object seems to them petty, superfluous, unimportant as against the chasing fear and the urge to save life and limb."[17]

To return to Anne O'Hare McCormick's question, what produced the Arab exodus from Israel in 1948? War during Israel's first year remade the new country's ethnic map, transforming Israel from a state with a very large Arab minority into a state with an overwhelming Jewish majority. Evacuations carried out by Arabs themselves contributed to the flight from some towns, but it is highly unlikely that this was the chief reason why more than half a million people left and then stayed away for good. In the 1980s a number of historians and writers, most notably the Israeli historian Benny Morris, began to cast doubt on this notion that Arabs fled by and large because they were told to do so by other Arabs.[18] Morris and other historians have sometimes been assailed as "revisionists" or as "new historians," but these labels do not address a larger problem raised by looking at other examples of mass flight in Europe and Western Asia. Where else do we find something analogous to what is supposed to have happened during the first Arab-Israeli war in 1948? A few other cases of voluntary evacuation in the midst of war can be found, so it is not surprising to learn that Arab authorities spoke at times of evacuating women and children from war zones, but such evacuations were not the chief cause of mass flight or migration in any other case. Why should we expect that the Arabs of Palestine were fundamentally different from all other peoples who had previously lost their homes during the many violent episodes that cleansed old imperial lands?

There were several causes of Arab flight in 1948. Arabs of Palestine behaved very much like many other peoples who fled their homes in earlier years and decades. Significant numbers left as

Palestinian society collapsed in major towns, but most left when Israeli forces attacked, or because they feared such attack. Anne O'Hare McCormick was probably correct when she observed, "Some were warned to leave by their own leaders, some were ordered out by Israeli troops, a vast multitude fled in sheer panic because of atrocity tales."[19]

Evacuation, expulsion, and panicked flight amounted to more than a list of reasons to flee; they had common roots as the logical and predictable results of ethnic war. Israeli leaders voiced surprise at the Arab exodus, and they may well have been sincere, but the Arab departures from Israel seem mysterious only if viewed in isolation from all comparable examples. Ethnic war in other former Ottoman regions had displaced entire peoples, and ethnic war in Israel and Palestine had much the same effect, though this war left some Arabs in Israel.

Opinion was varied within Israel about the Arab exodus. At one extreme, some figures such as Yosef Weitz, director of the Lands Department of the Jewish National Fund, a development fund long active in purchasing land, pressed for what he called "retroactive transfer" of Arab lands to Israelis. On the other hand, Mapam, a key political party in Israel's first government, objected to a plan for expulsion and called for an announcement that Arabs could return once there was peace. Still, the concept of a population exchange surfaced in the summer of 1948. In July the *New York Times*, citing Arthur Lourie of Israel's UN office, indicated that "Israeli Government circles are discussing a possible exchange of minorities between Israel and the Arab area of Palestine."[20] Transfer, in this case, also involved the idea of bringing Jews to Israel from Arab countries.

Efforts to prevent Arab return marked a key turning point in Israeli policy toward Arab refugees. Provisional Prime Minister Ben-Gurion did not sound like a man who wanted or expected large concentrations of Arabs to return to Israel any time soon. In a meeting on June 16, 1948, Ben-Gurion said, "But war is war. We did not start the war. They made the war. Jaffa waged war on us, Haifa waged war on us, Bet She'an waged war on us. And I do not want them again to make war. That would be not just but foolish. . . . Do we have to bring back the enemy, so that he again fights us . . . ? No! You made war [and] you lost."[21] Ben-Gurion also made explicit reference to the Greek-Turkish example. Perhaps he meant that he opposed such return as long as Israel was at war, but a real peace was far off. And in a book published a few years later, Ben-Gurion made much the same point: "Tel-Aviv did not wage war on Jaffa, Jaffa waged war on Tel-Aviv. And this should not happen again. . . . Bringing back the Arabs to Jaffa is not just but rather is foolish. Those who had gone to war against us—let them carry the responsibility after having lost."[22]

At the negotiating table and on the ground in former Palestinian villages there was dramatic evidence of Israeli policy to hinder return. Under international pressure, Israel made modest concessions on the issue of refugee return but never offered return to anything close to a majority of the Arabs who had left. By the early 1950s, Ben-Gurion made clear that the refugees would not return. Interviewing Israel's prime minister in 1952, *New York Times* reporter C. L. Sulzberger wrote that Israeli assistance for the refugees "would 'not under any conditions include permitting the return of Arab emigrants to Israel.'"[23]

Israel soon began to act as if most of these Arabs would never return. Many Arab villages were quickly destroyed or razed, and Israel swiftly put Arab land and property to new use. By early 1949 tens of thousands of Jews moved into property left by Arabs in urban neighborhoods. Jaffa was becoming a Jewish city.[24] Where Arab homes still stood in villages, the new residents were often immigrants to Israel from North Africa or elsewhere in the Middle East.

Some of these Jews who moved into old Arab neighborhoods or into new settlements were themselves pressured to leave their former homes in countries of the Middle East and North Africa. The state of Israel enthusiastically welcomed Jewish immigration, but at the same time several Arab governments did what they could to make life untenable for their own Jews once Israel gained independence. The government of Iraq, for example, arrested Zionists and enacted a citizenship deprivation law in 1950 that allowed Jews to leave Iraq if they relinquished their citizenship. By 1952 more than 100,000 Jews had left Iraq for Israel. Egypt also persecuted those accused of Zionism, and the Jews of Cairo suffered a mob attack; by 1950 tens of thousands of Jews had left Egypt for Israel. Egypt's Jews lived with extensive economic discrimination in the 1950s, and persecution of Egyptian Jews intensified in 1956 after Israel invaded the Sinai peninsula during the Suez crisis, leading to a new wave of emigration by more than 20,000 Jews through June 1957.[25]

The Berlin Wall of the Mediterranean

A little more than 150 miles northwest of Haifa, the island of Cyprus also fell into ethnic war when British withdrawal brought the end of imperial rule. British occupation in 1878 and annexation in 1914 postponed the end of empire on Cyprus. But as British imperial power faded after World War II, and Cyprus moved toward self-rule, the island celebrated by visitors for its scenery, its lemons and oranges, and its Mediterranean way of life became known for conflict between its Greek and Turkish residents. This was the final and long-delayed struggle for power between Greeks and Turks in a former Ottoman territory. The two had fought in the Morea in the 1820s, on Crete in the 1890s, in Thessaly in 1897, in Macedonia in 1912, and in Anatolia from 1919 until 1922. In the 1960s and 1970s a Greek-Turkish struggle for power led to mass flight and ethnic cleansing on Crete.

The slogan of the day for Greek Cypriots in the 1950s was *enosis*, or union with the Greek state. Arriving in Cyprus in 1953, the British writer Lawrence Durrell saw the demand for *enosis* everywhere. "We moved slowly inland . . . through little whitewashed villages bespattered by the slogan ENOSIS AND ONLY ENOSIS."[26] Durrell liked the island. He bought a house in a Greek village named Bellapais near the north coast and stayed in Cyprus until 1956, but in only three years Durrell saw the level of political tension and violence increase markedly.

In these calls for *enosis* Cyprus was reminiscent of Crete, another large island of the Mediterranean beset by ethnic violence between its Christians and Muslims. Crete finally gained *enosis* shortly before World War I, but if Crete's fate encouraged Greek Cypriot champions of *enosis*, the recent history of Greece also gave them cause for caution. The quest for a greater Greece uniting all Greeks had earlier ended in disaster. In 1897 only diplomatic arrangements overseen by the European great powers had saved Greek nationalists from themselves after their war with Turkey ended in rapid defeat. In 1922, however, no one was able to save the Greeks of Asia Minor after the collapse of the Greek campaign to realize a greater Greece culminated in the flight and departure of Greeks from the Black Sea, western Asia Minor, and Eastern Thrace.

In the end, neither Crete nor Asia Minor foreshadowed Cyprus's future. Cyprus never joined Greece, but neither did the island's Greeks suffer the same level of destruction, loss, and flight that had devastated Greeks of Turkey. Instead, in 1974, after years of escalating violence, they lost close to 40 percent of the island. This marked a victory for the concept of *taksim* or partition, ultimately favored by many Turkish Cypriots.

In the 1950s Cypriot Greek nationalists mounted a campaign against the island's British imperial rulers. Greek Cypriot opposition to British rule took two forms, a political movement led by Cypriot Archbishop Makarios III and a guerrilla war launched in 1955 by EOKA (National Organization of Cypriot Fighters) under the leadership of Georgios Grivas, a retired colonel in the Greek army. Durrell, who had taken a post with the government of Cyprus, witnessed the growing violence. "The attacks on police stations sharpened. Rioting and the hoisting of Greek flags everywhere kept the police busy."[27] The outcome, resolved in 1959 in negotiations between Greece and Turkey in Zurich, was neither *enosis* nor partition, both expressly banned, but an experiment in power-sharing between Greeks and Turks in an independent state created in 1960. Greeks elected the president, Archbishop Makarios, Turks the vice president, and the two communities divided up posts in the cabinet, civil service, and military according to quotas. Britain held on to two military bases, and Britain, Greece, and Turkey each retained the right to intervene in Cyprus if the treaty was violated.

The new Cyprus soon became synonymous with ethnic violence. After myriad disputes, fighting began on December 21, 1963, and intensified over the following days. Greek Cypriot fighters, led by Nikos Sampson, attacked Turkish Cypriots and expelled them from their homes in Omorphita, a Nicosia suburb. In the 1950s Sampson had assassinated British soldiers; he actually wrote about some of the killings in a newspaper he published. In 1964 Greek forces—police, irregulars, and soldiers—carried out attacks through much of the island. At Limassol on the south coast, Greek forces assaulted the town's Turkish quarter in February. "All they want to do is to kill us," one woman complained. After heavy fighting, *U.S. News and World Report* observed: "Houses were riddled with gaping holes. Whole walls had been blasted off many of them."[28] By the summer Cyprus was virtually in a state of civil war. The fighting stopped only in early August when Grivas's attack on Turkish Cypriots on the northwest coast prompted bombing raids by the Turkish air force.

As their leaders and diplomats struggled to find a solution for Cyprus, the island's civilians suffered something little short of localized ethnic cleansing. Neither community was swept off the island, but in many locales, civilians—most often Turks—fled their homes. Thousands abandoned homes in the suburbs for comparative safety in the Turkish Cypriot neighborhoods of Nicosia. As the fighting continued, Turkish Cypriots fled dozens of mixed communities. They left, as one refugee from a mixed village explained, because "armed Greeks began coming into the Turkish quarter at night, firing rifles in the air." They stole goods and set off explosions until the village's Turkish Cypriots "were so terrified that we asked the Turkish authorities to . . . take us away." Across the island such terror persuaded some twenty thousand to relocate to remaining Turkish enclaves where housing was in short supply. The psychiatrist Vamik Volkan, for example, "found four families crowded into my family's house" in 1968 when he returned from a visit to the United States.[29]

On the other side of the ethnic divide, Greek Cypriots did not emerge unscathed. Where Turks moved in, they moved out, and the island became ever more clearly delineated into distinct Greek and Turkish zones. As Sir David Hunt, the British high commissioner, later observed, "Many Greek Cypriots left places which had come under Turkish control and there were even a greater influx into them of Turkish Cypriots who felt it unsafe or inadvisable to remain in the more extensive areas still controlled by the government."[30]

Some of the Greek victims of the violence on Cyprus did not live on the island at all but far away in Istanbul. In 1955, as EOKA began its military campaign on Cyprus, demonstrations against EOKA in Turkey soon devolved into anti-Greek riots, including a virtual pogrom on the night of September 6, 1955, with the massive destruction of Greek houses and businesses. In 1964 Istanbul's dwindling population of Greeks again suffered a backlash after violence on Cyprus: Turkey revoked the right, based on a 1930 convention, for some ten thousand Greeks not holding Turkish passports to remain in the country. By September 1965 more than six thousand Greeks, their property seized, had been deported.[31]

The chief symbol of the new Cyprus was the so-called Green Line that divided the island's largest city, Nicosia. Named for the color of the pen used to draw a line on the city's map, the concept for the Green Line dated back to talks in late December 1963 at which British authorities tried to restore peace to Nicosia. Not a single wall as in Berlin but a mixed barrier of sandbags, emptied streets, blocked off houses, sides of buildings, barbed wire, and even oil drums, this neutral zone running through Nicosia and neighboring suburbs became a permanent landmark where United Nations peacekeepers separated Greek and Turkish Cypriot lines.

The end to the Cyprus crisis in 1964 briefly stemmed terror, but in 1967 a military coup in Greece, in which a group of colonels seized control of the Greek government, prompted a new round of violence. The campaign for *enosis* was now firmly identified with the Cypriot allies of the military junta in power in Greece. The colonels in Athens provided Grivas with a new chance to attack

Turkish Cypriots until November 1967 when Turkey threatened military intervention.

Despite their earlier setbacks, radical champions of *enosis* were not done. In 1971 Grivas returned to Cyprus to found a new break-away wing of EOKA, dubbed EOKA-B. Whereas EOKA had once attacked British and Turkish Cypriots, EOKA-B targeted figures in the Cypriot government led by Archbishop Makarios. Grivas died in early 1974, but his movement continued to fight the government of Cyprus. Makarios had grown more cautious and now recognized that *enosis* might not be feasible, at least not under current conditions. Certainly it was not worth another war, or, as one Greek Cypriot government official said, "The idea of *enosis* is a feeling, it's nothing more than that. Everybody believes it cannot be achieved." In an open letter to the Greek president, Makarios accused Greece of seeking to abolish the state of Cyprus and supporting EOKA-B. "The root of the evil," Makarios decried, "is very deep, reaching as far as Athens."[32]

Makarios's fears were warranted. Once again reckless military action undertaken in the name of *enosis* brought ruin for Greeks. A coup of July 15, 1974, dislodged Makarios, replacing him with Nikos Sampson, a stunning choice given Turkey's past record of threatening to intervene in Cyprus during times of crisis. Few, if any, other presidents could have so dismayed and angered Turkish Cypriots and Turkey. Sampson, a newspaper publisher, was best known for his killing of British soldiers during the uprising of the late 1950s and of Turkish Cypriots in 1963. Sampson was president for less than a week, just long enough to hold a press conference and see Turkey invade Cyprus. On July 20 Turkish forces landed on the island's north coast and pushed south toward Nicosia. Forced to concede that they could not defend Cyprus, the Greek government of the colonels— now generals—collapsed.

Outside the initial Turkish zone of occupation, Greek Cypriot forces blockaded and carried out the ethnic cleansing of Turkish Cypriots. One EOKA-B fighter from the village of Argaki in north-western Cyprus, recounting an attack on a neighboring Turkish village, told how he "just went berserk" after one of his comrades was shot. "I burst into a house. There were six or seven people inside and a child. I swung the machine-gun and mowed them down. All seven. Afterwards I noticed the child." Turkish Cypriots decided they could no longer live next to Greek Cypriots. As a teacher from a village northeast of Nicosia explained, "There is not a single Turk who thinks it is possible to live side by side with Greeks."[33] Refugees crammed into towns and villages still under Turkish Cypriot control. Some twelve thousand to thirteen thousand Turks, for example, held out in the old city of Famagusta on the east coast. This pattern of Turks fleeing to towns as Greeks took control of the countryside was reminiscent of Crete in the 1890s and of the Morea in 1821 at the start of the Greek War of Independence.

In August the balance of power on Cyprus shifted again, and so too did much of the island's population. Almost as soon as negotiations in Geneva collapsed on August 13, hundreds of Greeks, fearing a new Turkish attack, began to flee Nicosia. Sure enough, Turkish forces launched a second offensive on August 14 during which they quickly seized just under 40 percent of the island in a drive that culminated with the capture of Famagusta.

Turkish victory brought the ethnic cleansing of many Greek Cypriots. When Turkish forces approached, Greeks fled. As investigators for a U.S. Senate subcommittee discovered, "People moved the instant they saw or thought the Turkish army was advancing towards their town or village. And they moved *instantly*. . . ." Fear was the chief cause of flight. "The stories of rough and sometimes brutal treatment of civilians by Turkish forces in Kyrenia, after the first phase of the invasion, had spread over the island like wildfire." In this state of terror it took only a rumor for civilians to flee. That was the case, for example, for the Greek Cypriots of Argaki. As one refugee explained, "We'd heard what the Turks had done before [during the July invasion], how they'd dishonored women, raped, murdered."[34] These stories reinforced old images of Turks as enemies bent on Greek destruction. Then there was the bombing of the village to send Argaki's Greeks on their way.

In their haste the Cypriot Greeks' flight was not unlike that of
Greeks from Asia Minor in 1922, Christians and Muslims from various parts of Crete in 1896–1897, or Muslims from the Balkans in
1912 or 1877–1878. They made their way out of their towns and villages much like earlier waves of European refugees, their belongings piled into cars, tractors, or carts. Along with pots and pans and
furniture, the refugees on Cyprus also took appliances—televisions
and radios.

Some 150,000 to 200,000 Greek Cypriots fled northern Cyprus.
Within days, between 30,000 and 40,000 crammed into a small town
on the territory of the British Dhekelia base in southeastern Cyprus.
Refugees lined the roads of southern Cyprus. As the U.S. Senate subcommittee study mission observed, "To drive along the roads of
southern Cyprus, is to drive through an endless refugee camp."[35] The
throngs overtaxed the capacity of local authorities to provide shelter
in schools or other buildings, and many camped out in the open.

Bellapais, Lawrence Durrell's old home, was one of the few
places where Greeks remained in northern Cyprus in 1974. The
presence of United Nations troops made the village a safe haven for
Greek Cypriots. Some fled there from the northern port of Kyrenia
when the Turkish army invaded, and about a thousand Greek Cypriots remained in Bellapais behind Turkish lines.[36]

As Greeks moved south, a smaller stream of thirty thousand to
fifty thousand Turkish Cypriot refugees poured north. Turkish and
Greek explanations of their reasons for flight were almost inter-
changeable. As one Turkish Cypriot refugee leader told a *New York
Times* reporter, the Turks "have no confidence in going back to their
villages and living with the Greeks. They can't live with the people
who have been attacking them."[37]

The mass flight triggered by the coup and the Turkish invasion
of 1974 made Cyprus an island divided. The Green Line now extended out from Nicosia until it stretched for 112 miles across the
entire island. This new internal boundary made Cyprus a Germany
in the Mediterranean, long after the 1989 dismantling of the Berlin
Wall, though in April 2003 the Green Line was finally opened to

travel in the Turkish Cypriot north. To the south of the 112-mile-long line lies the Cyprus of the Greeks, or what remains of the Republic of Cyprus; to the north is the Cyprus of the Turks, since 1983 a Turkish Republic of Northern Cyprus that lacks international recognition. That very absence of international recognition created enormous pressure on the north to reunite with the south when Cyprus entered the European Union in 2004. But a large majority of Greek Cypriots voted against reunification in an April 2004 referendum at the same time a majority of Turkish Cypriots voted for reunification.

Mountain Turks

The same basic problem of how to divide into nation-states the multi-ethnic lands once ruled by empires has produced ethnic war, mass flight, and forced migration on both the western and eastern borders of the former Ottoman Empire. Along the western edges, conflicts between Jews and Arabs and between Greeks and Turks intensified with the delayed end of imperial rule when Britain moved out of Palestine and Cyprus. In the east, the states that succeeded the Ottoman Empire repeatedly clashed with Kurds.

Much like Armenians, Kurds once lived in the old empires of Western Asia: the Ottoman, Persian, and Russian empires. But where Armenians lived predominantly in towns or in farming villages, many Kurds maintained a semi-nomadic or nomadic way of life. Kurdish tribal leaders retained a large degree of autonomy in the Ottoman east, and they often held power over Armenian villages in regions that were ostensibly controlled by Ottoman authorities. Most but not all Kurds are Sunni Muslims. Kurds are not Turks or Arabs. Instead they speak languages related to Persian.[38]

Like Armenians, Kurds made progress toward gaining their own state after World War I. In 1920 the Treaty of Sèvres extended the promise of independence for Kurdish areas to the east of the Euphrates River, provided that Kurds, after one year, demonstrated that the majority desired independence and the council of the League

agreed that "the population in question is capable of such independence and recommends that it be granted."[39] This never came to
pass: resurgent Turkish Nationalists, led by Kemal Atatürk, took control of eastern Turkey.

Through the early twenty-first century, Kurds still had not
gained a state. They lived instead under the rule of several states
that succeeded the Ottoman Empire: the Republic of Turkey, Syria,
and Iraq. Kurds also lived in large numbers in Persia or Iran, and
there were smaller Kurdish populations in Russia and Lebanon.
Their population statistics were disputed because the states where
Kurds lived tended to minimize their numbers, but Kurds made up
some 20 percent of the population of Turkey, more than 20 percent
of the population of Iraq, and close to 10 percent of the population
of Iran. With a total population of some 24 million to 27 million by
the late twentieth century, Kurds made up the largest ethnic group
without a state in Europe or Western Asia.

Throughout the twentieth century, relations between Kurds and
their rulers were often hostile. Local uprisings by Kurdish tribes
continued after World War I, and from World War II onward various Kurdish political movements sought to gain self-rule and independence, especially at times when the governments with power
over them weakened. For their part, the governments that ruled
Kurds adopted no single policy—when weak they sometimes offered
concessions to Kurds, but the general trend was toward repression,
forced assimilation, and violent reprisal.

The Turkish Republic, for example, did not acknowledge the existence of Kurds as a people distinct from Turks. In 1924, Kemal
Atatürk set the tone for Turkish policy when he banned Kurdish
publications; denying Kurdish identity remained a cornerstone of
Turkey's treatment of Kurds for many decades. Much like the
Balkan states that sought to force some of their minorities to accept
the dominant national identity, Turkey resorted to cultural repression to try to make Kurds into Turks. Kurds, according to official
parlance, were not Kurds: they were mountain Turks, and these
mountain Turks were not allowed to speak Kurdish, at least not in

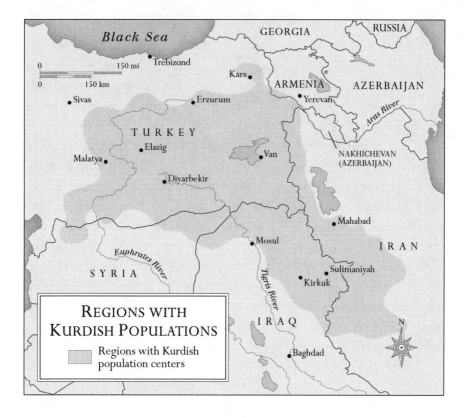

REGIONS WITH
KURDISH POPULATIONS

Regions with Kurdish
population centers

public. Indeed, they could actually be fined for using Kurdish to trade at markets.[40]

Kurdish armed resistance to the Turkish government occurred in two phases. Kurdish uprisings followed almost immediately after the founding of the Turkish Republic. These rebellions in the 1920s and 1930s were not full-scale nationalist revolutions but regional uprisings that continued the long Kurdish tradition of struggle against central authority. By 1938 Turkey had finally suppressed this first wave of Kurdish resistance, but it faced a renewed Kurdish challenge in the 1970s and 1980s. In 1984 the Kurdistan Workers' party (PKK), one of the most radical of all Kurdish parties, began a war in Turkey's east that intensified into the 1990s.[41] The PKK attacked Turkish installations and Kurdish guards recruited by the Turkish government. Both the PKK and Turkish forces carried out killings and summary executions. Turkey finally gained the upper hand in the late 1990s and in 1999 captured the PKK leader, Abdullah Öcalan.

Turkey struck back against Kurds in the 1920s and 1930s with deportations and the destruction of Kurdish villages. These never amounted to full-scale ethnic cleansing; that would not have made sense given that Turkish authorities repeatedly insisted that Kurds were Turks. But Turkish policy verged on ethnic cleansing in battle zones in eastern Anatolia. Commenting on a 1927 law that allowed for deportations of Kurds, British Ambassador Sir George Clerk noted the irony that "the Kurds who were the principal agent employed for the deportation of Armenians, should be in danger of suffering the same fate as the Armenians only twelve years later." Turkish authorities carried out some of their harshest reprisals in the Dersim, a region of central Anatolia to the north of Harput, which central governments had struggled to pacify since Ottoman times. Some Armenians took advantage of the weak government hold over Dersim by escaping there during World War I. After years of unrest, the Turkish government resolved to pacify the Dersim once and for all. Turkish authorities renamed the region Tunceli, placed it under a state of siege in 1936, and carried out a sweeping assault in 1937 and 1938 that included bombing, the destruction of villages, and deportations.[42]

Turkish forces carried out even more sweeping attacks and deportations during the war against the PKK in the 1980s and 1990s. The basic Turkish strategy consisted of forcing out villagers and burning their homes. "They ordered us to leave our houses," one witness told Human Rights Watch, "and told us to gather near the school. They told us we supported the PKK, and that they were going to burn the village." According to witnesses, Turkish soldiers, forces of the Ministry of the Interior known as Jandarma, special Jandarma units called the Özel Tim, and village guards recruited from local residents carried out such raids. The Turkish air force was also involved. According to Human Rights Watch, between 1984 and 1995 more than 2,000 Kurdish villages were destroyed, most by Turkish security forces. Even the Turkish minister of the interior said in 1995 that some 2,200 Kurdish villages had been "emptied or evacuated." All told, more than 3,000 villages were emptied of their inhabitants during the war. More than a million Kurds were either forced from their homes or fled the war zone, and estimates of the displaced reached as high as 3 million. Many of these internally displaced people left for slums in Turkey's large cities, including Istanbul.[43]

Turkey also resorted to political and cultural repression of the Kurds. The most prominent victims included the Zana family of the city of Diyarbekir in southeastern Turkey. Mehdi Zana was a Kurdish political activist who had been elected mayor of Diyarbekir in 1977, but three years later he was imprisoned. Released in 1991, Zana was returned to prison in 1994 and left for exile in Sweden upon his release in 1995. His wife, Leyla Zana, only fifteen years old when she married Mehdi, went to school and became a politician herself. She won a seat in Turkey's parliament in 1991, but her first act as a deputy created political shockwaves. She wore a headband with the Kurdish colors: yellow, green, and red, and after taking a loyalty oath in Turkish she added a few words in Kurdish: she intended to "struggle so that the Kurdish and Turkish peoples may live together in a democratic framework." Forced from her political party for this transgression, Zana and other deputies founded the new Democratic party, but in 1994 the Turkish Parliament lifted parliamentary immunity for Zana and her fellow deputies, claiming they were affiliated with the PKK. Leyla Zana and her fellow deputies received fifteen-year prison sentences.[44] A retrial, after the European Court of Human Rights found her original conviction unfair, confirmed her original sentence, but she was released in June 2004, pending yet another retrial.

To the south and east of Turkey, Kurds also repeatedly clashed with their rulers in Iran and even more so in Iraq. Iraq, like Turkey, had its origins as a successor state to the shattered Ottoman Empire. It would have emerged from the empire without a large Kurdish minority if Britain, for military and economic reasons, had not insisted on attaching the Ottoman province of Mosul to Mesopotamia. Turkey also claimed Mosul, but in 1925 the League of Nations accepted the British position, and Iraq, then a British mandate, received most of the region.[45] Britain soon entered into negotiations on granting Iraq independence, and the end of the British mandate in 1930 left the Kurds of the Mosul province in Iraq.

Kurds repeatedly staged uprisings in Iraq and in adjacent regions of Iran. Typically they launched rebellions when central government authorities appeared weak. Thus there is a long history of Kurdish uprising during or immediately after wars. The early uprisings were regional and tribal, but Kurdish revolutionary movements became increasingly nationalist during the twentieth century.

Mullah Mustafa Barzani of the Barzani tribe of northeastern Iraq was the most famous of all Kurdish revolutionaries. With his elder brother Sheikh Ahmad, he fought the government of Iraq in an uprising in 1931 and 1932 that was suppressed with the help of the Royal Air Force. In 1945 Barzani declared revolution but retreated under Iraqi pressure to the town of Mahabad in northern Iran. Mahabad flourished as a center of Kurdish nationalism during World War II after the Soviet Union took control of northern Iran in 1941. The Republic of Mahabad declared its independence in January 1946 but soon fell to Iranian forces, and in 1947 Barzani retreated to the USSR. He returned to Iraq from exile in 1958 after a revolution that briefly led to improved relations between the central government and Iraq's Kurds, but renewed fighting broke out in 1961.[46]

Kurdish nationalism developed a new intensity after the Baath party took control of Iraq in 1968. At first the new regime in Baghdad, uncertain of its power, offered Kurds in the north elements of self-rule, but the status of the city of Kirkuk and its oil fields proved a major problem. Saddam Hussein's regime and Kurdish leaders disputed whether Kirkuk would lie within the borders of a Kurdish region. In 1974 Baghdad unilaterally announced an autonomy measure that maintained central control over Kirkuk. Barzani refused to accept these terms and launched his last uprising. He depended on Iran for support, but Iraq concluded an agreement with Iran in 1975 and defeated Barzani.[47] This was Mullah Mustafa Barzani's final defeat—he died in 1979 in the United States. But in 1980 Iraq's invasion of Iran weakened the Iraqi military presence in Kurdish areas and sparked renewed Kurdish revolution by two competing Kurdish parties, the Kurdistan Democratic party (KDP) led by Mullah Mustafa's son Massoud Barzani, and the Patriotic Union of Kurdistan party (PUK) led by Jalal Talabani.

The governments of Iraq and Iran both employed selected deportations as a tool to suppress Kurdish uprisings, but in Iraq deportation gradually developed into ethnic cleansing. After suppressing Mullah Mustafa Barzani's final uprising, Iraq embarked on a campaign to remake the population of parts of northern Iraq. The government destroyed numerous Kurdish villages and provided incentives to Arabs to replace Kurds. Sunni Arabs from the desert south of Mosul, for example, moved north into Kurdish lands. As one Arab explained of his move into a Kurdish village in 1975, "We were very happy to go to the north because we had no irrigated lands in the south." Meanwhile tens of thousands of Kurds were deported south. In 1978 and 1979 Iraq cleared a zone of close to twenty miles along areas of its northern border, and destroyed hundreds more Kurdish villages. All told, Iraq pushed about a quarter of a million non-Arabs, including Kurds, out of their lands.[48]

Between 1987 and 1989 Iraq carried out an even more violent campaign against the country's Kurds. In 1987 Saddam placed his cousin Ali Hassan al-Majid in charge of retaking control over Iraq's north, and in April Iraqi forces first used the weapon that would give al-Majid the name that made him internationally notorious: "Chemical Ali." Iraqi forces released chemical weapons over Kurdish villages in the valley of Balisan. They also destroyed hundreds of villages. Peter Galbraith, a staff member for the U.S. Senate Foreign Relations Committee, saw some of the destruction in September 1987. The Iraqi ambassador to the United States offered to let Galbraith visit, and Iraqi forces surprisingly allowed Galbraith and an American diplomat to continue on their way into the Kurdish region where they found that most of the Kurdish towns and villages along the road had been destroyed.[49]

The war against Iraq's Kurds culminated in 1989 with the Anfal Operation in which Iraqi forces burned villages, launched chemical

attacks, and relocated Kurds. This was an ambitious program of ethnic cleansing. Al-Majid described his goals in a tape of an April 1988
meeting. "By next summer," he said, "there will be no more villages
remaining that are spread out here and there throughout the region,
but only camps." He spoke of prohibiting settlements in large areas
and of mass evacuations: "No human beings except on the main
roads." The most infamous Iraqi gas attack of the Anfal Operation
took place on March 16 at the town of Halabja; many other towns
and villages suffered a similar fate. On the afternoon of May 3, 1988,
Kurds at the village of Goktapa, for example, heard the sound of
Iraqi jets. Goktapa had been bombed many times before, but this
time was different. As one witness recounted, "When the bombing
started, the sound was different from previous times. . . . I saw smoke
rising, first white, then turning to gray. . . . The smoke smelled like
a matchstick when you burn it. I passed out."[50] In all, Iraqi forces
killed about 100,000 Kurds during the Anfal Operation and forced
hundreds of thousands out of their homes.

The final Iraqi campaign to remake the ethnic map of the country's north followed immediately after the Gulf War of 1991. With
the Allied victory, Kurds staged a nationalist revolution and took
over virtually all of the Kurdish areas of northern Iraq. After reaching a cease-fire, Saddam Hussein struck back against the Kurds. The
fall of Kirkuk in late March to Iraqi forces unleashed a wave of
flight. More than a million Kurds fled north. They crossed by the
thousands over mountains to the border of Turkey. The Turkish government did not welcome the refugees, though local Kurds did what
they could to provide food. One Kurdish baker in southeastern
Turkey increased his bread production more than threefold. "I don't
know if it's enough," he told a reporter. "But everyone from this
area is helping."[51]

This crisis so soon after the Allied victory in the Gulf War
gained international attention. Acting on humanitarian grounds, the
United States, Britain, and France created a "safe haven" close to
Iraq's northern border with Turkey and established a "no-fly zone"
for the Iraqi air force north of the thirty-sixth parallel. By October

1991 Iraqi forces and authorities withdrew from most Kurdish regions of Iraq's north with the exception of Kirkuk. The effective division of northern Iraq into Kurdish and Iraqi zones simultaneously advanced Kurdish interests and the Iraqi regime's campaign to Arabize the north. Kurds gained autonomy, but the Iraqi government accelerated its campaign to remake Kirkuk into an Arab city and region. Iraqi authorities deported 100,000 people from Kirkuk and other communities and encouraged Arabs to move north to replace them.[52]

Turks into Bulgarians

Through the late twentieth century there were many cases of ethnic and religious conflict and repression of undesired ethnic and religious groups in former Ottoman lands, including Bulgaria, Lebanon, and Syria. Bulgaria, for example, carried out several campaigns of repression against its Turks. Bulgaria's Turkish population declined after the Russo-Turkish War of 1877–1878 and the First Balkan War in 1912–1913, but the country nonetheless retained a Turkish minority. Turks remained a strong presence in districts along Bulgaria's southern central border and in some districts of the northeast. In all, they made up some 10 percent of Bulgaria's population, and 15 percent of Bulgarians were Muslims.

Bulgaria's Turks had reason to wonder whether their communities would survive the Communist regime that took power after World War II. In 1950 Bulgaria demanded that Turkey accept some 250,000 Bulgarian Turks termed "willing to emigrate" within three months. The movement did not proceed that quickly, but 155,000 Bulgarian Turks, many from the Varna region of the northeast, left by the end of 1951 when Turkey closed its borders.

Bulgaria's government renewed persecution of the country's Turks during the last decades of Communist rule. In a broad campaign that peaked in the 1980s, the Bulgarian regime denied the very existence of Bulgaria's Turks. Adopting what amounted to a theory of false identity, Bulgarian leadership under Todor Zhivkov, the country's last Communist dictator, decided that Bulgaria's Turks and Muslims were in fact Bulgarians deprived of their true identity by the conversion of their forebears. Acting much like one of the nationalizing Balkan states of the early twentieth century, Communist Bulgaria tried to restore Turks' supposed hidden Bulgarian identity by banning virtually all expression of Turkish identity as well as many features of Islam. Bulgaria shut down Turkish and Islamic institutions, abolished male circumcision, brought legal sanction against speaking Turkish in public, and abolished Turkish names. The forced name-changing campaign first targeted the Pomaks, Bulgarian-speaking Muslims concentrated in the Rhodope Mountains of southern Bulgaria, between 1971 and 1974, and by 1984 and 1985 expanded to cover Turks throughout most of the country. Fines for speaking Turkish in public and similar penalties prompted resistance, in turn countered by a violent crackdown by Bulgarian security forces. Reports received by Western diplomats told of hundreds of deaths among Bulgaria's Turks.[53]

In 1989, Todor Zhivkov began his last campaign against Bulgaria's Turks, forcing them to leave the country. Zhivkov may have decided to cleanse the Turks because he feared that the comparatively higher birthrate among Bulgaria's Turks would swell the country's Turkish minority. Perhaps, as when he spoke of "circles who harbor the hope of turning the wheel of history back to the times of the Ottoman Empire," he also hoped to cultivate support among Bulgarian nationalists. Whatever the motive, Bulgarian police and soldiers forced Turks out of their homes. "Policemen with dogs came in the night and told us to get out," explained one Turkish refugee in mid-June. Another refugee told of soldiers who arrived, "gave us our passports and told us to leave immediately."[54] Bulgarian officials claimed their newly liberal passport policy, not coercion, caused Turks to leave.

The town of Kapikule on the Turkish border with Bulgaria was the place to watch Bulgarian Turks leave the country in the late spring and summer of 1989, and they did so by the thousands. By mid-June, 3,000 a day were crossing from Bulgaria into Turkey, and by August the rate had increased to some 4,000 a day. The refugees arrived by car, train, bicycle, and by foot, and piled up at the border crossing in lines that grew ever longer: from six to thirteen to even fifteen miles long.[55] The Turks of 1989 were probably not as terrified as the Muslims of 1878 who had clung to the tops of trains in midwinter, or the civilians who had fled irregular bands in 1912, but Bulgaria's Turks nonetheless abandoned their homes and packed up their clothes, food, and, if they had a big enough vehicle, ovens, washing machines, and refrigerators. These were clearly people who did not expect to return home, though many eventually did. The stream of people continued until late August 1989, when Turkey, unable to absorb the torrent, shut its border to continued flight from Bulgaria. By that time some 300,000 or more had already left Bulgaria. This marked the largest single flight of refugees in Europe since the immediate aftermath of World War II, though as many as half or even more of the Turks later returned to Bulgaria.

Bulgaria itself suffered immediate economic damage as large segments of the labor force emptied out of entire districts, leaving factories and farms understaffed. The population of Razgrad in southern Bulgaria, for example, once 75,000, reportedly fell to 15,000 by early July.[56] The economic consequences were obvious: Bulgaria could ill afford to drive out its Turks. If Zhivkov's last campaign against Bulgarian Turks gratified nationalist circles, it utterly failed to bolster the government. As governments collapsed across the eastern bloc, Zhivkov too lost power in November 1989.

Bellapais and Jaffa

Mass flight and forced migration continued to transform the ethnic makeup of cities, towns, and villages in former Ottoman lands long after the empire had disappeared. The predominantly Greek village of Bellapais on Cyprus, for example, became a Turkish village. Greek Cypriots initially remained in Bellapais, but in 1976 they were expelled. Greek villagers were given the choice of leaving with their belongings or being expelled with nothing. Turkish Cypriot refugees from the south, in turn, settled in Bellapais. Most came from a single village near the southern town of Limassol.[57]

In Israel, ethnic war permanently changed the relationship between Tel Aviv and the port of Jaffa, where David Ben-Gurion had first arrived in 1906 as a young Zionist. The old city that predated the new Jewish city of Tel Aviv by thousands of years became the southern portion of the Tel Aviv metropolis. The rapid growth of Tel Aviv after 1948 testified to the success of Zionism, but Jaffa fell on hard times. Most of the city's Arab residents left for good in 1948, though a few thousand Arabs from Jaffa and from nearby villages stayed. In the 1950s Jewish immigrants moved into some of the old Palestinian Arab neighborhoods, but the Jewish newcomers soon moved elsewhere. In the 1960s Jaffa actually began to become more Arab, as Palestinian Arabs, seldom the city's original inhabitants, moved in. Urban renewal in the 1960s brought artists to the remaining sections of the old town, but the predominantly Arab neighborhood of Ajami became known in Tel Aviv for crime and neglect. In October 2000 Tel Aviv's mayor conceded, "Jaffa has been discriminated against for a long time."[58]

From the eastern Mediterranean to Iraq, the same basic problem of dividing up the lands of a diverse empire into nation-states generated ethnic war and in some cases ethnic cleansing, but the precise causes and the intensity of flight and forced migration varied greatly. Governments played a much greater role than ordinary people in planning and executing the deportations of Kurds in Turkey and Iraq. Their forced migration was never complete. Israel, as well, did not become a completely homogenous nation-state; it retained a significant Arab population. On Cyprus, in contrast, ethnic war divided old neighbors completely.

Ethnic cleansing is incomplete in several old Ottoman lands, but for that very reason these cases continued to promote conflict into the early twenty-first century. While no one expects a reversal of past ethnic cleansing in Central and Eastern Europe, the status of Palestinian refugees remains unresolved more than a half-century after Israel's founding. The division of Cyprus resurfaced as a major issue as recently as 2004, when the Republic of Cyprus, the island's southern region held by Greek Cypriots, gained membership in the European Union. The possibility that Turkey might gain EU membership also brought attention to the rights of Kurds in Turkey. And in Iraq the right of return of displaced Kurds emerged as a key issue after the American-led invasion in 2003.

CHAPTER EIGHT

"A Kind of Second Reality"

THE CAUCASUS AND YUGOSLAVIA, 1988–1999

In her book, *The Key to My Neighbor's House: Seeking Justice in Bosnia and Rwanda*, the *Boston Globe* correspondent Elizabeth Neuffer, who later died in an automobile accident while reporting on the war in Iraq, described the town of Kozarac in northwestern Bosnia. Situated at the foot of low mountains, Kozarac lies between the cities of Prijedor and Banja Luka. In 1992 it was a town of four thousand residents, mostly Bosnian Muslims, but Serbs also lived in Kozarac as well as in outlying villages. Kozarac was well known within Yugoslavia; it had been a center of partisan activity during World War II, and it was comparatively prosperous. The region's residents worked in tourism, in iron ore production, and in lumber, and the town also benefited from remittances by men who went to work in Germany and Austria and then invested their savings back home.[1]

In 1992 Kozarac was destroyed during the early weeks of the war for Bosnia-Herzegovina. On May 24 Serb forces, including Serbs from the Yugoslav army who had taken up arms with a Bosnian Serb army, began to shell Kozarac. Two days later they entered the town and carried out ethnic cleansing of Bosnian Muslims. Over loudspeakers, Serb fighters ordered residents to come out of their basements. They separated women from men, shot some men on the spot, forced the others onto buses, and took them to camps. Most of Kozarac, except for Serb houses, was burned.

Kozarac was one of many towns destroyed in Yugoslavia and in the Caucasus when Europe experienced its last major wave of ethnic cleansing in the twentieth century. Once again the breakup of empires generated terror and mass flight in ethnically mixed regions. This time two Communist "empires," the Soviet Union and Yugoslavia, fell apart. Neither state was in name an empire, but both bore a striking resemblance to the empires that had once ruled the border lands of Europe and Asia. Long after most of the countries in Central and Eastern Europe had become nation-states, the Soviet Union and Yugoslavia remained extremely diverse multinational states.[2]

The violence of the 1990s was especially shocking because people from different ethnic and religious groups in Yugoslavia and the Soviet Caucasus seemed to get along well enough. They lived close together, attended the same schools, and worked alongside one another. Bosnia, Croatia, Serbia, Azerbaijan, and Armenia did not appear near the top of lists of global hotspots in the 1960s or 1970s. Had Bosnia been a site of conflict then, its capital city of Sarajevo would certainly never have been chosen by the International Olympic Committee as the site of the 1984 Winter Olympic Games. In part this earlier era of ethnic and religious peace was the product of dictators who made previously hostile ethnic and religious groups into brothers in socialism. But ordinary people themselves also built cordial relations with their neighbors from different ethnic or religious groups. They had not forgotten the history of past violence, the killings during World War II in much of Yugoslavia or the deportations in the Caucasus, but they did not enshrine those memories as principles dictating their daily behavior and personal relationships. Serbs, for example, had suffered from Ustasha, or Croatian fascists, during World War II, but they did not usually regard their Croatian neighbors as killers.

A now familiar sequence of steps led to ethnic cleansing in both the Caucasus and Yugoslavia after years of peace under Communist

dictators. First, democratization and the opening of politics rein-
vigorated nationalism, and intellectuals and political leaders championed nationalist causes and called for the protection of national
homelands. Second, the breakup of empires in multiethnic regions
pitted neighbors against each other in power struggles to divide up
the former imperial lands. Finally, acts of violence revived stories
of ethnic and religious conflict and justified revenge killing.⁸ To
point out the links between democracy, extreme nationalism, and
violence in Yugoslavia and the Caucasus is certainly not to make an
argument in support of authoritarian regimes; but these connections should make us question the facile assumption that democracy will automatically create stability in other postimperial multiethnic regions.

Glasnost and Cleansing

It was no coincidence that ethnic violence struck the Caucasus only a
few years after Mikhail Gorbachev, the last leader of the USSR, initiated a reform program. Gorbachev sought to strengthen the USSR
with his policies of Perestroika (restructuring) and Glasnost (open-
ness), but his reforms created a series of extraordinary paradoxes.
Gorbachev himself never intended to be the Soviet Union's final
leader. He turned away from past repression, but his reforms brought
violence as well as liberty. The new freedom created an opening for
nationalist movements in Soviet borderlands. Rival nationalists often
coveted the same lands, and when the Soviet Union broke apart, they
went to war in the Caucasus.

In a land of fifteen republics, numerous autonomous regions,
and more than a hundred recognized ethnic groups, there were
many potential hotspots for ethnic conflict. In the Soviet west, earlier waves of pogroms, ethnic cleansing, and genocide reduced the
likelihood of new troubles. In the Baltic region, on the other hand,
the presence of large Russian populations caused tension with Esto-
nians and Latvians who viewed Russians as demographic threats to
their own national identities. But all Soviet successor states, close by

the much larger and more powerful Russian Republic, were highly unlikely to consider the ethnic cleansing of Russians, even if any political leader of influence had advocated such a policy. In the south, however, along the Soviet border across the Caucasus, all conditions were ripe for a new explosion of ethnic violence. It would have been impossible to superimpose a map of homogenous nation-states across this terrain even if the peoples of the Caucasus had trusted one another, and they did not. Many of the region's ethnic groups harbored deep resentments dating back to past genocide and deportations. Chechens and Ingush, for instance, remembered their sudden deportation by Stalin to the Soviet east during World War II, and Armenians remembered the genocide of 1915.

Old borders played a key role in shaping conflict as the Soviet empire weakened and then fell. Where peoples lived within the Russian Republic, nationalist movements directly confronted Russian power. In Chechnya in the north Caucasus, for example, successive Russian regimes sought to hold on to what they helped make a land of ruin and rubble. But ethnic groups who lived beyond Russia's borders could seek to cleanse each other in the newly independent states of Georgia, Armenia, and Azerbaijan.

"Go Back to Your Armenia"

By the Soviet map, Armenians and Azerbaijanis lived in different Soviet Republics, but in real life they often did not. Azerbaijanis made up a large minority in Armenia, the same was true of Armenians in Azerbaijan, and both groups lived in the region of Nagorno Karabakh or "Mountainous Black Garden" in western Azerbaijan. Despite its Armenian majority, Nagorno Karabakh had been assigned to Azerbaijan in the early Soviet era, as had the region of Nakhichevan. Over decades the Armenian population of Nakhichevan dwindled, but Armenians still clung to their position as the largest population group within Nagorno Karabakh.

Despite a past history of violence between Armenians and Azerbaijanis in 1905 and during the Russian civil war years of 1918 to

1920, it was not obvious that the collapse of the Soviet Union would lead to interethnic war in Armenia and Azerbaijan. After 1945 Armenians and Azerbaijanis often lived alongside or at least close by each other. There were many thousands of Armenians in Azerbaijani cities, including the capital Baku, and there were many Azerbaijani villages in Armenia. Even after war broke out, many refugees recalled previously cordial relations between Armenians and Azerbaijanis.[4] They had been neighbors, colleagues, even friends.

Armenians and Azerbaijanis did not always hate each other, but strong nationalist identities survived in the Caucasus throughout the Soviet era. This was especially true for Armenians. From the 1960s onward Armenian nationalism developed an increasingly strong focus on the memory of genocide. In 1965 a popular gathering on the fiftieth anniversary of the Armenian genocide made April 24 a day of commemoration in Armenia, and an official genocide monument was constructed in 1967.[5] Armenian memories of genocide also preserved an animosity against Azerbaijanis to the extent that Armenians identified Azerbaijanis, a Turkish people, as Turks.

A more open political climate in the 1980s radicalized nationalism in Armenia and Azerbaijan. As elsewhere in the USSR, Glasnost created more freedom for self-expression in Armenia and Azerbaijan, but Armenians and Azerbaijanis used their new freedom to voice irreconcilable goals: both peoples wanted Nagorno Karabakh.[6] Nationalists went into the streets to chant slogans and stake their competing claims to Nagorno Karabakh. Armenians, in the Armenian capital Yerevan and in Stepanakert, the chief city of Nagorno Karabakh, demanded the union of Nagorno Karabakh with Armenia. Azerbaijanis, to the contrary, went into the streets in Baku to insist that Nagorno Karabakh remain part of Azerbaijan.

Violence between Armenians and Azerbaijanis began in 1987, but the new conflict first gained widespread attention in February 1988 because of a pogrom in the Azerbaijani industrial city of Sumgait on the Caspian Sea coast, twenty miles north of Baku. Sumgait itself had little history of ethnic violence—it had been founded only

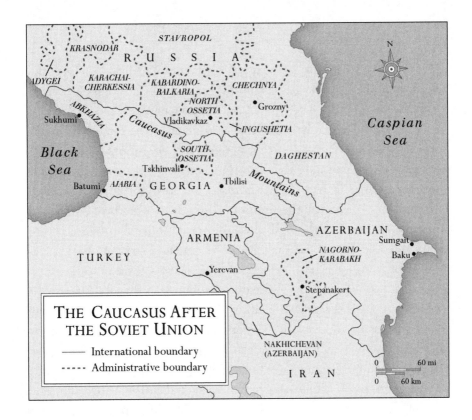

THE CAUCASUS AFTER
THE SOVIET UNION

——— International boundary
----- Administrative boundary

in 1949—and few of the city's ten thousand to twenty thousand Armenians imagined that a pogrom could occur in the Soviet Union in the late 1980s.

Crowds of Azerbaijanis gathered in Sumgait's Lenin Square on February 26 and 27, 1988. Reversing the slogans heard in Armenian demonstrations in Armenia and Nagorno Karabakh, they chanted "Karabagh! Karabagh! We won't give Karabagh to the Armenians!" One leader of the demonstrations was an Azerbaijani who had recently fled Armenia, and told of Armenian killings of his relatives. From chanting slogans, Azerbaijani demonstrators turned on February 27 to looting and attacking Armenians. They searched for Armenians on city buses. "Any Armenians in there? Out with you!" the crowds shouted as they stopped trolleys, beating Armenians. The next day Azerbaijanis, some armed with sharpened steel rods, hunted Armenians in Sumgait's large apartment complexes. "Death to the Armenians! Armenians come out!" they shouted before one apartment building.[7]

Amid the roar of a gathering mob, Armenian families had moments to barricade themselves into their apartments or seek shelter.
As members of one Armenian family discovered, help was hard to
find. "We'll kill you ourselves! Get out of here," the sons of an Azerbaijani neighbor shouted at them; and other neighbors told them to
go away before one neighbor let them into his bathroom. Some Armenians sought to transform themselves into Azerbaijanis, a difficult task on the spur of the moment, though turning on Azerbaijani
music could help. In the end, though, many Armenians closed their
doors, pushed furniture up against them, and armed themselves
with whatever lay at hand—belt buckles, knives, even boiling water.
First came the pounding on the door mixed with threats, but sooner
or later the mob entered. Recalling what happened next, one young
Armenian woman, Karine Grigorevna, explained, "It's like they
blew on it and it broke and fell right into the hall." As the
pogromists burst in, they shouted, "Get out of here, leave . . . go back
to your Armenia." They beat her mother and father, raped her, and
tried to throw her sister out of a window.[8] By the time the pogrom
had ended, some thirty-one or thirty-two people, according to official Soviet sources, had died, though Armenians listed a higher
death toll.

The Sumgait pogrom played a key part in reanimating and redi-
recting Armenian national fear and hatred of Turks. It was not simply the murders and other acts of violence that shocked Armenians.
As an isolated event Sumgait was dreadful, but Armenians saw it as
a new episode in a long history of violence against their people. From
this perspective Sumgait had a broader and more sinister significance
than any single massacre. It was more than a pogrom; it signaled the
start of a new genocide. Sumgait confirmed an Armenian vision of
history in which Turks always threatened to exterminate Armenians.
The pogrom, as Armenians saw it, fused the past of genocide with
the present of ethnic violence, and it identified Azerbaijanis as Turks.
Protesting trials held after the pogrom, Armenian demonstrators outside the Supreme Soviet in Moscow held signs with the slogan "Recognize the fact of Armenian genocide in Sumgait."[9]

During the last years of the Soviet Union, Azerbaijanis fled Armenia and Armenians fled Azerbaijan. By early December 1988 Soviet sources were referring to the flight of more than 100,000 people in Armenia and Azerbaijan. In some cases, such as at the village of Aidarli, the mass exodus actually saved lives from the earthquake that devastated much of Armenia on December 7, 1988.[10] In November local Armenians had blockaded Aidarli, and hundreds of Azerbaijanis had already left for the Republic of Azerbaijan before December 7. When the quake struck, only four people died. So many people had already gathered outside for a meeting to explain the newest evacuation plan that they escaped the collapse of homes they were soon due to leave.

Pogroms, ethnic cleansing, and population transfers continued as long as Armenians and Azerbaijanis lived near each other. In the countryside, Azerbaijanis and Armenians who lived in ethnically mixed areas found themselves besieged, their villages cut off and blockaded, their cars stoned, their animals killed, and their houses burned by their neighbors or by militias, often one and the same. In larger towns and cities, minority populations suffered attacks. In January 1990 a pogrom devastated Armenians in Baku. As in Sumgait almost two years earlier, crowds pounded on doors, hunted for Armenians, beat them, and injured and killed many, by the lowest count 74 and possibly hundreds. The pogrom ended with most of Baku's Armenians, some 50,000 people, ferried out of the city. This was symptomatic of a broader trend. Between 1988 and 1990, 250,000 Azerbaijanis left Armenia, and 300,000 Armenians left Azerbaijan.[11]

War for Nagorno Karabakh

With the collapse of the Soviet Union in 1991, the conflict between Azerbaijanis and Armenians entered a new phase: war for the disputed enclave of Nagorno Karabakh. In this war Armenia and Azerbaijan were now fully independent states, but only one, Azerbaijan, was an open combatant. In Nagorno Karabakh a breakaway

Armenian government declared the region's independence in January 1992. The Republic of Armenia was officially neutral, a position difficult to reconcile with reports of supplies entering Nagorno Karabakh from Armenia.

Victory in this war was tantamount to ethnic cleansing. Although outnumbered by Azerbaijan's military on paper, Armenian forces gained early victories, and as they advanced, Azerbaijanis fled. One of the most notorious Armenian attacks on Azerbaijanis took place in late February at the town of Khojaly, near the eastern border of central Karabakh. Armenian forces surrounded the town, told the population, according to survivors, to "get out or die," and attacked from three sides on the night of February 25–26. Azerbaijanis, who climbed over snowbound mountains to reach the nearby town of Agdam in Azerbaijan, told of a massacre of refugees trapped in a ravine and of hundreds left dead. "They were shooting, shooting, shooting," one woman said after she reached Agdam without her husband and son-in-law. Agdam itself was far from a secure safe harbor: thousands fled fearing a further Armenian advance. An American journalist on the scene described "a mass exodus of trucks, cars, horses, and people on bicycles."[12]

In May 1992 Armenian forces won further victories, including the capture of Shusha on the heights above Stepanakert. Shusha was the site of one of many past Armenian tragedies. In 1920 Azerbaijanis had suppressed an Armenian uprising at Shusha and destroyed much of the Armenian town. For Armenians, victory at Shusha on May 9 therefore revenged past wrongs and ended months of Azerbaijani rocket attacks. Armenians in Stepanakert stopped sleeping in basements and went uphill to loot Shusha. Some, chiefly refugees, stayed there. "Since our houses were reduced to ruin, we don't feel it's wrong to live here," explained one Armenian refugee who moved into an abandoned apartment in Shusha.[13] In the same month Armenians also seized a very narrow strip of land at the village of Lachin that had previously separated Nagorno Karabakh from the Republic of Armenia, thus opening up a direct route between the breakaway region and Armenia.

Armenian forces held the edge for much of early 1992, but when Azerbaijani forces advanced, Armenians fled. An Azerbaijani counteroffensive in northern Nagorno Karabakh in June and July 1992 propelled a stream of Armenians south. Some forty thousand fled toward Stepanakert, creating yet another humanitarian disaster. The military setback also stoked broader fears among Armenians, who continued to see events through a lens formed by genocide. They feared not just defeat but extermination. In June 1992 an Armenian who had originally fled from Baku told a reporter, "We are about to undergo our next genocide. Do you people in the West know what happened to us in 1915?" In July the Foreign Ministry of Armenia appealed to the UN to "end this new Armenian genocide."[14]

When Armenian forces, in turn, regained the initiative, Azerbaijani civilians fled. An April 1993 offensive by Karabakh Armenians (supported, according to many reports, by the Republic of Armenia) into the Azerbaijani province of Kelbajar prompted mass flight. Tens of thousands fled north from Kelbajar, climbing over mountain passes to an altitude of twelve thousand feet before storms blocked their exit. "People were running through the snow, falling . . . the wind was horrible," one refugee told of the mountain journey.[15] Some died in the snow, others suffered frostbite.

As the war for Nagorno Karabakh dragged on, the circle of civilians at risk expanded: first Armenians and Azerbaijanis in the enclave itself, then Azerbaijanis living between the enclave and the Republic of Armenia, and finally Azerbaijanis to the south and east of Nagorno Karabakh. Their position became perilous in 1993 when the Karabakh Armenian forces pushed out of the enclave with the aim of creating a security belt, but security for Armenians came at a high price for Azerbaijanis. The terror was almost palpable at the town of Agdam as Azerbaijani military positions collapsed in early June 1993. Azerbaijani civilians fled the town by any conveyance at hand: by car, by truck, in wagons, and on foot. Towns and villages were deserted across a broad swath of southwestern Azerbaijan as Armenian forces continued their push south toward the Iranian border, penning thousands of Azerbaijanis up against the Araks River on Azerbaijan's boundary with Iran. When Armenians began another offensive in autumn, civilians ran toward the Araks. "The Armenians were shelling us as we waited to cross the river," one twelve-year-old refugee told a journalist after fighting in October. "I was very scared. I saw several children of my age swept away by the current."[16]

A cease-fire in 1994, following a winter of combat between Armenian and Azerbaijani forces, ended hostilities, but the cold peace that followed only confirmed the results of ethnic cleansing. For Azerbaijanis and Armenians, freedom from Soviet authority meant freedom from each other. That sometimes meant living in each other's houses when refugees moved into an apartment left empty by another family's flight. In Baku, for example, Azerbaijanis moved into Armenians' apartments, while at Shusha several thousand Armenians, many refugees from Baku, moved into Azerbaijanis' apartments.[17] In effect this was population exchange on a personal level. Many refugees, however, ended up in emergency quarters. The more than 600,000 Azerbaijani refugees living in Azerbaijan outside of Nagorno Karabakh faced special hardship. Officially they were classified as internally displaced persons or IDPs rather than as refugees because they had crossed no internationally recognized boundary, but internal displacement looked much the same as ethnic cleansing. Internally displaced Azerbaijanis lived in camps, public buildings, factories, railway cars, stone huts, and even in pits carved from the earth.

The End of the "Red Riviera"

To the south of the high Caucasus peaks, the chain of ethnic violence generated by the breakup of the Soviet empire extended into Georgia as well as Armenia and Azerbaijan. The three new republics shared broadly similar causes of instability: a complex mix of ethnic and religious groups and multiple nationalist movements that seized the opportunity of Glasnost to contest ownership of the same lands. The outcomes were similar: war, ethnic cleansing, and the displacement of hundreds of thousands of refugees, many of them defined as internally displaced persons.

Like its neighbors, Georgia on the eve of Soviet collapse was divided by ethnicity, religion, and language. Georgians, mostly Orthodox Christians, made up some 70 percent of the population. Other Christians included Armenians, Greeks, Russians, and most of the republic's Ossetians, speakers of a Persian language. About 65,000 of Georgia's population of some 160,000 or more Ossetians lived in the Autonomous Region of South Ossetia. Georgia's chief Muslim populations included Ajars, Azerbaijanis, and most of the republic's Abkhazians. The vast majority of Georgia's Abkhazians were concentrated in the Abkhazian Autonomous Region along Georgia's northwestern Black Sea coast, but even there the approximately 90,000 Abkhazians made up less than one-fifth of the population.[18]

For Georgia's varied peoples, the chief issue of the era of independence was how to balance Georgian nationalist aspirations for separation from Russia against the wishes of other groups living within the Georgian Republic for greater autonomy, and perhaps even independence from Georgia. Ossetians and Abkhazians posed the chief challenges to Georgian authority. Ossetians favored either autonomy for South Ossetia or union with the adjacent region of North Ossetia in the Russian Federation, but in 1990 the Georgian Paliament abolished South Ossetia's autonomous status. Abkhazians, for their part, also split with Georgians over their political status. In March 1991 a referendum on the future of the Soviet Union signaled the growing rift between Georgians and both the Abkhazians and Ossetians. Georgians boycotted the vote, but a large majority of those voting in Abkhazia favored staying within the USSR, and Ossetians similarly voted in large numbers for remaining in the Soviet Union.

Bridging the gap between Georgians and Abkhazians and Ossetians would have required enormous tact and readiness to compromise. These were not the talents of Zviad Gamsakhurdia, Georgia's first post-Soviet leader. Gamsakhurdia was the son of a popular Georgian writer and had made a name for himself as a dissident in the late Soviet era. He briefly gained widespread popularity with his call for

Georgian independence while alienating other groups with his call for "Georgia for the Georgians."[19] Gamsakhurdia was elected president of Georgia in 1991, but his tenure in office was brief. He resorted to press censorship and human rights abuses to bolster his power and soon encountered strong opposition from Georgian politicians. He also fell afoul of powerful militias and fled Georgia's capital, Tbilisi, late in 1991 when civil war broke out. After Gamsakhurdia's loyalists fought against Georgia's new leadership, Gamsakhurdia himself died in late 1993 or early 1994 in uncertain circumstances.

The clash of nationalisms in Georgia produced wars in South Ossetia and Abkhazia. War in the highland region of South Ossetia began in January 1991. Gamsakhurdia suggested in February that Ossetians would have to leave Georgia. He denied that this was his intent, but he told a reporter, "There is terror and violations and a lot of Georgian houses have been burned. So in the end I think they will be all forced to leave Georgia. It is not my wish but I cannot control this process."[20] Many Ossetians fled, but so did Georgians. By the time the fighting ended with a July 1992 cease-fire, tens of thousands of Ossetians and between 10,000 and 23,000 Georgians had left South Ossetia, and Georgia still had not regained control over most of the breakaway region.

As the Soviet Union collapsed, Georgian and Abkhazian leaders moved toward a war that produced even greater destruction than the conflict in South Ossetia. From a Soviet perspective, the setting for this war was incongruous. Abkhazia was a kind of Soviet vacation land, a "Red Riviera." Much of the coast was not initially hospitable for tourism, but it had been transformed into a series of resorts during the Soviet era. As many as two million people a year visited Abkhazia. The visitors included Stalin and Brezhnev, both of whom had dachas in Abkhazia; the Ministry of Defense and *Pravda* both built facilities for their staff there.[21] War reached the beaches in August 1992 when Georgian military forces moved into Abkhazia. The fighting frightened away the last few vacationers. On paper Georgia possessed an advantage in population and resources over the Abkhazians, and Georgian units went on the offensive, taking the capital of Sukhumi in August and pushing north into resort towns such as Gagra near the Russian border. But the Georgian offensive soon stalled. Abkhaz forces regained all the towns north of Sukhumi by year's end and took Sukhumi in late September 1993 when remaining Georgian forces withdrew from Abkhazia.

Georgians blamed their defeat less on Abkhazians than on intervention by Russia and by other forces on behalf of the Abkhazians. Georgian witnesses routinely cited military action by volunteers from a Confederation of Mountain Peoples, including Shamil Basayev, later a leading Chechen commander during the Chechen-Russian wars. Improvements in Abkhaz weaponry and resources suggested their reliance on Russian military supplies, and both the press and human rights groups found strong evidence that Russians fought for the Abkhazians.[22] Georgians accused Russia of seeking to maintain its naval bases on the Black Sea.

Both sides in the war for Abkhazia carried out ethnic cleansing. During early offensives, Georgian soldiers, national guardsmen, and paramilitary forces or militias attacked Abkhazians along the Black Sea. Probably the best known of these militias was the Mkhedrioni or Horsemen. The Mkhedrioni's leader, Jaba Ioseliani, bridged the worlds of crime, culture, and politics. A onetime bank robber who spent years in prison, Ioseliani became a prominent theater critic and playwright. His Mkhedrioni engaged in banditry and killing. In Sukhumi, one Abkhazian refugee recalled, the Mkhedrioni drove through the streets shooting, and yelling, "Abkhaz! . . . This is your death!" This was grassroots ethnic cleansing: Abkhazians knew some of their Georgian assailants. "The Abkhaz population," Human Rights Watch reported, ". . . lived in terror of fighters from elsewhere in Georgia but also of its neighbors."[23]

Georgians suffered much the same fate when Abkhaz fighters counterattacked. Georgian refugees told of attacks by Abkhaz soldiers and armed bands as well as by Russians and Chechens. The Abkhaz fighters were often refugees themselves who fought to gain revenge. Looting was epidemic. One Georgian recounted how forces from Abkhaz military headquarters and Chechens took everything: cows, pigs, and turkeys. "They also took the television. They came every day, not the same people every time. . . . When we left the house, we had only furniture left: beds and so forth."[24] The war for Abkhazia ended in 1993 with looting on so vast a scale as to produce a traffic jam at Sukhumi.

With Georgian defeats, the Georgian majority emptied out of Abkhazia. In late 1992 Georgians made their way out along the Black Sea coast into the Russian resort city of Sochi. By 1993 there was no safe way out of Abkhazia. One refugee, a law student, told of escaping Sukhumi: "The only way to get out was by swimming. We swam for hours. The whole town was burning and the snipers did not see us." Wrecked cars and buses lined the mountain passes leading east out of Abkhazia, and some Georgians died when snow struck in early October. Those who climbed over the mountains then had to traverse the war zone in western Georgia, where Gamsakhurdia loyalists fought Georgia's government before they found safety in Tbilisi, a city free from war but short of food, supplies, and shelter. Along with Georgians, Pontic Greek residents of Abkhazia evacuated Sukhumi. They crossed the Black Sea for Greece and formed part of a larger migration of ninety thousand Pontic Greeks who left for a homeland they had never known when the Soviet Union collapsed.[25]

By the time the fighting ended, 350,000 people, almost two-thirds of Abkhazia's residents, had fled their homes. Many never returned. Some quarter of a million Georgians from Abkhazia took refuge in the Republic of Georgia. In Tbilisi close to 90,000 crammed into apartment buildings, hotels, schools, and medical clinics—any shelter they could find. In this fashion the Hotel Iveria, once Tbilisi's best, became home to a thousand internally displaced people.[26] The hotel was emptied of refugees only in 2004 and is scheduled to be demolished.

North Caucasus Wars

The same dynamic of political reform and nationalist conflict brought ethnic violence and refugee migrations to selected regions on the north slope of the Caucasus, within the Russian Federation. The two chief hot spots in the North Caucasus were North Ossetia and Chechnya. In North Ossetia ethnic violence in 1992 produced ethnic cleansing, and in Chechnya years of war during the 1990s displaced hundreds of thousands of people.

In North Ossetia, as in the republics south of the Caucasus, Glasnost exposed and intensified competing nationalist aspirations. Here the chief conflict was between Ossetians and the Ingush, both of whom laid claim to North Ossetia's Prigorodnyi District, a small region in the east of North Ossetia. Ingush had once lived there, but the region became part of North Ossetia in 1944 after Stalin deported them. In their absence, Soviet authorities resettled tens of thousands of new residents in Prigorodnyi, including Ossetians, and the Ossetian newcomers remained when the Ingush finally returned to the Caucasus after their 1957 rehabilitation by Stalin's successor, Khrushchev. Those Ingush who came back to Prigorodnyi found themselves a minority in their own land. The Ingush did not regain their land and houses, and they also claimed that they could not obtain jobs.[27]

With Glasnost, the tense relationship between the Ossetians and the Ingush deteriorated quickly. In a climate where open expression was possible, Ingush demanded return of their homes and of the Prigorodnyi District. Ossetians reacted with suspicion and fear. In 1991 a well-intentioned but poorly crafted Soviet law on rehabilitating repressed peoples further inflamed feelings on both sides. The law promised that peoples deported by Stalin could return to the places where they once lived, but it also pledged to protect those who now resided on the lands of the deported.[28] And it delayed any settlement of territorial issues until 1995. The law simultaneously raised Ingush expectations and Ossetian fears. Ingush lobbied for the return of their homes and lands, Ossetians defended their claims to the Prigorodnyi District, and both sides prepared for war.

After months of sporadic clashes, a short war for the Prigorodnyi District broke out on October 31, 1992. As one Ossetian left his village for a potato field that morning, his son told him, "A war has started." Soon Ingush armored trucks arrived. Ingush fighters briefly gained the upper hand in several villages and towns but fell back before North Ossetian forces and South Ossetian militias formed by refugees from the war to the south in Georgia. Ingush described the South Ossetian refugees as especially aggressive. "These southerners," one Ingush woman complained, "how many times I gave them things, they were refugees from South Ossetia. They looted all our things."[29] This was also a war of neighbors in which local residents manned roadblocks and acted as spotters for militia and troops, though some refugees also told of being rescued by neighbors.

It was also a war of arson. Ingush burned Ossetian houses, and Ossetians burned Ingush homes. Both sides used the same basic method: identify enemy homes, turn on the gas, wait, and then lob in a grenade or Molotov cocktail to set off an explosion. Local residents burned down their own neighbors' homes to settle outstanding quarrels. As one Ingush woman from Zavodskii explained, "A policeman burned our house down. He had had a fight with my son before the war broke out." Arson also had a broader purpose. Ossetians and Ingush did not just seek to win the war; they wanted to drive each other out and prevent the possibility of return. With this goal in mind, arson became logical. As one Ossetian said in late November 1992, "Perhaps it's not right to burn down their houses, but it's more difficult to return when you don't have a roof."[30]

By November 5 the military struggle was over, though looting and acts of revenge continued well into December. Ossetians had ethnically cleansed the Ingush from the Prigorodnyi District. Most fled to the neighboring republic of Ingushetia. By some estimates, the total number of refugees reached 60,000 or more. But the fact that the 1989 census counted only 32,000 Ingush in the disputed district suggested a lower figure.[31]

To the east of Ingushetia, far greater numbers of refugees fled their homes in the much longer conflict over Chechnya. Unlike the Ingush in the Prigorodnyi District, Chechens made up the largest part of the population of Chechnya, some two-thirds of a total of 1.2

million. Russia was not prepared to leave Chechnya, however, because Chechnya, in contrast to Armenia, Azerbaijan, or Georgia, was part of the Russian Federation.

The root causes of Chechen discontent stemmed from a long history of unrest and violence. Russia conquered the region only with great difficulty in the nineteenth century after decades of warfare against the Sufi imam Shamil, and rebellions continued through the early Soviet era. In 1944 Stalin deported the Chechens en masse. Rehabilitated by Khrushchev, they returned in the late 1950s. Thus many of the Chechen leaders who took up arms against Russia in the 1990s had experienced exile life in special settlements in Central Asia. Their memories of national and personal suffering helped propel the Chechen drive for independence in the early 1990s.[32]

Russia struggled for years to maintain control over Chechnya.[33] Led by Dzhokar Dudayev, a former Soviet general who had witnessed the nationalist wave of the Glasnost era firsthand from his post in Estonia between 1987 and 1990, Chechnya declared independence in November 1991. In 1994 Russian leaders sought to reestablish control. From a military standpoint, the results were mixed. A Russian attack on the Chechen capital of Grozny in late November 1994 failed, and only after months of fighting did Russia retake Grozny in March 1995. But Chechen resistance continued despite Dudayev's death in 1996, and Russian troops again left Grozny in August that year. Finally, in February 2000 Russian forces retook Grozny.

As in Russia's nineteenth-century wars for the Caucasus, warfare in Chechnya in the 1990s sometimes verged on ethnic cleansing. Like tsarist commanders, Russian authorities in the 1990s had no policy to empty Chechnya of Chechens. Russia wanted Chechens within the Russian Federation, and Russian authorities periodically forced Chechen civilians back into regions under Russian control. On the other hand, Russians did carry out massacres, and Russian assaults emptied cities and towns of their populations. In order to capture Grozny in 1995, Russian forces destroyed much of the city. Chechens fled by the tens of thousands to the countryside, leaving mainly Russian civilians to suffer the brunt of the Russian attack. In all, the war generated more than 300,000 displaced persons.[34]

The very language of Russian policy toward Chechnya equated war with cleansing or "filtering." Thus the Russian Interior Ministry set up filtration centers or camps in 1995 to separate fighters from Chechen civilians. The idea was to take in Chechen men and "filter" out rebels or *boyeviks.* Thousands entered the camps, usually located at Russian bases, such as the filtration center established by the Interior Ministry at the Mozdok military base in North Ossetia. Those Chechens who survived the experience told of beatings and torture, but many simply disappeared. By the summer of 1995 the number of missing reached more than one thousand.[35]

The language of cleansing also applied to so-called mop-up, or cleansing operations carried out by Russian troops. In theory, Russian forces were searching for rebels and weapons. In fact they carried out indiscriminate mass arrests and extra-judicial executions during "cleansing" operations. In one such sweep at the village of Mesker Yurt, just over nine miles from Grozny, Russian forces swept in on May 21, 2002, blocked roads, and seized all males twelve years and older for processing in a temporary "filtration" center. Those identified as Chechen fighters or rebel supporters were tortured and killed.[36]

"Something Seemed to Smolder"

While ethnic cleansing had begun on the borders of the Soviet Union in the late 1980s and early 1990s, no one used the phrase until the spring of 1992 when Serb paramilitaries drove Muslims from their homes through a broad swath of Bosnia. Serb radio, reflecting pride in the deeds of armed men who forced Muslims out of their villages and towns, actually reported the success of "ethnic cleansing." Almost immediately, however, it gained the reputation it deserves as a major abuse of human rights. The term "ethnic cleansing," then, emerged nearly fifty years after the creation of the term "genocide" during World War II by the legal scholar Raphael Lemkin.[37]

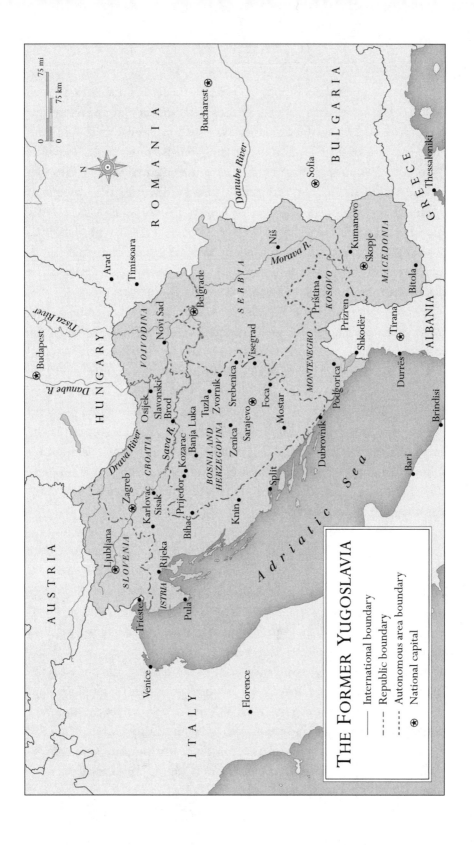

THE FORMER YUGOSLAVIA

— International boundary
- - - Republic boundary
····· Autonomous area boundary
⊛ National capital

In Yugoslavia the collapse of a multiethnic socialist state helped lead to ethnic cleansing. While Yugoslavia was not in name an empire, its leader, Tito, functioned as a sort of emperor for a socialist society. As one observer of his country's demise suggested, Tito was "the last Hapsburg, ruling a doomed multinational state." Tito was in effect Tito I. The key problem in this system was the absence of a Tito II. The Yugoslav League of Communists itself inadvertently revealed this with its slogan "After Tito, Tito!"[38] As no Tito was available after Tito himself died in 1980, Yugoslavia turned to an awkward rotating presidency among eight members representing the country's republics and two autonomous provinces.

The sudden collapse of a multiethnic society was one of the most puzzling aspects of the destruction of Yugoslavia. By some measures, ethnic relations remained sound until the country's final years. Most respondents to a 1990 survey described ethnic relations in the workplace and in neighborhoods as good or satisfactory.[39] Even after Yugoslavia fell apart, its former citizens recalled peaceful prewar relations between diverse ethnic and religious groups. At the town of Kozarac, for example, Hamdo Kahrimanović, an elementary school principal whom Elizabeth Neuffer interviewed, was on good terms with local Serbs. Serb students attended his school, and Kahrimanović had Serb neighbors.

In Kozarac and elsewhere, Yugoslavs of different ethnic and religious backgrounds generally got along with one another, but they remained divided by history. Tito's Yugoslavia promoted a common memory of partisan struggle and victory in World War II, but many Yugoslavs, depending upon their ethnic background, held very different memories of the war. Detecting these divisions in popular memory required penetrating beneath the surface of life in Tito's Yugoslavia, and that was no easy task. For one thing, recognizing the surviving ethnic tensions stood at odds with Tito's ideology, but there was also a more general problem. In any society people are most likely to reveal their most extreme prejudices when they are among friends and relatives, and these are not the kinds of conversations that typically leave an imprint on the public record.

Below the calm of everyday ethnic relations, some observers saw a submerged history of persistent ethnic hostility. When the Bosnian Serb historian and politician Milorad Ekmečić visited his village, "the stories they told were about the massacres during the war. They were possessed by the memories of 1941–45." Cvijeto Job, a Yugoslav diplomat, experienced both the promise of partisan solidarity and the failure to overcome past divisions. As a young man he had served as a partisan, but he came to realize that Yugoslavs had not reconciled their differences over the past. As a diplomat in Washington he took part in a "heated conversation that threatened to end in a brawl" with a Croatian leader and "distinguished" novelist over the number of Serbs killed by the Ustasha in the Jasenovac concentration camp. Job enjoyed traveling through Bosnia, but he felt that "something was amiss. . . . The visible evidence of an undisturbed ethnically mixed life was real. But something seemed to smolder beneath, a kind of second reality." Even foreign observers sometimes glimpsed this hidden anger. In the 1970s a Serb employee of the American consulate in Zagreb told the American diplomat Louis Sell that he got along with individual local Croatian colleagues all right. But he added that "sometimes when he looked into their eyes, he could not help recalling the blood that stained the hands of those responsible for the slaughter of Serbs during the Second World War."[40]

In Yugoslavia we see in stark form one of the central paradoxes of ethnic cleansing. As Cvijeto Job suggested, Yugoslavs lived with two realities. In the first, Serbs, Croats, and Muslims saw each other as acquaintances, colleagues, neighbors, friends, and sometimes even relatives. In the second reality, however, they identified others as members of groups marked by history as enemies. The people of Yugoslavia were not doomed to war and ethnic cleansing, but they lived with deep-seated and unresolved anger.

A revival of exclusive nationalist history accentuated the divisions between Yugoslavs in the years before the country broke apart. In the case of Serbs, for example, key turning points in an exclusive Serb history of victimization were already known before the collapse of Yugoslavia. These historical events included the Battle of Kosovo of 1389, Serbian defeat and flight in World War I in 1915, and the Ustasha killing of Serbs in World War II. As early as the 1970s, intellectuals and writers pieced these turning points together into a powerful story of Serb suffering, and by the 1980s politicians joined in this process. There was no single architect or even a plan for this Serb nationalist revival. The champions of Serb nationalism shared no single vision. Often they worked at cross-purposes. Only toward the very end of Yugoslavia did they begin to coalesce into a common movement, and even then their unity was fragile and short-lived.

The Serb nationalist revival began in the 1970s when the Serb novelist Dobrica Cosic brought attention to the Serb tragedy of World War I. In a four-volume epic, *Time of Death*, Cosic retold the story of the Serb catastrophe of 1915. He wrote of Serbian defeat, flight across Albania, and exile. Cosic's Serbia was a nation abandoned, but still unvanquished despite its suffering.[41] In 1984 a play based on *Time of Death* gained widespread acclaim and moved audiences to tears with its portrayal of Serb heroism in defeating Austria-Hungary in 1914.

The next step in the Serb nationalist renewal came with a wave of interest in the 1980s in commemorating the 1389 Battle of Kosovo. This medieval battle served as a symbol of the Serb claim to Kosovo, but by the 1980s Orthodox priests and Serb intellectuals were voicing increasing concerns about the viability of a Serb presence in Kosovo, where Albanians made up a large and rapidly growing majority.[42] Members of the Serbian Academy of Arts and Sciences drafted a *Memorandum*, leaked to the press in 1986, that spoke of threats to Serb survival in Kosovo and Croatia. In 1987, Slobodan Milosevic, a Socialist functionary not previously known as a nationalist, made the cause of Serb Kosovo his own when he told Serbs gathered at Kosovo field, "No one should dare to beat you!" Returning to Kosovo in 1989 for the six hundredth anniversary of the battle, Milosevic cloaked himself in national symbols and identified himself with a storied nationalist past.

The Serb nationalist revival also led to intense public discussion of World War II and of Ustasha genocide. Beginning in the 1980s, in memoirs, plays, and histories, Serbs began to speak much more openly about the Ustasha killings. They told of massacres, betrayal, and a continued cleft between Serbs and Croats.[43] In 1988 Serb media provided their own version of a popular history of genocide, publishing photos of disinterred graves of Ustasha victims.

By the 1980s these tragedies of the past formed a single coherent story in which Serbs were repeatedly victimized. According to this narrative, the Battle of Kosovo of 1389 and the Serb defeat in 1915 formed a prelude to the struggle for Kosovo in the 1980s. The bones of Lazar, the Serb prince said to have been betrayed in 1389, served as a physical symbol of the ongoing quest to defend a Serbian Kosovo. Lazar's bones were disinterred in 1986 and carried to Kosovo in 1989. Genocide under the Ustasha also fit into this story line of Serb victimization, because, for Serb nationalists, Ustasha crimes provided a warning of what was at stake: now in Kosovo, as in Yugoslavia during World War II, Serbs faced the danger of extermination. This story line fused together past, present, and future, presenting Serbia as a nation repeatedly victimized, betrayed, and threatened with destruction.

The revival of nationalism was not unique to Serbs. Croats developed a parallel story line of past glory and victimization. In the Croat case the key nationalist figure was Franjo Tudjman, a retired Yugoslav general who made his mark as a historian—though not necessarily because of his accuracy. In Tudjman's vision of the past, Croatia was a nation with a thousand-year-old history. Tudjman sought to find a respectable nationalist past in the Croatian state of World War II: he revised estimates of Ustasha victims downward and publicized partisan killings of Croats. Much as in Serbia, the Croatian media also popularized the history of wartime massacres, though Croats saw photos of the disinterred graves of Croat victims of partisan massacres rather than the bodies of the Ustasha's victims.

The Serb and Croat nationalist revivals cast each nation as a repeatedly victimized protagonist, but the nationalists' stories lacked a conclusion. The internal logic of their national narratives called for revenge against those responsible for oppression. Unfortunately for

Yugoslavia, these nationalist stories, whether Serb or Croat, encouraged hatred of other Yugoslavs. In principle it was possible for Serbs to distinguish between the individuals responsible for past massacres and the Croats they actually knew; Croats could make the same distinction. But the lines between past villains and present-day Yugoslavs blurred. Serbs and Croats in the streets of Yugoslavia's cities literally sang of their hatred, as folk "ditties" cited by Cviljovo Job reveal. "Comrade Slobo, send salads," a street song heard in Belgrade began. "There will be meat galore, We'll be slaughtering Croats." A song heard in Zagreb espoused much the same sentiments, exchanging only perpetrators and intended victims:

> Mother of God, Queen of Croats,
> Bring us back Ante Pavelic,
> So we can flush out Serbs again,
> Half put to knife, half string up on the willows.[44]

As in Transcaucasia, democratization strengthened and spread nationalism in Yugoslavia. Nationalist politicians thrived in elections in the individual Yugoslav republics. Nationalist parties did not always win majorities, but they soon gained political power. Democratic elections and referenda in 1991–1992 revealed widespread desire, outside of Serbia and Montenegro, to break away from Yugoslavia. Extremist nationalism flourished at the local level in towns such as Kozarac. Simo Drljača, a lawyer who gave legal advice to the Kozarac elementary school, became a local leader of the new Serb nationalist party, the Serbian Democratic Party or SDS. A café owner by the name of Duško Tadić, a neighbor of the elementary school principal Hamdo Kahrimanović, also joined the SDS even though both of Tadić's parents had been partisans during World War II.[45]

"Negative Geography"

Yugoslavia in the early 1990s was primed for nationalist conflict. Immediately after the republics of Croatia and Slovenia declared independence in 1991, Yugoslavia's military went to war against the breakaway regions. The army fought not to preserve a south Slav union but to hold on to Serb areas. Thus the presence or absence of Serbs led to very different experiences for Slovenia and Croatia. The declaration of independence by Slovenia, the northernmost Yugoslav republic, on June 25, 1991, led to a brief war, but the Yugoslav leadership, dominated by Serbs, was willing to let Slovenia depart. Serbs made up a very small minority—2 percent—of Slovenia's population in 1991. In contrast, the 600,000 Serbs in Croatia made up 12 percent of the population, and Serb forces fought to control the two areas of Croatia with large Serb populations: the Krajina region, east of the Adriatic Sea along the Bosnian border, and the region of Slavonia in eastern Croatia. In a striking testament to support for the Serb cause, Vuk Draskovic, one of Slobodan Milosevic's chief political rivals, told a rally on June 9, "The Serbian state must take it upon itself to defend the Serbian people in those parts of Croatia where they constitute a majority. . . . Serbia must punish those who threaten Serbs, demolish their homes, and force them to migrate, when Croatia is not doing so herself."[46]

From the start, this was a war of armies and of neighbors. A twenty-year-old Croatian woman driven out of the village of Struga, some sixty miles south of Croatia's capital of Zagreb, described this aspect of the war. She knew the men who attacked and beat her. "Almost all of them were schoolmates, the people with whom I used to meet for drinks."[47] These acts of violence convinced ordinary Serbs and Croats that nationalist rhetoric, with all its fear and hatred of enemy peoples, applied to people they themselves knew. Their mental boundary between past and present, between everyday life and a "second reality" of interethnic suspicion and hatred, eroded.

Gains by Serbian forces that relied on support from the Yugoslav National Army spurred on Croatian flight. Croats fled the Krajina when Yugoslav tanks approached or aircraft bombed their villages. The villages emptied of Croats in this rural area were often small. One Croatian opposition politician noted how the whole process served as a kind of grim geography lesson. "We call it negative geography," he said. "The first time you hear about them [these villages], it means you've lost them." The Serb campaign culminated in western Croatia with shelling of the historic Adriatic port of Dubrovnik, and in eastern Croatia with a drive on the town of Vukovar. Thousands of civilians fled the fighting at Dubrovnik, but the intent behind ethnic cleansing came ever more clearly into focus in the east. At Ilok, a town twenty miles southeast of Vukovar, Croats decided to leave en masse after the Yugoslav army ordered Croat forces to withdraw. "Ilok could be the start of something much bigger," one foreign diplomat suggested, "We could see an attempt at large-scale population transfers."[48] In late November 1991 Vukovar fell while Croat refugees streamed out of town.

The fighting in Croatia ended with a January 2, 1992, cease-fire that left between a quarter and a third of Croatia under Serb control. This was the first installment on a short-lived greater Serbia. Krajina and Eastern Slavonia were now almost entirely Serb: all except a few elderly Croats had fled. Most of their Croatian friends, neighbors, relatives, and colleagues now lived in what was left of Croatia.

"Where's Your Allah Now?"

In 1992 a second and still larger pulse of ethnic cleansing followed in Bosnia-Herzegovina. This land of Bosnian Muslims, Serbs, and Croats was the most precariously balanced of all the Yugoslav republics in terms of its ethnic makeup. According to the last Yugoslav census in 1991, Bosnian Muslims made up 44 percent of the population, Serbs 31 percent, and Croats 17 percent. Some 5.5 percent identified themselves as Yugoslavs; the remainder of the population consisted of minorities, including Gypsies and Jews. Most Croats lived in the west, in the region of Herzegovina; Serbs and Bosnian Muslims lived intermingled throughout much of Bosnia.

War broke out in Bosnia in early April 1992, soon after Bosnia-Herzegovina declared independence, and from the start Serb forces drove Bosnian Muslims from their homes.[49] The idea of pushing out members of an undesired ethnic or religious group was old, but here one thing was new. In the spring of 1992 Serb radio announced that "ethnic cleansing" was in progress. This new name for an old crime rapidly took hold among victims, bystanders, and observers. In one of the first cases of ethnic cleansing, Serb paramilitary forces attacked the town of Bijeljina in northeast Bosnia on April 1. At this point Serb paramilitaries were proud of their achievements: they wanted attention. Thus the American photojournalist Ron Haviv was able to follow a Serb force known as the Tigers, in what their commander Arkan, a former bank robber, described as a mission to "liberate this city of Muslim fundamentalists." In Bijeljina, Haviv witnessed murders of Muslim civilians. In perhaps the most famous photo from the entire war, he managed to photograph a Serb paramilitary commando kicking Muslim civilians who had just been executed. Days later, José Maria Mendiluce, a UNHCR (United Nations High Commissioner for Refugees) official, stumbled on ethnic cleansing in eastern Bosnia at Zvornik, a mixed town with a Muslim majority. He found the town under attack by forces attached to the Yugoslav army and by Serb paramilitaries. Officially the Yugoslav army had already disbanded in Bosnia, but witnesses spoke of soldiers wearing Yugoslav army uniforms and of military vehicles with Yugoslav symbols, and Mendiluce himself saw Yugoslav soldiers. Detained for several hours by Serb forces, Mendiluce saw "trucks full of dead bodies. I could see militiamen taking more corpses of children, women, and old people from their houses and putting them on trucks."[50] After his release by Serb forces, he met thousands of desperate refugees in a valley outside Zvornik.

Ethnic cleansing in Bosnia was both a policy and a grassroots phenomenon. Evidence of central planning was not hard to come by. As Vojislav Seselj, leader of the Chetnik paramilitaries, explained: "Milosevic organized everything. We gathered the volunteers and he gave us a special barracks. . . . Of course I don't believe he signed anything, these were verbal orders." There were many signs of planning and coordination just before attacks. Serb residents frequently received word to leave before Serb forces attacked, and Croat forces, for their part, extended similar courtesy to Croats. In some Bosnian towns, houses were even color coded to show attacking forces where to set fires.[51]

Directed from above, ethnic cleansing in Bosnia was also pursued at the personal level. Refugees repeatedly told of attacks by people they knew: neighbors and old classmates—the kind of people Bosnian Muslims had over for a snack or a drink. One woman told of her family's loss of their home near the southern Bosnian town of Foca on April 8, 1992, when a Serb neighbor showed up in the middle of the night armed with a machine gun. "We had coffee with him the day before."[52] Of course others were strangers, but the men who carried out cleansing were much like their victims. They had all lived together in a multiethnic state. The image of Arkan as a kind of criminal celebrity (the former bank robber had married a popular turbo-folk singer) should not obscure the fact that many of the men who carried out ethnic cleansing were comparatively ordinary. Some were called "weekend warriors" because they came to camps to kill on weekends.

Duško Tadić, the café owner from Kozarac, became one of the best known of all the men who took part in a campaign against their own neighbors. Tadić held no high rank, but his trial by the International Criminal Tribunal for the Former Yugoslavia provided a detailed picture of the Serb fighter as neighbor and buddy.[53] Tadić had grown up with Muslims, had trained with them in karate, and had even had many Muslim customers when his café first opened, before it became a gathering spot for Serb nationalists. But none of this restrained him once the war for Bosnia began. Instead, as numerous witnesses told the International Tribunal, their former neighbor drove Muslims out of their homes. Nasiha Klipic, a witness who had known Tadić for years, saw him separating Muslim men from women, children, and the elderly at Kozarac. Draguna Jaskic, a Muslim woman driven out of her house in a village near Kozarac in June 1992, told how she saw her longtime acquaintance Tadić drive men down the street and beat her father and other relatives.[54]

Another Bosnian Serb who gained notoriety for attacking people he knew was Milan Lukić from the southeastern Bosnian town of Visegrad. As the journalist Chuck Sudetic learned, Lukić was well known to his victims. As a boy, Lukić ate cheese pies and played soccer with Muslims. He even had a "crush" on one Muslim girl, but in May 1992 he became the leader of a gang of Serbs that, according to survivors, carried out numerous acts of violence and forced Muslims out of Visegrad. In 1995 he was also present at Srebrenica. The International Tribunal indicted Lukić, charging him with killing many Bosnian Muslims, but despite a reward of up to $5 million he was not found until he was arrested in 2005 in Argentina.[55]

No one fully understood the motives of Bosnian Serbs who attacked victims they knew. When the presiding judge hearing Tadić's case asked the Kozarac elementary school principal Hamdo Kahrimanović to explain how something like this could happen, he answered, "It is inexplicable what happened to those people. It was some kind of madness. I mean, one did not know whom to trust any more and I do not have a word of explanation for that." Those accused or convicted of ethnic cleansing tend not to speak about their actions, but in individual cases there are clues to their behavior. Family connections may have drawn Lukić into war, and personal experiences may have had the same effect on Tadić. Lukić had relatives in the army and police, and Tadić became involved in a feud with local Muslims after the window of his family's café was broken.[56]

The International Tribunal held those it convicted or indicted personally responsible for their acts, but there were other more general causes for grassroots ethnic cleansing in Bosnia. We should be cautious about dogmatically singling out any one of the many possible motives for taking part in ethnic cleansing. Some may have done so for personal gain, others because they enjoyed the feeling of power, but two other factors stand out. Popular stories of national victimization and the shock of war were critical in generating violence, though in isolation neither would have propelled people to drive out their own neighbors. War would have caused trauma in any event, but the struggle for Bosnia had a far more explosive effect than almost anyone could have predicted because many of the people of Bosnia were already prepared to think the worst of each other. Now war convinced many that the nationalist rhetoric of the prewar years really was accurate.

War brought history—history as Yugoslavs remembered it—alive. The mental boundary between past and present faded. Peoples of Bosnia resurrected uniforms, plans, and language from old wars. They began wearing old clothes or clothes that looked old: Serbs and Croats adopted the imagined trappings of World War II fighters. Serbs dusted off old plans from World War II for a greater Serbia: Milan Kovačević, deputy mayor of Prijedor, the nearby city west of Kozarac, called for securing the borders for a homogenous greater Serbia, sketched out in 1941 by Stevan Moljević, an adviser of the Chetnik leader Mihailović. Serbs and Croats also began referring to each other with terms from the past. They talked of Ustasha and Chetniks, and they identified Bosnian Muslims as Turks. Bosnian Serb commander Ratko Mladic invoked the idea of national vengeance against Turks when he entered the town of Srebrenica on July 11, 1995. "Finally, the time has come to take revenge on the Turks," he told Serb television.[57] Even when Serbian protesters later turned against Slobodan Milosevic, they called him "Ustasha," and "Turk."

The mixing of past and present was sometimes a fashion, but it also eased the path to killing. On the one hand, fighters adorned themselves with a confusing mélange of old symbols from World War II and the trappings of action movies. On the other hand, seeing present conflict as a continuation of past war stoked a very real hatred of enemies by identifying them with past oppressors. In this logic, enemy combatants and civilians were responsible not only for their own deeds but for those carried out by their ethnic and religious groups in World War II and in the more distant past. Soon after the war's end, Prijedor's former deputy mayor made this kind of argument when he described the Omarksa camp as a direct response to Croat killing of Serbs during World War II. "There is a direct connection. . . . During World War II the Croats and Muslims killed us; this time it was the other way round, we killed them."[58]

War for Bosnia created a kind of cognitive dissonance. For many, their own past experience of relations among Croats, Muslims, and Serbs contradicted claims that these groups were inherent enemies. It was precisely for this reason that so many stunned survivors expressed disbelief. It literally made no sense to identify longtime neighbors with Ustasha, Chetniks, or Turks, let alone to attack them.

Motives for ethnic cleansing were complex, but methods were simple. Serb troops and paramilitaries murdered Bosnian Muslims. Kozarac's experience was typical of many Bosnian towns. Estimates of the dead at Kozarac and in surrounding villages ranged from the hundreds to the thousands. The killing was not entirely random. Serb fighters read through lists of names at Kozarac to select local Bosnian Muslim leaders. Elsewhere in Bosnia, Serb forces carried out massacres large and small, in villages, on the roads, even at soccer stadiums taken over as holding pens for prisoners. At the town of Bratunac in eastern Bosnia, an international aid worker heard the sound of machine-gun fire every night from April 7 to April 10 as Muslim men were led out back behind a soccer stadium. "There was no return fire," the aid worker explained. "The men were taken out and they didn't come back."[59]

Rape and sexual assault were commonplace during all stages of ethnic cleansing. As Bosnian Muslims fled the attack on Kozarac, they met further terror on the road. Serb irregulars, one woman recalled asked: "Where's your Allah now?" and added, "We're going to fuck all you Muslim women." They did not, but it was no empty threat as mounting evidence of systematic rape demonstrated over the following months. Sexual assault of women and men occurred on all sides, but a lengthy report compiled for the United Nations Commission of Experts found especially extensive evidence of Bosnian Serb sexual assault of Bosnian Muslim women. Rape and sexual assault took place before, during, and after ethnic cleansing, often in camps, and some fighters took and held women as virtual sex slaves. In all, the UN commission compiled reports of rape and sexual assault from fifty-seven different locations in Bosnia as well as from numerous sites in Croatia.[60]

Especially in larger communities, Serb authorities established local bureaucracies of ethnic cleansing to create the fiction that the flight of Bosnian Muslims was voluntary. What terror meted out by Serb forces began, administrative coercion finished. Amidst continuing beatings and killings, Serb authorities deprived Muslims of the right to work and arranged for their departure if they ceded their homes and property. Not surprisingly, most Bosnian Muslim civilians sought escape whatever the price. As one refugee from the northeastern Bosnian town of Zvornik explained, "We were forced to leave. We were under threat. They were killing people during the night. Someone came from the local government and said it is better to leave." At the city of Banja Luka, southeast of Kozarac, Muslims desperately tried to arrange house trades with Serbs from other parts of the country. Visiting Banja Luka in August 1992, Richard Holbrooke, who later played a key role in American diplomatic efforts to end the war, witnessed what he termed this "'mild' form of ethnic cleansing. . . . At close to gunpoint, Muslims are signing papers giving up their personal property."[61]

Driven from their homes, tens of thousands of Bosnian Muslims spent time in camps set up by Serb military forces, both the army and police, in northern Bosnia. For many Bosnian Muslims, the camps were the last stop before they left the region for good. For others, the camps were the very last stop. Thousands died. Omarska, the former iron ore mine south of Kozarac, became the most notorious of all Serb camps after the American reporter Roy Gutman broke the story of the organized killing of prisoners there in the summer of 1992. Life at Omarska, according to survivors, could mean days held in open pits with little food. Serb guards periodically shot prisoners. "They would take them to a nearby lake. You'd hear a volley of rifles, and they'd never come back," one survivor told of his experiences. Other survivors told of nightly killings. "The guards would come in at 3 a.m. and take five people out . . . ," one former inmate said. "Next morning we would see the dead bodies. I am sure that 50 percent of those who disappeared would be killed."[62] In all, Gutman estimated, Omarska claimed well over one thousand victims.

Bosnian Serbs from Kozarac played a prominent role at Omarska. The elementary school principal Kahrimanović saw both Duško Tadić and Simo Drljača at Omarska. Tadić was not a guard, but he showed up from time to time and was later found guilty by the International Tribunal for beating several Bosnian Muslim men at the Omarska camp. Drljača, the lawyer who advised the Kozarac elementary school, helped to found and run Omarska. In his position as police chief of the city of Prijedor, Drljača actually escorted a small group of journalists, including Peter Maass, on a visit to several camps and detention centers that had been cleaned up after the international outcry over Omarska. At Keraterm, a ceramics factory where prisoners had been held, he gave the journalists a few minutes to look around and then said, "See, no blood."[63] Drljača was never brought to trial. He died in a brief shoot-out when British commandos tried to arrest him in July 1997.

The harassment and terror worked. Serb forces drove Bosnian Muslims out of a broad swath of northern and eastern Bosnia, and from the region south of Sarajevo. As Serbian forces established control across most of northern Bosnia, they pushed out a steady stream of refugees, about a thousand a day in late summer, via the central Bosnian town of Travnik. This journey was itself an ordeal. Serbians at one village shrieked "Butcher them! Butcher them!" when a convoy of Bosnian Muslim refugees passed through on their way to Travnik. By the fall of 1992 the Serb project was almost complete. When Serbs took the central Bosnian town of Jajce at the end of October, after a siege of many months, thousands of Bosnian Muslims, enough to make up a ten-mile column, left along a route dubbed the "Vietnam Road."[64] Most of the refugees pressed into whatever territory remained under the control of the Bosnian government: cities and towns like Sarajevo, Tuzla, and Srebrenica. Smaller numbers crossed into Croatia or made their way farther abroad.

As the term "ethnic cleansing" fell into ill repute, Bosnian Serb authorities denied that it was taking place, but why, then, some observers asked, had so many Bosnian Muslims left their homes? Radovan Karadzic, president of the Republic of Serbska, claimed their exodus was mostly voluntary. He explained in a September 1992 interview that "the Muslim population, considering that it was in Serbian regions, demanded the right to leave." Force, he asserted, had not led to their departure. He conceded that there might have been some bullies, though he claimed such people would face prosecution. Local Bosnian Serb authorities made much the same assertions. In the eastern Bosnian town of Visegrad, the self-styled executive mayor told Peter Maass, "The Muslims left voluntarily. Why, we even supplied the buses. We didn't force them to leave."[65]

For many Bosnian Serbs, including Karadzic and the military commander Ratko Mladic, it was Bosnia's Serbs who faced attack— from Croats, Muslims, and varied foreign forces. Mujhadin and foreign mercenaries, "even some blacks from some Islamic and African countries," Mladic announced in a November 1992 interview, as if this were a particularly horrifying detail, had come all the way to Bosnia to attack Serbs.[66] Croat special battalions were "predominantly specialists for murders, massacres, throwing people into pits, and so forth." And the Bosnian Serbs' own neighbors, "our former neighbors, colleagues, workmates, people, if one can call them that, who used to know us well," joined in the assault. Mladic's claims more or less agreed—a few key details aside—with how a growing number of journalists and human rights investigators described the conflict, but with one central exception: Serb paramilitaries and Serbs had displaced the largest number of people by late 1992. Although generally misleading, Bosnian Serb excuses for violence were still informative in one respect: they displayed the immense power of Serb stories of national victimization.

"He Had Best Friends Among Croats"

Serbs were undoubtedly the chief aggressors in the war for Bosnia-Herzegovina, but the conflict was not a simple affair of Serb advances and Bosnian Muslim retreats. Croatia's President Franjo

Tudjman also harbored ambitions to extend Croatia's power in Bosnia, and he was prepared to support Bosnia's Croats. "Bosnia has historically been a part of Croatia," he claimed in conversation with U.S. Ambassador Warren Zimmermann in 1990, "and has always been in Croatia's geopolitical sphere." In 1992 the only part of Bosnia-Herzegovina firmly within Croatia's geopolitical sphere was in the southwest, in Herzegovina, and there Croatian militia cleared out Serbs from towns and villages along the Neretva River.[67]

With Serbs out of the way, the Croats of western Herzegovina, supported by Croatia, went to war against their nominal allies—Bosnian Muslims. Using ethnic logic similar to that of the Ustasha leader Ante Pavlic, Tudjman in 1990 had told Zimmermann that "most Muslims in Bosnia consider themselves Croats." Evidently they did not. The erstwhile allies, united only by their common opposition to Serb expansion, fought against each other. Bosnian-Croatian forces built their own little state, which they called Herzeg-Bosnia. In late October 1992 they seized the mixed Muslim-Croat town of Prozor in northern Herzegovina. Croat fighters shelled and burned Muslims' homes. The town's Muslim residents, some clad only in slippers, fled for the hills. "Our homes are burned. We have nowhere to go except the mountains. The Croats have cleaned us out just like the Serbs would have done," one woman told a reporter.[68] Some did, however, return within a few days.

A major problem for the nationalists who ran Herzeg-Bosnia lay in the fact that Mostar, the chief city and capital of the new state (lacking international recognition), was in large part a city of Muslims. To make Mostar fully Croatian, Croat forces engaged in the ethnic cleansing of Muslims. In May 1993 the HVO (Croatian Defense Council), the armed forces of Croatian Herzeg-Bosnia, and assorted militias pushed Muslims into a crowded ghetto on the eastern side of the Neretva River. For months they expelled Muslims across the river and targeted them with mortar fire.

Some of the worst atrocities in the Croatian ethnic cleansing campaign against Muslims took place in the Lasva River Valley in central Bosnia. In an especially infamous massacre in this region, on

April 16, 1993, Croat forces attacked the village of Ahmici. One of the survivors was Fatima Ahmic, a Muslim who lived with her husband next door to her son Fahrudin, a factory manager and musician. She saw the attack by HVO soldiers. One soldier sprayed her curtains and sofa and set them alight with a cigarette lighter. When she arrived at her son's house, he was lying dead. Testifying before the International Tribunal, she asked how this could have happened. "He was good with everyone. He had best friends among Croats, he played music with them, he went to school with them, he worked with them, everything."[69] The day after the attack on her home, armed men seized her husband; she never saw him again.

The legal proceedings concerning the killings at Ahmici and in the Lasva River Valley were fraught with problems. Three Bosnian Croats from the nearby town of Vitez were convicted in January 2000 for taking part in the massacre at Ahmici, but their convictions were overturned on appeal the next year, in part because a Muslim from Ahmici testified that they were not guilty. The Croatian general Tihomir Blaskic was sentenced in 2000 to a forty-five year prison sentence by the war crimes tribunal, but his sentence was later reduced to nine years, and he was granted early release.

In June 1993 Muslim forces struck back against Croats in Bosnia. Ironically, Muslim setbacks in northern Bosnia helped them to launch successful counteroffensives against Croats in central Bosnia. The flood of Bosnian Muslim refugees forced out of towns and villages ethnically cleansed by Serbs rapidly shifted the demographics of central Bosnia. Most ominously for the region's Croats, the new arrivals included embittered refugee soldiers, most notably the 17th Brigade, composed of deportees and former prisoners in Serb camps. "We are doing to them what was done to us," a 17th brigade soldier told a reporter. "I feel sorry for them because we have suffered the same way but we have no choice. We cannot survive otherwise." In little more than a week, Bosnian Muslim forces seized several towns in central Bosnia, and thousands of Croats fled east.[70]

The Bosnian-Croat war for central Bosnia flared up again in October and November 1993. On October 23 Croatian forces massacred

Muslims at the village of Stupni Do. "Everything was on fire and we saw Ustase throwing bodies into the flames," said one survivor. Reports of the death toll ranged from twenty-five to eighty. But days later Croat defenses collapsed, and thousands of Croats, some of them already refugees, fled the town of Vares, long a comparative safe haven.[71] Police, driving through the streets in the middle of the night, told residents to leave immediately. Croats left an empty, looted Vares before Muslim soldiers entered and took whatever shops still had on their shelves.

As Croats and Bosnian Muslims fought for western Herzegovina and central Bosnia, refugees replaced refugees. Croats and Bosnian Muslims took over each other's houses and apartments. Herzeg-Bosnia housed Croatian refugees in Mostar and villages along the Neretva River, some still heavily damaged from war and ethnic cleansing. At Pocitelj, a small village on the Neretva, a Croat refugee from central Bosnia observed, "Some homes are only half destroyed. They said they would give us the materials to repair them." To the north, Muslims moved into Croats' old homes. Muslim refugees took over thousands of houses in Fojnica, a formerly mixed town once so renowned for its harmonious ethnic relations that its leaders had declared it a "Zone of Peace."[72]

By the time the fighting among Serbs, Croats, and Muslims slowed, the ethnic cleansers had separated Bosnia's people on the basis of their ethnic identity. With the exception of the small city of Bihac in the far northwest and several enclaves in the southeast, Bosnian Muslims had been pushed out of the north, east, and south: this territory, some 70 percent of the former Bosnia Herzegovina, now made up the Bosnian Serb Republic. Where Croats established their power center in the southwest, along the Croatian border, few but Croats remained. The Bosnian government hung on mainly in central Bosnia and retained the capital of Sarajevo. A cleansed Bosnia settled down into a state of stable misery. The world watched as Serb shells fell on Sarajevo, but Bosnian Serbs gained little new territory. Ethnic cleansing continued at a low level in cities such as the northern Bosnian Serb stronghold of Banja Luka.[73]

The End of Greater Serbia

In 1995 ethnic cleansing resumed on a massive scale. In May, Croats pushed Serbs out of the region of Western Slavonia in eastern Croatia; in July, Serbs completed the ethnic cleansing of several towns in southeastern Bosnia; and in August, Croats drove Serbs out of the Krajina. The events in Western Slavonia gave a hint that the war for the former Yugoslavia was taking a different turn. From the early phases of fighting, Serbs had typically held the military edge; Serbia had in fact taken Western Slavonia from Croatia in 1991. But this time Serb positions collapsed, and Serbs fled their homes en masse. Some ten thousand to fifteen thousand Serbs departed for either Serb-held areas of Bosnia or for the Serb enclave of Krajina.

Setbacks to the north did not blunt Bosnian Serb ambitions to complete ethnic cleansing in eastern and southeastern Bosnia. By 1995 there were only a few places left to cleanse, including Srebrenica and Zepa, towns crowded with Bosnian Muslim refugees forced out of the surrounding region. The only problem confronting Bosnian Serb troops and Serb paramilitaries surrounding these enclaves lay in the fact that the United Nations had designated these towns as safe havens. Serb forces decided to attack anyway.

Srebrenica was the site of the worst single massacre in a war of countless atrocities. At Srebrenica some 40,000 Bosnian Muslims, both residents of the town and refugees, depended for their safety on the presence of some 600 Dutch soldiers. Without heavy weapons or reliable NATO air support, these soldiers lacked the capacity— perhaps, events would suggest, even the will—to protect themselves, let alone civilians.[74] Bosnian Serb forces entered the town on July 11, 1995, and cleared out the Muslims. Some 23,000 women and children left by bus. Thousands of men scrambled through woods and over mountains seeking escape. But between 7,000 and 8,000 men and boys, some of them actually forced to leave a Dutch base, never made it out. A handful of survivors told of the mass murder of the rest, of executions in the fields of eastern Bosnia. One Serb native, complaining that Muslims had cut down the trees on hills surrounding the town, later explained, "They ruined this town. It used to be pretty. So, we killed them, we killed them all."[75]

Next came Zepa, another UN-designated safe haven, with some twelve thousand to sixteen thousand Bosnian Muslims, none with heavy weapons. All the seventy-nine or eighty Ukrainian UN peace-keeping troops stationed there could do to preserve Zepa's peace was wait to be shelled or taken hostage. When the Bosnian Serb commander demanded the enclave's surrender on July 14, 1995, few expected the town to hold out as long as it did. It finally fell on July 25, thousands ran into the mountains, and the Serbs deported the remainder by bus. "No Allah, no UN, no NATO can save you. Only me," Bosnian Serb commander General Ratko Mladic told the refugees.[76]

There was barely any time for Bosnian Serbs to celebrate before they suffered a series of massive defeats. In early August, Croat and Bosnian Muslim forces launched a counterattack in western Bosnia, and thirteen thousand Serbs joined the ever-growing ranks of Bosnia's refugees. Soon the news grew even worse for Serbs when Croatia took back the Krajina in a swift offensive dubbed Operation Storm. Once a testament to Serb power, Krajina was hollowed out by 1995. Cut off from nearby markets in Croatia, connected to Serbia by a circuitous and lengthy route, its economy little more than a black market, Krajina lay in ruins. Many Serbs had already left this outpost of Greater Serbia before the Croatian army, newly supplied and advised by retired American military officers, moved in. It was not much of a war. The Yugoslav army, so critical to the early Serb triumphs in Krajina, was nowhere to be seen, and within days Croatian forces seized the Krajina Serb capital of Knin. About all that was left to do was drive down the road, sometimes burning Serb houses. Croatian President Franjo Tudjman boasted that Serbs left Krajina so rapidly that they did not even have the time to take "their dirty hard currency and dirty underwear."[77]

Krajina's Serbs left because Croatia, despite having reached an agreement with the United Nations stipulating that previous residents could stay, wanted Serbs to go. Serbs almost expected this. As a Serb psychologist explained, "I realize that what is happening

now to us is a different side of the same coin of ethnic cleansing."
Spat at, showered with tomatoes, bricks, and stones by Croats who
lined village roads and in at least one case chanted "Go! Go! Go!,"
Krajina's departing Serbs made up the largest single mass flight so
far in Yugoslavia's new wars. The column of refugees stretched out
for sixty miles or more. That's how much space, cars, trucks, and
tractors placed end to end take up when some 150,000 people decide
to leave all at once with their furniture, clothes, and other possessions. Greater Serbia was finished—"Small Serbia survives but
Greater Serbia is in refugee convoys," one Belgrade commentator
observed.[78]

The exodus of Serbs bore more than a passing resemblance to
the outcome of other failed programs of national aggrandizement.
Perhaps the champions of Greater Serbia should have learned more
from the fate of ethnic Germans at the end of World War II and of
Greeks at the end of the Greek-Turkish War. It was true that the
crimes committed in the wars for Yugoslavia, even at Srebrenica,
and in the Greek-Turkish war did not match those of World War II
in numbers killed, but in each case a campaign that began with
armies moving out to unite a scattered nation brought ruin to that
nation itself. Soldiers and tanks (at least for the Germans and Serbs)
sallied forth, creating a greater Greece, a German New Order, or a
greater Serbia, but several years later refugee Greeks, Germans, and
Serbs lost their homes. As Zoran Djindjic, a Serbian political rival of
Milosevic's and later Serbian prime minister, said later after the catastrophic attempt to ethnically cleanse Kosovo in 1999, "Four times
the Serbs have gone forth on tanks, and four times they have come
back on tractors."[79]

The assault on Greater Serbia resumed in September 1995. After
a shell exploded in Sarajevo on August 28 killing thirty-eight people, NATO began bombing Serb positions, and Croatian and Bosnian
forces soon began an offensive in western Bosnia. In striking contrast
to 1992, no support was forthcoming from Serbia for the Bosnian
Serbs—Slobodan Milosevic had long since tired of the economic
and political costs of supporting the Bosnian Serb leadership. Day by

day, thousands of Serbs streamed north—in their tractors, cars, and carts—until fifty thousand to sixty thousand, perhaps as many as a hundred thousand, poured into the northern Serb stronghold of Banja Luka, a town already crowded with recent arrivals from the Krajina. For a few days these refugees wondered where they would go when and if Banja Luka fell, but the Croatian and Bosnian offensives slowed, and the fighting ended with an October 5 cease-fire.[80] Serb Banja Luka survived as a kind of giant refugee camp where tens of thousands struggled to stay warm as winter approached.

After weeks and months of fluid borders and refugees in motion, a cold peace set and hardened the new ethnic boundaries. The war ended in an unlikely place: Dayton, Ohio, where the United States brought the presidents of Serbia, Croatia, and Bosnia for talks that ended on November 21 with an agreement. In principle the Dayton Peace Accords supported the ideal of a single Bosnian state, but this Bosnia consisted of two entities, one Serb—now reduced from 70 to 49 percent of Bosnia—and the other a loose Bosnian-Croat Federation.

The peace accords ended the war and stopped the killing but contributed to a last pulse of flight as civilians left homes destined to lie within the bounds of another ethnic group's authority. News of the imminent transfer of Sarajevo suburbs to the Bosnian-Croat Federation caused many of the seventy thousand Serbs living outside the city to start packing. Arson and flight accompanied the transfer of suburbs. Richard Holbrooke noted that Bosnian Serbs, from their holdout in Pale above Sarajevo, actually "broadcast detailed instructions on how to set the fires." On March 10, 1996, days before the scheduled departure of Serb police from one suburb, Serb gangs set fires, wrecking houses and businesses and driving out Serbs who actually wanted to stay. "I hear these boys go up and down the stairs and smash things," one woman told a reporter. "I'm terrified they will burn my apartment block, but I am old and have nowhere to go."[81] Serbs who managed to stay in their homes soon faced new danger from Bosnian Muslims intent on forcing them out.

"All of Pristina Is Here"

Ethnic cleansing was over in Bosnia-Herzegovina and in Croatia, but there was one more wave of large-scale ethnic cleansing still to be finished, this time in Kosovo in 1999. The fate of Kosovo was both the first and the last issue to excite Serb nationalist passions during the disintegration of Yugoslavia. In the 1980s Serb nationalists celebrated past Serb heroism and tragedy in Kosovo, and Serbia sought to tighten its hold over Kosovo despite the fact that the large and growing Albanian majority amounted to some 90 percent of Kosovo's population. In 1989 Serbia rescinded the province's autonomy granted in 1974 under Tito.[82] Serb authorities ignored a Kosovar Albanian declaration of independence in July 1990 and the election of a president, Ibrahim Rugova, in 1992 balloting conducted by Kosovo's Albanians. Increasingly harsh Serbian repression fueled more radical Albanian opposition, most notably an Albanian guerrilla movement, the Kosovo Liberation Army (KLA), founded in 1996.

Slobodan Milosevic had sacrificed Serbs in Krajina and Bosnia when their cause threatened to damage his own interests, but Kosovo, the very place where he had announced his nationalism, was another matter. A summer's combat between Serbs and the KLA in 1998 led to NATO threats of air attacks in October. Even then, Milosevic suggested another possible solution to the problem of Kosovo. He told an astonished General Wesley Clark, Supreme Allied Commander, Europe, "we know how to handle these Albanians. . . . We have taken care of them before." Milosevic continued, "In Drenica, in 1946, we killed them. We killed them all."[83] Further warning of NATO intervention in January 1999 brought both sides to negotiations in Rambouillet, France, that yielded a plan for autonomy with NATO peacekeepers. When Serb authorities rejected the plan, NATO followed through on March 24 with its long-threatened air strikes.

As bombing began, Serb forces carried out ethnic cleansing of Kosovar Albanians. Serbia claimed that the Albanians fled to escape the bombing, but accounts from refugees and from the few foreigners who remained in Kosovo demonstrated that Serbs seized the new war as an opportunity to expel the Albanians. The message was clear. "Go, go; take something and go," soldiers shouted at Albanians at the town of Pec in northwest Kosovo. Death squads, staffed by police and paramilitaries, and sometimes made up simply of Serb civilians with guns, roamed the streets of Kosovo's capital, Pristina, carrying out assassinations such as the killing of the human rights lawyer Bajram Kelmendi and his two sons, abducted from their home and found dead outside the city. One Pristina resident, ordered by Interior Ministry soldiers to go, headed for a friend's house instead of leaving the city. She stayed, even as Pristina emptied out, until a Serb acquaintance, "someone I was friendly with," told her she was being foolhardy. "Hey you are still around?" he asked, "What the hell are you doing. Don't you know your life's in jeopardy?"[84] Some of his friends were headed for Macedonia, and she left with them, passing through burned-out neighborhoods.

Refugees soon piled up at Kosovo's borders with Macedonia, Montenegro, and Albania. By late March, twenty thousand struggled north from Pec through sleet and snow over mountains to Montenegro, where the line of refugees at the border extended to two or even four miles. Many Kosovar Albanians from Pristina headed south to Macedonia, by the map their most direct route out of the province, but they found the border blocked. "Albania is for the Albanians," Macedonian guards said as they pushed refugees back.[85] Macedonia let Albanians through at a trickle, but meanwhile the refugees jammed into a kind of no man's land at the border. By early April, tens of thousands of people were camped out in fields, sleeping in blankets, trying to stay dry, and waiting to go somewhere.

Blocked from easy entrance into Macedonia and pushed west by Serb soldiers and paramilitaries, the largest number of refugees ended up where it made least sense: in Albania. Albanians and Kosovar Albanians shared a common ethnic identity and language, but Albania was a country unprepared by almost any standard to accept, house, and support refugees. Still, Kosovo's Albanians crossed the mountains west into Albania in a line that extended thirty miles or more, over the border post at Morin, and into a narrow valley. They continued to arrive, as many as fifteen hundred or more an hour, until Serb authorities suddenly shut down the crossing on April 7. From the border, Kosovar Albanian refugees reached Kukes, a remote town in one of the poorest regions of Europe's poorest country. Lodging was scarce even for those who could pay: there was but one hotel. Many of the local residents, at least at first, did what they could to help the new arrivals, but conditions soon became almost indescribable. "All of Pristina is here," one refugee said in early April. Perhaps that was not literally accurate, but it was close enough to the truth.[86] Take a hundred thousand and more people and put them down suddenly in an impoverished town of twenty thousand and the results are predictable: crowding, lack of sanitation, and a resulting stench that rose up throughout and around Kukes. Albanian authorities tried to take refugees out of Kukes to the coast, but more kept arriving from Kosovo. They crowded into apartments, schools, and mosques, and many ended up out in the open.

After the main phase of ethnic cleansing was complete, the Serb terror campaign targeted remaining pockets of Albanians. At the village of Cuška, five miles east of Pec, for example, local Albanians somehow escaped the deportations that cleared out most of Pec's residents, but on May 14, 1999, paramilitaries and police entered the village, shot the father of a KLA commander, and, as one witness recalled, "set him on fire." At least some in the Serb forces seemed to know the village. They demanded, "Give us the keys to your van!" and addressed Albanian villagers by their names.[87] After setting women, children, and the elderly aside, the Serb force collected twenty-nine men, put them in three houses, shot them, and then burned down the houses.

After somewhere between half and three-quarters of all Kosovar Albanians had fled, the tide of refugees suddenly switched direction when Serbia, contrary to the predictions of many experts, announced on June 10 that its forces would withdraw from Kosovo. Why this happened was never adequately explained—perhaps it was because Slobodan Milosevic's key backers in Serbia were tired of seeing their property and economic assets bombed, or because Serbia feared intervention by NATO ground forces. In any case, ordinary Serbs in Kosovo paid the highest price for this decision. Albanians came back to Kosovo, and Serbs, at least the overwhelming majority, left. Serbs feared what would happen if they stayed. "We're in a panic," one explained, ". . . we'll be at the mercy of the KLA. I have two children; what can I do?"[88] Serbs poured out of Kosovo. By August 1999 as many as 150,000, or 75 percent of Kosovo's Serb population, had fled for Serbia and Montenegro. Once Kosovar Albanians returned, they forced out old neighbors. Serb witnesses placed the chief blame on KLA members, both uniformed and in civilian clothes, though the KLA leadership condemned such attacks. Soon towns such as Pec and Prizren were largely empty of Serbs, and many of the Serbs who remained in Kosovo moved to Serb strongholds such as the town of Mitrovica on the north bank of the Ibar River.

"Is the Glass Half Full or Half Empty?"

In many details the wave of terror and ethnic cleansing at the close of the twentieth century resembled many older cases, decades or even a century or more in the past. Once again people grabbed what they could carry and abandoned their homes. With some changes to account for new technology and vocabulary, press accounts of mass flight during ethnic cleansing could have been written at the end of World War II, in the early 1920s, in 1912, or even in the nineteenth century. Once again ethnic violence that accompanied the breakup of empires further homogenized the map of Europe. The very landscape of terror—Kosovo, Bosnia-Herzegovina, Croatia, Azerbaijan, Armenia, Georgia, North Ossetia, Chechnya—was familiar to those who remembered the past. This time ethnic cleansing in the Caucasus separated Armenians and Azerbaijanis, and drove Georgians out of Abkhazia and Ingush out of North Ossetia. In Yugoslavia, ethnic cleansing forced apart Croats, Serbs, and Bosnian Muslims, and separated Serbs and Kosovar Albanians. Scenes of mass flight suggested the portrayals of those decades or more than a century before. Aside from differences in transportation—refugees driving tractors—or baggage—refugees sometimes carried appliances—little was new.

Amidst the lingering misery there were, however, some hopeful signs at towns like Kozarac. For several years it seemed that ethnic cleansing had permanently transformed Kozarac into a small and heavily damaged Serb town, but in the late 1990s Bosnian Muslims began to return to Kozarac. By 1999 a few hundred had moved back. The rate of return accelerated, and by 2003 some ten thousand Bosnian Muslims had come back to Kozarac.[89] The power of Serb hard-liners in the nearby city of Prijedor had dissipated after the death of Simo Drljača, and a local foundation gained funding to re-build many of the destroyed houses.

Overall the record of refugee return after ethnic cleansing in the former Yugoslavia was very mixed. In 2001 a UNHCR publication summed up the challenge, asking, "Is the glass half full or half empty?" True, there had been progress. In September 2004 the UNHCR proudly announced that the one millionth refugee or dis-placed person had "returned home" to Bosnia. But that number was not easy to interpret. A million people had returned, but far fewer than a million had actually gone back to their former homes. While 446,795 had returned to areas where they lived in the minority, many remained in ethnically cleansed or divided communities. Ten years after the outbreak of war, the city of Mostar, for example, re-mained split into distinct and separate Croat and Bosnian Muslim sectors. In late 2003 a report for the International Crisis Group ob-served that "Mostar remains administratively and psychologically partitioned." A river, rather than a wall, divided the city, but much like Berlin in the cold war, it was a city with two of everything. In March 2004, Paddy Ashdown, the international governor of Bosnia, sought to begin the process of reuniting the city.[90]

CHAPTER NINE

A Continent Cleansed

The cities, towns, and villages of Central and Eastern Europe and Western Asia have been radically transformed over the past two centuries. The residents of thousands of communities now speak different languages, practice different religions, and have different national identities from the people who once lived there. They make their homes in the same cities, towns, and villages where now-vanished communities of Turks, Greeks, Armenians, Jews, Germans, Ukrainians, Poles, Bosnian Muslims, Bulgarians, Serbs, Azerbaijanis, Georgians, Palestinians, Kurds, and others once lived. Some Europeans inhabit the very apartments and houses vacated by refugees during previous waves of flight, population transfer, and ethnic cleansing.

By the end of the twentieth century, ethnic cleansing had remade the ethnic and religious map of Central and Eastern Europe and Western Asia, erasing diversity across most of the region. Violence was not the only cause of migration—some people left their homes to find better opportunities elsewhere. But millions were forced out or killed. Successive waves of ethnic cleansing and genocide created new maps with new borders between new nation-states. Greeks live without Turks, Turks without Greeks, Czechs and Poles without Germans, Armenians without Azerbaijanis, Christian Cypriots without Muslim Cypriots. And in many countries virtually no one lives with Jews.[1]

Ethnic cleansing and related violence created new identities for victims and survivors. The experience of having been ethnically cleansed or transferred for many survivors became the pivotal event in their lives. Some clung to their memories of the past: they never forgot their old homes, they held on to maps and photos of their lost homelands. Some even tried to obtain plants from gardens they had been forced to leave. And they frequently identified themselves by referring to places and institutions that no longer existed. Adam Zagajewski, whose family moved from Lvov to the new Polish city of Gliwice (formerly the German city of Gleiwitz), wrote of people he knew growing up who seemed to live in a place and time that did not exist: "Living shadows, emigrants in their own country: ex-professors of a university that no longer existed; ex-officers of an army that no longer existed, with eastern accents of a no longer extant East."[2]

Many of the ethnically cleansed and their descendants retain a visceral anger and mistrust toward the perpetrators of expulsion and *their* offspring. Decades after ethnic cleansing, a sense of victimization remains a core element of their identity. The sense of victimization extends even to diaspora communities whose members have moved far away from Europe.[3]

Past ethnic cleansing also leaves those who live in place of the expelled with a sense of unease. Some simply insist they have every right to their homes, but others display curiosity about the past by commemorating the history of vanished and destroyed communities. Some also live with anxiety. They fear return, not by invading armies, but by lawyers and real estate agents representing the previously expelled or their heirs with demands for compensation or for the return of land, buildings, and businesses. Some worry that the expelled and their descendants will simply buy up what they lost, though these concerns are sometimes tempered by economic desperation. Farmers in rural Polish towns that used to be German may be eager to find a buyer. Germans may move back to Pomerania by buying up vacation homes, and Italians may return to Istria in the same way.

On the other side of the coin, some communities publicly celebrate the triumph of ethnic cleansing. Often the connection between a holiday and the ethnic violence of the past is unstated. In Bulgaria, Greece, and Turkey the date of national holidays commemorates independence, but in each case independence is also linked to mass flight and forced migration. The connection with ethnic cleansing can be still more direct when it comes to the commemoration of national heroes. For most Europeans, Nazi leaders were permanently discredited; but champions of ethnic and religious war from World War II, such as the OUN-Bandera and the Ustasha, later won honor in nationalist circles. Some of the key figures implicated in ethnic cleansing in the late twentieth century have become outlaw heroes. Radovan Karadzic and Ratko Mladic have both been indicted for war crimes, but T-shirts sold in the town of Banja Luka call Karadzic a "Serbian Hero." A 2002 tape released by a band called Serbian Taliban, with songs dedicated to Karadzic, Mladic, and Slobodan Milosevic, was a hit.[4]

Shirts and songs that honor men indicted of crimes against humanity might seem like acts of tasteless bravado, but ethnic cleansing and ethnic violence are deeply rooted in the politics and culture of modern Europe. Ethnic cleansing occurred under a variety of political systems and political leaders. Dictatorships carried out mass expulsions, but so too did democracies, though in some cases only as an "unfortunate necessity." Interest in ethnic cleansing and in population transfers crossed all political boundaries. Even if we remove Nazi and Soviet leaders from the equation because their crimes were unique, it is startling to list some of the other figures accused of supporting forced migration: Atatürk, Truman, Churchill, Beneš, David Ben-Gurion, Slobodan Milosevic, Saddam Hussein. Polemical false comparisons should be avoided: it is a slander to accuse Truman, Churchill, Beneš, or Ben-Gurion of supporting genocide. But what other policy could this unlikely assortment of leaders share?

Ethnic cleansing and violence took place under both strong and weak regimes. Powerful dictatorships such as Stalin's Soviet Union carried out swift and efficient deportations, but state power was neither a necessary precondition for conducting ethnic cleansing nor a guarantee that efforts to do so would succeed. Few states concentrated more power than Nazi Germany, but even Nazi leaders displayed frustration with the gap between their vision of moving entire nations and the results they were able to achieve. On the other hand, pogroms, ethnic war, and ethnic cleansing repeatedly occurred in very weak states, especially when empires broke down and collapsed.

European ethnic cleansing is not just something that bad states have done to good people. Ordinary people themselves have helped to create cleansed nation-states. A concentration on individual cases—the Holocaust or the Armenian genocide, for example—may make it easier to depict Germans or Turks as evil, even though some Germans or Turks did try to help the victims. But a broader, longer examination of ethnic cleansing in this region expands considerably on the list of both perpetrator and victim groups.

Ethnic cleansing united Europeans even as it drove them apart. They shared a common desire for nation-states of their own, untarnished by the presence of large ethnic or religious minorities. These dreams of purity created a sense that something was amiss with normal daily life: nationalist myths and stories depicted as traitors and enemies the very same people that many residents of Europe and Western Asia lived comfortably alongside. Many Europeans lived with what Cvijeto Job described as two realities, a concept described earlier. The first reality was of peaceful everyday relations with neighbors or fellow citizens of a different ethnic identity. The second reality—at odds with the first—was of ethnic hatred and fear that neighbors were traitors. For many, war confirmed those fears. Cycles of revenge killing suggested that the worst suspicions had been correct all along: neighbors were indeed enemies, and ethnic cleansing provided a way to build a better and more secure future.

Over decades it proved almost impossible to realize the dream of national purity peacefully and democratically—a failing of both empires and of nation-states. Old empires in which unity derived from loyalty to a common monarch began to fracture in the era of nationalism and democracy, and collapsed from the shock of World War I. New nationalist and racist empires, notably Nazi Germany, made purity and hate core values and collapsed in pursuit of their own grandiose and delusional aims. Communist empires, in contrast, at times provided homes for many nations but relied on repression and collapsed almost as soon as they began to democratize.

Nation-states proved no more successful at peacefully reconciling democracy with diversity. Even the fledgling democracies that succeeded empires often took part in ethnic wars and ethnic cleansing to carve up and purify old mixed imperial lands. Democracies that retained large minorities suffered from deep divisions and instability, and frequently came under authoritarian rule. Today Europe is mostly democratic, but it has also been ethnically cleansed. The arrival of new minority populations now offers European nations a second chance to reconcile democracy with diversity. Immigrants have arrived from former colonial possessions in Africa, South Asia, and the Caribbean, and economic migrants have also come from Turkey. But integrating these populations has proved extremely difficult for democracies of Western and Central Europe.

Europe's calamitous history of ethnic cleansing and violence shares common roots with tragedies in other regions, including Africa. In Africa as in Europe and Western Asia, the end of empire in ethnically mixed regions generated ethnic war and ethnic cleansing. The best-known case occurred in Rwanda. Imperial rule by Belgium accentuated the divisions between Hutus and Tutsis, the majority and minority ethnic groups in both Rwanda and the neighboring state of Burundi, and Belgian withdrawal sparked ethnic power struggles in both countries. In the case of Rwanda, repeated episodes of mass killing culminated in 1994 with the genocide of Tutsis. Rwanda provides one of the worst-case scenarios; many African countries escaped any comparable violence. But the end of empire also helped to spark ethnic war in several other key African countries, including Nigeria, Sudan, and the Congo (Zaire). The death toll in Sudan alone from years of fighting between the Arab-dominated central government and varied peoples in the south numbered at least 1.5 million.[5]

The most infamous case of mass killing in East Asia, the Cambodian genocide differs considerably from the genocides and ethnic violence of Europe and Western Asia. In Cambodia the genocide carried out by the Khmer Rouge after its seizure of power in 1975 did not aim to purify a country chiefly by expelling or exterminating another ethnic or religious group. The Khmer Rouge did target some of Cambodia's ethnic minorities for persecution, but primarily they wished to purify the Khmer people themselves. In this case a cohort of Khmer extremists launched genocide against their own people to rid the Khmer of what they saw as impure or alien influences, including people with too much education or with too close ties to the West. For this reason the Cambodian tragedy has been described as "auto-genocide."

No precise formula exists for predicting the next outbreak of ethnic cleansing or genocide, but the history of the past two centuries indicates when and where ethnic cleansing is most likely to occur. Searching for powerful modern states alone reveals almost nothing; most such states are actually quite unlikely to carry out ethnic cleansing. It is only slightly more helpful to scan the globe for malevolent leaders. Such a leader may be more inclined than the average head of state to consider and execute atrocities, but most such leaders will never carry out any policy that closely resembles ethnic cleansing. Europe's experience suggests a different approach to identifying likely trouble spots for future ethnic cleansing: we should look for an ethnically and religiously diverse region, a border zone of civilizations, especially one undergoing rapid modernization, where the boundaries of major ethnic and religious groups do not match the boundaries of states.

In Europe itself there is still potential for bitter ethnic conflict in the Balkans and in the Caucasus, but Europe is not the most likely site for large-scale future ethnic cleansing. The very success of past ethnic cleansing makes future recurrences less likely in much of Europe, and there are increasingly powerful incentives against further ethnic cleansing. Kosovo, for example, was an obvious flashpoint for ethnic conflict after the NATO intervention that reversed the Serbs' ethnic cleansing of Kosovar Albanians. Almost five years after the Yugoslav war, a renewed outbreak of ethnic violence in 2004 caused

NATO members to dispatch additional troops for peacekeeping in Kosovo. The possibility of membership in the European Union nonetheless provides strong motivation to refrain from ethnic cleansing. Balkan leaders may decide that they have more to gain from membership in one of the world's largest economies than in clinging to national pride at the cost of remaining an economic backwater. In the Transcaucasus as well, war-weary states have strong economic and political reasons to avoid renewed ethnic war and ethnic cleansing.

Future ethnic cleansing reminiscent of past European violence is most likely to strike several cultural, ethnic, and religious border zones in Asia and Africa. The eastern edge of the former Ottoman Empire remains highly unstable. In Iraq, for example, Kurdish political leaders speak hopefully of autonomy, but the overwhelming majority of Kurds wants a truly independent state. Relations between Kurds and non-Kurds, including Turkmens and Arabs, remain extremely tense in the city of Kirkuk. Major ethnic and religious divisions persist in other states and regions of Western and Central Asia, including Pakistan, Afghanistan, and Kashmir.[6]

At least two major zones of severe ethnic and religious conflict can be located in Africa. One such zone stretches from Sudan to the Congo in East and Central Africa. The government of Sudan and rebels in the country's south signed a peace agreement in January 2005, but ethnic cleansing carried out in western Sudan, in the Darfur region, has been so severe that U.S. Secretary of State Colin Powell said in September 2004 that "genocide has been committed in Darfur." Congo meanwhile staggered through years of war, including fighting in the northeast between ethnic militias, after the fall of Mobutu Sese Seko's despotic dictatorship.

A second vast zone of ethnic and religious conflict stretches across much of West Africa from Nigeria through Senegal. West Africa is certainly not doomed to ethnic cleansing, but a resurgence of ethnic violence in Nigeria beginning in the 1990s forced hundreds of thousands of people to flee their homes. In 2004 Nigerian President Olusegun Obasanjo declared six months' martial law to

stop "near mutual genocide" between Muslims and Christians in
central Nigeria.[7] As in Nigeria, tensions between Islam and other religions, including Christianity and animism, reinforced ethnic and
economic conflicts across the coastal states of West Africa in countries such as the Ivory Coast in 2002.

South and Southeast Asia are other places where religions, cultures, and ethnic groups meet with potential for future ethnic and
religious violence. Violence in Indonesia actually subsided in the
early twenty-first century. The conflict over East Timor ended, and
the level of ethnic and religious violence diminished on several In-
donesian islands, including Sulawesi and Sumatra. Still, Indonesia
faces immense challenges as the country struggles to forge a common national identity in a vast and diverse archipelago. Sharp divisions also exist in the southern Philippines and even in southern
Thailand.

The continued threat of violence in several regions of the world
lends urgency to the tasks of redressing and preventing ethnic
cleansing. Some of the most obvious remedies have already failed.
Democratization, for example, provides a very uncertain cure for
ethnic cleansing. In its early stages, democracy may sometimes make
ethnic cleansing more—not less—likely.[8] In Yugoslavia and in
Transcaucasia, democratization immediately preceded ethnic
cleansing, and the early phases of democratization also pose a challenge for Iraq after the fall of Saddam Hussein. More sustained and
developed democratization may reduce the chances of ethnic cleansing, but this requires going beyond holding elections and drafting
constitutions, which mark only the tentative first stages in democratization. The further steps in building a broader and deeper democracy include the establishment of a civil society and institutions that
protect minority rights and encourage tolerance.

The effectiveness of economic incentives as deterrents to ethnic
cleansing varies enormously. Substantial economic rewards may discourage ethnic cleansing and promote reconciliation between rival
ethnic groups, but even the prospect of economic ruin has seldom
stopped ethnic cleansing. Of course, the same wars that cause mis-

ery for many often enrich the few. Thus while the former Yugoslavia experienced immense economic damage from ethnic cleansing and war, some individuals made fortunes. Perhaps those who profited during years of general ruin will look back fondly on the years of war as good times, long after Serbia-Montenegro has gained membership in the European Union and raised its standard of living for the average person.

Preventing and ending ethnic cleansing is difficult but possible. Based on experience from Yugoslavia, we already know how to end the process if it is imminent or already underway: a strong international coalition with military force at its disposal can block and reverse ethnic cleansing. NATO halted ethnic cleansing in Bosnia and reversed it in Kosovo. Military intervention in such cases must be robust; some of the catastrophes in Yugoslavia, such as the Srebrenica massacre, indicate the dangers of weak intervention or peacekeeping carried out by inadequate forces. The Dutch troops at Srebrenica made mistakes, but most important they lacked the numbers and arms necessary to carry out their mission.

But stopping ethnic cleansing once it has begun requires the marshaling of political support. The wars of the 1990s placed ethnic cleansing front and center as an international human rights issue, but the catastrophe in Darfur in Sudan only a few years later has taught us that shocking news stories alone are not sufficient to build support for military intervention on the scale necessary to stop ethnic cleansing. In a world of nation-states, it is apparently no one's job to stop ethnic cleansing. Political leaders in democracies must determine how many of their countries' citizens would choose to volunteer for an international military force with the express tasks of intervening to stop ethnic cleansing and genocide and providing humanitarian relief in crises.

Outrage at ethnic cleansing and genocide during the 1990s gave rise to an international movement to create new legal institutions to punish crimes against humanity. The International Criminal Tribunal for the Former Yugoslavia (ICTY) began its work in 1994, and an International Criminal Tribunal for Rwanda (ICTR) held its first trial in 1997.[9] A UN conference in Rome voted in 1998 to establish a permanent international court, and in 2002 the treaty creating the International Criminal Court (ICC) was ratified. In the short run the mere threat of punishment has not dissuaded ethnic cleansing, but international courts may prove more effective in discouraging crimes against humanity once there are well-known examples of convictions for such offenses.

The ICTY made important strides in initiating legal proceedings against individuals charged with violations of international law at the local level. It held numerous trials, and in 2001 Serbia's government sent Slobodan Milosevic to be tried in the Hague. Still, several prominent suspects evaded arrest. Years after the end of the Yugoslav war, the chief political and military leaders of the Bosnian Serbs, Radovan Karadzic and Ratko Mladic, remain at large. Their continued freedom, despite indictments and rewards for information leading to their apprehension, has embarrassed the international community.

While stopping ethnic cleansing has proven difficult, repairing its damage is even more complicated. The window for action is brief. Unless refugees return very soon to their homes, they are unlikely ever to go back, except as visitors. George Seferis, the Noble Prize–winning Greek poet, went back to Izmir, but he knew that his Smyrna was gone. Izmir and Elâziğ (the city spread out below the former Harput) will remain Turkish cities, just as Jaffa will remain Israeli, Thessaloniki will remain Greek, Lviv will remain Ukrainian, and Gdansk will remain Polish.

The former Yugoslavia has provided a testing ground for a host of local and regional projects by governments and by nongovernmental organizations, addressing the damage caused by ethnic cleansing. These include local economic development projects as well as cultural and educational initiatives. One such project brought Serbs and Bosnian Muslims together for work on strawberry cultivation. It proved possible to encourage local cooperation in very specific tasks, but changing ethnic relations at the political level was far more challenging. The United Nations High Commissioner for

Refugees carried out pilot projects as part of an initiative to "Imagine Coexistence" at sites including the Bosnian town of Kozarac. On the other hand, efforts by the United Nations Mission in Kosovo to promote coexistence between Kosovar Albanians and Serbs achieved little success in building ties between these ethnic rivals in the years after NATO intervention in Kosovo.[10]

The most promising approach to reversing ethnic cleansing combines local reconciliation projects with economic development, legal proceedings, and an effective guarantee of security. The work must begin quickly, as soon as possible after ethnic cleansing ends, and it is expensive. Local cooperative projects can rebuild trust between communities that once lived alongside each other, but establishing security is also vital. While no one can guarantee an end to ill feeling between neighbors who recall past violence, it is possible to apprehend and try those charged with committing ethnic cleansing and related violence. Such action goes beyond providing local policing or security; it means removing culprits from the community. Strong local projects that build on memories of previous cooperation, as well as effective action against those who initiated and led the violence, can make possible the next critical step: encouraging refugees to return in numbers large enough for them to gain a significant share of local political power. With progress in all three of these tasks—rebuilding cooperation, apprehending criminals, and sharing political power—it is possible to speak of repairing some of the damage of ethnic cleansing. Nongovernmental organizations pioneered this approach in pockets of Bosnia, but there has been little progress rebuilding ethnically mixed towns and villages elsewhere in the former Yugoslavia and in Georgia, Armenia, and Azerbaijan.

History itself provides a final remedy, because ethnic cleansing is in large part a crime that begins with the misuse of history. Time and again, advocates of ethnic cleansing provide compartmentalized narratives of the past in which their own nation is always victimized and betrayed, and they repeatedly identify their present-day victims with their past national enemies. At best this style of extremist nationalist history is simplistic, at worst it is dishonest. Creating a new history to

replace these nationalist stories of age-old hatred and repeated betrayal by rival groups requires the pursuit of honest, balanced, and
comprehensive history, which has never been easy. On the one hand,
a new history of Europe and Western Asia cannot simply ignore past
grievances and suffering, advising people to forget the past and start
over again. Denial of history as a strategy has already failed. On the
other hand, the new history of Europe should not devolve into a com-
petition over the scale of past suffering (whose genocide was worse?),
but it also should not falsely equate all past episodes of persecution,
ethnic cleansing, and genocide, which is just a different kind of historical falsification. As a first step, a new history should persuade the
peoples of Central and Eastern Europe and Western Asia to look beyond their own people's suffering to acknowledge the tragedies of
their neighbors and former neighbors.[11]

This new history cannot be just "correct." Historians have begun
to break down barriers between previously exclusive national histories. German, Czech, and Slovak historians have worked together to
investigate World War II and its end, while German and Polish historians have carried out similar joint research. Even Armenian and
Turkish historians have begun to break down the walls between
their national histories. But it is not enough for historians to pursue
an accurate and balanced interpretation of ethnic conflict unless a
broader public also takes interest in and accepts this new history.

New and balanced history is vital for reconciliation in conflicts
where ethnic cleansing, forced migration, or population transfers are
already complete. Despite insistence on the "right of return," it is
highly unlikely that any Israeli government will ever under any conditions agree to let most Palestinian refugees, however defined, return to what were their homes in 1948, and there is no reason to believe that Armenians will ever regain their families' former homes
in Turkey. Arriving at a new understanding of history will not resolve all legal and diplomatic issues, but it should make it easier for
these and other ethnic and religious groups to live together in peace.

Acknowledgments

IN WRITING THIS BOOK I ranged into many areas of history, and I thank the experts who graciously answered inquiries on specific issues. I am especially grateful to Cathie Carmichael, Suzanne Marchand, Hunt Tooley, and Anita Fábos for reading drafts of the manuscript and offering valuable insights and suggestions.

I also wish to thank my colleagues at Fitchburg State College, in particular Pasquale Micciche, for their ongoing interest and encouragement. I am especially grateful to colleagues René Reeves, Joshua Spero, and Sean Goodlett for their critical careful reading and ideas.

Questions and comments from panel members and audiences at conferences and seminars were extremely helpful. I thank Hunt Tooley and Steven Béla Vardy, Stefan Wolff, and Omer Bartov for these opportunities. Thanks also to, among others, Dennis P. Hupchick, Peter Holquist, and David Curp for sharing their insights. I am grateful to Peter Holquist and Eyal Ginio for permission to cite papers.

I received valuable assistance from the Fitchburg State College Library, and I owe an enormous debt to the extraordinary efforts and effective work of Lisa Field and Mary Leger in tracking down and obtaining materials. In effect they transformed a college library into the collection of a large research university, and I could not have written this book without their help. Thanks also to Fitchburg State College history librarian Jean Missud for his assistance. I also thank Louise Richardson, executive dean of the Radcliffe Institute for Advanced Study at Harvard University, for her assistance.

I wish to express my particular gratitude to the Fitchburg State College Foundation and to President Robert V. Antonucci for supporting the preparation of maps.

The support, comments, and encouragement of friends and colleagues helped me bring this project to a conclusion, but any mistakes are my own. Translations are either my own or are quoted from the sources cited in the notes. I have also consulted translations from www.armenocide.com for help with some documents.

Ivan R. Dee brought care and attention to preparing the manuscript, and I thank him for his significant contribution.

I am grateful to Marcia Lieberman for her careful reading, and I thank her and Philip Lieberman, Daniel Lieberman, and Tonia Prescott for their encouragement and interest. Isabel and Sam provided high spirits and good cheer, and yes, Isabel, I really did start this book before Sam was born, and it is now finished.

Most of all, I thank my wife, Nancy Waters, for everything (her support, encouragement, sharp pencil, skillful editing, and keen eye), and it is to her that I dedicate this book with all my love.

Notes

BRITISH DIPLOMATIC RECORDS: FO refers to the British Foreign Office. Papers of the Foreign Office are classified by type, region, and chronology. FO 424, for example, refers to a series of 297 volumes from the Confidential Print on affairs of Turkey between 1841 and 1957. On occasion, reports on particular issues were also sent to Parliament. These were then listed in sequence. They were also known as Blue Books after the color of the covers.

AMERICAN DIPLOMATIC RECORDS: U.S. Department of State, Internal Affairs of Armenia and Relations Between Armenia and Other States, are microfilms of records from the National Archives.

PREFACE

1. The literature on nationalism is immense. For two of the most influential studies, see Benedict Anderson, *Imagined Communities: Reflections on the Origins and Spread of Nationalism*, rev. ed. (New York, 1991), and Ernest Gellner, *Nations and Nationalism* (Ithaca, 1983). For a somewhat different interpretation see Rogers Brubaker, *Ethnicity Without Groups* (Cambridge, Mass., 2004).

2. The rise of nationalism has prompted growing efforts to differentiate among the languages of Serbs, Croats, and Bosnian Muslims. See Robin Okey, "Serbian, Croatian, Bosnian? Language and Nationality in the Lands of Former Yugoslavia," *East European Quarterly* 38 (2004), pp. 419–441.

3. For a discussion of modern states, ethnic cleansing, and genocide see Norman M. Naimark, *Fires of Hatred: Ethnic Cleansing in Twentieth-Century Europe* (Cambridge, Mass., 2001), p. 8; Eric D. Weitz, *A Century of Genocide: Utopias of Race and Nation* (Princeton, N.J., 2003); and Benjamin A. Valentino, *Final Solutions: Mass Killing and Genocide in the Twentieth Century* (Ithaca, 2004). For a reassessment, see Mark Mazower, "Violence and the State in the Twentieth Century," *American Historical Review* 107 (2002), pp. 1158–1178.

4. Jasmina Dervisevic-Cesic, *The River Runs Salt, Runs Sweet: A Memoir of Viseg-rad, Bosnia*, as told to Joanna Vogel and Bruce Holland (Eugene, Ore., 1994, 2003), p. 3.

5. For discussion of definitions, see Drazen Petrovic "Ethnic Cleansing—An At-tempt at Methodology," *European Journal of International Law* 5 (1994), pp. 342–359; Daphna Shraga and Ralph Zacklin, "The International Criminal Tribunal for the For-mer Yugoslavia," *European Journal of International Law* 5 (1994), pp. 360–380; An-drew Bell-Fialkoff, *Ethnic Cleansing* (New York, 1996); Naimark, *Fires of Hatred*, pp. 2–4; Cathie Carmichael, *Ethnic Cleansing in the Balkans: Nationalism and the Destruc-tion of Tradition* (London, 2002), p. 2; Eagle Glassheim, "National Mythologies and Ethnic Cleansing: The Expulsion of Czechoslovak Germans in 1945," *Central European History* 33 (2000), pp. 465–466; Michael Mann, "Explaining Murderous Ethnic Cleans-ing: The Macro-level," in *Understanding Nationalism*, ed. Montserrat Guibernau and John Hutchinson (Cambridge, England, 2001), pp. 210–216; and Michael Mann, *The Dark Side of Democracy: Explaining Ethnic Cleansing* (Cambridge, England, 2005), p. 12. For an argument that stresses the primacy of religion, see Jack Goody, "Bitter Icons and Ethnic Cleansing," *History & Anthropology* 13 (2002), pp. 1–13.

6. Harassment and economic discrimination can lead to slower migration over longer periods of time. See Rogers Brubaker, *Nationalism Reframed: Nationhood and the National Question in the New Europe* (Cambridge, England, 1996), pp. 166–169. In some cases the term "unmixing of peoples," coined by the British diplomat Lord Curzon, may be useful. But the concept of "unmixing" fails to convey the level of force, intimidation, and violence that played a key part in driving many ethnic and religious groups out of their homes.

7. For a discussion of the distinction between the terms "deportation," most often used to describe cleansing within state borders, and "expulsion," used in con-trast to describe cleansing across state borders, see Philip Ther, "A Century of Forced Migration: The Origins and Consequences of 'Ethnic Cleansing,'" in *Redrawing Na-tions: Ethnic Cleansing in East-Central Europe, 1944–1948*, ed. Philipp Ther and Ana Siljak (Lanham, Md., 2001), p. 13. In practice, however, the term "deportation" is fre-quently used to describe movement across state boundaries.

8. Specialists on Spanish history debate whether the expulsion order of 1492 was intended to expel all or only some Jews from Spain. See Norman Roth, *Conversos, In-quisition, and the Expulsion of the Jews from Spain* (Madison: Wisc., 1995). On the Aca-dians, see John Mack Faragher, *"A Great and Noble Scheme" The Tragic Story of the Expulsion of the French Acadians from Their American Homeland* (New York, 2005).

9. There was one possible exception: between 1904 and 1907 German forces suppressed a revolt by the Herero people of South West Africa with a murderous cam-paign of deportations and killings. The legacy of the German colonial experience in Africa extended to World War II: the term "Askari," used to describe African soldiers who fought for the Germans in East Africa, resurfaced as a term for East European auxiliaries of the Germans in that war. On the genocide in Namibia, see Jürgen Zim-merer and Joachim Zeller, eds., *Völkermord in Deutsch-Südwestafrika: der Kolo-nialkrieg (1904–1908) in Namibia und seine Folgen* (Berlin, 2003). For an argument that stresses the influence of Namibia on World War II, see Benjamin Madley, "From Africa to Auschwitz: How German South West Africa Incubated Ideas and Methods Adopted and Developed by the Nazis in Eastern Europe," *European History Quar-terly* 35 (2005), pp. 429–464.

CHAPTER 1: BAG AND BAGGAGE: ETHNIC CLEANSING BEGINS

1. Edmund Spencer, *Travels in European Turkey in 1850*, vol. 2 (London, 1851), pp. 371, 376.

2. Henry Austen Layard, *Autobiography and Letters from his Childhood Until his Appointment as the Ambassador at Madrid*, ed. William N. Bruce, vol. 1 (New York, 1903), p. 146; Layard, *Autobiography and Letters*, vol. 2, p. 24.

3. Some historians note that the millet system was completed officially only in the nineteenth century, but nineteenth-century laws creating and recognizing millets elaborated and confirmed a preexisting system of conceptualizing Ottoman communities and their relationship to the empire in terms of religion.

4. Misha Glenny, *The Balkans: Nationalism, War, and the Great Powers, 1804–1999* (New York, 2000); Dennis P. Hupchick, *The Balkans: From Constantinople to Communism* (New York, 2002); Mark Mazower, *The Balkans: A Short History* (New York, 2000); and Carmichael, *Ethnic Cleansing in the Balkans*, pp. 10–15. For examples of some of the many studies on nationalism and other forms of identity, see Gerasimos Augustinos, *The Greeks of Asia Minor: Confession, Community, and Ethnicity in the Nineteenth Century* (Kent, Ohio, 1992); Thomas A. Meininger, *The Formation of a Nationalist Bulgarian Intelligentsia, 1835–1878* (New York, 1987); and Fatma Müge Göçek, *Rise of the Bourgeoisie, Demise of the Empire: Ottoman Westernization and Social Change* (New York, 1996).

5. Justin McCarthy, *Death and Exile: The Ethnic Cleansing of Ottoman Muslims, 1821–1922* (Princeton, N.J., 1995).

6. Tim Judah, *The Serbs: History, Myth, and the Destruction of Yugoslavia* (New Haven, 1997), pp. 51–53, 75; André Gerolymatos, *The Balkan Wars: Conquest, Revolution, and Retribution from the Ottoman Era to the Twentieth Century and Beyond* (New York, 2002), p. 114. On massacres, see Jacques Sémelin, "Toward a Vocabulary of Massacre and Genocide," *Journal of Genocide Research* 5 (2003), pp. 193–210.

7. Sir William Gell, *Narrative of a Journey in the Morea* (London, 1823), pp. 116–117. Even during the Greek War of Independence, foreign observers were surprised at the difficulty in distinguishing Turks from Greeks. See George Jarvis, *George Jarvis, His Journal and Related Documents*, ed. George Georgiades Arnakis, with the collaboration of Eurydice Demetracopoulou (Thessaloniki, 1965), p. 75.

8. Quoted in J. A. R. Marriott, *The Eastern Question: An Historical Study in European Diplomacy*, 4th ed. (Oxford, 1940), p. 205; Theodoros Kolokotrones, *Kolokotrones: The Klepht and the Warrior*, trans. with an Introduction by Mrs. Edmunds (London, 1892), p. 129.

9. Philip James Green, *Sketches of the War in Greece* (London, 1827), pp. 27, 56–58.

10. Maxime Raybaud, *Mémoires sur la Grèce: pour server à l'histoire de la guerre de l'indépendance* (Paris, 1824), vol. 1, p. 466; Sir Thomas Gordon, *History of the Greek Revolution*, vol. 1 (Edinburgh, 1844), p. 244. See also Douglas Dakin, *The Greek Struggle for Independence, 1821–1833* (Berkeley, 1973), p. 56. For a Greek witness, see Kolokotrones, *Kolokotrones*, p. 157. Note also the killing of prisoners at the Acropolis, and a massacre of refugees killed when they landed at the island of Cerigo (Kithira). See Green, *Sketches of the War in Greece*, pp. 80, 113.

11. Gordon, *History of the Greek Revolution*, vol. 1, p. 191. There were also reports of terror against Greeks at Smyrna, and Greeks were killed at Patras. See also David Brewer, *The Greek War of Independence: The Struggle for Freedom from Ottoman Oppression and the Birth of the Modern Greek Nation* (New York, 2001), pp. 101–106; Gerolymatos, *Balkan Wars*, pp. 160–161, 164–165; Green, *Sketches of the War in Greece*, pp. 28, 52–53; and Jarvis, *George Jarvis*, p. 42.

12. On the Klephts, see John Koliopoulos, "Brigandage and Irredentism in Nineteenth-Century Greece," *European History Quarterly* 19 (1989), p. 199. On the war's outcome and population change, see McCarthy, *Death and Exile*, p. 12.

13. Quoted in Victor Roudometof, "Invented Traditions, Symbolic Boundaries, and National Identity in Southeastern Europe: Greece and Serbia in Comparative Historical Perspective (1830–1880)," *East European Quarterly* 32 (1999), p. 434. See also Theodore George Tatsios, *The Megali Idea and the Greek Turkish War of 1897: The Impact of the Cretan Problem on Greek Irredentism 1866–1897* (Boulder, Colo., 1984).

14. Cathie Carmichael, "'Neither Serbs, nor Turks, Neither Water nor Wine, but Odious Renegades': the Ethnic Cleansing of Slav Muslims and Its Role in Serbian and Montenegrin Discourses since 1800," in *Ethnic Cleansing in Twentieth-Century Europe*, ed. Steven Béla Várdy and T. Hunt Tooley (Boulder, Colo., 2003), pp. 114–117; Judah, *Serbs*, pp. 61–65, 76–77. See also Roudometof, "Invented Traditions," pp. 447–448.

15. Raoul Motika and Michael Ursinus, ed., *Caucasia Between the Ottoman Empire and Iran, 1555–1914* (Wiesbaden, 2000).

16. Michael Khodarkovsky, *Russia's Steppe Frontier: The Making of a Colonial Empire, 1500–1800* (Bloomington, Ind., 2002); Michael Khodarkovsky, "Of Christianity, Enlightenment, and Colonialism: Russia in the North Caucasus, 1550–1800," *Journal of Modern History* 71 (1999), pp. 394–430; and Brian Glyn Williams, "Hijra and Forced Migration from Nineteenth-Century Russia to the Ottoman Empire: A Citical Analysis of the Great Crimean Tatar Emigration of 1860–1861," *Cahiers du Monde Russe* 41 (2000), p. 82.

17. John F. Baddeley, *Russian Conquest of the Caucasus*, with a new Foreword by Moshe Gammer (Richmond, England, 1999); Nicholas Griffin, *Caucasus: Mountain Men and Holy War* (New York, 2001).

18. Quoted in Robert Seely, *Russo-Chechen Conflict, 1800–2000: A Deadly Embrace* (Portland, Ore., 2001), p. 51. See also Baddeley, *Russian Conquest of the Caucasus*, p. 153; and Friedrich Bodenstedt, *Die Völker des Kaukasus und ihre Freiheitskämpfe gegen die Russen* (Frankfurt am Main, 1849), pp. 465, 467.

19. Leo Tolstoy, *The Complete Works of Count Tolstoy*, vol. 2, trans. and ed. by Leo Wiener (New York, 1968), p. 241.

20. Moshe Gammer, *Muslim Resistance to the Tsar: Shamil and the Conquest of Chechnia and Daghestan* (Portland, Ore., 1994), pp. 176–179, 218–221.

21. See Willis Brooks, "Russia's Conquest and Pacification of the Caucasus: Relocation Becomes a Pogrom in the Post-Crimean War Period," *Nationalities Papers* 23 (1995), p. 680; and Peter Holquist, "To Count, to Extract, and to Exterminate: Population Statistics and Population Politics in Late Imperial and Soviet Russia," in *A State of Nations: Empire and Nation-Making in the Age of Lenin and Stalin*, ed. Ronald Grigor Suny and Terry Martin (Oxford, 2001), pp. 116–117.

22. Quoted in Williams, "Hijra and Forced Migration," p. 93. See also Paul B. Henze, "Circassian Resistance to Russia," in *The North Caucasus Barrier: The Rus-*

sian Advance Towards the Muslim World, ed. Marie Bennigsen Broxup (London, 1992), pp. 62–111.

23. Quoted in Holquist, "To Count, to Extract, and to Exterminate," p. 119. See also McCarthy, *Death and Exile*, p. 36; and Williams, "Hijra and Forced Migration," p. 93.

24. Quoted in Williams, "Hijra and Forced Migration," p. 92. See also pp. 100–101.

25. Holquist, "To Count, to Extract, and to Exterminate," p. 117; Robert Crews, "Empire and the Confessional State: Islam and Religious Politics in Nineteenth Century Russia," *American Historical* Review 108 (2003), pp. 50–83.

26. Layard, *Autobiography and Letters*, vol. 2, p. 126; Meininger, *Formation of a Nationalist Bulgarian Intelligentsia*, pp. 100, 113.

27. Quoted in Mari A. Firkatian, *The Forest Traveler: Georgi Stoikov Rakovski and Bulgarian Nationalism* (New York, 1996), pp. 159–160; Hristo Botev, *Selected Works*, Selection, Foreword and Explanatory Notes by Stefana Tarinska (Bucharest, 1976), p. 55.

28. Botev, *Selected Works*, p. 79. See also McCarthy, *Death and Exile*, pp. 59–60; Glenny, *Balkans*, pp. 107–108; and British Foreign Office (FO) 424, vol. 43, p. 61.

29. Januarius MacGahan, *The Turkish Atrocities in Bulgaria* (London, 1876), pp. 22, 27, 29; James J. Reid, "Batak 1876: A Massacre and Its Significance," *Journal of Genocide Research* 2 (2000), p. 376; James J. Reid, *Crisis of the Ottoman Empire: Prelude to Collapse, 1839–1878* (Stuttgart, 2000); and Robert Jasper More, *Under the Balkans: Notes of a Visit to the District of Philippopolis in 1876* (London, 1877), p. 86. Only the previous year, a rebellion of mainly Christian peasants in Herzegovina and Bosnia had also ended with harsh punishment. See Arthur J. Evans, *Illyrian Letters* (London, 1878).

30. R. T. Shannon, *Gladstone and the Bulgarian Agitation 1876*, 2nd ed. (Hassocks, 1975), p. 110.

31. FO 424, vol. 55, p. 113; MacGahan, *Turkish Atrocities*, p. 12.

32. Colonel Epauchin, *Operations of General Gurko's Advance Guard in 1877* (London, 1900), pp. 35–36.

33. Archibald Forbes, *Czar and Sultan: The Adventures of a British Lad in the Russo-Turkish War of 1877–78* (New York, 1895), p. 37; Frederick Boyle, *The Narrative of an Expelled Correspondent* (London, 1877), p. 143. For a similar account of Tirnova, see Richard Graf Von Pfeil, *Experiences of a Prussian Officer in the Russian Service During the Turkish War of 1877–78*, trans. Colonel C. W. Bowdler (London, 1893), p. 79.

34. *The War Correspondence of the 'Daily News' 1877 with a Connecting Narrative Forming a Continuous History of the War Between Russia and Turkey to the Fall of Kars* (London, 1878), p. 237.

35. FO 424, vol. 57, pp. 127, 132; Wentworth Huyshe, *The Liberation of Bulgaria: War Notes in 1877* (London, 1894), p. 181. See also FO 424, vol. 59, p. 198.

36. FO 424, vol. 59, p. 9.

37. *War Correspondence of the 'Daily News,'* p. 400; Valentine Baker, *War in Bulgaria: A Narrative of Personal Experiences*, vol. 1 (London, 1879), p. 243. Note that Baker had previously suffered disgrace and imprisonment because of a sex scandal.

38. FO 424, vol. 66, pp. 17, 42.

39. Forbes, *Czar and Sultan*, p. 357; FO 424, vol, 67, p. 39; Henry O. Dwight, *Turkish Life in Wartime* (New York, 1881), p. 214; and Richard von Mach, *Elf Jahre Balkan: Erinnerungen eines preussischen Officiers aus den Jahren 1876 bis 1887* (Breslau, 1889), p. 134.

40. On the low end, see Richard J. Crampton, *Bulgaria 1878–1918: A History* (Boulder, Colo., 1983), p. 179; and Alexandre Toumarkine, *Les Migrations des Populations Musulmanes Balkaniques en Anatolie (1876–1913)* (Istanbul, 1995), p. 33. On the high end, see McCarthy, *Death and Exile*, p. 90; and Kemal H. Karpat, *Ottoman Population, 1830–1914: Demographic and Social Characteristics* (Madison, Wisc., 1985), p. 75. See also Dennis P. Hupchick, "Bulgaria's 'Turks': A Muslim Minority in a Christian Nation-State, 1878–1989," in *Ethnic Cleansing in Twentieth-Century Europe*, ed. Várdy and Tooley, p. 145–147.

41. Richard J. Crampton, *Bulgaria 1878–1918*, p. 179.

42. FO 424, vol. 59, p. 17; FO 424, vol. 60, p. 165; and FO 424, vol. 59, p. 181. See also FO 424, vol. 59, p. 296.

43. Walter G. Wirthwein, *Britain and the Balkan Crisis 1875–1878* (New York, 1935), p. 253.

44. FO 424, vol. 59, pp. 89, 211; FO 424, vol. 60, p. 65. For a critique of Layard, see R.W. Seton-Watson, *Disraeli, Gladstone, and the Eastern Question: A Study in Diplomacy and Party Politics* (New York, 1972), pp. 286–287. See also Wentworth Huyshe, *The Liberation of Bulgaria: War Notes in 1877* (London, 1894), pp. 158–161; and Boyle, *Narrative of an Expelled Correspondent*, p. 199.

45. Boyle, *Narrative of an Expelled Correspondent*, p. 197; FO 424, vol. 60, p. 165; Baker, *War in Bulgaria*, vol. 1, p. 330; and FO 424, vol. 60, p. 42. For an argument that Circassians were also primarily responsible for Muslim flight, see Reid, *Crisis of the Ottoman Empire*, p. 353.

46. FO 424, vol. 60, p. 214; FO 424, vol. 66, p. 79. See also FO 424, vol. 57, p. 144; and McCarthy, *Death and Exile*, pp. 66, 68, 74.

47. *Acktenstücke aus den Correspondenzen des Kais. Und Kön. Gemeinsamen Ministeriums des Äussern über orientalische Angelegenheiten vom 7. April 1877 bis 3. November 1878*, p. 52.

48. Antonio Gallenga, *Two Years of the Eastern Question*, vol. 1 (London, 1877), p. 101; and Boyle, *Narrative of an Expelled Correspondent*, pp. 195, 198. On the other hand, the British military attaché, Lieutenant Colonel Fred Wellesley, doubted Ignatieff's sincerity. See B. H. Sumner, *Russia and the Balkans 1870–1880* (London, 1962), pp. 614–615.

49. As McCarthy puts it, "Unless researchers find the war orders for the 1877–78 war in Russian archives, there will be no way to see what specific orders were given to the Cossacks." See McCarthy, *Death and Exile*, p. 69; Peter Holquist, "The Russian Empire as a 'Civilized Nation': International Law as Principle and Practice in Imperial Russia, 1874–1917," paper presented to American Historical Association 118th Annual Meeting, 2004; Seton-Watson, *Disraeli, Gladstone, and the Eastern Question*, p. 286; and *War Correspondence of the 'Daily News,'* p. 248.

50. Boyle, *Narrative of an Expelled Correspondent*, pp. 195–196; Francis Stanley, *St. Petersburg to Plevna: Containing Interviews with Leading Russian Statesmen and Generals* (London, 1878), p. 101.

51. FO 424, vol. 59, p. 12.

52. FO 424, vol. 59, pp. 184–185.

53. FO 424, vol. 59, pp. 10, 85; FO 424, vol. 60, p. 41; and Boyle, *Narrative of an Expelled Correspondent*, pp. 199–200.

54. FO 424, vol. 59, p. 85; FO 424, vol. 59, p. 184. See also FO 424, vol. 59, p. 182.

55. FO 424, vol. 60, p. 108; FO 424, vol. 59, p. 186. Vice Consul Dupuis described his source as "a respectable member of the Israelite community." See also FO 424, vol. 59, p. 228.

56. The village was Kazadjik. See FO 424, vol. 59, p. 11.

57. James F. Clarke, *The Pen and the Sword: Studies in Bulgarian History*, ed. Dennis P. Hupchick (Boulder, Colo., 1988), pp. 37–43, 50–53; More, *Under the Balkans*, pp. 27, 59, 65; and FO 424, vol. 43, p. 332. See also FO 424, vol. 57, p. 163.

58. FO 424, vol. 59, p. 84.

59. FO 424, vol. 125, pp. 25, 53; Justin McCarthy, "Muslims in Ottoman Europe: Population from 1800 to 1912," *Nationalities Papers* 28 (2000), p. 32.

60. William J. Stillman, *American Consul in a Cretan War*, rev. ed. of *The Cretan Insurrection of 1866–7–8*, Introduction and Notes by George Georgiades Arnakis (Austin, Tex., 1966), pp. 38, 63, 67.

61. *Correspondence Respecting the Affairs of Crete (August 1896), Turkey No. 7*, pp. 11, 72–73, 110–112; Tatsios, *Megali Idea*, pp. 79–80; and *Further Correspondence Respecting the Affairs of Crete (July 1897), Turkey No. 10*, pp. 125–128, 189.

62. *Correspondence Respecting the Affairs of Crete and the War Between Turkey and Greece (1897), Turkey No. 11*, p. 146.

63. *Further Correspondence Respecting the Affairs of Crete (July 1897), Turkey No. 10*, p. 25.

64. Ibid., pp. 116, 135–137.

65. *Reports on the Situation in Crete (May 1897), Turkey No. 9*, p. 9.

66. Ibid., pp. 9–10.

67. *Further Correspondence Respecting the Affairs of Crete (July 1897), Turkey No. 10*, p. 116. See also *Documents Diplomatiques. Affaires d'Orient. Affaire de Crète . . . Février-Mai 1897* (Paris, 1897), p. 161; Toumarkine, *Migrations des Populations Musulmanes*, p. 36; and *Britannica* 1911.

68. Halidé Edib, *The Turkish Ordeal* (New York, 1928), p. 8. The identity of Muslims from Crete was also distinct from that of other Turks. See Sophia Koufopoulou, "Muslim Cretans in Turkey: The Reformulation of Ethnic Identity in an Aegean Community," in *Crossing the Aegean: An Appraisal of the 1923 Compulsory Population Exchange Between Greece and Turkey*, ed. Renée Hirschon (New York, 2003), pp. 209–219.

69. Tatsios, *Megali Idea*, p. 93; *Correspondence Respecting the Affairs of Crete and the War Between Turkey and Greece (1897), Turkey No. 11*, p. 42.

70. W. Kinnaird Rose, *With the Greeks in Thessaly* (Boston, 1898), p. 140.

71. Rose, *With the Greeks in Thessaly*, pp. 140, 211; Ellis Ashmead-Bartlett, *The Battlefields of Thessaly* (London, 1897), p. 171; and Stephen Crane, *The War Dispatches of Stephen Crane*, ed. R. W. Stallman and E. R. Hagemann (New York, 1964), pp. 34–35.

72. Ashmead-Bartlett, *Battlefields of Thessaly*, pp. 184–185.

73. G. W. Steevens, *With the Conquering Turk: Confessions of a Bashibazouk* (London, 1897), p. 183.

74. Dominic Lieven, *Empire: The Russian Empire and Its Rivals* (New Haven, 2001), p. 277.

75. Quoted in William O. Oldson, *A Providential Anti-Semitism: Nationalism and Polity in Nineteenth-Century Romania* (Philadelphia, 1991), p. 118; David Vital, *A People Apart: The Jews in Europe, 1789–1939* (Oxford, 1999), pp. 171–176; Brian Porter, *When Nationalism Began to Hate: Imagining Modern Politics in Nineteenth-Century Poland* (Oxford, 2000), pp. 176–182, 227–232.

76. Quoted in Vital, *A People Apart*, p. 489. See also pp. 503–507; and Radu Ioanid, *The Holocaust in Romania: The Destruction of Jews and Gypsies Under the Antonescu Regime, 1940–1944*, with a Foreword by Elie Wiesel and a Preface by Paul A. Shapiro (Chicago, 2000), pp. 7–9.

77. Vital, *A People Apart*, p. 283.

78. Ibid., pp. 287–288, 291; Hans Rogger, *Jewish Policies and Right Wing Politics in Imperial Russia* (Berkeley, 1986), pp. 29–30; and Hans Rogger, "Conclusion and Overview," in *Pogroms: Anti-Jewish Violence in Modern Russian History* (Cambridge, England, 1992), ed. John D. Klier and Shlomo Lambroza, pp. 317, 333–337.

79. Benjamin Rubinstein, Eulogy for Minnie Rubinstein.

80. Edward H. Judge, *Easter in Kishinev: Anatomy of a Pogrom* (New York, 1992); Shlomo Lambroza, "The Pogroms of 1903–1906," in *Pogroms*, ed. Klier and Lambroza, pp. 196–204.

81. Lambroza, "Pogroms of 1903–1906," p. 208.

82. Ibid., pp. 214–215.

83. Quoted in Lambroza, "Pogroms of 1903–1906," p. 225; a newspaper reference to M. Dubrovin was likely an error. *Die Judenpogrome in Russland* (Cologne and Leipzig, 1910), vol. 2, pp. 151, 200, 281.

84. *Judenpogrome in Russland*, vol. 2, pp. 86–87, 92–93, 99–101. The hooligans arriving by train attacked Jews at the town of Kalarsch.

85. Quoted in Robert Weinberg, *The Revolution of 1905 in Odessa: Blood on the Steps* (Bloomington, Ind., 1993), pp. 164–167.

86. Hans Rogger, "Conclusion and Overview," in *Pogroms*, ed. Klier and Lamborza, p. 344.

87. *Correspondence Relative to the Armenian Question (February 1896), Turkey No. 2*, pp. 22, 34–35.

88. Sir Telford Waugh, *Turkey Yesterday, To-day and To-morrow* (London, 1930), pp. 49–50; *Correspondence Relative to the Armenian Question (February 1896), Turkey No. 2*, p. 66.

89. *Correspondence Relative to the Armenian Question (February 1896) Turkey No. 2*, pp. 149–150, 207, 216, 298–337.

90. Edwin Munsell Bliss, *Turkey and the Armenian Atrocities: A Reign of Terror* (Philadelphia, 1896), p. 461.

91. Ronald Grigor Suny, *Looking Toward Ararat: Armenia in Modern History* (Bloomington, Ind., 1993), pp. 105–106; Vahakn N. Dadrian, *Warrant for Genocide: Key Elements of Turko-Armenian Conflict* (New Brunswick, N.J., 1999), pp. 85–90. *Correspondence Relative to the Armenian Question (February 1896) Turkey No. 2*, pp. 214, 238; and James L. Barton, *'Turkish Atrocities' Statements of American Missionaries on the Destruction of Christian Communities in Ottoman Turkey, 1915–1917* (Ann Arbor, Mich., 1998), p. 75.

92. Sir Robert Graves, *Storm Centres of the Near East: Personal Memories 1879–1929* (London, 1933), p. 157.

93. Luigi Villari, *Fire and Sword in the Caucasus* (London, 1906), pp. 156–157.

94. Tadeusz Swietochowski, *Russian Azerbaijan, 1905–1920: The Shaping of National Identity in a Muslim Community* (Cambridge, England, 1985), pp, 21–22, 37–41; J. D. Henry, *Baku: An Eventful History* (London, 1905), pp. 3, 149; and Villari, *Fire and Sword in the Caucasus*, p. 195.

95. Villari, *Fire and Sword in the Caucasus*, pp. 286, 199; Henry, *Baku*, p. 172; and Swietochowski, *Russian Azerbaijan*, p. 41.

96. Quoted in Andrew Mango, *Atatürk* (Woodstock, N.Y., 2000), p. 11. Jews also left for economic opportunity, but the few survivors of pogroms that I met left no doubt that escaping violence was also a reason to leave Russia.

97. James George Minchin, *Bulgaria Since the War: Notes of a Tour in the Autumn of 1879* (London, 1880), pp. 36–39; Glenny, *Balkans*, p. 168; and Reginald Rankin, *The Inner History of the Balkan War* (London, 1914), p. 44.

98. Peter Mentzel, "Conclusion: *Millets*, States, and National Identities," *Nationalities Papers* 28 (2000), p. 201.

99. Mazower, *Balkans*, pp. 39–40. For a study of the borderland of Right Bank Ukraine, see Kate Brown, *Biography of No Place: From Ethnic Borderland to Soviet Heartland* (Cambridge, Mass., 2004).

CHAPTER 2: FAREWELL TO SALONICA

1. Leon Sciaky, *Farewell to Ottoman Salonica* (Istanbul, 2000, first published as *Farewell to Salonica*, 1946). For the authoritative history of Salonica, see Mark Mazower, *Salonica, City of Ghosts: Christians, Muslims, and Jews, 1430–1950* (London, 2004).

2. FO 424, vol. 243, pp. 89–90.

3. Loring M. Danforth, *The Macedonian Conflict: Ethnic Nationalism in a Transnational World* (Princeton, N.J., 1995); Steevens, *With the Conquering Turk*, p. 3. Greeks and Macedonians disputed the right to use symbols of the ancient Macedonia of Alexander the Great. Fans preparing to see Greece play at the 1994 soccer World Cup in the United States could see the slogan "Macedonia is Greece" on banners pulled by aircraft.

4. M. E. Durham, *Twenty Years of Balkan Tangle* (London, 1920), p. 94. See also Glenny, *Balkans*, pp. 195–206; and Mazower, *Salonica, City of Ghosts*, pp. 269–271.

5. There is a massive literature on the Young Turks. For some recent works, see M. Sükrü Hanioğlu, *Preparation for a Revolution: The Young Turks, 1902–1908* (New York, 2001); and M. Naim Turfan, *Rise of the Young Turks: Politics, the Military, and Ottoman Collapse* (London, 2000).

6. Sciaky, *Farewell to Ottoman Salonica*, p. 135; Noel Malcolm, *Kosovo: A Short History*, updated with a new Preface (New York, 1998, 1999), pp. 239–249; Glenny, *Balkans*, p. 228; and M. E. Durham, *The Struggle for Scutari (Turk, Slav, and Albanian)* (London, 1914), pp. 55–56.

7. FO 424, vol. 236, p. 188.

8. Philip Gibbs and Bernard Grant, *The Balkan War: Adventures of War with Cross and Crescent* (Boston, 1913), p. 127.

9. Durham, *Struggle for Scutari*, pp. 195, 252–253, 268, 295–296.

10. Leon Trotsky, *The Balkan Wars 1912–13: The War Correspondence of Leon Trotsky*, trans. Brian Pearce, ed. George Weissman and Duncan Williams (New York, 1980), pp. 267, 270.

11. Rebecca West, *Black Lamb and Grey Falcon: A Journey Through Yugoslavia*, vol. 1 (New York, 1940, 1964), p. 20. For reports on massacres, see FO 424, vol. 243, pp. 89–91.

12. *The Other Balkan Wars: 1914 Carnegie Endowment Report of the International Commission to Inquire into the Causes and Conduct of the Balkan Wars*, Introduction by George F. Kennan (Washington, D.C., 1993), p. 277. The Carnegie Report described the Commission members as "Bulgarian notables." Harry Lamb suggested that release might come if six of seven members of the Commission declared the suspect "to have been a good man." See FO 424, vol. 236, p. 275. See also W. H. Crawfurd Price, *The Balkan Cockpit: The Political and Military Story of the Balkan Wars in Macedonia* (London, 1914), p. 179.

13. *Carnegie Report*, pp. 72, 279–280; FO 424, vol. 236, pp. 185, 276, 347.

14. FO 424, vol. 236, p. 76; FO 424, vol. 241, p. 130.

15. FO 424, vol. 243, p. 300; *Carnegie Report*, pp. 72, 281; and FO 424, vol. 236, p. 185.

16. Price, *Balkan Cockpit*, p. 176; FO 424, vol. 243, p. 298; and *Carnegie Report*, pp. 72, 282–284.

17. FO 424, vol. 236, p. 185; FO 424, vol. 241, p. 206. See also Price, *Balkan Cockpit*, pp. 177, 181.

18. *Carnegie Report*, p. 76; FO 424, vol. 236, p. 189; FO 424, vol. 236, p. 76; and FO 424, vol., 241, p. 185.

19. Noel-Buxton, *With the Bulgarian Staff* (London, 1913), p. 90.

20. *Carnegie Report*, p. 151.

21. Ibid.

22. FO 424, vol. 236, p. 276; Price, *Balkan Cockpit*, p. 97.

23. FO 424, vol. 243, p. 299; Price, *Balkan Cockpit*, pp. 108–110.

24. Gibbs, *Balkan War*, pp. 154, 161.

25. Ellis Ashmead-Bartlett and Seabury Ashmead-Bartlett, *With the Turks in Thrace* (New York, 1913), pp. 96, 134.

26. Ibid., pp. 220, 231, 250.

27. Rankin, *Inner History of the Balkan War*, p. 304; Katrin Boeckh, *Von den Balkankriegen zum Ersten Weltkrieg: Kleinstaatenpolitik und ethnische Selbstbestimmung auf dem Balkan* (Munich, 1996), p. 258; and McCarthy, *Death and Exile*, p. 160.

28. Sciaky, *Farewell to Ottoman Salonica*, pp. 154, 156–157.

29. Ibid., p. 156; Mazower, *Salonica, City of Ghosts*, pp. 296–297; and *Carnegie Report*, p. 56.

30. FO 424, vol. 249, p. 47. See also Price, *Balkan Cockpit*, pp. 350, 353; and *Carnegie Report*, p. 298.

31. *Carnegie Report*, p. 95.

32. FO 424, vol. 248, p. 168; Sciaky, *Farewell to Ottoman Salonica*, pp. 160–161. See also FO 424, vol. 248, pp. 170–175; *Carnegie Report*, p. 99.

33. FO 424, vol. 248, pp. 168, 170.

34. *Carnegie Report*, pp. 104–105, 308–309.

35. *Carnegie Report*, pp. 307–308, 311.

36. Ibid., pp. 308–309.

37. Ibid., pp. 95–97.

38. Ibid., p. 123.

39. Taner Akçam, *Armenien und der Völkermord: Die Istanbuler Prozesse und die türkischer Nationale Bewegung* (Hamburg, 1996), p. 39; Aviel Roshwald, *Ethnic Nationalism and the Fall of Empires: Central Europe, Russia and the Middle East,*

1914–1923 (New York, 2001), pp. 106–107; and Eyal Ginio, "Paving the Way for Ethnic Cleansing: Eastern Thrace (Doğu Trakya) During the Balkan Wars (1912–1913)."

40. *Carnegie Report*, pp. 124, 127.

41. Ibid., p. 131; Alexander Papadopoulos, *Persecutions of the Greeks in Turkey before the European War*, trans. Carroll N. Brown (New York, 1919), pp. 34–36.

42. *Carnegie Report*, p. 348; FO 424, vol. 248, p. 28. See also Trotsky, *Balkan Wars*, p. 254.

43. FO 424, vol. 243, p. 298; FO 424, vol. 242, p. 266.

44. *Carnegie Report*, p. 199. See also Boeckh, *Von den Balkankriegen zum Ersten Weltkrieg*, p. 228.

45. *Carnegie Report*, pp. 176, 165; Boeckh, *Von den Balkankriegen zum Ersten Weltkrieg*, p. 177. See also *Carnegie Report*, pp. 173–174.

46. Boeckh, *Von den Balkankriegen zum Ersten Weltkrieg*, pp. 155, 165; Malcolm, *Kosovo*, pp. 257–258.

47. Richard von Mach, *Briefe aus dem Balkankriege 1912 1913: Kriegsberichte der Kölnischen Zeitung* (Berlin, 1913), p. 117; FO 424, vol. 243, p. 299; Boeckh, *Von den Balkankriegen zum Ersten Weltkrieg*, p. 166; and Carmichael, *Ethnic Cleansing in the Balkans*, p. 82.

48. Mazower, *Salonica, City of Ghosts*, pp. 301–303, 317–321, 339.

49. Trotsky, *Balkan Wars*, p. 286; Price, *Balkan Cockpit*, p. 181; and *Carnegie Report*, p. 148.

50. Von Mach, *Briefe aus dem Balkankriege*, p. 117. On images of the Balkans, see Maria Todorova, *Imagining the Balkans* (New York, 1997), pp. 3, 19, 28, 121.

CHAPTER 3: "HOW MUCH WORSE IT IS THAN MASSACRE!"

1. Richard G. Hovannisian, "Armenian Tsopk/Kharpert," and Robert H. Hewsen, "Golden Plain: The Historical Geography of Tsopk/Kharpert," in *Arme-nian Tsopk/Kharpert*, ed. Richard G. Hovannisian (Costa Mesa, Calif., 2002), pp. 1–58.

2. See T. Hunt Tooley, "World War I and the Emergence of Ethnic Cleansing in Europe," in *Ethnic Cleansing in Twentieth-Century Europe*, ed. Várdy and Tooley, pp. 63–97. For a more general discussion of the interaction between the war, nationalism, and ethnic conflict, see Roshwald, *Ethnic Nationalism and the Fall of Empires.*

3. John Reed, *The War in Eastern Europe* (New York, 1916), pp. 39, 282, 299, 325.

4. Ibid., pp. 76, 84, 87.

5. Alice Askew and Claude Askew, *The Stricken Land: Serbia as We Saw It* (New York, 1916), p. 147; Milutin Krunich, *Serbia Crucified: The Beginning* (Boston, 1918), p. 139. For a scene of Serbs fleeing advancing German and Austrian forces, see Gordon Gordon-Smith, *Through the Serbian Campaign: The Great Retreat of the Serbian Army* (London, 1916), p. 57.

6. Askew, *Stricken Land*, p. 200.

7. Fortier Jones, *With Serbia into Exile: An American's Adventures with the Army That Cannot Die* (New York, 1916), pp. 231, 234.

8. Ibid., p. 229.

9. Marko Zivkovic, "Stories Serbs Tell Themselves: Discourses on Identity and Destiny in Serbia Since the Mid-1980s," *Problems of Post-Communism* 44 (1997), pp. 22–29. On Serbia's occupation see Dragon Živojnović, "Serbia and Montenegro: The Home Front, 1914–18," in *East Central European Society in World War I*, ed. Béla K. Király and Nándor F. Dreisziger (Boulder, 1985), pp. 239–259.

10. *Report of the Inter-Allied Commission in Eastern Macedonia* (London, 1919), pp. 5–6.

11. Ibid., pp. 22–28. The Commission was of course making no comparison to death camps.

12. Ibid., p. 29; Bulgarian Delegation, *The Accusations Against Bulgaria: Official Documents Presented to the Peace Conference* (1919), p. 6.

13. See Joshua A. Sanborn, *Drafting the Russian Nation: Military Conscription, Total War, and Mass Politics, 1905–1925* (DeKalb, Ill., 2003).

14. S. Ansky, *The Enemy at His Pleasure: A Journey Through the Jewish Pale of Settlement During World War I*, ed. and trans. Joachim Neugroschel (New York, 2003), p. 3.

15. Ansky, *Enemy at His Pleasure*, pp. 3–5.

16. Eric Lohr, "The Russian Army and the Jews: Mass Deportation, Hostages, and Violence During World War I," *Russian Review* 60 (July 2001), p. 407; Eric Lohr, *Nationalizing the Russian Empire: The Campaign Against Enemy Aliens During World War I* (Cambridge, Mass., 2003), pp. 137–138.

17. Ansky, *Enemy at His Pleasure*, pp. 13–14. See also Rogger, *Jewish Policies and Right-Wing Politics*; Mark Levene, "Frontiers of Genocide: Jews in the Eastern War Zones, 1914–1920 and 1941," in *Minorities in Wartime: National and Racial Groupings in Europe, North America, and Australia During the Two World Wars*, ed. Panikos Panayi (Providence, R.I., 1993), pp. 83–117; Peter Gatrell, *A Whole Empire Walking: Refugees in Russia During World War I* (Bloomington, Ind., 1990); and Lohr, "Russian Army and the Jews," pp. 404–419.

18. Ansky, *Enemy at His Pleasure*, pp. 68, 91. See Gatrell, *Whole Empire Walking*, p. 18.

19. Gregor Alexinsky, *Russia and the Great War*, trans. Bernard Miall (New York, 1915), p. 203. See Lohr, *Nationalizing the Russian Empire*, p. 138.

20. Lohr, "Russian Army and the Jews," pp. 409–410; Levene, "Frontiers of Genocide," p. 95; and Rogger, *Jewish Policies and Right Wing Politics*, p. 100.

21. Ansky, *Enemy at His Pleasure*, pp. 163–164, 155, 29–30; Reed, *War in Eastern Europe*, p. 133; Lohr, "Russian Army and the Jews," p. 417; Alexinsky, *Russia and the Great War*, p. 203; and Christoph Mick, "Ethnische Gewalt und Pogrome in Lemberg 1914 und 1941," *Osteuropa* 53 (2003), pp. 1810–1829.

22. Lohr, "Russian Army and the Jews," pp. 411–412; Rogger, *Jewish Policies and Right Wing Politics*, pp. 104–105; and Gatrell, *Whole Empire Walking*, p. 146.

23. Charles J. Vopicka, *Secrets of the Balkans: Seven Years of a Diplomatist's Life in the Storm Centre of Europe* (Chicago, 1921), p. 271.

24. Theodor Schieder, ed., *Das Schicksal der Deutschen in Rumänien* (Bonn, 1957), p. 24.

25. Ansky, *Enemy at His Pleasure*, p. 183. See Lohr, *Nationalizing the Russian Empire*, pp. 129–134; and Hans Freiherr von Rosen, *Wolhynienfahrt 1926* (Siegen, 1982), p. 17.

26. Schieder, *Schicksal der Deutschen in Rumänien*, p. 24. See Lohr, *Nationalizing the Russian Empire*, pp. 94–120.

27. Reed, *War in Eastern Europe*, 196.

28. Henry Morgenthau, *Ambassador Morgenthau's Story* (Ann Arbor, Mich., 2000), p. 34. On the rise of Turkish nationalist ideology and the campaign against

Greeks, see Taner Akçam, *From Empire to Republic: Turkish Nationalism and the Armenian Genocide* (New York, 2004), pp. 137–145.

29. Alexander Papadopoulos, *Persecutions of the Greeks in Turkey Before the European War*, trans. Carroll N. Brown (New York, 1919), pp. 74–84. This was very much a Greek document. On Phocaea, see Harry Stuermer, *Two War Years in Constantinople* (New York, 1917), p. 169.

30. Papadopoulos, *Persecutions of the Greeks in Turkey Before the European War*, p. 121. Ayhan Aktar, "Homogenising the Nation, Turkifying the Economy: The Turkish Experience of Population Exchange Reconsidered," in *Crossing the Aegean*, ed. Hirschon, pp. 83–84; and Henry Morgenthau, *I Was Sent to Athens* (Garden City, N.Y., 1929), p. 16.

31. George Horton, *Recollections Grave and Gay: The Story of a Mediterranean Consul* (Indianapolis, 1927), p. 224.

32. *Tragedy of the Sea of Marmora* (New York, 1918), pp. 5–6. This was a pamphlet published by the Relief Committee for Greeks of Asia Minor.

33. Hypourgeio Exoterikon (Greek Ministry of Foreign Affairs), *Persecutions of the Greeks in Turkey Since the Beginning of the European War*, trans. Carrol N. Brown and Theodore P. Ion (New York, 1918), pp. 45, 52; Institut für Armenische Fragen, *Armenian Genocide Documentation*, vol. 2, pp. 409–410.

34. Morgenthau, *Ambassador Morgenthau's Story*, p. 216.

35. Quoted in Mazower, *Salonica, City of Ghosts*, p. 275. See also Akçam, *From Empire to Republic*, pp. 128–137; and Peter Balakian, *The Burning Tigris: The Armenian Genocide and America's Response* (New York, 2003), pp. 163–166. For an argument that traces an Ittihadist path toward genocide to the 1911 party congress and suggests that the Ittihadists even consulted with Abdul Hamid on the Armenian issue, see Dadrian, *Warrant for Genocide*, pp. 93–103, 155–157.

36. Henry H. Riggs, *Days of Tragedy in Armenia: Personal Experiences in Harput, 1915–1917* (Ann Arbor, Mich., 1997), p. 22; James Bryce and Arnold Toynbee, *The Treatment of Armenians in the Ottoman Empire, 1915–1916*, uncensored ed., ed. with an Introduction by Ara Sarafian (Princeton, N.J., 2000), p. 268. See Akçam, *Armenien und der Völkermord*, p. 58; and Dadrian, *Warrant for Genocide*, pp. 115–116.

37. Leslie A. Davis, *The Slaughterhouse Province: An American Diplomat's Report on the Armenian Genocide, 1915–1917*, ed. with an Introduction and Notes by Susan K. Blair (New Rochelle, N.Y., 1989), p. 61.

38. Morgenthau, *Ambassador Morgenthau's Story*, p. 198; Clarence Ussher, *An American Physician in Turkey: A Narrative of Adventures in Peace and War* (Boston, 1917), pp. 237, 239, 244. See Donald Bloxham, "The Beginning of the Armenian Catastrophe: Comparative and Contextual Considerations," in *Der Völkermord an den Armeniern und die Shoa*, ed. Hans-Lukas Kieser and Dominik J. Schaller (Zurich, 2002), p. 118.

39. Ussher, *American Physician in Turkey*, p. 285. See also Hovannisian, *Armenian Van/Vaspurakan*.

40. Morgenthau, *Ambassador Morgenthau's Story*, pp. 223, 229; McCarthy, *Death and Exile*, pp. 191–195; and "Armenocide," 1915-05-29-DE-011, Aufzeichnung des Generalkonsuls in Konstantinopel (Mordtmann), www.armenocide.net (February 2005).

41. Riggs, *Days of Tragedy in Armenia*, pp. 47–48, 53; Barton, '*Turkish Atrocities*,' p. 59; and Tacy Atkinson, "*The German, the Turk and the Devil Made a Triple Alliance*": *Harpoot Diaries, 1908–1917*, with a Foreword by J. Michael Hagopian (Princeton, N.J., 2000), p. 35; Balakian, *Burning Tigris*, p. 213.

42. Akçam, *From Empire to Republic*, pp. 164–168; Akçam, *Armenien und der Völkermord*, p. 61; and Vahakn N. Dadrian, *The History of the Armenian Genocide: Ethnic Conflict from the Balkans to Anatolia to the Caucasus* (Providence, 1997), p. 221.

43. Wolfgang Gust, ed., *Der Völkermord an den Armeniern 1915/16: Dokumente aus dem Politischen Archiv des deutschen Auswärtigen Amts* (Springe 2005), pp. 223–224, 267–268; "Armenocide," 1915-05-18-DE-012, Der Verweser in Erzerum (Scheubner-Richter) an die Botschaft Konstantinopel, www.armenocide.net (February 2005); ibid., 1915-06-02-DE-012; ibid., 1915-06-26-DE-013. For an account of genocide at Erzerum, see Hilmar Kaiser, "'A Scene from the Inferno': The Armenians of Erzerum and the Genocide, 1915–1916," in *Der Völkermord an den Armeniern und die Shoa*, ed. Kieser and Schaller, pp. 129–186.

44. Gust, *Völkermord an den Armeniern*, p. 195; *Armenian Genocide Documentation*, vol. 2, pp. 196, 203–204; Barton '*Turkish Atrocities*,' p. 78; Bryce and Toynbee, *Treatment of Armenians in the Ottoman Empire*, p. 356; and *Armenian Genocide Documentation*, vol. 1, p. 321.

45. Gust, *Völkermord an den Armeniern*, pp. 185, 227.

46. Davis, *Slaughterhouse Province*, p. 54; Riggs, *Days of Tragedy in Armenia*, p. 88.

47. Davis, *Slaughterhouse Province*, pp. 55–57; Riggs, *Days of Tragedy in Armenia*, p. 90; and Atkinson, "*The German, the Turk and the Devil*," pp. 44, 48.

48. *Armenian Genocide Documentation*, vol. 2, p. 214; Barton, '*Turkish Atrocities*,' p. 149.

49. *Armenian Genocide Documentation*, vol. 2, p. 266.

50. "Armenocide," 1915-06-02-DE-012, Der Verweser in Erzerum (Scheubner-Richter) an die Botschaft Konstantinopel, www.armenocide.net (February 2005); ibid., 1915-06-18-DE-013; and Gust, *Völkermord an den Armeniern*, p. 219.

51. *Armenian Genocide Documentation*, vol. 2, p. 205. See also Gust, *Völkermord an den Armeniern*, p. 208, for similar predictions from the town of Samsun.

52. Davis, *Slaughterhouse Province*, p. 52; Riggs, *Days of Tragedy in Armenia*, p. 140.

53. Barton, '*Turkish Atrocities*,' p. 146; "Armenocide," 1915-07-02-DE-011, Der Konsul in Trapezunt (Bergfeld) an die Botschaft Konstantinopel, www.armenocide .net (February 2005).

54. Gust, *Völkermord an den Armeniern*, p. 269.

55. Barton, '*Turkish Atrocities*,' pp. 23, 68; Davis, *Slaughterhouse Province*, p. 60; and Gust, *Völkermord an den Armeniern*, p. 198.

56. Akçam, *From Empire to Republic*, pp. 158–174. On early killings by the Special Organization in the east, see Bloxham, "The Beginning of the Armenian Catastrophe," p. 117.

57. Akçam describes killing by the Special Organziation, gendarmes, Kurds, and civilians. Military units were most likely to carry out massacres toward the east. See Akçam, *Armenien und der Völkermord*, pp. 72–75; and Vahakn N. Dadrian, "Comparative Aspects of the Armenian and Jewish Cases of Genocide: A Sociohistorical Per-

spective," in *Is the Holocaust Unique?: Perspectives on Comparative Genocide*, ed. Alan S. Rosenbaum (Boulder, Colo., 1996), pp. 121–122.

58. Gust, *Völkermord an den Armeniern*, p. 228. See also Atkinson, "*The German, the Turk and the Devil,*" p. 40; and Bryce and Toynbee, *Treatment of Armenians in the Ottoman Empire*, pp. 330–331.

59. "Armenocide," 1915-07-27-DE-011, Der Konsul in Aleppo (Rössler) an die Botschaft Konstantinopel, www.armenocide.net (February 2005); Barton, *'Turkish Atrocities,'* pp. 33, 18; and Gust, *Völkermord an den Armeniern*, p. 353.

60. *New York Times*, May 10, 2000.

61. Davis, *Slaughterhouse Province*, pp. 80, 86; Barton, *'Turkish Atrocities,'* pp. 51, 60. Atkinson soon died of typhus.

62. "Armenocide," 1915-07-16-DE-012, Der Vizekonsul in Mossul (Holstein) an die Botschaft Konstantinopel, www.armenocide.net (February 2005); ibid., 1915-07-21-DE-012.

63. Gust, *Völkermord an den Armeniern*, pp. 279–280, 418–420; "Armenocide," 1915-11-20-DE-001, Der Geschäftsträger in Konstantinopel (Neurath) an den Reichskanzler (Bethmann Hollweg), www.armenocide.net (May 2005).

64. Morgenthau, *Ambassador Morgenthau's Story*, p. 205; *Armenian Genocide Documentation*, vol. 2, pp. 208, 243.

65. Morgenthau, *Ambassador Morgenthau's Story*, p. 233; Gust, *Der Völkermord an den Armeniern*, p. 171.

66. Morgenthau, *Ambassador Morgenthau's Story*, pp. 224–225.

67. Akçam, *Armenien und der Völkermord*, pp. 66–67; McCarthy, *Death and Exile*, p. 193.

68. Riggs, *Days of Tragedy in Armenia*, p. 96; Barton, *'Turkish Atrocities,'* p. 47; and Tooley, "World War I and the Emergence of Ethnic Cleansing in Europe," p. 91.

69. Peter Balakian, *Black Dog of Fate: An American Son Uncovers His Armenian Past* (New York, 1998), pp. 192–205.

70. Frank Bajohr, *"Aryanisation in Hamburg": The Economic Exclusion of Jews and the Confiscation of Their Property in Nazi Germany* (New York, 2002).

71. *Armenian Genocide Documentation*, vol. 2, pp. 182, 186, 195. For the ongoing debate, see Dadrian, *History of the Armenian Genocide*, pp. 248–294; and Vahakn N. Dadrian, *German Responsibility in the Armenian Genocide: A Review of the Historical Evidence of German Complicity* (Watertown, Mass., 1996). For discussion of the range of German responses, see Donald Bloxham, "A Reassessment of the German Role in the Armenian Genocide," in *Der Völkermord an den Armeniern und die Shoah*, ed. Kieser and Schaller. See also Ulrich Trumpener, *Germany and the Ottoman Empire, 1914–1918* (Princeton, N.J., 1968).

72. Gust, *Der Völkermord an den Armeniern*, pp. 143, 224. For Lepsius's deletions, see "Armenocide," www.armenocide.com.

73. Riggs, *Days of Tragedy in Armenia*, p. 157; Davis, *Slaughterhouse Province*, pp. 78–79; Hewsen, "Golden Plain," pp. 50–51.

CHAPTER 4: ETHNIC CLEANSING BETWEEN THE WORLD WARS

1. Balakian, *Burning Tigris*, pp. 342–344; Balakian, *Black Dog of Fate*, pp. 254–258.

2. See Philip Mansel, *Constantinople: City of the World's Desire, 1453–1924* (New York, 1995), pp. 380–414.

3. Glenny, *Balkans*, pp. 379–382; Harold Armstrong, *Turkey in Travail: The Birth of a New Nation* (London, 1925), p. 84: and Çağrı Erhan, *Greek Occupation of Izmir and Adjoining Territories: Report of the Inter-Allied Commission of Inquiry (May–September 1919)* (Ankara, 1999), pp. 58, 65. See *Greek Atrocities in the Vilayet of Smyrna (May to July, 1919): Inedited Documents and Evidence of English and French Officers* (Lausanne, 1919), pp. 42–44.

4. FO 406, vol. 41, pp. 211–212. For an account sympathetic to Greece, see Marjorie Housepian, *The Smyrna Affair* (New York, 1971).

5. Alexis Alexandris, *The Greek Minority of Istanbul and Greek-Turkish Relations 1918–1974* (Athens, 1983), p. 65.

6. *Greek Atrocities in the Vilayet of Smyrna*, p. 63; FO 406, vol. 42, p. 211; Erhan, *Greek Occupation of Izmir*, p. 62; FO 406, vol. 41, p. 175; and E. L. Woodward and Rohan Butler, *Documents on British Foreign Policy, 1919–1939*, 1st Series, vol. 4 (London, 1952), p. 655.

7. *Documents on British Foreign Policy, 1919–1939*, 1st Series, vol. 4, pp. 758–759.

8. Bristol to the Secretary of State, July 1, 1920, U.S. Department of State, Internal Affairs of Armenia, 1910–1929.

9. Erhan, *Greek Occupation of Izmir*, p. 65; Michael Llewellyn Smith, *Ionian Vision: Greece in Asia Minor, 1919–1922* (New York, 1973), p. 100.

10. Arnold J. Toynbee, *The Western Question in Greece and Turkey: A Study in the Contact of Civilizations* (New York, 1970), pp. 277, 283, 287–288, 291; FO 406, vol. 46, p. 64.

11. Armstrong, *Turkey in Travail*, p. 162.

12. Quoted in Smith, *Ionian Vision*, p. 203.

13. *Documents on British Foreign Policy, 1919–1939*, 1st Series, vol. 4, p. 873.

14. Alfred Rawlinson, *Adventures in the Near East, 1918–1922* (New York, 1924), p. 328; Lysimachos Oeconomos, *The Martyrdom of Smyrna and Eastern Christendom* (London, 1922), p. 26. For a searing account of deportation, see Thea Halo, *Not Even My Name* (New York, 2000).

15. *Documents on British Foreign Policy, 1919–1939*, 1st Series, vol. 17, p. 397. Foreign Greeks were deported; and affected native Greeks were sent to the interior.

16. Mabel Evelyn Elliott, *Beginning Again at Ararat* (New York, 1924), p. 150. See also Toynbee, *Western Question in Greece and Turkey*, p. 297; and *Documents on British Foreign Policy, 1919–1939*, 1st Series, vol. 17, p. 282.

17. Second Section of the General Staff of the Western Front, *Greek Atrocities in Asia Minor, First Part* (Constantinople, 1922); 2me bureau d'Etat-Major du front d'occident, *Atrocites greques en Asie-Mineure, 3me Partie* (Constantinople, 1922).

18. *Greek Atrocities in Asia Minor, First Part*, pp. 10, 13; *Atrocites greques en Asie-Mineure 3me Partie*, p. 31.

19. Armstrong, *Turkey in Travail*, p. 209; *Documents on British Foreign Policy, 1919–1939*, 1st Series, vol. 17, p. 422; Lausanne Conference on Near Eastern Affairs, 1922–1923, *Records of Proceedings and Draft Terms of Peace* (London, 1923), p. 547; and *Greek Atrocities in Asia Minor, First Part*, p. 3.

20. Oeconomos, *Martyrdom of Smyrna*, p. 56.

21. *Greek Atrocities in Asia Minor Part 4* (Constantinople, 1922), p. 15; Halidé Edib, *The Turkish Ordeal: Being the Further Memoirs of Halidé Edib* (New York, 1928), p. 375; and Lausanne Conference, *Records of Proceedings*, pp. 53, 551.

22. Lausanne Conference, *Records of Proceedings*, p. 552; Horton, *Blight of Asia*, p. 118; and Oeconomos, *Martyrdom of Smyrna*, p. 62.

23. Oeconomos, *Martyrdom of Smyrna*, p. 79.

24. Ibid., p. 64.

25. Ibid., p. 70; *New York Times*, September 17, 1922. For a detailed account, see Housepian, *Smyrna Affair*.

26. Oeconomos, *Martyrdom of Smyrna*, p. 67; *Greek Atrocities in Asia Minor, Part 4*, p. 21.

27. Ernest Hemingway, *By-Line: Selected Articles and Dispatches of Four Decades*, ed. William White (New York, 1967), p. 51; Oeconomos, *Martyrdom of Smyrna*, p. 195.

28. Oeconomos, *Martyrdom of Smyrna*, p. 169; Mazower, *Salonica, City of Ghosts*, p. 346.

29. Rear Admiral Mark Bristol, November 1, 1920, U.S. Department of State, Relations Between Armenia and Other States, 1910–1929.

30. *Documents on Ottoman Armenians*, vol. 3 (Ankara, 1986), pp. 135, 145; Publication du Congrès National, *Documents Relatifs aux Atrocités commises par les Arméniens sur la Population Musulmane* (Constantinople, 1919), p. 52; Twerdo Khlebof, *Notes of Superior Russian Officer on the Atrocities at Erzeroum* (1919), p. 11.

31. Firuz Kazemzadeh, *The Struggle for Transcaucasia, 1917–1921* (New York, 1951), p. 107. Note that Kazemzadeh is critical of Armenian attacks on Muslims during this period.

32. Quoted in McCarthy, *Death and Exile*, pp. 227–228; *The Armenian Genocide*, vol. 2, p. 456.

33. C. E. Bechhofer, *In Denikin's Russia and the Caucasus, 1919–1920* (London, 1921), p. 13.

34. *Documents on Ottoman Armenians*, vol. 3, p. 221. For an account of refugees, see James L. Barton, *The Story of Near East Relief (1915–1930)* (New York, 1930), pp. 121–122. See also Ronald Grigor Suny, *Looking Toward Ararat: Armenia in Modern History* (Bloomington, Ind., 1993), pp. 124–131. Richard G. Hovannisian's monumental history provides the most detailed account of these years. See his *The Republic of Armenia*, 4 vols. (Berkeley, 1971–1996).

35. Rawlinson, *Adventures in the Near East*, pp. 189, 204, 212.

36. Ibid., p. 218; *Documents on Ottoman Armenians*, vol. 3, p. 217.

37. *Documents on British Foreign Policy, 1919–1939*, 1st Series, vol. 3, p. 601. Richard Hovannisian argues that repeated exaggerated charges of Armenian assaults on Muslims gradually influenced Wardrop. See Hovannisian, *Republic of Armenia*, vol. 3, pp. 124–125, 127–128. See also Bechhofer, *In Denikin's Russia*, pp. 261, 275.

38. Bechhofer, *In Denikin's Russia*, pp. 276, 283. Bechhofer insisted that Armenians did not share equal blame.

39. Ronald Grigor Suny, *The Baku Commune: Class and Nationality in the Russian Revolution* (Princeton, N.J., 1972); Tadeusz Swietochowski, *Russian Azerbaijan: The Shaping of National Identity in a Muslim Community* (Cambridge, England, 1985), pp. 115–117; and U.S. Department of State, Internal Affairs of Armenia, 1910–1929, April 28, 1920.

40. Suny, *Baku Commune*, 337; Swietochowski, *Russian Azerbaijan*, p. 139; and U.S. Department of State, Internal Affairs of Armenia, 1910–1929, April 28, 1920.

41. Rhea to Admiral Mark Bristol, December 1, 1919; U.S. Department of State, Internal Affairs of Armenia, 1910–1929; Hovannisian, *Republic of Armenia*, vol. 1, p. 177; and Hovannisian, *Republic of Armenia*, vol. 3, p. 152.

42. Osip Mandelstam, *The Complete Poetry of Osip Emilevich Mandelstam*, trans. Burton Raffel and Alla Burago (Albany, N.Y., 1973), p. 201; Shahen Mkrtchian and Schors Davtian, *Shushi, The City of Tragic Fate* (Yerevan, 1999), p. 89.

43. To Director General N.E.R. Alexandropol, November 15, 1920, U.S. Department of State, Relations Between Armenia and Other States, 1910–1929. There is conflicting evidence on the treatment of Armenians under Turks. Near East Relief workers reported seeing few excesses against Armenians who stayed in Alexandropol, but a Soviet official later reported the number killed by Turks at sixty thousand. See Dadrian, *History of the Armenian Genocide*, p. 360.

44. See Peter Kenez, *Civil War in South Russia, 1919–1920: The Defeat of the Whites* (Berkeley, 1977).

45. Henry Abramson, *A Prayer for the Government: Ukrainians and Jews in Revolutionary Times, 1917–1920* (Cambridge, Mass., 1999), pp. 80, 100; Elias Heifetz, *The Slaughter of the Jews in the Ukraine* (New York, 1921), p. 46; and Committee of the Jewish Delegations, *The Pogroms in Ukraine Under the Ukrainian Governments, 1917–1920* (London, 1927), p. 206.

46. *Pogroms in Ukraine*, pp. 178–179; Abramson, *Prayer for the Government*, p. 129.

47. On the Directory's attitude and policy toward Jews, see Abramson, *Prayer for the Government*, pp. 71–72, 142–144; *Pogroms in Ukraine*, p. 170.

48. Heifetz, *Slaughter of the Jews in the Ukraine*, pp. 259, 262, 267, 308.

49. *Documents on British Foreign Policy, 1919–1939*, 1st Series, vol. 3, p. 785.

50. Quoted in Peter Kenez, "Pogroms and White Ideology in the Russian Civil War," in *Pogroms*, ed. Klier and Lambroza, p. 305; Heifetz, *Slaughter of the Jews in the Ukraine*, p. 111; *Pogroms in Ukraine*, p. 239; and Emma Goldman, *My Disillusionment in Russia*, Introduction by Rebecca West (Gloucester, Mass., 1983), pp. 136–137.

51. Abramson, *Prayer for the Government*, p. 154; Mick, "Ethnische Gewalt und Pogrome in Lemberg," pp. 5–6.

52. George Seferis, *A Poet's Journal: Days of 1945 1951*, trans. Athan Anagnostopoulos (Cambridge, Mass., 1974), pp. 164, 177–178, 187; Roderick Beaton, *George Seferis: Waiting for the Angel: A Biography* (New Haven, 2003), p. 288.

53. Mick, "Ethnische Gewalt und Pogrome in Lemberg."

54. For a useful discussion, see Mark Mazower, *Dark Continent: Europe's Twentieth Century* (New York, 1999), pp. 41–42.

55. Istavan Mócsy, *The Effects of World War I: The Uprooted: Hungarian Refugees and Their Impact on Hungary's Domestic Politics, 1918–1921* (New York, 1983), p. 12.

56. On the population exchange, see Stephen Ladas, *The Exchange of Minorities: Bulgaria, Greece, and Turkey* (New York, 1932); Hirschon, *Crossing the Aegean*; and *Documents on British Foreign Policy, 1919–1939*, 1st Series, vol. 17, p. 661.

57. Mazower, *Salonica, City of Ghosts*, pp. 345–351.

58. Renée Hirschon, *Heirs of the Greek Catastrophe: The Social Life of Asia Minor Refugees in Piraeus*, with a new Preface by the author and a Foreword by

Michael Herzfeld (New York, 1998), p. 37; Beaton, *George Seferis*, p. 287; and Seferis, *Poet's Journal*, pp. 133, 182.

59. C. A. Macartney, *National States and National Minorities* (London, 1934), p. 444; Bulgarian Red Cross, *The Refugee Question in Bulgaria* (Sofia, 1925), pp. 17–19.

60. See Horace Alexander, *The League of Nations and the Operation of Minority Treaties* (Nendeln, 1978); Christian Raitz von Frentz, *A Lesson Forgotten: Minority Protection Under the League of Nations: The Case of the German Minority in Poland, 1920–1934* (New York, 1999); and Roshwald, *Ethnic Nationalism and the Fall of Empires*, pp. 163–167.

61. Robert Conquest, *Stalin: Breaker of Nations* (New York, 1991); Terry Martin, "Origins of Soviet Ethnic Cleansing," *Journal of Modern History* 70 (1998), p. 825. For an argument on Soviet pressure to create nations into the 1930s, see Brown, *Biography of No Place*.

62. Shimon Redlich, *Together and Apart in Brzezany: Poles, Jews, and Ukrainians, 1919–1945* (Bloomington, Ind., 2002), pp. 39–41, 56–57; Timothy Snyder, *Reconstruction of Nations: Poland, Ukraine, Lithuania, Belarus, 1569–1999* (New Haven, 2003), pp. 149–151.

63. Glassheim, "National Mythologies and Ethnic Cleansing," pp. 467–469; Friedrich Prinz, ed., *Böhmen and Mähren* (Berlin, 1993); and Carol Skalnik Leff, *National Conflict in Czechoslovakia: The Making and Remaking of the State, 1918–1987* (Princeton, N.J., 1988).

64. On the early history of nationalism and nationalist tension in Yugoslavia, see Ivo Banac, *The National Question in Yugoslavia: Origins, History, Politics* (Ithica, 1984).

65. Vera Ranki, *The Politics of Inclusion and Exclusion: Jews and Nationalism in Hungary* (St. Leonards, New South Wales, 1999); William W. Hagen, "Before the 'Final Solution': Toward a Comparative Analysis of Political Anti-Semitism in Interwar Germany and Poland," *Journal of Modern History* 68 (1996), pp. 370–373; and Eva Hoffman, *Shtetl: The Life and Death of a Small Town and the World of Polish Jews* (Boston, 1997).

66. Mick, "Ethnische Gewalt und Pogrome in Lemberg"; Mihail Sebastian, *Journal, 1935–1944: The Fascist Years* (Chicago, 2000); Waldemar Lotnik with Julian Preece, *Nine Lives: Ethnic Conflict in the Polish-Ukrainian Borderlands* (London, 1999), p. 14; and Rivka Lozansky-Bogomolnaya, *Wartime Experiences in Lithuania*, ed. Susan Logan, trans. Miriam Beckerman (London, 2000), p. 15.

67. Götz Aly and Susanne Heim, *Architects of Annihilation: Auschwitz and the Logic of Destruction*, trans. A. G. Blunden (Princeton, N.J., 2002), p. 59; Ingo Haar and Michael Fahlbusch, ed., *German Scholars and Ethnic Cleansing, 1920–1945* (New York, 2005); Corneliu Zelea Codreanu, *Eiserne Garde* (Berlin, 1939), pp. 66, 111; and A. L. Easterman, *King Carol, Hitler and Lupescu* (London, 1942), p. 230.

68. Magnus Brechtken, *'Madagaskar für die Juden,' Antisemitische Idee und politische Praxis 1885–1945* (Munich, 1997), pp. 87, 103–104, 109–113, 141; Aly and Heim, *Architects of Annihilation*, pp. 50–51.

69. Quoted in Malcolm, *Kosovo*, p. 284.

70. Snyder, *Reconstruction of Nations*, pp. 143, 164–165; Tadeusz Piotrowski, ed., *Genocide and Rescue in Wołyń: Recollections of the Ukrainian Nationalist Ethnic Cleansing Campaign Against the Poles During World War II* (Jefferson, N.C., 2000), pp. 176–177.

71. Detlef Brandes, *Der Weg zur Vertreibung, 1938–1945: Pläne und Entschei-dungen zum 'Transfer' der Deutschen aus der Tschechoslowakie und aus Polen* (Munich, 2001), pp. 5–6; Eagle Glassheim, "National Mythologies and Ethnic Cleansing," p. 471.

72. Amir Weiner, *Making Sense of War: The Second World War and the Fate of the Bolshevik Revolution* (Princeton, N.J., 2001), pp. 138–139, 143, 146–147. Note that the Bolsheviks briefly considered a program of "De-Cossackization" in 1919 during the Civil War. See Peter Holquist, "To Count, to Extract, and to Exterminate," p. 129; ⟨illegible⟩ Ethnic Cleansing," pp. 848–849.

73. Benny Morris, *Righteous Victims: A History of the Zionist-Arab Conflict, 1881–2001* (New York, 2001), pp. 95–97, 101, 113–115, 120, 125–132, 144–151.

74. Quoted in Morris, *Righteous Victims*, pp. 138–139, 143. Note that Efraim Karsh, a critic of Morris, argues that the idea of transfer originated with the Peel commission. See Efraim Karsh, *Fabricating Israeli History: The New Historians*, 2nd rev. ed. (London, 2000), pp. 39–40.

CHAPTER 5: "THERE WAS NO ONE LEFT FOR ME"

1. Samuel Drix, *Witness to Annihilation: Surviving the Holocaust, A Memoir* (Washington, D.C., 1994), p. 1.

2. Götz Aly, *'Final Solution': Nazi Population Policy and the Murder of the European Jews*, trans. Belinda Cooper and Allison Brown (London, 1999), p. 19.

3. Quoted in Robert Lewis Koehl, *RKFDV German Resettlement and Population Policy 1939–1945: A History of the Reich Commission for the Strengthening of Germandom* (Cambridge, Mass., 1957), p. 51. See also Jürgen von Hehn, *Die Umsiedlungen der baltischen Deutschen: das letzte Kapitel baltischdeutscher Geschichte* (Marburg, 1982), p. 87. Hitler may also have initially seen resettlements as a way to reduce tension with Italy and the Soviet Union. See Valdis O. Lumans, *Himmler's Auxilliaries: The Volksdeutsche Mittelstelle and the German National Minorities of Europe, 1939–1945* (Chapel Hill, N.C., 1993), p. 153.

4. Michael Burleigh, *Germany Turns Eastwards: A Study of Ostforschung in the Third Reich* (Cambridge, England, 1988), pp. 168–171.

5. Johann Wolfgang Brügel, *Tschechen und Deutsche, 1939–1946* (Munich, 1974), pp. 104, 115 (Konstantin von Neurath took notes on Hitler's comments); Czeslaw Madajczyk, *Vom Generalplan Ost zum Generalsiedlungsplan* (Munich, 1994), p. 468.

6. Martin Seckendorf, *Die Okkupationspolitik des deutschen Faschismus in Jugoslawien, Griechenland, Albanien, Italien und Ungarn (1941–1945)* (Berlin, 1992), p. 224. See also Jozo Tomasevich, *War and Revolution in Yugoslavia, 1941–1945: Occupation and Collaboration* (Stanford, 2001), pp. 82–94.

7. Madajczyk, *Generalplan Ost*, p. 62.

8. Ibid., pp. 64, 69; Burleigh, *Germany Turns Eastwards*, p. 217.

9. Madajczyk, *Generalplan Ost*, pp. 134, 173, 265.

10. Matin Broszat, *Nationalsozialistische Polenpolitik (1939–1945)* (Frankurt am Main, 1965), p. 89.

11. Quoted in Christopher R. Browning, *Ordinary Men: Reserve Police Batallion 101 and the Final Solution in Poland* (New York, 1993), p. 39.

12. Polish Ministry of Information, *The German New Order in Poland* (London, 1942), pp. 179, 181, 185; and Czeslaw Madajczyk, *Die Okkupationspolitik Nazideutschlands in Polen, 1939–1945* (Berlin, 1987), p. 407.

13. Note that there were also economic reasons to seek work in Germany. On this complex topic, see Ulrich Herbert, *Fremdarbeiter: Politik und Praxis des "Ausländer–Einsatzes" in der Kriegswirtschaft des Dritten Reiches* (Bonn, 1999).

14. Madajczyk, *Okkupationspolitik*, p. 408. On the overall problem, see Aly, *'Final Solution.'*

15. Quoted in Aly and Heim, *Architects of Annihilation*, p. 102.

16. Madajczyk, *Generalplan Ost*, pp. 514–515. See Madajczyk, *Okkupationspolitik*, p. 422; and Aly and Heim, *Architects of Annihilation*, p. 277.

17. Broszat, *Nationalsozialistische Polenpolitik*, pp. 97–98; Madajczyk, *Okkupationspolitik*, pp. 419–420.

18. Karel C. Berkhoff, *Harvest of Despair: Life and Death in Ukraine Under Nazi Rule* (Cambridge, Mass., 2004), pp. 259–274; Alexander Dallin, *German Rule in Russia, 1941–1945: A Study of Occupation Policies* (New York, 1957); and Wendy Lower, "'Anticipatory Obedience' and the Nazi Implementation of the Holocaust in the Ukraine: A Case Study of Central and Peripheral Forces in the Generalbezirk Zhytomyr, 1941–1944," *Holocaust and Genocide Studies* 16 (2002), pp. 1–22.

19. Quoted in Aly *'Final Solution,'* pp. 116, 67. On expulsions, see also Christopher R. Browning, with contributions by Jürgen Matthäus, *The Origins of the Final Solution: The Evolution of Nazi-Jewish Policy, September 1939–March 1942* (Lincoln, Nebr., 2004), pp. 36–110.

20. See Aly, *'Final Solution.'*

21. Raul Hilberg, *The Destruction of the European Jews*, student ed. (New York, 1985), pp. 95–96.

22. Lumans, *Himmler's Auxilliaries*, pp. 155–156; Aly, *Final Solution*, pp. 25, 93, 110; and Koehl, *RKFDV*, p. 45.

23. R. G. Waldeck, *Athene Palace* (New York, 1942), p. 100.

24. Schieder, *Schicksal der Deutschen in Rumänien*, pp. 7, 24–25; Dirk Jachomowski, *Die Umsiedlung der Bessarabien-, Bukowina- und Dobrudschadeutschen: Von der Volksgruppe in Rumänien zur 'Siedlungsbrücke' an der Reichsgrenze* (Munich, 1984), p. 80.

25. Aly and Heim, *Architects of Annihilation*, p. 90.

26. Jachomowski, *Umsiedlung*, p. 147.

27. Aly and Heim, *Architects of Annihilation*, p. 90.

28. Schieder, *Schicksal der Deutschen in Rumänien*, p. 25.

29. Note that the Nazi leadership still saw Germany as victimized by Jews. See Omer Bartov, "Defining Enemies, Making Victims: Germans, Jews, and the Holocaust," *American Historical Review* 103 (1998), pp. 782–786.

30. Aly, *'Final Solution,'* p. 63. There is a massive literature on persecution of German Jews. For some examples, see Saul Friedländer, *Nazi Germany and the Jews* (New York, 1997); and Marion A. Kaplan, *Between Dignity and Despair: Jewish Life in Nazi Germany* (New York, 1998).

31. Leigh White, *The Long Balkan Night* (New York, 1944), p. 41.

32. See Aly, *'Final Solution.'* There is an immense literature on the causes of the Holocaust. For another major position, see Christian Gerlach, "The Wannsee

Conference, the Fate of the German Jews, and Hitler's Decision in Principle to Exterminate All European Jews," *Journal of Modern History* 70 (1998), pp. 759–812.

33. Thomas Sandkühler, *"Endlosung" in Galizien: Der Judenmord in Ostpolen und die Rettungsinitiativen von Berthold Beitz, 1941–1944* (Bonn, 1996), pp. 114–116; Thomas Sandkühler, "Anti-Jewish Policy and the Murder of the Jews in the District of Galicia, 1941/42," in *National Socialist Extermination Policies: Contemporary German Perspectives and Controversies*, ed. Ulrich Herbert (New York, 2000), p. 108. For an argument that stresses German responsibility and direction of pogroms, see Dieter Pohl, *Nationalsozialistische Judenverfolgung in Ostgalizien 1941–1944: Organisation und Durchführung eines staatlichen Massenverbrechens* (Munich, 1996), pp. 55–59.

34. For an example, see Richard C. Lukas, *The Forgotten Holocaust: The Poles Under German Occupation, 1939–1944* (Lexington, Ky., 1986).

35. Stefan Szende, *The Promise Hitler Kept* (New York, 1945), pp. 12–16; Thomas Held, "Vom Pogrom zum Massenmord: Die Vernichtung der jüdischen Bevölkerung Lembergs im Zweiten Weltkrieg," in *Lemberg, Lwów, Liviv: Eine Stadt im Schnittpunkt europäischer Kulturen*, ed. Peter Fässler, Thomas Held, and Dirk Sawitzki (Cologne, 1993), p. 118.

36. Harry Gordon, *The Shadow of Death: The Holocaust in Lithuania* (Lexington, Ky., 1992), p. 9. See also Sima Ycikas, "Lithuanian-Jewish Relations in the Shadow of the Holocaust," in *Bitter Legacy: Confronting the Holocaust in the USSR*, ed. Zvi Gitelman (Bloomington, Ind., 1997), pp. 185–213. See also Alfonsas Eidintas, *Jews, Lithuanians, and the Holocaust* (Vilnius, 2003).

37. See Roger Dale Petersen, *Understanding Ethnic Violence: Fear, Hatred, and Resentment in Twentieth-Century Eastern Europe* (Cambridge, England, 2002); Bogdan Musial, *"Konterrevolutionäre Elemente sind zu erschiessen": die Brutalisierung des deutsch-sowjetischen Krieges im Sommer 1941* (Berlin, 2000); Eidintas, *Jews, Lithuanians, and the Holocaust*; Alexander B. Rossino, "Polish 'Neighbours' and German Invaders: Anti-Jewish Violence in the Bialystok District During the Opening Weeks of Operation Barbarossa," *Polin: Studies in Polish Jewry*, 16 (2003); and Ben-Cion Pinchuk, *Shtetl Jews Under Soviet Rule: Eastern Poland on the Eve of the Holocaust* (Oxford, 1990).

38. Szende, *Promise Hitler Kept*, p. 17. See also Thomas Held, "Vom Pogrom zum Massenmord," pp. 118–119; and Jacob Gerstenfeld-Maltiel, *My Private War: One Man's Struggle to Survive the Soviets and the Nazis* (London, 1993), p. 29.

39. Musial describes NKVD killings, but Musial's key chapter on those killings concentrates less attention on the actual identity of perpetrators. See Musial, *"Konterrevolutionäre Elemente sind zu erschiessen,"* pp. 106–139, 270–283.

40. Drix, *Witness to Annihilation*, p. 26.

41. David Kahane, *Lvov Ghetto Diary*, trans. Jerzy Michalowicz (Amherst, Mass., 1990), p. 6; Szende, *Promise Hitler Kept*, p. 48; Gerstenfeld-Maltiel, *My Private War*, p. 54; Sandkühler, *"Endlosung" in Galizien*, pp. 117, 120–121; Held, "Vom Pogrom zum Massenmord," p. 124; Drix, *Witness to Annihilation*, pp. 22, 27; and Musial, *"Konterrevolutionäre Elemente sind zu erschiessen,"* pp. 175–191.

42. Shimon Redlich, "Metroplitan Sheptyts'kyi and Ukrainian-Jewish Relations," in *Bitter Legacy*, ed. Gitelman, p. 68; Held, "Vom Pogrom zum Massenmord," p. 125; and Kahane, *Lvov Ghetto Diary*, p. 13.

43. Martin Dean, *Collaboration in the Holocaust: Crimes of the Local Police in Belorussia and Ukraine* (New York, 2000), p. 20; Shmuel Spector, *The Holocaust of*

Volhynian Jews, 1941–1944 (Jerusalem, 1990), p. 64; and quoted in Spector, *Holocaust of Volhynian Jews*, p. 65.

44. Quoted in Sandkühler, *"Endlosung" in Galizien*, p. 121; Sandkühler, "Anti-Jewish Policy," p. 109; Ralf Ogorreck, *Die Einsatzgruppen und die "Genesis der Endlösung"* (Berlin, 1996); and Weiner, *Making Sense of War*, pp. 276–277.

45. Solly Ganor, *Light One Candle: A Survivor's Tale from Lithuania to Jerusalem* (New York, 1995), p. 57; Avraham Tory, *Surviving the Holocaust: The Kovno Ghetto Diary*, ed. with an Introduction by Martin Gilbert, Notes by Dina Porat, trans. Jerzy Michalowicz (Cambridge, Mass., 1990), p. 6.

46. Gordon, *Shadow of Death*, p. 30; William W. Mishell, *Kaddish for Kovno: Life and Death in a Lithuanian Ghetto, 1941–1945* (Chicago, 1988), p. 27; Tory, *Surviving the Holocaust*, p. 8; Ernst Klee, Willi Dressen, and Volker Riess, *"Schöne Zeiten": Judenmord aus der Sicht der Täter und Gaffer* (Frankfurt am Main, 1988), pp. 33–43; and Daniel Jonah Goldhagen, *Hitler's Willing Executioners: Ordinary Germans and the Holocaust* (New York, 1997), p. 191.

47. Herman Kruk, *The Last Days of the Jerusalem of Lithuania: Chronicles from the Vilna Ghetto and the Camps, 1939–1944*, ed. and Introduced by Benjamin Harshav, trans. Babara Harshav (New Haven, 2002), pp. 52, 62, 91; Klee, *"Schöne Zeiten,"* p. 48; and Petersen, *Understanding Ethnic Violence*, pp. 100–101.

48. Lozansky-Bogomolnaya, *Wartime Experiences in Lithuania*, pp. 15, 25, 45, 55, 68.

49. Jan T. Gross, *Neighbors: The Destruction of the Jewish Community in Jedwabne, Poland* (Princeton, N.J., 2001), pp. 79–80. For debate over Gross's book, see *Slavic Review* 61 (2002), pp. 453–489; Dariusz Stola, "Jedwabne: Revisiting the Evidence and Nature of the Crime," *Holocaust and Genocide Studies* 17 (2003), pp. 139–152; and Antony Polonsky and Joanna B. Michlic, ed., *The Neighbors Respond: The Controversy Over the Jedwabne Massacre in Poland* (Princeton, N.J., 2004).

50. Boris Kacel, *From Hell to Redemption: A Memoir of the Holocaust* (Niwot, Colo., 1998), pp. 7–8; Bernhard Press, *The Murder of the Jews in Latvia, 1941–1945*, trans. Laimdota Mazzarins (Evanston, Ill., 2000), p. 45. See also Hans-Heinrich Wilhelm, " 'Inventing' the Holocaust for Latvia: New Research," in *Bitter Legacy*, ed. Gitelman, pp. 104, 117–120.

51. For a start, see Hilberg, *Destruction of the European Jews*.

52. Mazower, *Salonica, City of Ghosts*, pp. 428–433; and Primo Levi, *Survival in Auschwitz*, trans. Stuart Woolf (New York, 1961), pp. 24, 64–65, 72.

53. Tomasevich, *War and Revolution in Yugoslavia*, pp. 47–64.

54. Seckendorf, *Okkupationspolitik des deutschen Faschismus in Jugoslawien*, pp. 168, 173, 176–179; see also Walter Manoschek, "Serbia: The War Against the Partisans, 1941," in *The German Army and Genocide: Crimes Against War Prisoners, Jews and Other Civilians, 1939–1944*, ed. Hamburg Institute for Social Research, trans. Scott Abbott (New York, 1999), pp. 34–75; and Walter Manoschek, *"Serbien is Judenfrei": militärische Besatzungspolitik und Judenvernichtung in Serbien 1941/42* (Munich, 1993).

55. Ladislaus Hory and Martin Broszat, *Der Kroatische Ustascha-Staat, 1941–1945* (Stuttgart, 1964), p. 77; *This Is Artukovic*, p. 34. Judah, *Serbs*, p. 126; and quoted in Marcus Tanner, *Croatia: A Nation Forged in War* (New Haven, 1997), p. 151. See also Tomasevich, *War and Revolution*, pp. 387–392.

56. Tanner, *Croatia*, p. 144; Edmund Paris, *Genocide in Satellite Croatia, 1941–1945: A Record of Racial and Religious Persecution and Massacres*, trans. Lois Perkins (Chicago, 1961), pp. 61–62.

57. Judah, *Serbs*, p. 125. See also Tomasevich, *War and Revolution*, pp. 397–409; and Hory and Broszat, *Der Kroatische Ustascha-Staat*, p. 101.

58. Hory and Broszat, *Der Kroatische Ustascha-Staat*, pp. 102, 126.

59. The number killed has been the subject of intense debate. See Seckendorf, *Okkupationspolitik des deutschen Faschismus*, pp. 45–46; Tanner, *Croatia*, p. 152; and Philip J. Cohen, *Serbia's Secret War: Propaganda and the Deceit of History* (College Station, Tex.,1996), pp. 106–107.

60. Noel Malcom, *Bosnia: A Short History*, new, updated ed. (New York, 1996), p. 188; *The Trial of Draglojub-Draža Mihailović: Stenographic Records and Documents from the Trial* of *Draglojub-Draža Mihailović* (Belgrade, 1946), p. 361.

61. *Trial of Draglojub-Draža Mihailović*, pp. 358–359. For an indictment of Chetnik violence against non-Serbs, see Cohen, *Serbia's Secret War*.

62. Malcom, *Bosnia*, p. 188.

63. Quoted in Malcom, *Kosovo*, p. 294.

64. White, *Long Balkan Night*, p. 95.

65. C. L. Sulzberger, *A Long Row of Candles: Memoirs and Diaries, 1934–1954* (New York, 1969), p. 109.

66. Mark Mazower, *Inside Hitler's Greece: The Experience of Occupation, 1941–1944* (New Haven, 1993), p. 20; Glenny, *Balkans*, p. 481; and Eugene M. Kulischer, *Europe on the Move: War and Population Changes, 1917–47* (New York, 1948), pp. 258–259.

67. White, *Long Balkan Night*, p. 107.

68. Kulischer, *Europe on the Move*, p. 259; Robert Parker, *Headquarters Budapest* (New York, 1944), p. 240; and Derek Patmore, *Balkan Correspondent* (New York, 1941), p. 152.

69. Sebastian, *Journal*, p. 293; White, *Long Balkan Night*, p. 119.

70. Ioanid, *Holocaust in Romania*, pp. 41–42.

71. Sebastian, *Journal*, p. 377.

72. Dinu C. Giurescu, "Romania During the Second World War, September 1, 1939–August 23, 1944," in *Romania: A Historic Perspective*, ed. Dinu C. Giurescu and Stephen Fischer-Galați (Boulder, Colo., 1998), p. 356; Ioanid, *Holocaust in Romania*, pp. 43–50.

73. Sebastian, *Journal*, p. 313; White, *Long Balkan Night*, p. 148. See also Clare Hollingworth, *There's a German Just Behind Me* (London, 1942), p. 185.

74. Sebastian, *Journal*, pp. 391, 405, 431–432, 447, 479; Matatias Carp, *Holocaust in Romania: Facts and Documents on the Annihilation of Romania's Jews 1940–1944*, ed. Andrew L. Simon, trans. Sean Murphy (Safety Harbor, Fla., 2000), pp. 43–44; and Giurescu, "Romania During the Second World War," p. 360.

75. Sebastian, *Journal*, pp. 369, 375.

76. Quoted in Radu Ioanid, "The Holocaust in Romania: The Iasi Pogrom of June 1941," *Contemporary European History* 2 (1993), pp. 127–128, 142–143; Carp, *Holocaust in Romania*, p. 139; Ioanid, *Holocaust in Romania*, pp. 67, 80–86; and Jean Ancel, "The Jassy Pogrom—June 29, 1941," in *Rümanien und der Holocaust: Zu den Massenverbrechen in Transnistrien, 1941–1944*, ed. Mariana Hausleitner, Brigitte Mihok, and Julianne Wetzel (Berlin, 2001), pp. 62–64.

77. Carp, *Holocaust in Romania*, pp. 127, 21–24; Ioanid, *Holocaust in Romania*, pp. 94, 97, 101, 104–106.

78. Ancel, "The Jassy Pogrom," p. 54; quoted in Ioanid, *Holocaust in Romania*, p. 92; Armin Heinen notes a killing order of June 1941 from Bucharest to gendarmes. See Armin Heinen, "Gewalt-Kultur: Rümanien, der Krieg und die Juden (Juni bis Oktober 1941) in *Rümanien und der Holocaust*, ed. Hausleitner, Mihok, and Wetzel, p. 42.

79. On conflicting German and Romanian policies, see Andrej Angrick, "Rümanien, die SS, and die Vernichtung der Juden," in *Rümanien und der Holocaust*, ed. Hausleitner, Mihok, and Wetzel, p. 128; and Ioanid, *Holocaust in Romania*, pp. 122, 128–129.

80. Avigdor Shachan, *Burning Ice: The Ghettos of Transnistria*, trans. Shmuel Himelstein (Boulder, Colo., 1996), p. 102.

81. Quoted in Shachan, *Burning Ice*, pp. 130–133.

82. Shachan, *Burning Ice*, p. 199; Felicia Carmelly, *Shattered! Fifty Years of Silence: History and Voices of the Tragedy in Romania and Transnistria* (Scarborough, Ontario, 1997), p. 295; and Ioanid, *Holocaust in Romania*, p. 26.

83. Shachan, *Burning Ice*, pp. 74, 79; Carmelly, *Shattered*, p. 295. See also Mirjam Korber, *Deportiert: jüdische Überlebensschicksale aus Rümanien 1941–1944. Ein Tagebuch*, trans. Andrei Hoisie, ed. Erhard Roy Wiehn, with "Familiengeschichte" by Sylvia Hoisie-Korber and "Bericht über das Massaker in Jassy 1941," by Henry L. Eaton (Konstanz, 1993), pp. 53–54.

84. Korber, *Deportiert*, pp. 100, 103; Ioanid, *Holocaust in Romania*, pp. 148, 289; and Carp, *Holocaust in Romania*, p. 18.

85. Emil Dorian, *The Quality of Witness: A Romanian Diary, 1937–1944*, ed. Marguerite Dorian, trans. Mara Soceanu Vamos, with an Introduction by Michael Stanislawski (Philadelphia, 1982), pp. 173, 182, 228, 237; Sebastian, *Journal*, p. 509. Other possible factors included protest by prominent Romanians. See Mariana Hausleitner, "Grossverbrechen in rümanischen Transnistrien," in *Rümanien und der Holocaust*, ed. Hausleitner, Mihok, and Wetzel, p. 19.

86. For another discussion of this comparison, see Mark Levene, "The Experience of Genocide: Armenia 1915–16 and Romania 1941–42," in *Der Völkermord an den Armeniern und die Shoa*, ed. Kieser and Schaller, pp. 423–462.

87. Estimates range to up to a million and more. See Jan T. Gross, *Revolution from Abroad: The Soviet Conquest of Poland's Western Ukraine and Western Belorussia* (Princeton, N.J., 1998), p. 194; Keith Sword, *Deportation and Exile: Poles in the Soviet Union, 1939–1948* (New York, 1994), p. 25; and Wlodzimierz Borodziej and Hans Lemberg, *"Unsere Heimat is uns ein fremdes Land geworden . . .": Die Deutschen östlich von Oder und Neisse, 1945–1950: Dokumente aus polnischen Archiven*, vol. 1 (Marburg, 2000), p. 39. See also N. S. Lebedeva, "The Deportation of the Polish Population to the USSR, 1939–41," *Journal of Communist Studies & Transition Politics*, 16 (2000), pp. 28–45.

88. Christina Soltan, *Under Strange Skies* (London, 1948), pp. 125, 179, 186. Soltan later left Japan by way of Mozambique.

89. Gerhard Simon, *Nationalism and Policy Toward the Nationalities in the Soviet Union: From Totalitarian Dictatorship to Post-Stalinist Society*, trans. Karen Forster and Oswald Forster (Boulder, Colo., 1991), p. 200; Nikolaĭ Fedorovich Bugaĭ, *The Deportation of Peoples in the Soviet Union* (New York, 1996), pp. 181–186; Eric J.

Schmaltz and Samuel D. Sinner, "'You Will Die Under Ruins and Snow': The Soviet Repression of Russian Germans as a Case Study of Successful Genocide," *Journal of Genocide Research* 4 (2002), p. 332; and J. Otto Pohl. "Stalin's Genocide Against the 'Repressed Peoples,'" *Journal of Genocide Research* 2 (2000), pp. 279–281.

90. Aleksandr M. Nekrich, *The Punished Peoples: The Deportation and Fate of Soviet Minorities at the End of the Second World War*, trans. George Saunders (New York, 1978), pp. 20–21, 72–76, 84.

91. Walter Comins-Richmond, "The Deportation of the Karachays," *Journal of Genocide Research* 4 (2002), pp. 431–439; Nekrich, *Punished Peoples*, p. 85; and Curtis Richardson, "Stalinist Terror and the Kalmyks' National Revival: A Cultural and Historical Perspective," *Journal of Genocide Research* 4 (2002), p. 445.

92. Quoted in Bugaĭ, *Deportation of Peoples in the Soviet Union*, pp. 104, 81, 105–106; N. F. Bugai and A. M. Gonov, "The Forced Evacuation of the Chechens and Ingush," *Russian Studies in History* 41 (2002), pp. 43–61; and Brian Glyn Williams, "Commemorating 'The Deportation' in Post-Soviet Chechnya: The Role of Memorialization and Collective Memory in the 1994–1996 and 1999–2000 Russo-Chechen Wars," *History and Memory* 12 (2000), p. 108.

93. Quoted in Nekrich, *Punished Peoples*, p. 86; quoted in Bugaĭ, *Deportation of Peoples*, p. 106.

94. Brian Glyn Williams, "Hidden Ethnocide in the Soviet Muslim Borderlands: The Ethnic Cleansing of the Crimean Tatars," *Journal of Genocide Research* 4 (2002), pp. 357–373. Quoted in Nekrich, *Punished Peoples*, pp. 110–111.

95. Bugaĭ, *Deportation of Peoples*, p. 98. On the Karachai, see Walter Comins-Richmond, "The Karachay Struggle After the Deportation," *Journal of Muslim Minority Affairs*, 22 (2002), pp. 63–79.

96. Snyder, *Reconstruction of Nations*, pp. 159–168. Snyder suggests that work in the Holocaust accustomed a contingent of Ukrainian police to mass murder and notes that Ukrainian police joined the UPA in 1943.

97. Nahum Kohn and Howard Roiter, *A Voice from the Forest: Memoirs of a Jewish Partisan* (New York, 1980), pp. 94, 121; Drix, *Witness to Annihilation*, p. 201.

98. Lotnik, *Nine Lives*, pp. 63, 65, 70.

99. Snyder, *Reconstruction of Nations*, p. 170; Timothy Snyder, "'To Resolve the Ukrainian Problem Once and for All': The Ethnic Cleansing of Ukrainians in Poland, 1943–1947," *Journal of Cold War Studies* 1 (1999), pp. 86–120. For other estimates of numbers of Poles killed, see Piotrowski, ed., *Genocide and Rescue in Wołyń*, p. 21.

100. Quoted in Piotrowski, *Genocide and Rescue in Wołyń*, pp. 64, 4, 13. Note that most of this work is organized by Ukrainian rescuers of Poles. See also Snyder, *Reconstruction of Nations*, pp. 170–171. Quoted in Dean, *Collaboration in the Holocaust*, p. 145.

101. Leo Cooper, *In the Shadow of the Polish Eagle: The Poles, the Holocaust, and Beyond* (New York, 2000), p. 105.

102. Quoted in Sebastian Siebel-Achenbach, *Lower Silesia from Nazi Germany to Communist Poland, 1942–1949* (New York, 1994), pp. 33, 50; Brandes, *Der Weg zur Vertreibung*, pp. 215–216. The Polish Workers' party (PPR) was originally less nationalist, but moved toward a more radical nationalist position by 1944. See

T. David Curp, "The Politics of Ethnic Cleansing: The P.P.R., the P.Z.Z. and Wielkopolska's Nationalist Revolution, 1944–1946," *Nationalities Papers* 29 (2001), pp. 577–579.

103. Quoted in Sulzberger, *Long Row of Candles*, pp. 203–204; Václav Kural, "Tschechen, Deutsche und die sudetendeutsche Frage während des Zweiten Weltkrieges," in *Erzwungene Trennung: Vertreibungen und Aussiedlungen in und aus der Tschechoslowakei, 1938–1947: im Vergleich mit Polen, Ungarn und Jugoslawien,* ed. Detlef Brandes, Edita Invaničková and Jiří Pešek (Essen, 1999), pp. 85–87; Brandes, *Der Weg zur Vertreibung,* pp. 147, 184; and Emilia Hrabovec, *Vertreibung and Abschub: Deutsche in Mähren 1945–1947* (Frankfurt am Main, 1995), pp. 41, 43.

104. Drix, *Witness to Annihilation,* pp. 223–225, 234; Gerstenfeld-Maltiel, *My Private War,* p. 262. See also Philipp Ther, "Chancen und Untergang einer multinationalen Stadt: Die Beziehungen zwischen den Nationalitäten in Lemberg in der ersten Hälfte des 20. Jahrhunderts," in *Nationalitätenkonflikte im 20.Jahrhundert: Ursachen von inter-ethnischer Gewalt im Vergleich,* ed. Phillip Ther and Holm Sundhaussen (Wiesbaden, 2001), pp. 137–140.

105. Adam Zagajewski, *Two Cities: On Exile, History, and the Imagination,* trans. Lillian Vallee (Athens, Ga., 2002), p. 4.

106. See, Browning, *Ordinary Men;* and Goldhagen, *Hitler's Willing Executioners,* p. 379.

CHAPTER 6: "THE LAND OF THE POLES THAT IS LOST TO THE GERMANS"

1. Günter Grass, *The Danzig Trilogy,* trans. Ralph Manheim (New York, 1987), p. 80.

2. The literature on these expellees is vast. In the years after World War II, the Ministry for the Expelled and Refugees in the Federal Republic of Germany collected numerous testimonies and included some in a multivolume series. For background on this project see Robert G. Moeller, "War Stories: The Search for a Usable Past in the Federal Republic of Germany," *American Historical Review* 101 (1996), pp. 1023–1024; and Robert G. Moeller, *War Stories: The Search for a Usable Past in the Federal Republic of Germany* (Berkeley, 1999). There is also a very dense specialized literature on the subject in German. More recently, collaborative studies involving German, Czech, Slovak, and Polish historians have provided still more information. Figures on German deaths vary widely. Estimates of more than two million German deaths have been common. See, for example, Gerhard Ziemer, *Deutscher Exodus: Vertreibung und Eingliederung von 15 Millionen Ostdeutschen* (Stuttgart, 1973), pp. 94–96. On the other hand, recent research has estimated German deaths in expulsion from Czechoslovakia at thirty thousand to forty thousand. See Rüdiger Overmans, "'Amtlich und wissenschaftlich erarbeitet'—Zur Diskussion über die Verlüste während Flucht und Vertreibung der Deutsche aus der ČSR," in *Erzwungene Trennung,* ed. Brandes, pp. 149, 176–177.

3. Churchill's evocative accounts of conversations between himself and Stalin suggested that new boundaries—with the exception of the western Neisse River—resulted from informal negotiations, but more often than not, new boundaries reflected military reality on the ground.

4. Theodor Schieder, ed., *Die Vertreibung der deutschen Bevölkerung aus den Gebieten östlich der Oder-Neisse*, vol. I/1 (Berlin, 1953), p. 147. Georg Weber, Renate Weber-Schlenther, Armin Nassehi, Oliver Sill, and Georg Kneer, ed., *Die Deportation von Siebenbürger Sachsen in die Sowjetunion 1945–1949*, vol. 3 (Cologne, 1995), pp. 652, 655.

5. Omer Bartov, *Hitler's Army: Soldiers, Nazis, and War in the Third Reich* (New York, 1992).

6. Schieder, *Schicksal der Deutschen in Rumänien*, pp. 4E, 74–75E.

7. Theodor Schieder, ed., *Das Schicksal der Deutschen in Jugoslawien* (Munich, 1984), pp. 101–103, 121–122, 134–135.

8. Schieder, *Vertreibung . . . östlich der Oder-Neisse*, vol. I/1, p. 3; Borodziej and Lemberg, *"Unsere Heimat is uns ein fremdes Land geworden . . . ,"* vol. 1, p. 445.

9. Schieder, *Vertreibung . . . östlich der Oder-Neisse*, vol. I/1, pp. 83, 91, 102.

10. Ibid., pp. 81, 126.

11. Eberhard Beckherrn and Alexej Dubatow, *Die Königsberg Papiere: Schicksal einer deutschen Stadt: Neue dokumente aus russischen Archiven* (Munich, 1994), p. 40; Schieder, *Vertreibung . . . östlich der Oder-Neisse*, vol. I/1, pp. 45E–49E.

12. Schieder, *Vertreibung . . . östlich der Oder-Neisse*, vol. I/1, pp. 151–153.

13. Paul Peikert, *"Festung Breslau" in den Berichten eines Pfarrers, 22. January bis 6. Mai 1945*, ed. Karol Jonca and Alfred Konieczny, 3rd ed. (Berlin, 1970), pp. 25, 30; Siebel-Achenbach, *Lower Silesia*, p. 72. Johannes Kaps, *Die Tragödie Schlesiens in Dokumenten unter besonderer Berücksichtigung des Erzbistums Breslau* (Munich, 1952/3), p. 421.

14. Manfred Zeidler, *Kriegsende im Osten: die Rote Armee und die Besetzung Deutschlands östlich von Oder und Neisse, 1944–45* (Munich, 1996), pp. 115–121, 138, 140. See also Norman M. Naimark, *The Russians in Germany: A History of the Soviet Zone of Occupation, 1945–1949* (Cambridge, Mass., 1995), p. 72.

15. Lisa Barendt, *Danziger Jahre: Aus dem Leben einer jungen Frau bis 1945/46* (Oldenburg, 1994), pp. 172–174, 178–179. Barendt also met nuns who had been assaulted. Schieder, *Vertreibung . . . östlich der Oder-Neisse*, vol. I/2, p. 241. On rape in East Prussia, Silesia, and in the Soviet zone of occupation in Germany, see Naimark, *Russians in Germany*, pp. 69–140.

16. Barendt, *Danziger Jahre*, p. 175.

17. Egon Buddatsch, *Abschied von Danzig: Meine Vertreibung und Flucht 1945–1946*, ed. Jürgen Kleindienst (Berlin, 2004), p. 45; Schieder, *Vertreibung . . . östlich der Oder-Neisse*, vol. I/2, p. 327; and Zeidler, *Kriegsende im Osten*, p. 154.

18. Weber, *Deportation von Siebenbürger Sachsen*, pp. 449, 451. On overall numbers, see Siebel-Achenbach, *Lower Silesia*, p. 65.

19. Robert Bishop and E. S. Crayfield, *Russia Astride the Balkans* (New York, 1948), pp. 128–133.

20. Schieder, *Vertreibung . . . östlich der Oder-Neisse*, vol. I/2, p. 93.

21. Weber, *Deportation von Siebenbürger Sachsen*, pp. 403, 405–406.

22. Schieder, *Schicksal der Deutschen in Jugoslawien*, pp. 198–201, 213, 225, 262, 264; John R. Schindler, "Yugoslavia's First Ethnic Cleansing: The Expulsion of the Danubian Germans, 1944–1946," in *Ethnic Cleansing in Twentieth-Century Europe*, ed. Várdy and Tooley, p. 367; and Željko Šević, "The Unfortunate Minority Group: Yugoslavia's Banat Germans," in *German Minorities in Europe: Ethnic Identity and Cultural Belonging*, ed. Stefan Wolff (New York, 2000), pp. 154–155. Schieder, *Schicksal der Deutschen in Jugoslawien*, p. 264.

23. Dušan Kovac, "Die Evakuierung und Vertreibung der Deutschen aus der Slowakei," in *Nationale Frage und Vertreibung in der Tschechoslowakei und Ungarn 1938–1948*, ed. Richard G. Plaschka, Horst Haselsteiner, Arnold Suppan, and Anna M. Drabek (Vienna, 1997), p. 114; Tomáš Staněk, *Verfolgung 1945: Die Stellung der Deutschen in Böhmen, Mähren und Schlesien (ausserhalb der Lager und Gefängnisse)*, trans. Otfrid Pustejovsky, ed. and partial translation by Walter Reichel (Vienna, 2002), pp. 155–157.

24. On Landskron, see Staněk, *Verfolgung 1945*, pp. 110–114; and Theodor Schieder, ed., *Die Vertreibung der deutschen Bevölkerung aus der Tschechoslowakei* (Berlin, 1957), p. 257. On Komotau, see Staněk, *Verfolgung 1945*, pp. 141–142; and Schieder, *Vertreibung ... aus der Tschechoslowakei*, pp. 293, 412. Czech sources gave a slightly lower death toll.

25. Grass, *Danzig Trilogy*, pp. 311–312; Schieder, *Vertreibung . . . östlich der Oder-Neisse*, vol. I/2, p. 653.

26. Schieder, *Vertreibung ... östlich der Oder-Neisse*, vol. I/2, pp. 167, 554.

27. Ibid., p. 377; Kaps, *Tragödie Schlesiens*, pp. 195, 212.

28. Kaps, *Tragödie Schlesiens*, pp. 340–341. The camp was part of the Gross Rosen concentration camp.

29. Schieder, *Vertreibung ... aus der Tschechoslowakei*, p. 305.

30. Eagle Glassheim, "National Mythologies and Ethnic Cleansing," pp. 467–475; Hrabovec, *Vertreibung und Abschub*, p. 69; and Joseph B. Schechtman, *Postwar Population Transfers in Europe, 1945–1955* (Philadelphia, 1962), p. 66.

31. Quoted in Bernard Linek, "'De-Germanization' and 'Re-Polonization' in Upper Silesia, 1945–1950," in *Redrawing Nations*, ed. Ther and Siljak, p. 126; Borodziej and Lemberg, *"Unsere Heimat is uns ein fremdes Land geworden...,"* vol. 1, p. 139; Andreas R. Hofmann, *Die Nachkriegszeit in Schlesien: Gesellschafts- und Bevölkerungspolitik in den polnischen Siedlungsgebieten 1945–1948* (Cologne, 2000), p. 192; Philipp Ther, *Deutsche und polnische Vertriebene: Gesellschaft und Vertriebenenpolitik in der SBZ/DDR und in Polen 1945–1956* (Göttingen, 1998), pp. 56–57; Glassheim, "National Mythologies," p. 473; Stanisław Jankowiak, "'Cleansing' Poland of Germans: The Province of Pomerania, 1945–1949," in *Redrawing Nations*, ed. Ther and Siljak, p. 89; and Hrabovec, *Vertreibung und Abschub*, p. 66.

32. Borodziej and Lemberg, *"Unsere Heimat is uns ein fremdes Land geworden...,"* vol. 1, p. 178; Glassheim, "National Mythologies," p. 473; Hofmann, *Nachkriegszeit in Schlesien*, pp. 194, 196; and Curp, "Politics of Ethnic Cleansing," p. 581.

33. Borodziej and Lemberg, *"Unsere Heimat is uns ein fremdes Land geworden...,"* vol. 1, pp. 72–73, 161, 163.

34. Schieder, *Vertreibung ... östlich der Oder-Neisse*, vol. I/2, pp. 665, 667–669.

35. Borodziej and Lemberg, *"Unsere Heimat is uns ein fremdes Land geworden...,"* vol. 1, p. 160.

36. Kaps, *Tragödie Schlesiens*, pp. 255, 408.

37. Schieder, *Vertreibung ... östlich der Oder-Neisse*, vol. I/2, p. 812.

38. Ibid., vol. I/1, p. 74e; Siebel-Achenbach, *Lower Silesia*, pp. 122–123; and Schieder, *Vertreibung ... östlich der Oder-Neisse*, vol. I/2, pp. 694–695.

39. Staněk , *Verfolgung 1945*, pp. 44–45; Hrabovec, "Neue Aspekte zur Ersten Phase der Vertreibung der Deutschen aus Mähren 1945," in *Nationale Frage und Vertreibung*, ed. Plaschka, pp. 123, 133–134; and Hrabovec, *Vertreibung und Abschub*, pp. 114–115.

40. Tomáš Staněk, "1945—Das Jahr der Verfolgung. Zur Problematik der aussergerichtlichen Nachkriegsverfolgungen in den böhmischen Ländern, in *Erzwungene Trennung*, ed. Brandes, p. 126; Hrabovec, "Neue Aspekte zur Ersten Phase der Vertreibung," p. 123; and Schieder, *Vertreibung . . . aus der Tschechoslowakei*, pp. 404, 410.

41. Schieder, *Vertreibung . . . aus der Tschechoslowakei*, pp. 445–449. On the "death march," see Staněk, *Verfolgung 1945*, pp. 116–119; Glassheim, "National Mythologies," p. 477; and Eagle Glassheim, "The Mechanics of Ethnic Cleansing: The Expulsion of Germans from Czechoslovakia, 1945–1947," in *Redrawing Nations*, ed. Ther and Siljak, p. 206.

42. Schieder, *Vertreibung . . . aus der Tschechoslowakei*, p. 369; Hrabovec, "Neue Aspekte zur Ersten Phase der Vertreibung," pp. 127–128.

43. Siebel-Achenbach, *Lower Silesia*, p. 111. For a critique of the Allies, see Alfred de Zayas, *Nemesis at Potsdam: The Expulsion of the Germans from the East*, 3rd ed. rev. (Lincoln, Nebr., 1989).

44. Schieder, *Vertreibung . . . östlich der Oder-Neisse*, vol. I/2, pp. 536, 630.

45. Hofmann, *Nachkriegszeit in Schlesien*, p. 197; Kaps, *Tragödie Schlesiens*, pp. 463, 471.

46. Buddatsch, *Abschied von Danzig*, pp. 81, 87; Schieder, *Vertreibung . . . östlich der Oder-Neisse*, vol. I/2, p. 307.

47. Beckherrn, *Königsberg Papiere*, pp. 91, 104, 128–131.

48. Staněk, "1945–Das Jahr der Verfolgung," pp. 138–140; Schieder, *Vertreibung . . . aus der Tschechoslowakei*, p. 198.

49. Barendt, *Danziger Jahre*, pp. 210–213.

50. Schieder, *Vertreibung . . . östlich der Oder-Neisse*, vol. I/2, pp. 741–742, 752–753; Borodziej and Lemberg, "*Unsere Heimat is uns ein fremdes Land geworden . . . ,*" vol. 1, pp. 99–100, 517, 522; and Hofmann, *Nachkriegszeit in Schlesien*, pp. 212–216.

51. Hrabovec, *Vertreibung und Abschub*, pp. 145–147, 153–156.

52. Ibid., pp. 287, 320–321.

53. Schieder, *Vertreibung . . . östlich der Oder-Neisse*, vol. I/2, p. 796. On crowding in trains, see Jankowiak, "'Cleansing' Poland of Germans," p. 98.

54. Quoted in de Zayas, *Nemesis at Potsdam*, 123; Hofmann, *Nachkriegszeit in Schlesien*, pp. 227–228; Borodziej and Lemberg, "*Unsere Heimat is uns ein fremdes Land geworden . . . ,*" vol. 1, pp. 226–227.

55. Hrabovec, *Vertreibung und Abschub*, p. 287; Schieder, *Vertreibung . . . aus der Tschechoslowakei*, pp. 474, 483, 497.

56. Beckherrn, *Königsberg Papiere*, pp. 199, 201, 212–215.

57. Krystyna Kersten, "Forced Migration and the Transformation of Polish Society," in *Redrawing Nations*, ed. Ther and Siljak, p. 82; Jerzy Kochanowski, "Gathering Poles into Poland: Forced Migration from Poland's Former Eastern Territories," in *Redrawing Nations*, ed. Ther and Siljak, p. 141.

58. Zagajewski, *Two Cities*, p. 12.

59. Siebel-Achenbach, *Lower Silesia*, pp. 137, 193; Kochanowski, "Gathering Poles into Poland," p. 138. National identity in Silesia was often fluid and sometimes changed from generation to generation. See Karl Cordell, "Poland's German Minority," in *German Minorities in Europe*, ed. Wolff, pp. 85–87.

60. Snyder, "'To Resolve the Ukrainian Problem Once and for All,'" pp. 106, 108, 113; Orest Subtelny, "Expulsion, Resettlement, Civil Strife: The Fate of Poland's Ukrainians, 1944–1947," in *Redrawing Nations*, ed. Ther and Siljak, pp. 157–159, 163, 166; Marek Jasiak, "Overcoming Ukrainian Resistance: The Deportation of Ukrainians Within Poland in 1947," in *Redrawing Nations*, ed. Ther and Siljak, p. 178.

61. Pamela Ballinger, "Who Defines and Remembers Genocide After the Cold War? Contested Memories of Partisan Massacre in Venezia Giulia in 1943–1945," *Journal of Genocide Research* 2 (2000), p. 13; Pamela Ballinger, *History in Exile: Memory and Identity at the Borders of the Balkans* (Princeton, N.J., 2003), pp. 81–82, 120. For another interpretation, see Glenda Sluga, *The Problem of Trieste and the Italo-Yugoslav Border: Difference, Identity, and Sovereignty in Twentieth Century Europe* (Albany, N.Y., 2001). Bogdan Novak argues that communism rather than nationalism was the predominant factor. See Bogdan C. Novak, *Trieste, 1941–1954: The Ethnic, Political, and Ideological Struggle* (Chicago, 1970), p. 184.

62. Alfred Connor Bowman, *Zones of Strain: A Memoir of the Early Cold War* (Stanford, 1982), p. 120; Geoffrey Cox, *The Road to Trieste* (London, 1947); and Ballinger, *History in Exile*, p. 197.

63. Flight, expulsion, or transfer were the most common fates for Germans of Eastern Europe, but a minority remained. For discussion of German minorities, see Wolff, ed. *German Minorities in Europe*.

CHAPTER 7: AFTER THE OTTOMANS

1. Shabtai Teveth, *Ben-Gurion: The Burning Ground, 1886–1948* (Boston, 1987), p. 39. Gruen did return to Jaffa several weeks later for a political conference.

2. Teveth, *Ben-Gurion*, pp. 75–98.

3. Mark Levine, *Overthrowing Geography: Jaffa, Tel Aviv, and the Struggle for Palestine 1880–1948* (Berkeley, 2005); *Jerusalem Post*, March 25, 2005.

4. Benny Morris, *The Birth of the Palestinian Refugee Problem Revisited* (Cambridge, England, 2004), pp. x–xviii, 602; Walid Khalidi, ed., *All That Remains: The Palestinian Villages Occupied and Depopulated by Israel in 1948* (Washington D.C., 1992), pp. 581–582, 585–594.

5. *New York Times*, December 22, 1948.

6. Rashid Khalidi, *Palestinian Identity: The Construction of Modern National Consciousness* (New York, 1997), pp. 28, 80–83, 89–117.

7. Quoted in Tom Segev, *One Palestine, Complete: Jews and Arabs Under the British Mandate*, trans. Haim Watzman (New York, 2000), p. 116.

8. Quoted in Karsh, *Fabricating Israeli History*, p. 66; Morris, *Righteous Victims*, p. 122; Morris, *Birth of the Palestinian Refugee Problem Revisited*, pp. 14, 18.

9. On the idea of transfer, see Morris, *Birth of the Palestinian Refugee Problem Revisited*, pp. 39–61; Segev, *One Palestine, Complete*, pp. 406–407; and Karsh, *Fabricating History*, pp. 39, 41–58. Karsh stresses that Zionists, rather than initiating this notion, discussed transfer in response to the British Peel Commission. Karsh also critiques Benny Morris's discussion of David Ben-Gurion's thinking about transfer. The bulk of Karsh's discussion concerns three meetings in 1937 as well as a letter from David Ben-Gurion to his son Amos. For a work that emphasizes Zionist interest in

transfer, see Nur Masalha, *Expulsion of the Palestinians: The Concept of 'Transfer' in Zionist Political Thought, 1882–1948* (Washington, D.C, 1992).

10. Morris, *Birth of the Palestinian Refugee Problem Revisited*, pp. 99–100, 103–105, 196–197; Efraim Karsh, "Nakbat Haifa: Collapse and Dispersion of a Major Palestinian Community," *Middle Eastern Studies* 37 (2001), pp. 55–56.

11. Morris, *Birth of the Palestinian Refugee Problem Revisited*, pp. 110–111, 211–214, 217–218.

12. Ibid., pp. 217–218.

13. Ibid., pp. 237–239; Meron Benvenisti, *Sacred Landscape: The Buried History of the Holy Land Since 1948*, trans. Maxine Kaufman-Lacusta (Berkeley, 2000), pp. 114–117; and Karsh, "Nakbat Haifa," p. 46.

14. Quoted in Morris, *Birth of the Palestinian Refugee Problem Revisited*, pp. 164–165. In his critique of Benny Morris, Efraim Karsh says little about Plan D. See Karsh, *Fabricating Israeli History*.

15. Morris, *Birth of the Palestinian Refugee Problem Revisited*, pp. 262–265; quoted in Benvenisti, *Sacred Landscape*, pp. 117–118.

16. Benvenisti, *Sacred Landscape*, pp. 116–117. There is considerable debate about Jordan's war goals and about the significance of a meeting between Golda Meir and Jordan's King Abdullah. See Avi Shlaim, *Collusion Across the Jordan: King Abdullah, the Zionist Movement and the Partition of Palestine* (Oxford, 1988).

17. Quoted in Morris, *Birth of the Palestinian Refugee Problem Revisited*, pp. 415, 473–490; quoted in Benvenisti, *Sacred Landscape*, pp. 144–145.

18. Benny Morris, *The Birth of the Palestinian Refugee Problem, 1947–1949* (Cambridge, England, 1987). This was a most influential book, but there were several others with varied styles and approaches. See Simha Flapan, *The Birth of Israel: Myths and Realities* (New York, 1987); Ilan Pappé, *The Making of the Arab-Israeli Conflict, 1947–1951* (London, 1992); and Michael Palumbo, *The Palestinian Catastrophe: The 1948 Expulsion of a People from Their Homeland* (London, 1987).

19. *New York Times*, December 22, 1948.

20. Morris, *Birth of the Palestinian Refugee Problem Revisited*, pp. 312–314, 320, 349. Efraim Karsh critiques Morris's use of quotes from Weitz, but there is little discussion of "retroactive transfer" in Karsh, *Fabricating History*, pp. 219–231. In a book published in 1950, Weitz himself spoke of Arab flight as "a miracle." See Michael R. Fischbach, *Records of Dispossession: Palestinian Refugee Property and the Arab-Israeli Conflict* (New York, 2003), p. 8; Benvenisti, *Sacred Landscape*, pp. 173–174; and *New York Times*, July 23, 1948. Note misspelling in *New York Times* as Arthur Lowrie.

21. Quoted in Karsh, *Fabricating Israeli History*, pp. 214, 228–229. Note that in the full quote Ben Gurion first discusses the need to employ Arab workers in Jaffa, and says Arabs should have civil rights, but the concluding section of the quote is nonetheless striking. Morris and Karsh dispute the significance of the June 16, 1948, cabinet meeting. See Morris, *Birth of the Palestinian Refugee Problem Revisited*, pp. 326–334; and Karsh, *Fabricating Israeli History*, pp. 206–207. On Ben Gurion and the Greek-Turkish exchange, see Morris, *Birth of the Palestinian Refugee Problem Revisited*, p. 318.

22. Quoted in Karsh, *Fabricating Israeli History*, pp. 211–212.

23. Morris, *Birth of the Palestinian Refugee Problem Revisited*, pp. 326–334, 549–580; Morris, *Righteous Victims*, p. 258; and *New York Times*, December 15, 1952. See also Sulzberger, *Long Row of Candles*, pp. 801–802.

24. Fischbach, *Records of Dispossession,* p. 11.

25. Itamar Levin, *Locked Doors: The Seizure of Jewish Property in Arab Countries,* trans. Rachel Neiman, Foreword by Abraham Hirchson and Israel Singer (Westport, Conn., 2001); Aha Aharoni, "The Forced Migration of Jews from Arab Countries," *Peace Review* 15 (2003), pp. 53–60.

26. Lawrence Durrell, *Bitter Lemons* (New York, 1957), p. 25.

27. Ibid., p. 207.

28. Pierre Oberling, *The Road to Bellapais: The Turkish Cypriot Exodus to Northern Cyprus* (Boulder, Colo., 1982), pp. 97–100; *The Guardian,* February 14, 1964; and *U.S. News and World Report,* February 24, 1964, p. 39, in Oberling, *Road to Bellapais,* p. 107.

29. *The Guardian,* February 3, 1964; Vamik D. Volkan, *Bloodlines: From Ethnic Pride to Ethnic Terrorism* (Boulder, Colo., 1997), p. 95.

30. Sir David Hunt, *Footprints in Cyprus* (London, 1990), p. 285, in Andrew Borowiec, *Cyprus: A Troubled Island* (Westport, Conn., 2000), p. 62.

31. Alexandris, *Greek Minority of Istanbul,* pp. 259, 283.

32. *New York Times,* July 16, 1974; Oberling, *Road to Bellapais,* p. 247.

33. Peter Loizos, *The Heart Grown Bitter: A Chronicle of Cypriot War Refugees* (Cambridge, England, 1981), p. 90; *New York Times,* August 14, 1974.

34. *Crisis on Cyprus: A Report Prepared for the Subcommittee to Investigate Problems Connected with Refugees and Escapees for the Committee on the Judiciary of the United States Senate* (Washington, D.C., 1975), p. 27; Loizos, *Heart Grown Bitter,* p. 105.

35. *New York Times,* August 19, 1974; *Crisis on Cyprus,* p. 19.

36. *New York Times,* August 2, 1974; ibid., November 3, 1974.

37. Ibid., January 17, 1975.

38. David McDowall, *A Modern History of the Kurds* (London, 1996), pp. 1–18. On non-Muslim Kurds, see Christiane Bird, *A Thousand Sighs, A Thousand Revolts: Journeys in Kurdistan* (New York, 2004), pp. 121–123.

39. Quoted in John Bulloch and Harvey Morris, *No Friends But the Mountains: The Tragic History of the Kurds* (New York, 1992), p. 90. The borders of such a Kurdish region were imprecise and incomplete. See McDowall, *Modern History of the Kurds,* p. 137.

40. Philip G. Kreyenbroek, "On the Kurdish Language," in *The Kurds: A Contemporary Overview,* ed. Philip G. Kreyenbroek and Stefan Sperl (London: Routledge, 1992), pp. 73–74; and Bulloch and Morris, *No Friends But the Mountains,* p. 172.

41. Bulloch and Morris, *No Friends But the Mountains,* pp. 172–173, 181–184; McDowall, *A Modern History of the Kurds,* pp. 191–196; and Michael M. Gunter, *The Kurds in Turkey: A Political Dilemma* (Boulder, Colo., 1990), p. 77.

42. Quoted in McDowall, *A Modern History of the Kurds,* pp. 199–200, 206–209; Kreyenbroek, "On the Kurdish Language," p. 73; David McDowall, "The Kurdish Question," in *Kurds,* ed. Kreyenbroek and Sperl, p. 18; and Martin van Bruinessen, "Kurdish Society, Ethnicity, Nationalism and Refugee Problems," in *Kurds,* ed. Kreyenbroek and Sperl, p. 60.

43. Human Rights Watch, *Weapons Transfers and Violations of the Laws of War in Turkey* (November 1995), pp. 2, 15; and Norwegian Refugee Council/Global IDP Project, Profile of Internal Displacement: Turkey. "Compilation of the Information Available in the Global IDP Database of the Norwegian Refugee Council (as of 5 April 2004)."

44. Ertugrul Kürkçü, "Leyla Zana: Defiance Under Fire," *Amnesty Magazine* (2003).

45. McDowall, *Modern History of the Kurds*, pp. 143–146; Bulloch and Morris, *No Friends But the Mountains*, pp. 91–93.

46. Bulloch and Morris, *No Friends But the Mountains*, pp. 98–123; McDowall, *Modern History of the Kurds*, pp. 178–180, 240–246, 308–313; Jonathan C. Randal, *After Such Knowledge, What Forgiveness? My Encounters with Kurdistan* (Boulder, Colo., 1999), pp. 112–131.

47. McDowall, *Modern History of the Kurds*, pp. 335–339; McDowall, "Kurdish Question," pp. 28–30; Human Rights Watch, *Iraq's Crime of Genocide: The Anfal Campaign Against the Kurds* (New Haven, 1995), pp. 4, 19–20; and Edmund Ghareeb, *The Kurdish Question in Iraq* (Syracuse, N.Y., 1981).

48. Human Rights Watch, *Iraq's Crime of Genocide*, pp. 24–25; Human Rights Watch, *Claims in Conflict: Reversing Ethnic Cleansing in Northern Iraq* (August 2004), vol. 16, no. 4 (E), pp. 2, 8, 10; and Samantha Power, *"A Problem from Hell": America and the Age of Genocide* (New York, 2002), p. 175. On Iran, see Fereshteh Koohi-Kamali, "The Development of Nationalism in Iranian Kurdistan," in *The Kurds*, ed. Kreyenbroek and Sperl, p. 17.

49. Human Rights Watch, *Iraq's Crime of Genocide*, pp. 40–47, 49–51; Power, *"A Problem from Hell,"* p. 183.

50. Quoted in Human Rights Watch, *Iraq's Crime of Genocide*, pp. 255, 118; Power, *"A Problem from Hell,"* pp. 188–189; and Randal, *After Such Knowledge*, pp. 212–214, 230–232.

51. Power, *"A Problem from Hell,"* pp. 238–241; Randal, *After Such Knowledge*, pp. 53–57; and *New York Times*, April 7, 1991.

52. Human Rights Watch, *Claims in Conflict*, pp. 13–15.

53. *New York Times*, February 7, 1985; *Washington Post*, April 2, 1985; and Raymond Detrez, *Historical Dictionary of Bulgaria* (Lanham, Md., 1997), p. 275.

54. *The Independent*, July 10, 1989; *Financial Times*, June 16, 1989; and *New York Times*, June 22, 1989.

55. For some of the accounts of the exodus, see *The Times* (London), June 23, 1989; *New York Times*, June 22, 1989.

56. *The Independent*, July 4, 1989.

57. Oberling, *Road to Bellapais*, pp. 231–233; *Washington Post*, August 31, 1980.

58. Levine, *Overthrowing Geography*, pp. 217–220; *Jerusalem Post*, June 5, 2003.

CHAPTER 8: "A KIND OF SECOND REALITY"

1. Elizabeth Neuffer, *The Key to My Neighbor's House: Seeking Justice in Bosnia and Rwanda* (New York, 2001), pp. 15–16, 20, 35–36, 41, 43, 315. See also Judah, *Serbs*, p. 233; and Peter Maass, *Love Thy Neighbor: A Story of War* (New York, 1996), pp. 28–29.

2. For a brief comparison of the Soviet and Hapsburg empires, see Mazower, *Dark Continent*, p. 49.

3. For a discussion of how democracy can contribute to ethnic cleansing, see Michael Mann, "The Dark Side of Democracy: The Modern Tradition of Ethnic and

Political Cleansing," *New Left Review* 235 (1999), pp. 18–45; and Mann, *Dark Side of Democracy*.

4. For an excellent discussion, see Thomas de Waal, *Black Garden: Armenia and Azerbaijan Through Peace and War* (New York, 2003), pp. 45–47, 169.

5. Suny, *Looking Toward Ararat*, p. 186.

6. See Mark Malkasian, *Gha-ra-bagh! The Emergence of the National Democratic Movement in Armenia* (Detroit, 1996).

7. Samvel Shahmuratian, *Sumgait Tragedy: Pogroms Against Armenians in Soviet Azerbaijan*, with a Foreword by Yelena Bonner, trans. Steven Jones (New Rochelle, N.Y., 1990), pp. 23, 75, 249; de Waal, *Black Garden*, pp. 18–19, 32.

8. Shahmuratian, *Sumgait Tragedy*, pp. 96, 310.

9. Ronald Grigor Suny, "Constructing Primordialism: Old Histories for New Nations," *Journal of Modern History* 73 (2001), p. 885; Associated Press, May 20, 1988.

10. *New York Times*, September 12, 1988; *New York Times*, December 2, 1988; *The Guardian*, December 29, 1988; and *Christian Science Monitor*, January 19, 1989. On the cleansing of Azerbaijanis in rural Armenia in 1988, see de Waal, *Black Garden*, p. 62.

11. De Waal, *Black Garden*, pp. 169, 272; Michael P. Croissant, *The Armenia-Azerbaijan Conflict: Causes and Implications* (Westport, Conn., 1998), p. 37; and Thomas Greene, "Internal Displacement in the North Caucasus, Azerbaijan, Armenia, and Georgia," in *The Forsaken People: Case Studies of the Internally Displaced*, ed. Roberta Cohen and Francis M. Deng (Washington, D.C., 1998), p. 259.

12. Thomas Goltz, *Azerbaijan Diary: A Rogue Reporter's Adventures in an Oil-Rich War-Torn Post-Soviet Republic* (Armonk, N.Y., 1998), pp. 122, 125; *The Sunday Times* (London), March 1, 1992.

13. Griffin, *Caucasus*, pp. 185–186; *Christian Science Monitor*, June 17, 1992; and *The Guardian*, May 25, 1992.

14. De Waal, *Black Garden*, p. 195; *The Independent*, June 20, 1992; and *The Independent*, July 6, 1992. See also Nora Dudwick, "The Cultural Construction of Political Violence in Armenia and Azerbaijan," *Problems of Post-Communism* 42 (1995), pp. 18–23.

15. Human Rights Watch, *Azerbaijan: Seven Years of Conflict* (New York, 1994), p. 11.

16. For an account of flight near Fizuli, see Human Rights Watch, *Azerbaijan*, p. 30. On flight across the Araks, see *The Guardian*, November 1, 1993.

17. *New York Times*, May 27, 2001.

18. Stuart J. Kaufman, *Modern Hatreds: The Symbolic Politics of Ethnic War* (Ithica, N.Y., 2001), p. 87.

19. Greene, "Internal Displacement in the North Caucasus," p. 288.

20. *The Guardian*, February 14, 1991; Greene, "Internal Displacement in the North Caucasus," pp. 284–285, 288–289; and International Crisis Group, "Georgia Avoiding War in South Ossetia," November 2004, 26, p. 5.

21. See Georgi M. Derluguian, "The Forgotten Abkhazia: A Historical Anatomy of Ethnic Conflict," Washington, D.C., Council on Foreign Relations: *PONARS Working Paper Series* No. 18 (January 2001), p. 6; Georgi M. Derluguian, "The Tale of Two Resorts: Abkhazia and Ajaria Before and Since the Soviet Collapse," pp. 268–269, in *The Myth of "Ethnic Conflict": Politics, Economics, and*

"Cultural" Violence, ed. Beverly Crawford and Ronnie D. Lipschutz (Berkeley, 1998), pp. 261–292; and *The Independent*, July 29, 1993.

22. Thomas Goltz, "Letter from Eurasia: The Hidden Russian Hand," *Foreign Policy*, (1993), p. 107. On Russian fighters, see Human Rights Watch, *Georgia/Abkhazia: Violations of the Laws of War and Russia's Role in the Conflict* (New York, 1995), p. 34. A controversy also ensued over the shooting down of a Russian military helicopter in 1992, including whether Georgians had shot down the helicopter and whether it was carrying chiefly civilians or armed fighters.

23. Human Rights Watch, *Georgia/Abkhazia*, pp. 15–16, 19.

24. Ibid., pp. 17–19; *The Times* (London), October 4, 1993; and *The Guardian*, October 7, 1993.

25. Human Rights Watch, *Georgia/Abkhazia*, pp. 20–21; *The Guardian*, October 3, 1992; Agence France Presse (AFP), December 31, 1992; *The Times* (London), October 11, 1993; and Sebastian Smith, *Allah's Mountains: Politics and War in the Russian Caucasus* (London, 1998), p. 84.

26. Greene, "Internal Displacement in the North Caucasus," p. 291; *New York Times*, April, 16, 2002.

27. Human Rights Watch / Helsinki Human Rights Watch, *Russia: The Ingush Ossetian Conflict in the Prigorodnyi Region* (New York, 1996), pp. 6–7.

28. Ibid., p. 9.

29. Ibid., pp. 18, 27.

30. Ibid., p. 38; AFP, November 28, 1992.

31. Smith, *Allah's Mountains*, p. 106; Greene, "Internal Displacement in the North Caucasus," p. 245.

32. Brian Glyn Williams, "Commemorating 'The Deportation,'" pp. 120–123.

33. Carlotta Gall and Thomas de Waal, *Chechnya Calamity in the Caucasus* (New York, 1998); Robert Seely, *Russo-Chechen Conflict*; and Smith, *Allah's Mountains*.

34. Greene, "Internal Displacement in the North Caucasus," p. 241.

35. Gall and de Waal, *Chechnya*, pp. 229–233; Smith, *Allah's Mountains*, p. 190.

36. Gall and de Waal, *Chechnya*, p. 244; Anna Politkovskaya, "'Cleansing' Chechnya," trans. John Crowfoot, *Amnesty Now* 28 (2002), pp. 14–17.

37. Note that other terms for "cleansing" had previously been used in languages other than English, though none had ever gained the wide usage of ethnic cleansing. See Ther, "Century of Forced Migration," p. 43; Tooley, "World War I and the Emergence of Ethnic Cleansing in Europe," p. 63; Klejda Mulaj, "Ethnic Cleansing in the Former Yugoslavia in the 1990s: A Euphemism for Genocide?," in *Ethnic Cleansing in Twentieth-Century Europe*, ed. Várdy and Tooley, pp. 693–696; and *The Sunday Times* (London), May 31, 1992.

38. Bogan Denitch, *Ethnic Nationalism: The Tragic Death of Yugoslavia* (Minneapolis, 1994), p. 58; Mazower, *Balkans*, p. 138.

39. Anthony Oberschall, "The Manipulation of Ethnicity: From Ethnic Cooperation to Violence and War in Yugoslavia," *Ethnic and Racial Studies* 23 (2000), p. 988.

40. Quoted from Carmichael, *Ethnic Cleansing in the Balkans*, p. 80; Cvijeto Job, "Yugoslavia's Ethnic Furies," *Foreign Policy* (Fall 1993), issue 92, pp. 52–75; Cvijeto Job, *Yugoslavia's Ruin: The Bloody Lessons of Nationalism, A Patriot's Warning* (Lanham, Md., 2002), pp. 76–78, 167; and Louis Sell, *Slobodan Milosevic and the Destruction of Yugoslavia* (Durham, N.C., 2002), p. 34.

41. Jasna Dragović-Soso, *Saviours of the Nation?: Serbia's Intellectual Opposition and the Revival of Nationalism* (London, 2002), pp. 89–93; Sell, *Milosevic*, p. 43.

42. The story of the reemergence of nationalism among Serbian intellectuals and in Serbia, has been told many times. See for example Norman Cigar, *Genocide in Bosnia: The Policy of "Ethnic Cleansing"* (College Station, Tex., 1995), pp. 27–29; Misha Glenny, *The Fall of Yugoslavia: The Third Balkan War* (London, 1992); Judah, *Serbs*, pp. 158–160; and Laura Silber and Allan Little, *Yugoslavia: Death of a Nation*, rev. and updated ed. (New York, 1997), pp. 31–36.

43. Dragović-Soso, *Saviours of the Nation?*, pp. 104–114; Branimir Anzulovic, *Heavenly Serbia: From Myth to Genocide* (New York, 1999), pp. 99–114.

44. Job, "Yugoslavia's Ethnic Furies."

45. Neuffer, *Key to My Neighbor's House*, p. 22.

46. Quoted in Robert Thomas, *The Politics of Serbia in the 1990s* (New York, 1999), pp. 99–100.

47. *New York Times,* July 31, 1991; Roger Cohen, *Hearts Grown Brutal: Sagas of Sarajevo* (New York, 1998), pp. 154–155.

48. Silber and Little, *Yugoslavia: Death of a Nation*, pp. 170–172; *Toronto Star,* July 29, 1991; and *The Guardian*, October 18, 1991. The statement on Ilok came from a "Western diplomatic source in Belgrade."

49. Killings actually began in late March. See Judah, *Serbs*, p. 203.

50. Human Rights Watch, "Bosnia and Hercegovina Unfinished Business: The Return of Refugees to Bijeljina," vol. 12, no. 7 (D); Ron Haviv, *Blood and Honey: A Balkan War Journal*, Essays by Chuck Sudetic and David Rieff, Afterword by Bernard Kouchner (New York, 2000) (some authors prefer to call Arkan by his real name, Zeljko Raznatovic, but it was under the name Arkan that he carried out ethnic cleansing); quoted in Silber and Little, *Yugoslavia: Death of a Nation*, p. 223. See also Hannes Tretter, et al., "'Ethnic Cleansing Operations' in the Northeast Bosnian City of Zvornik from April Through June 1992," Ludwig Boltzmann Institute of Human Rights, 1994.

51. Quoted in Judah, *Serbs*, p. 188; Silber and Little, *Yugoslavia Death of a Nation*, p. 224; "'Ethnic Cleansing Operations'"; Ed Vulliamy, *Seasons in Hell: Understanding Bosnia's War* (New York, 1994), p. 226; and Cigar, *Genocide in Bosnia*, pp. 47–53.

52. *Washington Post,* August 22, 1992; Carmichael, *Ethnic Cleansing in the Balkans*, pp. 50, 91. See also Vulliamy, *Seasons in Hell*, pp. 147–148; *The Daily Telegraph*, September 19, 1992; *The Times* (London), July 25, 1992 ; and Judah, *Serbs*, p. 227. On the importance of coffee drinking, see Tone Bringa, *Being Muslim the Bosnian Way: Identity and Community in a Central Bosnian Village* (Princeton, N.J., 1995), pp. 66–67. For examples of ordinary people who provided help, see Svetlana Broz, *Good People in an Evil Time: Portraits of Complicity and Resistance in the Bosnian War*, trans. Ellen Elias-Bursać, ed. Laurie Kain Hart (New York, 2004).

53. Neuffer, *Key to My Neighbor's House*.

54. International Criminal Tribunal for the Former Yugoslavia, "Tadic (IT-94-1) 'Prijedor,'" www.un.org/icty/transe1/960613IT.htm and www.un.org/icty/transe1/960731IT.htm (April 2005).

55. Chuck Sudetic, *Blood and Vengeance: One Family's Story of the War in Bosnia* (New York, 1998), pp. 120–121, 296; International Criminal Tribunal for the Former Yugoslavia, "The Prosecutor of the Tribunal Against Milan Lukic, Sredoje Lukic, Mitar Vasiljevic," www.un.org/icty/indictment/english/vas-ii000125e.htm (April 2005).

56. Sudetic, *Blood and Vengeance*, pp. 120–121; Neuffer, *Key to My Neighbor's House*, p. 22. On the possible individual factors, see Mann, *Dark Side of Democracy*, pp. 401–403.

57. Vullimay, *Seasons in Hell*, pp. 8–9; Cohen, *Hearts Grown Brutal*, pp. 478–480; Carmichael, *Ethnic Cleansing in the Balkans*, p. 44; Jill A. Irvine, Ultranationalist Ideology and State-Building in Croatia, 1990–1996, *Problems of Post-Communism* 44 (1997), pp. 30–43; Volkan, *Bloodlines*, pp. 68–69, 73; quoted in Eric Stover, *The Graves: Srebrenica and Vukovar*, Photographs by Gilles Peress (Berlin, 1998), pp. 88–89; Stacy Sullivan, "Milosevic's Willing Executioners," *New Republic*, May 10, 1999, p. 35.

58. Cohen, *Hearts Grown Brutal*, p. 479.

59. *Manchester Guardian Weekly*, August 9, 1992.

60. Ibid.; Adam Jones, "Gender and Ethnic Conflict in Ex-Yugoslavia," *Ethnic and Racial Studies* 17 (1994), pp. 115–134; and Final Report of the United Nations Commission of Experts Established Pursuant to Security Council Resolution 780 (1992), Annex IX, Rape and Sexual Assault, United Nations Security Council, S/1994/674—27 May 1994.

61. *Newsday*, July 3, 1992; *The Guardian*, September 29, 1992; and Richard C. Holbrooke, *To End a War*, rev. ed. (New York, 1999), p. 37.

62. Roy Gutman, *A Witness to Genocide: The 1993 Pulitzer Prize–Winning Dispatches on the "Ethnic Cleansing" of Bosnia* (New York, 1993), pp. 44, 97.

63. Maass, *Love Thy Neighbor*, pp. 39–40; Neuffer, *Key to My Neighbor's House*, pp. 41–42, 304.

64. Vulliamy, *Seasons in Hell*, pp. 133, 179.

65. BBC Summary of World Broadcasts, September 28, 1992; Maass, *Love Thy Neighbor*, p. 9.

66. For summaries of Mladic interviews broadcast on November 23, 2002, see BBC Summary of World Broadcasts, November 25 and November 27, 1992.

67. Warren Zimmermann, *Origins of a Catastrophe: Yugoslavia and Its Destroyers—America's Last Ambassador Tells What Happened and Why* (New York, 1996), p. 74; Mart Bax, "Warlords, Priests and the Politics of Ethnic Cleansing: A Case-Study from Rural Bosnia Hercegovina," *Ethnic and Racial Studies* 23 (2000), p. 16; and Tanner, *Croatia*, pp. 286–287.

68. Zimmermann, *Origins of a Catastrophe*, 74; *The Guardian*, October 28, 1992; Vulliamy, *Seasons of Hell*, p. 222; *The Daily Telegraph*, October 29, 1992; and Silber and Little, *Yugoslavia: Death of a Nation*, p. 294.

69. International Criminal Tribunal for the Former Yugoslavia, "Blaskic (IT-95-14) 'Lasva Valley,'" www.un.org/icty/transe14/971118ed.htm (April 2005).

70. *The Guardian*, June 9, 1993; *Daily Mail*, June 19, 1993.

71. *The Guardian*, October 26, 1993; *The Independent*, November 4, 1993.

72. *The Daily Telegraph*, September 7, 1993; *Christian Science Monitor*, September 3, 1993.

73. Maass, *Love Thy Neighbor*, p. 116.

74. In April 2002 the Dutch government resigned after a report by the Netherlands Institute for War Documentation criticized the role of the government as well as the UN in the tragedy at Srebrenica.

75. *Christian Science Monitor*, January 18, 1996. See also David Rhode, *Endgame: The Betrayal and Fall of Srebrenica: Europe's Worst Massacre Since World War II* (New York, 1997).

76. *The Guardian*, July 27, 1995.

77. *International Herald Tribune*, September 4, 1995.

78. *New York Times*, August 7, 1995; *Los Angeles Times*, August 10, 1995; and *The Times* (London), September 2, 1995.

79. *New York Times*, October 31, 1999.

80. In September 1995, Richard Holbrooke advised Croatian leaders that Croatian forces should not try to take Banja Luka. See Holbrooke, *To End a War*, pp. 160, 166.

81. Ibid., pp. 335–336; *New York Times*, March 11, 1996.

82. Zimmermann, *Origins of a Catastrophe*, 57.

83. Wesley K. Clark, *Waging Modern War: Bosnia, Kosovo, and the Future of Combat* (New York, 2002), pp. 129, 148, 151–152.

84. *Los Angeles Times*, March 30, 1999; *Boston Globe*, March 28, 1999; *The Independent*, April 5, 1999; and Tim Judah, *Kosovo: War and Revenge* (New Haven, 2000), pp. 241–247.

85. *The Times* (London), March 25, 1999.

86. *Christian Science Monitor*, April 2, 1999.

87. Human Rights Watch, *A Village Destroyed: War Crimes in Kosovo* (October 1999), vol. 11, no. 13 (D), pp. 5–6.

88. Human Rights Watch, *Abuses Against Serbs and Roma in the New Kosovo* (August 1999), vol. 11, no. 10 (D), p. 8.

89. Neuffer, *Key to My Neighbor's House*, p. 315; Elizabeth Neuffer, "Homecoming," *New Republic*, August, 23, 1999, pp. 15–16; "Coming Home," *Economist*, December 12, 2003, p. 74; and International Crisis Group, "The Continuing Challenge of Refugee Return in Bosnia & Herzegovina," Europe Report, no. 137, 13, December 2002, pp. 25–26.

90. "The Editor's Desk," *Refugees*, vol. 3, no. 124 (2001), p. 2; International Crisis Group, "Building Bridges in Mostar," Europe Report, no. 150, 20, November 2003, p. 1; and *Manchester Guardian Weekly*, July 30, 2004–August 5, 2004.

CHAPTER 9: A CONTINENT CLEANSED

1. The Jewish population of Central Europe began to rebound slightly after the end of the Soviet Union because of the emigration of Jews from former Soviet republics.

2. Zagajewski, *Two Cities*, p. 15.

3. Michael Ignatieff, "Afterword Reflections on Coexistence," in *Imagine Coexistence: Restoring Humanity After Violent Ethnic Conflict*, ed. Antonia Chayes and Martha Minow (San Francisco, 2003), p. 332. On a diaspora dipute, see Danforth, *Macedonian Conflict*.

4. Goran Tarlac, "Turbo Folk Politics," *Transitions Online*, April 14, 2003; Michael Logan, "Radovan Karadzic, 'Serbian Hero,'" *Transitions Online*, March 15, 2004. See also Russ Baker, "Catch Me If You Can," *Washington Monthly*, January/February 2004, pp. 38–41.

5. Hiram A. Ruiz, "The Sudan: Cradle of Displacement," in *Forsaken People*, ed. Cohen and Deng, pp. 139–170

6. Peter W. Galbraith, "A Tenuous Leadership Deal in Iraq," *Boston Globe*, April 7, 2005.

7. IDP News Alert, February 17, 2005, www.idpproject.org/weekly_news/weekly_news.htm#2 (March 2005).

8. Mann, *Dark Side of Democracy.*

9. Power, *Problem from Hell*, pp. 483–484; Neuffer, *Key to My Neighbor's House*, p. 168.

10. Aneelah Afzali and Laura Colleton, "Constructing Coexistence: A Survey of Coexistence Projects in Areas of Ethnic Conflict," in *Imagine Coexistence*, ed. Chayes and Minow, pp. 8–9; Diana Chigas and Brian Ganson, "Grand Visions and Small Projects: Coexistence Efforts in Southeastern Europe," in ibid., pp. 64–69; Cynthia Burns, Laura McGrew, and Ilija Todorovic, "Imagine Coexistence Pilot Projects in Rwanda and Bosnia," in ibid., pp. 90–93; and Antonia Chayes, "Bureaucratic Obstacles to Imagining Coexistence," in ibid., pp 166–167.

11. Job, *Yugoslavia's Ruin*, p. 221.

Index

A NOTE ON THE AUTHOR

Benjamin Lieberman was born in Boston, Massachusetts, and studied history at Yale and the University of Chicago, where he received a Ph.D. In addition to a number of articles on modern European history, he has also written *From Recovery to Catastrophe*, a study of Weimar Germany. Mr. Lieberman is now professor of history at Fitchburg State College in Massachusetts and lives with his wife and two children in Maynard, Massachusetts.